WORDSWORTH'S LIBRARY

GARLAND REFERENCE LIBRARY
OF THE HUMANITIES
(VOL. 102)

Room at Rydal Mount

WORDSWORTH'S LIBRARY,
A Catalogue

Including a List of Books
Housed by Wordsworth
for Coleridge
from c. 1810 to c. 1830

Chester L. Shaver
Alice C. Shaver

GARLAND PUBLISHING, INC. • NEW YORK & LONDON
1979

Library of Congress Cataloging in Publication Data

Shaver, Chester L
  Wordsworth's library.

    (Garland reference library of the humanities ; v. 102)
    1. Wordsworth, William, 1770–1850—Library.
2. Coleridge, Samuel Taylor, 1772–1834—Library.
3. Bibliography—Rare books. I. Shaver, Alice C.,
joint author. II. Title.
Z8985.S46 [PR5885]   016.821'7   77-83348
ISBN 0-8240-9842-0

Printed on acid-free, 250-year-life paper
Manufactured in the United States of America

CONTENTS

ILLUSTRATIONS

Frontispiece:
Room at Rydal Mount, 1840, from an engraving of a sketch by William Westall, reproduced through the courtesy of Mr. Peter Laver and the University of Newcastle upon Tyne

PREFACE

This book originated a number of years ago when the late Professor William Jackson, Director of the Houghton Library, Harvard University, gave permission to bring out as an independent volume an unpublished Manuscript Catalogue (1829) of Wordsworth's library which belonged to the Houghton Library. As time went on, it seemed that the proposed work would be more useful if the contents of the Manuscript Catalogue were embodied in a form which amalgamated its titles with the titles listed in the printed catalogue (1859) of the sale of Wordsworth's books, the Manuscript Catalogue containing some titles absent from the printed catalogue and vice versa. Professor Jackson graciously agreed to this change of plan. Later, Miss Elizabeth C. Ford, Curator of the Harry Elkins Widener Collection at Harvard, gave leave to publish as a separate volume a Widener Collection notebook recording loans made from Wordsworth's library at Rydal Mount between 1824 and 1858. Still later, having discovered that this notebook includes certain items not found in the two catalogues, we asked for and received from the present director of the Houghton Library, Mr. William H. Bond, permission to consolidate the loan-notebook titles with those occurring in the two catalogues. These three sources of information have served as the basis for the first section of this book (Composite List).

Here and there we have supplemented both this section and the one following (Appendix I: Wordsworth) with either additional or corroborative facts from a fourth source, the so-called Hudson List. This document, now at Wordsworth Library, Grasmere, is labelled: "Inventory of the Books, Prints, and Pictures of the late Wm. Wordsworth Esq. of Rydal Mount, taken by me [John Hudson, bookseller, of Kendal] this 7th day of May 1850." Miss Marilyn Kuhar of Georgetown University has generously provided us with a photocopy of her transcription and has allowed us to cite this as needed.

Besides the items thus accumulated, we have gleaned by correspondence with libraries and private owners some titles not otherwise accounted for. These appear in Appendix I.

The titles which make up Appendix II: Coleridge derive mainly from the 1829 Manuscript Catalogue,[1] where they are mingled indiscriminately with Wordsworth's books, but are identified as Coleridge's by a system of markings. As they remained on Wordsworth's shelves for twenty years (from about 1810 to about 1830), we have felt justified in incorporating them, though separately, in a catalogue of Wordsworth's books because they were, in effect, part of his library during that interval.

While our original plan was being modified in the ways mentioned, various books and articles were published from which our undertaking benefited materially. Certain titles which we had not heard about were revealed. Others which we had described incorrectly or inadequately we were enabled to amend. The present whereabouts of many items came to light. Among these publications two which served us greatly were the late Professor George Healey's *The Cornell Wordsworth Collection* (1957) and Professor Kathleen Coburn's *The Notebooks of Samuel Taylor Coleridge* (1957–1973).

We are much indebted, furthermore, to various persons, among them four members of the Wordsworth family. The late Mrs. Dorothy Dickson, the poet's great-granddaughter, kindly allowed Chester L. Shaver to examine in 1959 every book in her library at "The Stepping Stones," Rydal, for evidence of Wordsworth's former ownership. From Wordsworth's great-grandson, the late Rev. Christopher W. Wordsworth, and from

---

1. Twelve titles bearing Coleridge's name appear in the Sale Catalogue and consequently are listed in the Composite List as well as in Appendix II.

the latter's son Richard Wordsworth we have learned of some titles which were unknown to us and of their locations. Jonathan Wordsworth, of Exeter College, Oxford, a collateral descendant, has similarly helped us to identify certain books as having belonged to the poet.

To Peter Laver, Administrative Librarian of Wordsworth Library, Grasmere, and to Professor George Whalley of Queen's University, Kingston, Ontario, we are grateful indeed for several kinds of assistance. Mr. Laver has been indefatigable in answering our questions about books once Wordsworth's which are now in Wordsworth Library and in obtaining (with the cooperation of the University of Newcastle upon Tyne) a photograph of the engraving used as our frontispiece. Professor Whalley, the editor of Coleridge's *Marginalia* for the new edition of Coleridge, has shared most generously his unrivaled knowledge of Coleridge's books. As a result, we have not only been able to avoid the consequences of several wrong guesses about Coleridge's titles in Appendix II, but also have been supplied with titles of which we were ignorant.

Another group of persons have aided us substantially in a variety of ways. Professor Paul F. Betz of Georgetown University and Professor Mark L. Reed of the University of North Carolina have described books in their possession which were formerly the poet's. Professor Betz has also furnished us with photocopies of two sales lists: (1) the contents of Rydal Mount auctioned in August 1871; (2) furnishings and effects from "The Stepping Stones" belonging to Mrs. Dorothy Dickson auctioned in April 1970.

To two Grasmere ladies, both devoted Wordsworthians, we are indebted for help of several kinds. Miss Nesta Clutterbuck graciously replied to many queries when she was Librarian of Wordsworth Library, and since her retirement has continued unfailingly to do so. The late Miss Helen Darbishire, long a student of the Wordsworths' handwriting, aided us in solving certain puzzles created by poor penmanship and bad spelling in the Loan Book. It was she, moreover, who suggested that the monogram "JC" used as a check-mark in the Manuscript

Catalogue probably stands for John Carter, Wordsworth's clerk at Rydal Mount for almost forty years—a suggestion so convincing that we have adopted it.

We wish to thank Miss Margaret Goalby, also a devoted Wordsworthian, for the information that some of Wordsworth's books which were formerly Mrs. Dickson's are now in the hands of J. Goalby, her father.

Our thanks are due to Professor Ian Jack, of Pembroke College, Cambridge, for describing one of Wordsworth's books which he owns and for helping us to trace another belonging to Cambridge University Library.

Professor Russell L. Noyes of Indiana University, Curator Emeritus of its Wordsworth Collection, has, with his customary readiness to cooperate, given needed information about the relevant volumes in this collection.

Many persons besides the foregoing have generously responded to our appeals for assistance. To these also we wish to offer our warm thanks: Mrs. Mildred K. Abraham (Alderman Library, University of Virginia); Jean Archibald (The British Library); Rodney Armstrong (Library of the Boston Athenaeum); Carey S. Bliss (The Henry E. Huntington Library); Benjamin C. Bowman (The Milton S. Eisenhower Library, The Johns Hopkins University); A.P. Burton (The Library, Victoria and Albert Museum); Leslie S. Clarke (The Bancroft Library, The University of California, Berkeley); Mrs. Nancy N. Coffin (The Robert H. Taylor Collection, Princeton University Library); Mrs. Susan Dean (The Newberry Library); the Bishop of Derby; the Rev. Geoffrey Dickenson (Burton-on-Trent); Donald D. Eddy (Cornell University Library); Mrs. C.M. Gee (Keats House, Hampstead, London); Walter G. Glascoff, III (The Joseph Regenstein Library, The University of Chicago); Charles E. Green (Princeton University Library); Mrs. Holly Hall (Washington University Libraries, St. Louis); Dr. Brian Hillyard (National Library of Scotland); W.S. Hutton (Librarian, Pembroke College, Cambridge); Mair Jones (National Library of Wales); Miss Harriet C. Jameson (University Library, University of Michigan); Mrs. Nati H. Krivatsky (The Folger Shakespeare Library); John Lancaster (Amherst College Library); Thomas V. Lange (The Pierpont Morgan Library); Mrs. Sally S. Leach (Humanities Research Center, University of Texas); Guy Lee (Librarian, St. John's College, Cambridge); Kenneth A. Lohf (Butler Library, Columbia University); Miss Lucy Marks (Beinecke Library, Yale University); J.C. Oates (Cambridge University Library); Miss Ellen M. Oldham (Boston Public Library); R. Julian Roberts and David Rogers (The Bodleian Library, Oxford); Florian J. Shasky (The Stanford University Libraries); John H. Stanley (The John Hay Library, Brown University); Miss Rachel Stuhlman (Library of the Boston Athenaeum); Dr. Heiko Uecker and Frau Gerhard Rambow (Bonn, West Germany); Miss Katharine Watson (Director, Bowdoin College Museum of Art); Betsy Wilson (University Library, University of Illinois at Urbana-Champaign); Robert F. Wiseman (Berg Collection, New York Public Library); Thomas F. Wright (The William Andrews Clark Memorial Library, University of California at Los Angeles); Robert Yampolsky (The Carl H. Pforzheimer Library, New York); and Professor Paul M. Zall (California State University, Los Angeles).

We wish to offer particular thanks to the staffs of the two institutions most closely associated with our enterprise: to that of the Houghton Library, Harvard University, and its director, Mr. William H. Bond, for their patience in answering inquiries about Harvard-owned books once Wordsworth's and for their cooperativeness in providing us with photographic copies not only of the two Harvard manuscripts we have been permitted to publish, but also of several pages of these manuscripts which we have used as illustrations; and to that of Mudd Learning Center, Oberlin College, primarily its acquisitions, cataloguing, reference, and special collections divisions, for assistance of various kinds.

To Oberlin College itself we are much indebted for a summer grant-in-aid to cover typing services when our project was in its early phase. We are also much indebted to Mrs. Dwain Kibler, who later typed the final version of Appendix II with exceptional care.

We are grateful to several Oberlin colleagues, chiefly in the Departments of Classics and English, for answering queries about subjects in their areas of special competence.

Professor John C. Olmsted of Oberlin's Department of English has always obligingly lent us his expertise in matters bibliographical, has drawn our attention to several pertinent articles we had overlooked, and, together with Dr. Jeffrey E. Welch of the Department of English, Cranbrook School, has helped us to secure photocopies of materials inaccessible in Oberlin. Both he and Dr. Welch, moreover, have constantly aided us with timely advice and encouragement during the final stages of our enterprise. To these helpers and well-wishers we owe a debt greater than we know how to express adequately.

Oberlin, Ohio
November 1978

CHESTER L. SHAVER
ALICE C. SHAVER

INTRODUCTION

It is often said that Wordsworth depended less on books to in-
itiate and fund his writing, especially his poetry, than Coleridge
did. This assertion may be true, generally speaking. In 1907,
however, Lane Cooper, an eminent Wordsworthian, in "A
Glance at Wordsworth's Reading,"[1] insisted: "The dominant im-
pulse of Wordsworth's life owed the normal debt of poetry to
books." During the years following, several books and articles
have given support to Cooper's view. In 1908 Kurt Lieneman
published in Berlin a survey of Wordsworth's acquaintance with
books in a monograph entitled *Die Belesenheit von William
Wordsworth*. Jane Worthington's *Wordsworth's Reading of Roman
Prose* (1946) and C.N. Coe's *Wordsworth and the Literature of Travel*
(1953) examined two specific areas of Wordsworth's obligations
to books. Similarly, in 1950, Charles L. Pittman contributed to
Furman Studies (Vol. XXXIII, No. 5) a lengthy article, "An Introduction to a Study of Wordsworth's Reading in Science."
These and other investigations suggest that Wordsworth did indeed rely more on his reading to fructify his writing than was
formerly supposed.

Believing that further efforts to explore the subject might
be aided by a volume which would reconstruct the contents of
Wordsworth's library as fully as possible, we have made our first
aim a compilation of what we have been able to learn about his
library from various printed and manuscript sources and from
information furnished by a number of librarians and private
book collectors.[2] A second aim has been to ascertain which volumes belonging to Coleridge were housed with Wordsworth's
books for about two decades and thus available during that

period for Wordsworth's use. We cannot call our compilation definitive. It may serve, nevertheless, to indicate most of the works which Wordsworth could consult under his own roof.

The term "Wordsworth's library" as we employ it here means not only the poet's books, but also books belonging to members of his immediate family for whom Rydal Mount was home or more or less home from 1813 onward. These included his wife, Mary; his sister, Dorothy; his sister-in-law, Sara Hutchinson; his daughter, Dora (later Mrs. Edward Quillinan); and his sons, John and William. The ownership of several volumes inscribed "W.W." is uncertain because it is not clear whether the initials represent the father or the son. The term also embraces a very few titles which were published after the poet's death, but which we have included because they remained in the Rydal Mount library until Mary's death in 1859, when the entire collection was dispersed.

We have divided our catalogue into three parts. The first (Composite List) is made up of titles obtained from three sources: the Sale Catalogue of Wordsworth's books (1859); a manuscript listing his books and books he stored for Coleridge (1829); and a manuscript identifying books lent from his library at Rydal Mount (1824–1858).[3] The second part (Appendix I: Wordsworth) brings together titles derived from other sources than these.[4] The third part (Appendix II: Coleridge) consists chiefly of works designated as Coleridge's in the manuscript of 1829.

Besides grouping titles in this way, we have shown in each division, whenever we could, the present whereabouts of an item and have used the word "annotated" (abbreviated to "Ann") to indicate that an item contains one or more of the following: (1) Wordsworth's autograph or his initials; (2) Coleridge's autograph or initials; (3) inscriptions in the hand of either poet; (4) presentation inscriptions; (5) autographs or initials of members of Wordsworth's family; (6) annotations in the stricter sense of marginal or other notes. Limitations of space have precluded our reproducing every so-defined "annotation." Here and there, however, we have quoted them, especially some printed in the

Sale Catalogue of 1859, some which are not in the public domain of libraries, and some from volumes whose location, once known, is now uncertain. In these instances our intent has been the wish to authenticate a work.

For some entries our authority is only one of the sources mentioned above, but for many there are at least two and sometimes three. It may be useful, therefore, to differentiate our sources more precisely and to explain our system of reference to them.

The Sale Catalogue

On 20 June 1859, John Burton, auctioneer, of Preston, Lancashire, issued a catalogue offering for sale "at Rydal Mount, near Ambleside, Windermere," on the following 19, 20, and 21 July, "the varied and valuable Historical, Poetical, Theological and Miscellaneous Library of the late venerated Poet-Laureate, William Wordsworth Esq."

In November 1925, the poet's grandson, Gordon Graham Wordsworth, transcribed into his own copy of this catalogue (now at Wordsworth Library, Grasmere) information, chiefly concerning prices brought, which he had found in another copy (present whereabouts unknown) called the "Queen's Hotel, Ambleside" copy. In 1974, Gordon Wordsworth's edited copy was reprinted photographically by Roy Park, Fellow of University College, Oxford, with an introduction.[5]

Meanwhile, in 1884, Burton's catalogue was republished, with a very few emendations, by Professor William Knight of the University of Edinburgh in *Transactions of the Wordsworth Society.*[6]

In many respects Park's and Knight's reprints are alike. Both list the same number of lots (700) put up at auction; both retain the original enumeration of the lots, which includes the omission of Lot 185 and the doubling of Lot 451.[7] Both retain the same classifications of titles and in the same order.[8]

Both, moreover, often repeat the typographical and arithmetical errors of the original. The typographical errors comprise misspellings of authors' names and of words in titles, misdatings of publication, and inexact descriptions of book-size. Both reprints, for example, give "T.K. Kervey" (Lot 533) for "T.K. Hervey," "Josias Holmesby" (Lot 560) for "Josias Homely," and "J. Conybeare" (Lot 579) for "J. Conington." Similarly, "Conquests in Ireland" (Lot 15) is a mistake for "Contests in Ireland"; *Il Pastore Incantato* stands in Lot 548 as *Il Pestore Incantata,* and *The Omnipotence of the Deity* in Lot 555 for *The Omnipresence of the Deity.* Again, Lot 60, which contains but one volume, is listed as containing eight, and Lot 89, said to contain eight items, has only two.

Two peculiarities shared by the reprints are their failure at times to specify each title in a lot and their always giving the same count of titles in a lot. In both, for example, Lot 291, after particularizing six theological works, teasingly concludes "and six other bks." In both, similarly, Lot 661, after listing two volumes of poems with titles, adds "and twelve other poetical Productions by various authors." In such instances it is a fair guess that the unspecified items belong to the same category as the specified ones, and we have accordingly so classified them: e.g., "*Theology. SC.*291: 'six other books.'" Now and then, however, a lot is numerically vague in both reprints, such as Lot 405, which reads "Pamphlets, and Ephemera—French, a bundle," or is not only numerically vague, but vaguely entitled as well: e.g., Lot 116, which is made up partly of "Miscellaneous Periodicals. A Bundle." In such cases we have had no choice but to index the first as "Pamphlets" and the second as "Periodicals, Miscellaneous." The number of items rendered unidentifiable in the original catalogue by these kinds of imprecision is considerable.

The phraseology of Park's reprint is sometimes more exact than that of Knight's—e.g., "Sectaries" (Lot 9) instead of "Secretaries"—but more often the converse is true; Knight, for example, corrects "Prohibition" (Lot 304) to "Probabilities" and "National" (Lot 296) to "Natural." Knight's printer, furthermore, was usually quite scrupulous in supplying requisite accent marks in foreign-language titles—omitted entirely by the printer of the original and therefore lacking in Park's reproduction of it. A lot-by-lot comparison shows Knight's reprint to be the more accurate of the two in a ratio of about three to one.

Park's version is the more interesting one, to be sure, because the compiler of the original often subjoined to items brief comments quoted from bibliophiles such as Dibdin and Lowndes or literary figures such as Pope and Schlegel, none of which were retained by Knight. Especially interesting in Park's reprint is Gordon Wordsworth's transcribed record of the price each lot fetched, data which Knight either lacked or decided to omit.[9] From the standpoint of mere bibliographical exactitude, however, Knight's reprint is the more generally reliable.[10] For this reason we have preferred to use it as the source from which to reconstruct the titles in the sale of 1859, and the abbreviation "*SC*" therefore signifies Knight's reprint, though here and there we have cited Park's (RP.QH) as well.

Surprisingly, nine titles in *SC*, most of them Greek or Latin authors, bear evidence of having belonged to both Coleridge and Wordsworth, Coleridge's name preceding Wordsworth's in each.[11] These books may have been given to Wordsworth by Coleridge or they may have been overlooked when Coleridge's books were sent to London. Another kind of ambiguous ownership is exemplified by William Newcome's *Historical View of English Biblical Translations*. It is listed in *SC*.674, with "Newcome" misprinted as "Newsom." It is also listed on MC.24 as "Newcome on Bib: Transla: C," the "C" supposedly indicating Coleridge to be the owner. Not knowing whether there were two copies of the volume in Wordsworth's hands or only one, we have included it in both the Composite List and Appendix II.

Two other titles in *SC*, both Coleridge's only, are there for other reasons. Lot 117 (Frend's *Evening Amusements*) was a gift from Coleridge to his son Hartley (1796–1849), who spent much time with the Wordsworths and had the run of the Rydal Mount library. Another, Lot 491, an edition of Chapman's Homer, was given by Coleridge to Sara Hutchinson (1775–1835). An unexplained anomaly, however, is a set of Shadwell in four volumes, Lot 650, which has only Coleridge's autograph.

The Manuscript Catalogue

Sometime before 20 January 1925 (the date of the accession stamp) Harvard University acquired a manuscript catalogue of Wordsworth's library (MS. Eng 880) which had formerly belonged to Mr. Norton Perkins.[12] On the verso of the front cover there is inscribed in longhand: "A/ Catalogue of Wordsworth's Library/ W/ rendered in the handwriting of his daughter."/ [accession stamp]/ Norton Perkins [in a different hand]." Above this inscription, in still another hand, is written "18467.5*/ 83 written leaves/ 24 blank leaves."[13] On the verso of the back flyleaf, on an unfinished pencil sketch of what seems to be a clown's head and written in ink in the poet's hand, are the words "Wm. Wordsworth/ Rydal Mount/ Kendal."

Roy Park correctly describes this volume as "a small notebook in a brown cartridge paper wrapper."[14] The leaves measure 14.5 cm x 9 cm. In the upper right-hand corner of the first there is a penned monogram and a date: "JC—Octr/ 1829," the two lines joined by a brace on the right. The first two leaves, which are unnumbered, provide an index of the contents by classes.[15]

Although the volume is said to be in the handwriting of the poet's daughter, Dora (1804–1847), the late Helen Darbishire, a specialist in the various hands of Wordsworth and his family, doubted this; and after comparing a photographic copy with specimens of both Dora's hand and that of John Carter (1796–1863), Wordsworth's clerk, she was inclined to favor Carter as the scribe. After making a similar comparison, we are of the same opinion, supported by the evidence on page 7 of four lines written in ink and in a clearly different hand under which someone has pencilled "the aut[o]g [of] the Poet's daughter."[16]

It is true, of course, that other hands than the scribe's are found in the manuscript, but chiefly where interlinear or marginal additions, corrections, and notes have been made and in the last eight pages as a whole. Thus, "Claudiani opera HC," written aslant in the left margin of page 2 and with a thicker nib or quill, adds an omitted title which was probably on loan to Hartley

Coleridge. Similarly, the phrase "Jackson's Treatise" (in Wordsworth's hand and in darker ink), written on page 24 above the scribe's "On the divine Essence," clarifies the entry. Very often these annotations in other hands than the scribe's are such brief memoranda as "gone to Derwent [Coleridge, Coleridge's younger son (1800–1883)]" or "sent to D[erwent]," always or almost always in a hand recognizably Wordsworth's. But more frequent than such exceptions is the monogram already mentioned, "JC," which we take to be the initials of John Carter, the reason for this frequency being that this monogram, penned in the left margin beside every item believed to belong to Coleridge, was the final device of three used to verify his ownership.

Harvard MS. Eng 880 is, in truth, a catalogue of *two* book collections, of which roughly a fourth (about three hundred titles) was Coleridge's. In October 1829, these had been in Wordsworth's care for about twenty years, for over fifteen years at Rydal Mount, following Coleridge's removal to London from the Lake District. On 17 September 1829, when Coleridge drew up and signed his will, he bequeathed to "Joseph Henry Green, of Lincoln's Inn Fields, Surgeon, all my Books . . . upon Trust," with instruction that the trustee sell these and invest the proceeds for the benefit of Coleridge's widow and children.[17] It became essential, therefore, to separate from Wordsworth's books the volumes Coleridge had left in Wordsworth's keeping; and that this segregating was completed some time in the following October is implied by the date on the first leaf of the Manuscript Catalogue.

It would appear, however, that the catalogue already existed in more or less final form. Page 20, for instance, has in the left margin and beside several volumes of sermons the memorandum "sent to Derwent 1827" (the year when Derwent became Vicar of Helston, Cornwall). Furthermore, the loan of John Harris' *Navigantium atque Itinerantium Bibliotheca* on 2 April 1828 (Loan Book, p. 9), a title indicated as Coleridge's on MC.71, suggests that Coleridge's books had not been sent to him by that date. Page 53 has a puzzling interlineation in Wordsworth's hand under Coleridge's "Wallenstein 2 Co." It reads: "1 Copy

sent to Derwent at Mr. Hopwood's/ His Father's desire." Derwent was a tutor in the household of a Mr. Hopwood at Ul-
verston, Lancashire, from 1817 to late 1819, before he entered
St. John's College, Cambridge, in 1820.[18] It is therefore con-
ceivable that the catalogue was compiled before 1820. On the
other hand, it is possible that Wordsworth remembered having
sent the *Wallenstein* when requested, but did not record the fact
in the catalogue until later, perhaps at the time when Coleridge's
books were being got ready for shipment to him. Alternatively,
the *Wallenstein* might have been dispatched while Derwent was
visiting the Hopwoods during his Cambridge vacations. A similar puzzle was created when Wordsworth wrote beside a folio of
Beaumont and Fletcher belonging to Coleridge: "Hartley took
Mar: 4th 1824." No other internal evidence has been found that
the catalogue was finished before this date, but it almost certainly was.[19]

In the first state of the catalogue, books known or believed
to be Coleridge's were designated by a capital "C" written beside
them in the right margin and in the hand of the scribe. Later,
these items were again identified as Coleridge's, this time by an
"X" pencilled, now and then inked, beside them in the left margin. A third and final check-mark, generally superimposed on
the "X," was the monogram "JC" in ink.[20] It might be assumed,
therefore, that final responsibility for determining which volumes belonged to Coleridge was delegated to John Carter if the
monogram was, as we believe, his. That "JC" did his job carefully
is shown by an addendum of thirteen items (pages 105–106)
headed "Mr: Coleridge's Books/ not traced out & marked/ off in
preceding Catalogue" and signed "JC."[21] But so conscientious
was Wordsworth about deciding which books were Coleridge's
that he seems to have gone over the checked list himself, for the
last eight pages of the catalogue record, in his own pencilling,
113 titles, of which all but seven had already been ticked off as
Coleridge's.[22]

A major enigma of the Manuscript Catalogue is that
twenty-three entries are followed by an "O" in the scribe's hand.
This letter seems, like the "C" indicating books belonging to

Coleridge, to refer to a person who was neither Coleridge nor Wordsworth. Three of the twenty-three are also marked "JC," as if they were intended for Coleridge; and one of these, "La Pucelle Voltaire," is in Wordsworth's pencilled checklist of the books sent to Coleridge. Certainly the contents of the books marked "O" are such as would have been of particular interest to Coleridge: philosophy, theology, poetry, and dictionaries of foreign languages. Yet at least seven "O" titles appear in the Sale Catalogue.

Who or what "O" represents we can only guess. It may stand for the Rev. Owen Lloyd (1803–1841), who was Curate at Ambleside from 1826 to 1830 and Vicar of nearby Langdale from 1830 until his death. He was the nephew of Wordsworth's sister-in-law, Priscilla Lloyd, Christopher Wordsworth's wife, and he is often mentioned in various Wordsworth family letters as having been at Rydal Mount. His name appears as borrower in seven entries in LB between 1828 and 1837. It is therefore possible either that the "O" books were found, when the checking of titles was done in 1829, to be his property. On the other hand, the "O" may signify books which were meant to be given to him.

Another individual for whom books were marked was Edward Irving (1792–1834), minister of the Caledonian Church, Hatton Garden, London, from 1822 to 1830, a close friend and disciple of Coleridge. As three entries designated as Coleridge's books have the notation "Gone to Mr. Irvine," presumably Coleridge had requested that they be sent to Irving.

The Rydal Mount Loan Book

In the Harry Elkins Widener Collection at Harvard there is a small calf-bound manuscript on the front cover of which is written in ink: "Account of the Books lent out of the Library from Rydal Mount."[23] A slip of paper pasted above this title expands it in an unidentified hand to "A Library Book kept by Mr./ Wordsworth in which are/ entered the titles of the/ books lent out and/ the names of the/ borrowers." In the lower left corner of the slip and in the autograph of James Dykes Campbell (1838–1895), the biographer of Coleridge, are the words "Bought from a/ London Catalogue/ (Wallers, I think) soon/ after the sale JDC."[24] Campbell's own library was sold in 1904, and Mr. Widener (A.B. Harvard 1907) acquired the volume sometime before 15 April 1912, when he perished in the *Titanic* disaster.[25] In order to simplify references to it, we are calling it "The Rydal Mount Loan Book" and abbreviating this to "LB."

Besides being a record of titles borrowed, borrowers, and dates of borrowing or return between 25 August 1824 and 25 November 1858, LB served as a catchall for various memoranda: addresses; disbursements to carriers (e.g., for two boxes of soap candles on 21 February 1829) and to coach drivers for freight delivered (e.g., "Barrel of Oys^rs" on 11 January 1829); and "D^r W^s recipe for Rheumatis & Lumbago." This extraneous material occupies only the first page and the last eight, the borrowings forming an uninterrupted sequence.

At the beginning, entries were made in three columns divided by vertical lines and headed "Name & description of Books," "By whom taken out," and "Date"; but as time went on columns were abandoned for entries running straight across the page, and the date when a book was either lent or returned was sometimes omitted.[26] That is to say, many entries consist of only the title and the borrower's name. Sometimes merely the name of a borrower's residence (e.g., "Green Bank") was entered. Periodically, columns were reinstated, but very soon afterwards the practice again lapsed.

When a lent volume came back, the entry was cancelled, usually by a horizontal line drawn through it, sometimes by a series of slanting lines, and sometimes by criss-crosses or squiggles.[27] This obscuring or near-obliterating of an entry makes the deciphering of it difficult. About a dozen items are illegible.

A variety of hands appears. Generally, Wordsworth or some member of his household was responsible for noting the loan. Occasionally, however, a borrower made the entry himself and signed his name or his initials.

Many names familiar in Wordsworth's circle appear as borrowers, among them Sara Coleridge, Hartley Coleridge, De Quincey, and Dr. Thomas Arnold. Members of the poet's family, no less than friends, were expected to write down borrowed titles that were taken away from Rydal Mount. There are many listed to William Wordsworth, Junior (1810–1883) (WW2), for instance, when he was living at Carlisle and conducting the Stamp Office business there, the earliest entry being 1832 and the latest (the last in the notebook) 1858. Edward Quillinan's borrowings, both before and after his marriage to Dora, were recorded. Jane Wordsworth, aged nine, visiting doting grandparents at Christmas, was charged with "Arabian Knights [*sic*]," but four years later with "Elegant Extracts in Verse."

LB amply demonstrates that Wordsworth's library constituted a lending library for many persons, chiefly relations and friends, who were either settled neighbors or transient visitors, usually the guests of relations and friends. It names about two hundred borrowers and shows what types of book they borrowed. By 1830 the Ambleside Book Society, which in that year had thirty paying members (including Wordsworth) living in the area, had come into existence. But only members were privileged to borrow from this source and borrow only one volume at a time for no more than seven days without incurring a fine. Meanwhile, Wordsworth's books were circulating free of charge among his intimates.

Besides its value for Wordsworth's biography, LB provides information about the contents of his library which is not revealed by either *SC* or MC. It furnishes about two hundred additional titles. It also vouches for about 470 named in the other two lists; and sometimes the date of a borrowing in it makes it possible to deduce which edition of a book was lent.

Appendix I: Wordsworth

Appendix I consists of titles which we believe to have been in Wordsworth's library, but which do not appear in the Sale Catalogue, the Manuscript Catalogue, or the Loan Book. All are annotated (in the sense in which we are using the word), but although the great majority bear evidence of having been Wordsworth's, the others, though probably shelved with his, belonged to members of his household. Two, J.J. Scaliger's *Epistola de Vetustate et Splendore Gentis Scaligerae* and L.A. Seneca's *Philosophi,* are inscribed with either the autograph or the initials of Coleridge in addition to Wordsworth's autograph. These have not been included in Appendix II.

Our knowledge of these items comes from reports made by libraries and private individuals. The largest number are in university and other libraries; some are in private hands; some are described in printed catalogues of sales since 1859 and in articles dealing with these. A large group which belonged to Wordsworth's great-granddaughter, Mrs. Dorothy Dickson (d. 1969), was examined and inventoried by Chester L. Shaver in 1959.[28] Many of these items are now in Wordsworth Library, Grasmere. Some are known to have been sold or given to persons and institutions. About forty, however, according to our calculation, have dropped out of sight.

Editorial Method and Apparatus

As a standard of bibliographical information we have used the printed catalogue of the British Museum (*L*), relying on its description of an item, but not citing it overtly except when we quote its description of a volume once belonging to Wordsworth or Coleridge. When data in our sources (e.g., year of publication, size of volume, etc.) conflict with the data of this norm, we have indicated the discrepancy. Other printed catalogues, especially that of the Bibliothèque Nationale (*BN*) and the *National Union Catalogue* (*NUC*), we have cited when they furnish information not found in our primary authority.[29] In the same way we have utilized the printed catalogues of such Wordsworth collections as those of Amherst and Cornell, and have drawn upon articles dealing with Wordsworthiana at the Huntington Library, various libraries in and near Philadelphia, and the Coleridge Collection of Victoria University, Toronto. Finally, the verification of a number of books as Wordsworth's, particularly those in the

Wordsworth Library, Grasmere, has been made by means of letters received from libraries and private owners.

An entry in each of the three sections of the catalogue typically consists of most or some of the following data standing in the following order: (1) author's or authors' names or the first word of the title when the authorship is anonymous; when an author adopts a pseudonym, a title is indexed under his real name (if known) with his pseudonym (abbreviated to *pseud.*) in square brackets following (e.g., Procter, Bryan Waller [Cornwall, Barry, *pseud.*]) and the pseudonym is indexed as a cross reference to the real name: e.g., Cornwall, Barry, *pseud.* See Procter, Bryan Waller; (2) title, truncated if exceptionally long, transliterated if wholly or partly in Greek or Hebrew; (3) number of edition if not the first: e.g., Echard, Laurence. *The History of England* . . . Third edition, with additions;[30] (4) number of volumes if more than one; (5) place or places of publication other than London, which is always presupposed, except when London is one of two or more places of publication, those in foreign languages, especially those in Latin, being reproduced as found on the title-page: e.g., "Argentorati" for Strasbourg and "Parigi" for Paris;[31] (6) year or years (if a span) of publication; (7) size of volume, stated sometimes in the traditional forms (folio, quarto, octavo, duodecimo), sometimes in centimeters or inches; (8) the bibliographical authority or authorities, cited in square brackets, if not the printed catalogue of the British Museum: e.g., [Wing: AU]; (9) present or last-known whereabouts of an annotated item, enclosed in square brackets: e.g., [WL: Ann]; (10) the lot number of the Sale Catalogue in which an item appears (*SC*.4), the page number of the Manuscript Catalogue (MC.102), the page number of the Loan Book (LB.43), or the item number in the Hudson List as transcribed by Marilyn Kuhar (HL.MK.424)—but never all four of these.

What has just been said about a typical entry calls for a little qualification. First, a number of items in *SC*, MC, and LB, though giving the title of a work, fail to add the name of the author—a deficiency which we have supplied when we could. Again, when the name of an author *is* stated, how to index it has sometimes created a problem: e.g., Mindanus, whose actual name was Peter Frider, Mindanus (the city of Minden in Westphalia) being a kind of epithet. In this and similar cases involving a so-called scholar-in-*us* we have entered both the real name and the epithet, with a cross reference from one to the other. Second, keeping the practice of *L*, we have arranged an author's works (Cicero's, for example) in the following order: (1) an unspecified work or works: e.g., "Cicero (*Latin*)"; (2) collected works; (3) translations of collected works; (4) individual works; (5) translations of individual works. Once or twice, furthermore, in describing Latin titles we have retained such a printer's mode of spelling as the substitution of "v" for "u." Generally, too, we have noted only the first occurrence of a title in LB, the exception being a later occurrence which provides a more exact description. Third, when the year of publication is omitted from *SC*, we have cited as our authority the earliest edition of the work listed in *L* or in some other library catalogue; when the year is given in *SC* (it almost never appears in MC and LB and is sometimes lacking in *SC*), we have retained it if it agrees with the year given in *L* or in some other library catalogue. Fourth, it is proper to point out that all entries in MC and LB and some in *SC* fail to indicate the place of publication. Fifth, the size of a volume is seldom shown in MC and LB and is often stated erroneously in *SC*. Neither *CN*, moreover, nor H.O. Dendurent's article listing Coleridge's books in the library of Victoria University, Toronto, notes dimensions. Last, we have sometimes quoted the wording, in full or in part, of an entry in *SC*, MC, or LB in order to show that it agrees with the description given in *L* or in some other authority, or to draw attention to discrepancies, usually of publication date or size, between it and *L* or some other authority, for example, the entries for Mark Akenside and for Charles Thomas Browne's *Irene*.

A word, finally, about our use of signs and abbreviations. An asterisk preceding an entry denotes that we have not succeeded in identifying an author or a title. A question mark before an item registers our uncertainty either about our description of it or about which of two or more alternative descriptions is the correct one: e.g., our uncertainty about the name of an author, as in "Almanacco-Italiano"; about which of several works by the same author is meant (see the first entry under "Faber, George"); about which edition of a work, what place of publication, or what year of publication is signified: e.g., "Aristotle— Ethica." We have employed square brackets for several reasons: in general, to set off editorial insertions; specifically, to enclose the name of an author now known but not revealed when a work was first published: e.g., [Addison, Joseph]. *The Freeholder*; and to separate two or more titles offered in the same entry as alternatives (see the entry for *The Dublin Magazine*). Abbreviations of the titles of library catalogues, published and unpublished, correspond to those standardized in the *National Union Catalogue* (*NUC*) or Donald Wing's *Short-Title Catalogue of Books . . . 1641– 1700* (Wing) or the *British Union-Catalogue of Periodicals* (*BUCP*).

We have not attempted to draw from a list of Wordsworth's books conclusions about their possible influence on his writing. Such an endeavor would be out of place, we believe, in a volume intended to be simply a catalogue of his books (and some of Coleridge's). We hope, however, that the materials we have assembled will be of service to whoever may undertake such a study in the future.

Notes

1. *Modern Language Notes*, XXII, Part I, 83–89; Part II, 110–117.

2. Occasionally we have alluded to titles referred to in *The Letters of William and Dorothy Wordsworth* (Oxford, 1967–), as supplementary evidence.

3. Only those works by Wordsworth (some of them annotated) are included in the Composite List which are found in *SC*, MC, or LB.

4. Only those works by Wordsworth are included in Appendix I which are annotated.

5. *Sale Catalogues of Libraries of Eminent Persons* (general editor, A.N.L. Munby), Vol. 9 (*Poets and Men of Letters*), London, 1974, pp. 1–74.

6. No. VI, pp. 195–257.

7. We have renumbered the repeated one "Lot 451a."

8. History (Civil, Naval, and Military), Political Economy, Jurisprudence, etc. (Lots 1–86). Biography, Topography, Geography, Physical Science, and Natural History (Lots 87–184). Theology and Ethics, Ecclesiastical History, and Polemical Divinity (Lots 186–320). Philology, Bibliography, Belles-Lettres, and Miscellanea (Lots 321–451). Histrionic Literature, Fiction, and Fine Arts (Lots 451a–700).

9. The sum realized by the sale was only £380.11.9.

10. Park's reprint contains, however, as Knight's does not, indications that some sets of books were incomplete when the original catalogue was issued. After Lot 61 the compiler observed of its two items: "The missing volumes of these works having been lent, (to whom is not known,) may possibly be returned in time for the sale, and if so, will be sold with the above." With cross references to Lot 61 he plaintively reiterated this hope after half a dozen subsequent lots.

11. Lots 20, 141, 204, 344, 372, 385, 436, 556, and 679. Books that have both Coleridge's and Wordsworth's autographs are listed in both the Composite List and Appendix II.

12. A.B. Harvard 1898; d. 14 July 1925.

13. According to our count, one hundred written leaves and seventeen blank leaves.

14. *Op. cit.*, p. 4.

15. Classics: 1–10; Books illustrat: of the Classics: 11–15; Books illustrative of Modern Languages &c: 16–18; [blank, 19]; Theology: 20–29; Philosophy: 30–37; Law & Politics: 38–41; [blank, 42]; Poetry: 43–54; [blank, 55]; [blank, 56]; History: &c: &c: 57–67; [blank, 68]; Voyages, Travels, Geog: &c: 69–72; [blank, 73]; [blank, 74]; Natural History &c: &c: &c: 75–76; [blank, 77]; [blank, 78]; Books of Amusemt: &c: &c: 79–84; [blank, 85]; [blank, 86]; Novels & Romances: 87–88; [blank, 89]; [blank, 90]; Translations: 91–93; [blank, 94]; Modern Languages: 95–102; [blank, 103]; [blank, 104]; Mr. Coleridge's Books/ not traced out & marked/ off in preceding Catalogue./ JC: 105–106; [blank, 107]; eight unnumbered pages in pencil, 108s–115s ("s" indicating page numbers editorially supplied) in Wordsworth's hand, followed on 115s by "The above sent to Coleridge," also in Wordsworth's hand, but in ink. Below, in another hand, is a pencilled notation: "All above in Wordsworth's hand." See Plate II.

16. In the Manuscript Catalogue there are occasional misspellings, which suggest that the scribe failed to hear correctly some titles and authors' names as these were read to him: for example, "Moralisches Bademecum" (page 101) for "Moralisches Vademecum"; and "Harrington" (page 40) for "Barrington." What such errors tell about the identity of the scribe we do not know.

17. *CL*, VI, 998.

18. *CL*, V, 37, footnote 2.

19. Professor George Whalley discusses the question of date in *CM*.

20. See Plate I.

21. Of these thirteen items, four, in spite of "JC's" enumeration, had already been marked in the catalogue as Coleridge's.

22. Three of these are so illegible as to make it uncertain whether they repeat earlier items or not, and Wordsworth cancelled one (Harrington's *Oceana*, p. 115s) as being not Coleridge's but his own.

23. Shelfmark 12.11.14. It consists of seventy pages measuring 19.5 cm x 12.5 cm. Two pages, 31 and 62, are blank, and some are unnumbered.

24. If by "the sale" he meant the auction of Wordsworth's books in July 1859, the purchase probably occurred before April 1860, when, according to *DNB*, he went to Canada, not returning to Scotland until 1862.

25. It is described by A.S.W. Rosenbach in *A Catalogue of the Books and Manuscripts of Harry Elkins Widener* (Philadelphia, 1918).

26. See Plate III.

27. See Plate IV.

28. See, for example, the Aristotle entry. The sale catalogue of Mrs. Dickson's effects, auctioned on 9 April 1970, lists only a few books clearly identified as having been Wordsworth's, a case in point being *The Works of Burns, with His Life by Allan Cunningham.*

29. For authors following "Stimpfl" in *NUC,* the present limit of this catalogue, the catalogue of the Library of Congress (*DLC*) has been consulted.

30. The names of the publisher and printer are included only when these are necessary to authenticate an edition.

31. Charles Du Cange's *Glossarium ad Scriptores Mediae et Infimae Latinatis* (1678) is a help in discovering the English equivalents of Latin place names.

Signs and Abbreviations

*	An unidentified title.
X	A check-mark in MC usually identifying a title as STC's.
ABL	*Allgemeines Bücher-Lexikon oder vollständiges Alphabetisches Verzeichniss der von 1700 bis zu Ende 1810 erschienen Bücher in Deutschland und in den durch Sprache und Literatur damit verwandten Ländern gedruckt worden sind.* Ed. Wilhelm Heinsius. Vier Bände [in two volumes]. Leipzig, 1812.
ADB	*Allgemeine Deutsche Biographie.* 45 Bände. Leipzig, 1875-1900.
Allibone	Samuel Austin Allibone. *A Critical Dictionary of English Literature and British and American Authors.* 3 vol. Philadelphia, 1872, 1871.
Ann	A volume containing annotation (initials, autograph, inscription) identifying WW or a member of his immediate family as former owner.
AU	Aberdeen University Library.
AWC	*The Amherst Wordsworth Collection: A Descriptive Bibliography.* By Cornelius Howard

Patton. Published by the Trustees of Amherst College. 1936.

BB *Bibliotheca Britannica or a General Index to British and Foreign Literature.* By Robert Watt, M.D. 4 vol. Edinburgh, London, 1824.

BBel *Bibliotheca Belgica.* 6 tomes. Bruxelles, 1964-1970.

BN *Catalogue Général des Livres Imprimés de la Bibliothèque Nationale.* 226 tomes. Paris, 1897-1977 (unfinished).

Brunet *Manuel du Libraire et de l'Amateur de Livres* ... Par Jacques-Charles Brunet. 6 tomes. Paris, 1860-65.

BSic *Bibliographia Siciliana.* Comp. by Giuseppe M. Mira. 2 vol. Palermo, 1875; reprinted New York, n.d.

BU *Biographie Universelle Ancienne et Moderne.* 52 tomes. Paris, 1811-1828.

BUCP *British Union-Catalogue of Periodicals.* New York, London, 1955-1958, and *Supplement,* 1962.

C An abbreviation for "Samuel Taylor Coleridge" in MC.

CaOKQ Queen's University, Kingston, Ontario.

CaOTV.HD H.O. Dendurent, "The Coleridge Collection in Victoria University Library, Toronto," *TWC,* V (Autumn, 1974), 225-286.

CaOTV. HD.Ann A book annotated by STC (as indicated in the above article).

CaOTV. HD.GW Professor George Whalley's corrections of HD's article as communicated to the authors by letter.

CF   Coleridge family (a work owned by).

CM   *The Collected Works of Samuel Taylor Coleridge*. General editor Kathleen Coburn. [12. *Marginalia*. Edited by George Whalley. 6 vol. London and Princeton, 1979-].

CN   *The Notebooks of Samuel Taylor Coleridge*. Edited by Kathleen Coburn. 3 vol. (Text); 3 vol. (Notes). London, 1957- . T: Text; N: Notes.

CSJ   St. John's College Library, Cambridge.

CSmH   Henry E. Huntington Library and Art Gallery, San Marino, California.

CSmH.   P.M. and W.W. Zall ... and Doris Braendel,
ZZB:Ann   "Wordsworth in the Huntington Library: A Preliminary Check-list," *TWC*, (Autumn, 1970), 141-160.

CtY   Yale University Library.

CtY.BL   Yale University, Beinecke Library.

CWC   *The Cornell Wordsworth Collection: A Catalogue of Books and Manuscripts Presented to the University by Mr. Victor Emanuel ...* Compiled by George Harris Healey. Ithaca, N.Y., 1957.

CWW   Books annotated by WW or members of his immediate family owned in 1957 by the Rev. Christopher William Wordsworth (1879-1961).

D or   Derwent Coleridge, son of STC.
Derwent

DAB   *Dictionary of American Biography*.

DAL   *Deutsche Anonymen-Lexicon, 1501-1850*. Compiled by Michael Holzmann and Hanns Bohatta. 4 vol. Weimar, 1902.

DAP   *Dictionary of Anonymous and Pseudonymous English Literature. (Samuel Halkett and John Laing). New and Enlarged Edition.* By Dr. James Kennedy, W.A. Smith, and A.F. Johnson. 7 vol. London, 1926–1934.

DD   Books annotated by WW or members of his immediate family owned in 1959 by Mrs. Dorothy Wordsworth Dickson (d. 1969).

DDSC   Mrs. Dorothy Dickson Sale Catalogue *(Catalogue of Furnishings and Effects Removed from Stepping Stones, Rydal, for Sale by Auction at North Terrace, Bowness-on-Windermere. Thursday 9th April 1970, Commencing 12:00 Noon).*

DFo   The Folger Shakespeare Library, Washington, D.C.

DFo.AC   The Folger Shakespeare Library, Association Collection.

DLC   *A Catalog of Books Represented by Library of Congress Printed Cards Issued to July 31, 1942.* 167 vol. Ann Arbor, Michigan, 1943.

DNB   *Dictionary of National Biography.*

DW   Dorothy Wordsworth, WW's sister.

DWQ   Dora Wordsworth Quillinan, daughter of WW and wife of Edward Quillinan.

E   *Catalogue of the Printed Books in the Library of the Faculty of Advocates.* 6 vol. Edinburgh, London, 1863–1878; *Supplementary Volume,* 1879. (Now merged with the National Library of Scotland, Edinburgh).

EU   *Catalogue of the Printed Books in the Library of the University of Edinburgh.* 3 vol. Edinburgh, 1918–1923.

EY   *The Letters of William and Dorothy Words-*
worth. Arranged and Edited by the Late Er-
nest de Selincourt. Second edition. The
Early Years 1787-1805. Revised by Chester
L. Shaver. Oxford, 1967.

GBD   *A General Bibliographical Dictionary, from*
the German of Frederic Adolphus Ebert. 4
vol. Oxford, 1837.

GGW   Gordon Graham Wordsworth (1860-1935), WW's
grandson and son of WW2.

GM   *The Gentleman's Magazine; or, Monthly Intelli-*
gencer. 103 vol. London, 1731-1833; New
series, 45 vol., 1834-56.

Graesse *Trésor de Livres Rares et Précieux* ... par
Jean George Théodore Graesse. 7 vol. [in 8].
Berlin, 1922.

GS   *Catalogue of the Library of Joseph Henry*
Green Which Will Be Sold by Auction. Sotheby,
Wilkinson, and Hodge. London, 1880.

GW   Professor George Whalley, Queen's University,
Kingston, Ontario, Canada.

H, HC, or Hartley Coleridge, son of STC.
Hartley

HL   The John Hudson List (of WW's books) as cited
by Peter Laver.

HL.MK   The John Hudson List (of WW's books) as
transcribed by Marilyn Kuhar.

ICN   The Newberry Library, Chicago.

ICN.Bon The Newberry Library, Chicago, Lucien Bona-
parte Collection.

ICN.RBC The Newberry Library, Chicago, Rare Book Collection.

ICU   The University of Chicago Library.

InU   Indiana University Library, Bloomington.

InU.WC   Indiana University Library, Bloomington,
             the Wordsworth Collection.

IS   Kathleen Coburn, *Inquiring Spirit: A New
             Presentation of Coleridge from his Published
             and Unpublished Writings*. New York, 1951.

IU   University of Illinois Library, Urbana.

JB   James Butler, "Wordsworth in Philadelphia
             Area Libraries, 1787-1850," *TWC*, IV (Winter,
             1973), 41-64.

JC   John Carter, WW's clerk and amanuensis.

[JC]   John Carter (monogram extrapolated by the
             authors from a single entry to thirteen en-
             tries on MC.105 and MC.106).

KC   Professor Kathleen Coburn, Victoria Univer-
             sity, Toronto.

L   *British Museum General Catalogue of Printed
             Books*. Photolithographic Edition to 1955.
             263 vol. London, 1965-66; *Ten-Year Supple-
             ment*, 1956-65. 50 vol. London, 1968.

LB   "A Library Book kept by M^r. Wordsworth in
             which are entered the titles of the books
             lent out and the names of the borrowers."
             Harvard University Library, The Harry Elkins
             Widener Collection, Shelfmark 12.11.14 (MS.).

LLA   *Catalogue of the London Library, St. James's
             Square, London*. By C.T. Hagberg Wright ...
             and C.J. Parnell. 2 vol. London, 1913-
             1914. (and *Supplements*, 1913-20, 1920-28,
             1928-50).

Lowndes   William Thomas Lowndes. *Bibliographer's Manual of English Literature*. 10 vol. London, 1864, and *Appendix*, 1880-82.

LVA.DC   The Victoria and Albert Museum and Library, London, Dyce Collection.

LY   *The Letters of William and Dorothy Wordsworth. The Later Years*. Arranged and edited by Ernest de Selincourt. 3 vol. Oxford, 1939.

MA   Amherst College Library, Amherst, Massachusetts.

McAC   *Catalogue of the McAlpin Collection of British History and Theology* [in Union Theological Seminary, New York], compiled by Charles Ripley Gillett. 5 vol. New York, 1927-30.

MB   Boston Public Library, Boston, Massachusetts.

MBAt   *Catalogue of the Library of the Boston Athenaeum*. 5 vol. Boston, 1874-1882.

MC   "A Catalogue of Wordsworth's Library rendered in the handwriting of his daughter," Harvard University, The Houghton Library, MS Eng 880.

MdBJ   The Johns Hopkins University Library, Baltimore, Maryland.

MH   Harvard University Library, Cambridge, Massachusetts.

MiU   The University of Michigan Library, Ann Arbor.

MoSW   Washington University Library, St. Louis, Missouri.

MoSW.   Washington University Library, St. Louis,
GNMC   Missouri. The George N. Meissner Collection.

MR   *Catalogue of the Printed Books and Manu-*
              scripts in the John Rylands Library, Man-
              chester, 3 vol. Manchester, 1896-99.

MW   Mary Wordsworth, wife of WW.

MY   *The Letters of William and Dorothy Words-*
              worth. The Middle Years. Arranged and
              edited by Ernest de Selincourt. Second edi-
              tion. Revised by Mary Moorman and Alan G.
              Hill. 2 vol. Oxford, 1969-70.

N&Q   *Notes and Queries, a Medium of Intercommuni-*
              cation. 12 vol. London, [1849]-55; *Ninth*
              series, 1898- .

n.d.   No date of publication.

NIC   Cornell University Library, Ithaca, New York.

NjP   Princeton University Library.

NN.BC   New York Public Library. Berg Collection.

NNMor   The Pierpont Morgan Library, New York.

NN.RBD   New York Public Library, Rare Book Division.

NN.SC   Columbia University Library, Special Collec-
              tions.

NNUT   Union Theological Seminary Library, New York.

n.p.   No place of publication.

n.s.   No size indicated.

NUC   *The National Union Catalogue: Pre-1956 Im-*
              prints. 569 vol. London, 1968-1978 (com-
              pleted through "Stimpfl, Hugo").

O   ? Owen Lloyd (1803-1841).

OO.SC   Oberlin College (Ohio) Library, Special Col-
               lections.

Ox   The Bodleian Library, Oxford University.

P   An unidentified person (or place) so labeled
               in MC.

PL   Peter Laver, Administrative Librarian, The
               Wordsworth Library, Dove Cottage, Grasmere,
               Cumbria.

PPRF   The Rosenbach Foundation, Philadelphia.

PSC.WWC   Swarthmore College, Wells Wordsworth Collec-
               tion.

PSC.WWC.   A book annotated by WW as indicated in JB.
JB:Ann

RP   Roy Park, ed., *Poets and Men of Letters*, Vol.
               9 (1974) of the twelve-volume series *Sale
               Catalogues of Libraries of Eminent Persons*,
               general editor A.N.L. Munby (London, 1971-
               75), "William Wordsworth," pp. 1-75.

RPB.HLKC   Brown University, The John Hay Library,
               Harry Lyman Koopman Collection.

RPB.RBC   Brown University, The John Hay Library,
               Rare Book Collection.

RP.QH   RP's reproduction of GGW's transcription from
               the Queen's Hotel (Ambleside, Cumbria) copy
               of the 1859 Sale Catalogue (*SC*) into a copy
               of the 1859 Sale Catalogue.

RS   Robert Southey.

s   A supplemental page-number in MC assigned
               by the authors.

SB   *Shakespeare Bibliography*. Compiled by Will-
               iam Jaggard. Stratford-on-Avon, 1911.

SC   *Catalogue of the Varied and Valuable Histori-*
            cal, Poetical, Theological, and Miscellaneous
            Library of the Late Venerated Poet-Laureate,
            William Wordsworth, Esquire, D.C.L.... To-
            gether Nearly Three Thousand Volumes: Which
            Will Be Sold by Auction, by Mr. John Burton
            (of Preston) at ... Rydal Mount, near Amble-
            side, Windermere, on Tuesday the 19th, Wed-
            nesday the 20th, and Thursday the 21st, Days
            of July, 1859. At Eleven O'Clock 'Fore Noon
            Each Day: In Pursuance of Instructions from
            the Executors. (As reprinted by Professor
            William Knight in *Transactions of the Words-*
            worth Society, No. 6 [1884], pp. 195-257.

SH   Sara Hutchinson, sister-in-law of WW.

SM   *A Bibliography of English Law.* 3 vol. Lon-
            don, 1925-33. (Vol. I, "to 1650," of Sweet
            and Maxwell's *Complete Law Book Catalogue.*
            By W. Harold Maxwell; Vol. II, "1651-1800,"
            compiled by Leslie F. Maxwell, 1931; Vol.
            III, "1801-1932," completed by Leslie F.
            Maxwell, 1933).

STC   Samuel Taylor Coleridge.

STL   *Serie dei Testi di Lingua.* Comp. by Barto-
            lommeo Gamba da Bassano. Venezia, 1839.

TC   Edward Arber. *The Term Catalogues,* 3 vol.,
            London, 1903-06.

TWC   *The Wordsworth Circle.* Philadelphia, 1969- .

TxU.An   The University of Texas Library, Austin, The
            George A. Aitken Collection.

TxU.Wn   The University of Texas Library, Austin, The
            John Henry Wrenn Library.

VCL   Victoria College Library. See CaOTV.

Wing   *Short-Title Catalogue of Books Printed in England, Scotland, Ireland, Wales, and British America and of English Books Printed in Other Countries, 1641-1700.* Compiled by Donald Wing of the Yale University Library. 3 vol. New York, 1945-51.

WL   The Wordsworth Library, Dove Cottage, Grasmere, Cumbria.

Woodward   G. Woodward, compiler, *Early Nonconformity 1566-1800. A Catalogue of Books in Dr. Williams's Library..* 10 vol. Boston, 1968.

WR   William Roberts, "Books from Wordsworth's Library," *The Athenaeum*, 30 May 1896, p. 714.

WW   William Wordsworth.

WW2   William Wordsworth, Junior (1810-1883).

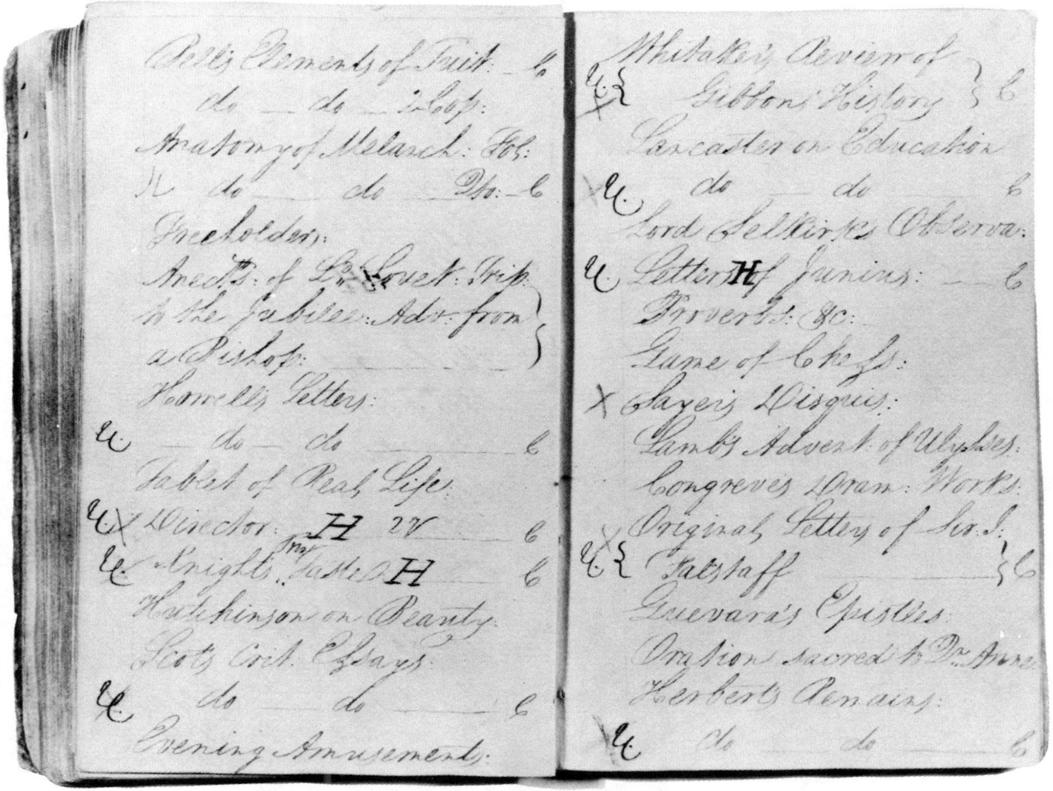

[illegible] Elements of [illegible] — 6
do — do — 2 Cop:
Anatomy of Melanch: Fol:
H do — do — 8vo — 6
Freeholder:
Anecd: of Dr. Swift: Trip to the Jubilee: Adv. from a Bishop:
Howell's Letters:
e — do — do — 6
Tablet of Real Life:
e X Director: H 2V — 6
e Knight's: Taste H — 6
Hutchinson on Beauty:
Scots Crit. Essays:
e — do — do — 6
Evening Amusements:

e X { Whitaker's Review of Gibbon's History } 6
Lancaster on Education
X e — do — do — 6
Lord Selkirk's Observa:
e Letters H of Junius: — 6
Proverbs: &c:
Game of Chess:
X Sayer's Disquis:
Lamb's Advent. of Ulysses:
Congreve's Dram: Works:
e X { Original Letters of Sir J. Falstaff } 6
Guevara's Epistles:
Oration sacred to Dr. [illegible]
Herbert's Remains:
X e — do — do — 6

Plate I

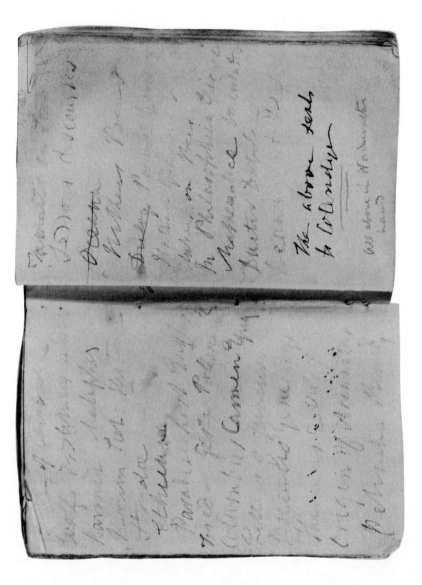

Plate II

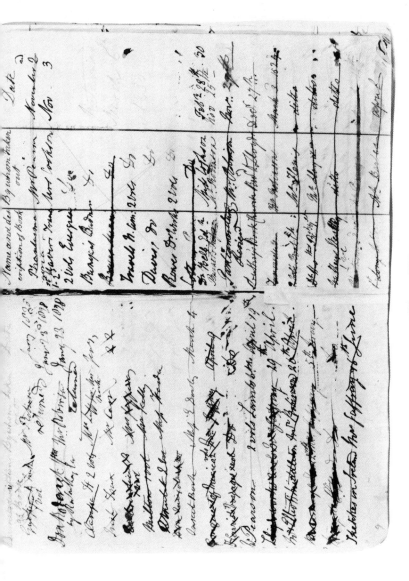

Plate III

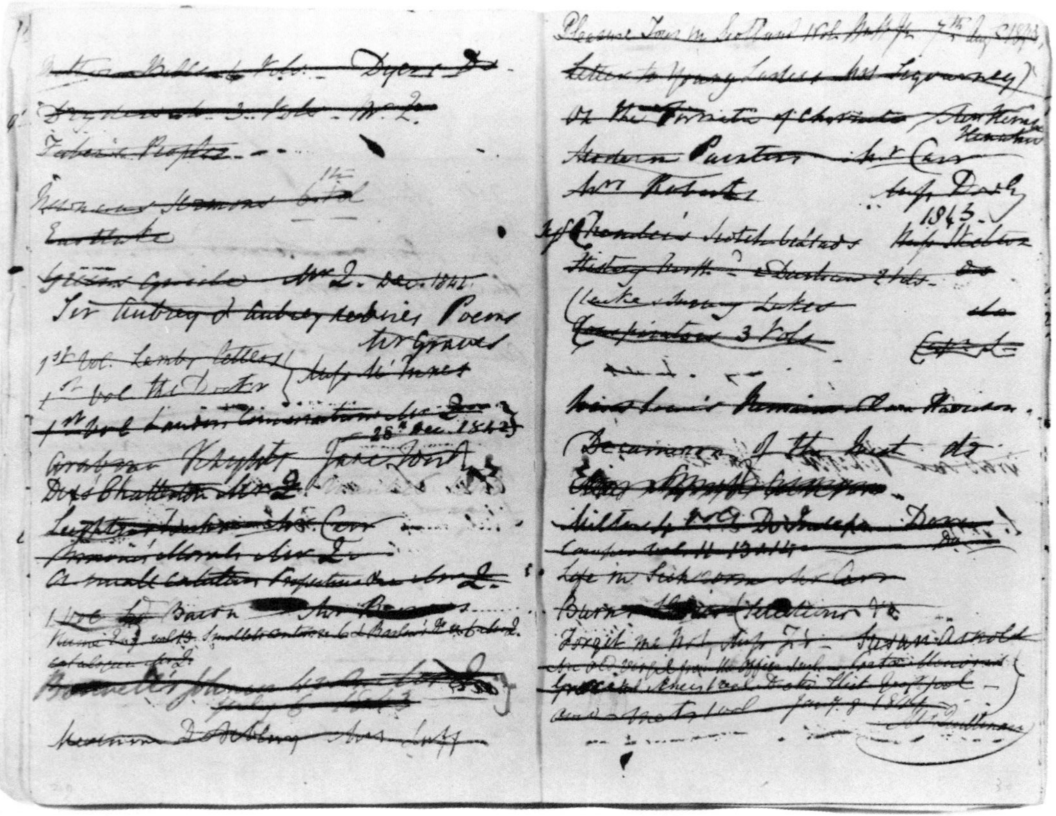

Plate IV

COMPOSITE LIST

Books belonging to Wordsworth
as found in
the Sale Catalogue,
the Manuscript Catalogue,
or the Loan Book

Abercrombie, John. The gardener's pocket journal.
1789. 12°. MC.75: "Abercrombie's Pocket Journ:"

The accomplish'd letter-writer. Newcastle-upon-Tyne,
1778. 12°. MC.84: "Accomp: Letter Writer:"

*An account of some matters relating to the Long
Parliament, by a Person of Honor. 1670.
SC.37.

*Account of the Kingdom of Hungary. 1717. SC.78.
MC.66: "Historical Account of Hungary."

An account of the principal pleasure tours in Scotland and the great lines of road in that country.
Maps. Edinburgh, 1819. 8°. LB.30.

Acosta, Joseph de. The naturall and morall historie
of the East and West Indies. Translated into
English by Edward Grimstone. 1604. 8°. SC.67:
"4to." MC.61: "Hist: of Indies:"

Adam, Alexander. Roman antiquities. Edinburgh,
1791. 12°. MC.15: "Adam's Rom: Antiqui:"

Adamson, John. Lusitania illustrata; notices of the
history, antiquities, literature, etc. of Portugal. Literary department. Part I. Selection
of sonnets, with biographical sketches of the
authors. (Part II. Minstrelsy). Newcastle
upon Tyne, 1842-46. 8°. SC.514: "Selection of
Sonnets, etc., of Portugal, by J. Adamson, 1842."
SC.531: "Notices of the Minstrelsy of Portugal,
by J. Adamson, 1846."

Addison, Joseph. See Steele, Sir Richard. The
tatler.

————. The evidences of the Christian religion. 1730. 12°. LB.11.

[————]. The freeholder, or political essays. 4th ed. 1729. 16.5cm. [*NUC*]. *SC*.46: "12mo, 1739."

[———— and Sir Richard Steele]. The spectator. 8 vol. 1744. 12°. *SC*.434: "9 vols., 8vo, 1744." MC.79: "Spectator: 9 Vol:" [Lowndes: "*London*, Tonson, 1744, 12 mo. 8 vols; or with the addition of a 9th volume, Tonson and Watts"].

[————]. The spectator; corrected from the originals. With a new biographical preface, by N[athaniel] Ogle. 8 vol. 1827. 8°. *SC*.435: "12mo."

Addison, Lancelot. The primitive institution; or, a seasonable discourse of catechizing. 2nd ed. 1690. 12°. *SC*.199: "Addison on Catechising, 1690." MC.28: "Primitive Institution."

Advice from a bishop: in a series of letters to a young clergyman. 1759. 8°. [Woodward: "T. Lindsey in ms. note attrib. this to Fer. Warner; this seems unlikely; also attrib. to Rob. Clayton"]. MC.82: "Adv: from a Bishop."

Aeschines. Aischinou ho kata Ktesiphontos kai Demosthenous ho peri stephanou logos [in Greek]. Interpretationem latinam et vocum difficiliorum explicationem adjecerunt P[eter] Foulkes, J[ohn] Friend. Editio secunda. Gr. & Lat. 2 pt. Oxonii, 1715. 8°. *SC*.409.

*Aeschylus. MC.1 "Aeschiles:"

————. The Agamemnon; the Greek text with a translation into English verse, and notes critical and explanatory by John Conington. 1848. 22cm. [*NUC*]. *SC*.579: "by John Conybeare."

African Association. See Proceedings of.

Aikin, afterwards Barbauld, Anna Letitia. See Aikin,
John.

————. The British novelists; with an essay; and pre-
faces, biographical and critical, by Mrs. Barbauld.
50 vol. 1810. 12°. [WW appears to have owned
twelve volumes of this set. See Burney, Frances;
Defoe, Daniel; Fielding, Henry; Hawkesworth, John;
Johnson, Samuel; Mackenzie, Henry; Radcliffe, Mrs.
Ann; Reeve, Clara; Smollett, Tobias; Walpole,
Horace]. MC.87: "Brit: Novelist: 12 Vol: Viz:
Evelina.--Romance of the Forest.--Rob: Crusoe.--
Hump: Clinker.--Jos: Andrews.--Rascilas [*sic*].--
Almeron [*sic*].--Old Eng: Baron.--Castle of Otranto.
--Man of Feeling.--Julia de Rubina [*sic*]." ["H.A."
pencilled beside "Almeron"]. LB.55: "26th v.
[Rasselas, and Almoran and Hamet]."

Aikin, Arthur. The annual review and history of literature, 1802-1808. Arthur Aikin, editor. 7 vol.
1803-09. 8°. MC.79: "Annual Review: 4 Vol:"

————. The natural history of the year, being an en-
largement of Dr. [John] Aikin's Calendar of nature.
1798. 12°. *SC*.142. MC.76: "Natural Hist: of the
Year:"

Aikin, John. See Milton, John. The poetical works;
Spenser, Edmund.

[———— and Aikin, afterwards Barbauld, Anna Letitia].
Evenings at home; or, the juvenile budget opened.
Consisting of a variety of miscellaneous pieces,
for the instruction and amusement of young persons.
6 vol. 1792-96. 12°. MC.80: "Evenings at Home:"

Aikin, Lucy. See Barbauld, Mrs. Anna Letitia.

Ainsworth, Robert. Thesaurus linguae compendarius ...
a new edition [by Thomas Morell] carefully revised ... by J[ohn] Carey. 2 pt. 1816. 4°.
SC.321: "Ainsworth's Latin Dictionary, by Morell,
8vo, 1816." [? MC.14: "Latin Diction^y:"].

[Ainsworth, William Harrison and John Partington Aston].
Sir John Chiverton; a romance. 1826. 12°. *SC*.634.
LB.8.

[Akenside, Mark]. The pleasures of imagination. A
poem, in three books. 1744. 4°. *SC*.451a: "(*the
first edition*) ... 4to, *with MS. Notes by W. Wordsworth.*"

Akerman, John Yonge, ed. Moneys received and paid for
secret services of Charles II. and James II. from
30th March, 1679, to 25th December, 1688. 1851.
4°. *SC*.15.

Alciati, Andrea. See Sanchez de las Brozas, Francesco.

————. Emblemata. Elucidata Claudij Minois ... commentariis; quibus additae sunt eiusdem auctoris
notae posteriores. Lugduni Batavorum, 1614. 8°.
SC.323. MC.10: "Alciati Emblemata." LB.27: "Alciati Emblemata."

————. Rerum patriae Andreae Alciati ... libri IIII.
Ex m. s. Bibliothecae Ambrosianae. Mediolani, 1625.
16.5cm. [Paul F. Betz: Ann]. *SC*.324: "4to."

Alea, Josef Miguel. See Saint-Pierre, Jacques Henri
Bernardin de.

Alemán, Mateo. The rogue; or, the life of Guzman de
Alfarache. Translated by ... James Mabbe. 2 pt.
Oxford, 1630. fol. *SC*.421: "folio ... 1630."
MC.87: "Life of Guzman de Alfer [*sic*]:"

Alethe. See Derivations from the Welsh.

Alfieri, Vittorio, Count. The tragedies of Vittorio
Alfieri. Translated from the Italian by C[harles]
Lloyd. 3 vol. 1815. 12°. MC.54: "Lloyd's Trag:
of Alfieri: 3 Vol:" LB.38: "Lloyd's translation
of Alfieri 1st vol."

Alford, Henry. Chapters on the poets of ancient Greece.
1841. 22.5cm. [NIC:Ann: "vol. 1"]. *SC*.452: "vol.
1, 8vo, 1841."

————. [? The poetical works of Henry Alford. 2 vol.
1845. 8°.]--[? 2 vol. in 1. 1845. 17cm.].
[*NUC*]. LB.57: "Alford's Poems."

————. Prose hymns, chiefly from Scripture, printed
for chanting. 1844. 12°. *SC*.453.

————. Psalms and hymns adapted to the Sundays and
holydays throughout the year; to which are added
some occasional hymns. 1844. 12°. *SC*.453.
[? LB.44: "Hymns & Psalms"].

————. The school of the heart and other poems. 2
vol. Cambridge, London, 1835. 7.75 in. [*CWC*:
Ann]. *SC*.598: "8vo." LB.19 "'The School of the
Heart'."

Alhacen. See Life of Tamerlane.

Alison, Sir Archibald. The principles of population,
and their connection with human happiness. 2 vol.
Edinburgh, 1840. 8°. *SC*.87.

Alison, William Pulteney. Remarks on the report of Her
Majesty's commissioners on the poor laws of Scotland in 1844 and on the dissent of Mr. Twisleton
from that report. Edinburgh, 1844. 8°. *SC*.1.

[Allestree, Richard]. The government of the tongue.
3rd ed. Oxford, 1675. 8°. *SC*.199: "1675." MC.29:
"Govt: of the Tongue."

[————]. The whole duty of man, necessary for all
families, with private devotions for severall occasions. 2 pt. 1660. 8°. MC.28: "The whole duty
of Man:"

Allott, Robert. England's Parnassus. 1600. 15.4cm.
[DFo:Ann]. *SC*.611: "12mo." MC.45: "Eng: Parnassus:"

Allston, Washington. Monaldi; a tale. 1842. 7.75 in.
[*CWC*:Ann]. *SC*.634.

————. [Another copy]. [CtY.BL: "Autograph and presentation inscription from Washington Allston"].
SC.454: "*(with the Artist-author's Autograph)*."

Almon, John. The debates and proceedings of the British
House of Commons, during the ... sessions ... 1743-
1774. [Compiled by J. Almon and others]. 11 vol.
1766-75. 8°. *SC*.25: "during the years 1743, '44,
'45, and 1746; 2 vols., 8vo ... 1766." MC.39:
"Commons Deb: 2 vol:"

An amateur. See Barton, Bernard.

The amulet. See Hall, Samuel Carter.

Amyot, Jacques. See Plutarch.

*Anacreon. *SC*.668: "Anacreon, Gr. et La., interlinear,
8vo."

The ancient British drama. See Scott, Sir Walter.

*Ancient history. MC.57: "Ancient History:"

Ancillon, Johann Peter Friedrich. Mélanges de la littérature et de philosophie. 2 tom. Paris, 1809.
8°. MC.100: "Anc: Melanges: 2 Vol:"

Andersen, Hans Christian. Tales from Denmark. Translated by Charles Boner. 1847. 17cm. [*NUC*].
[DD:Ann]. LB.40: "Andersen's Tales."

Anderson, Christopher. Historical sketches of the
ancient native Irish and their descendants. Edinburgh, 1828. 20cm. [MA:Ann]. *SC*.2: "8vo."

Anderson, Robert, M.D. The works of the British poets.
With prefaces, biographical and critical by Robert
Anderson, M.D. 13 vol. London, Edinburgh, [1792-]
1795. 8°. [Vol. XI is dated 1794]. [WL:Ann].

MC.43: "Anderson's Brit: Poets 13 Vol:" LB.8 "[?
1st ? 6th Vol B. Poets"].

Anderson, Robert, of Carlisle. See Cumberland ballads;
Sanderson, Thomas.

————. The poetical works of Robert Anderson ... To
which is prefixed the life of the author, written
by himself. An essay on the character, manners,
and customs of the peasantry of Cumberland; and observations on the style and genius of the author,
by Thomas Sanderson. 2 vol. Carlisle, 1820. 16°.
[WL (2 copies):Ann]. LB.58: "Andersons Works. 2
Vol."

Anderson, Robert, Perpetual Curate of Trinity Chapel,
Brighton. A practical exposition of the Gospel
according to St. John. 2 vol. 1841. 12°. [? LB.
28: "St John Gospel"]. See Sumner, John Bird.

*Anecdotes of [Simon Fraser,] Lord Lovat. MC.82: "An-
ects: of Ld Lovet [sic]:"

Anfrie (or Amfrye) de Chaulieu, Guillaume. Oeuvres de
l'abbé de Chaulieu. Nouvelle édition, augmentée
d'un grand nombre de pièces qui n'étoient point
dans les précédentes, & corrigée dans une infinité
d'endroits sur des copies autentiques par M. de
Saint-Marc. 2 vol. Amsterdam, Paris, 1750. 15cm.
[NUC]. SC.492. MC.102: "Chaulieu 2 [? vol.]."

The annual anthology, 1799-1800 [ed. Robert Southey].
2 vol. Bristol, [1799-1800]. 8°. SC.653.
MC.49: "Annual Anthology: 2 Vol:"

The annual register; or, a view of the history, poli-
ticks, and literature of the year 1758 (-1851).
Vol. 1-93. 8°. SC.4: "1758 to 1792, 35 vols.;
1794 to 1796, 4 vols.; 1800, 1 vol.; 1802 to 1807,
8 vols.... 1808 to 1811, 4 vols.; 1814 and 1820,
2 vols.... in all 54 vols. 8vo." MC.58: "Annual
Register 1777:" LB.43: "4 vols of Annual Register
Review."

The annual review. See Aikin, Arthur.

Another hand. See Lindsay, Robert.

Anster, John. See Goethe, Johann Wolfgang von.

Anstey, Christopher. The new Bath guide; or, memoirs
    of the B--r--d family: in a series of poetical epis-
    tles. A new edition. 1832. 8°. *SC*.11: "1832."

An answer to a late pamphlet intituled, The judgment
    and doctrine of the clergy of the Church of England
    concerning one special branch of the king's pre-
    rogative, viz. in dispensing with the penal laws
    ... In a letter to a friend. 1687. 4°. [Ox].
    [? MC.28: "An Answer--Clergy-- --"].

Antoninus Atheniensis. See Gale, Thomas.

Antoninus Liberalis. See Gale, Thomas.

Apollodorus. MC.1: "Apollodorus:" See Statius, Publius
    Papinius.

Apostolic instruction, exemplified in the First Epistle
    General of St. John. 1840. 12°. *SC*.310. HL.MK.
    424. See *GM*, April, 1840, p. 405.

Arabian nights entertainments. Translated from the
    French of M. [Antoine] Galland. [Vol. 18 of The
    novelist's magazine]. [? LB.15: "Arabian Nights"].

The Arabian nights entertainments, carefully revised
    ... To which is added a selection of new tales, now
    first translated from the Arabic originals. Also,
    an introduction and notes ... By Jonathan Scott.
    6 vol. 1811. 12°. *SC*.456: "Oxford." [? LB.15:
    "Arabian Nights"].

Arabian tales. LB.17: "Arabian Tales." [? Arabian
    tales: or, a continuation of the Arabian nights
    entertainments ... Newly translated from the ori-
    ginal Arabic into French by Dom Chaves [i.e. Dom

Denis Chavis, an Arab monk] ... and M[onsieur
Jacques] Cazotte. 3 vol. 1794. 12°]. [L; *BU*].

Arago, Dominique François Jean. Historical éloge of
James Watt. Translated from the French, with ad-
ditional notes and an appendix, by J[ohn] P[atrick]
Muirhead. 1839. 4°. *SC*.89.

Arblay, Madame D'. See Burney, Frances.

Arbuthnot, John, M.D. The miscellaneous works of the
late Dr. Arbuthnot. The second edition, with additions. 2 vol. Glasgow, 1751. 12°. *SC*.325: "2
vols., 8vo ... *Glasgow*, 1751." MC.81: "Arbuthnot's Works:"

Argentine; an auto-biography. 1839. 12°. *SC*.452:
"8vo, 1839 (*Presentation Autograph*)." LB.70:
"Argentine."

Ariosto, Ludovico. Opere in versi e in prosa, italiane
e latine, con dichiarazioni. [ed. Giovanni Andrea
Barotti]. 4 tom. Venezia, 1741. 12°. *SC*.458:
*"with Charles Lloyd's Book-plate and Laureate's
Autog."* [? MC.99: "Ariosto:" [classified under
"Modern Languages"]. LB.17: [? Ariosto] [MS.
unclear].

————. Orlando furioso. [WL: "My companion in the
Alps with Jones [front page]. I carried this book
on my pedestrian Tour in the Alps with Jones, W.
Wordsworth [last page]." n.d., small]. MC.100:
"Orlando Furioso:" LB.17: [? Ariosto] [MS. unclear].

————. Orlando Furioso in English heroical verse.
By J[ohn] Harington. 1591. fol. *SC*.457: "folio."
MC.46: "Harrington's [*sic*] Orlando Furis: [*sic*]."
LB.38: "Harrington's [*sic*] Ariosto."

Aristophanes. Comoediae duae, Plutus et Nubes. 1695.
8°. *SC*.670. MC.1: "Aristoph: 2 Plays: 2 Cop."

————. A metrical version of the Acharnians, the Knights, and the Birds, in the last of which a vein of peculiar humour and character is for the first time detected and developed. By John Hookham Frere. 3 pt. 1840. 4°. *SC*.537.

*Aristotle. Ethica Nicomachea. MC.34: "H[artley] C[oleridge] Ethica: (qy ?) Arist: Eth: HC."

*————. [Rhetoric]. LB.18: "Aristotles Rhetoric."

Armistead, Wilson. A tribute for the negro: being a vindication of the capabilities of the coloured portion of mankind. Manchester, 1848. 8°. *SC*.13.

*Armistice and convention in Portugal. MC.62: "Armist: & Conven: in Portug:"

[Armstrong, John]. The art of preserving health; a poem. 1744. 4°. *SC*.451a.

[————]. Sketches; or, essays on various subjects. By Launcelot Temple, Esq. [*pseud*., i.e. John Armstrong]. 1758. 8°. [*NUC*]. [? MC.80: "Temple's Essays:"].

Arnold, Mary. See Arnold Thomas. Christian life.

Arnold, Thomas. See Stanley, Arthur Penrhyn; Thucydides.

————. Christian life, its hopes, its fears, and its close. Sermons. 1842. 8°; 3rd ed. [ed. Mary Arnold]. 1845. 8°. LB.46: "Miss Arnold's Pamphlet."

————. History of Rome. 3 vols. 1838-1843. 8°. LB.24: "Arnolds History."

————. Passages from the sermons of Dr. Arnold. 1857. 8°. *SC*.291: "Passages from Dr. Arnold's Sermons; and six other bks. [? by Thomas Arnold]."

————. Sermons. 3 vol. 1829-34. 8°. LB.19:
"1 v." LB.20: "2ᵈ vol." LB.20: "3ᵈ Vol."

Arouet de Voltaire, François Marie. The history of
Charles XII., king of Sweden, translated from the
French. 1732. 8°. *SC*.171. MC.58: "History of
Charles 12:"

Aston, John Partington. See Ainsworth, William Harrison.

Atkinson, Thomas. The chameleon. 1832. 8°. *SC*.454.
LB.59.

*Attempts at verse. 1836. 6.625 in. [*CWC*.757].
[? Attempts at verse. 1838. *SC*.677]. [? Attempts in verse, 1836. *SC*.518].

*Attempts in verse, by divers authors, various dates.
[Apparently nine volumes]. *SC*.566.

Atterbury, Francis. See Donne, John.

————. Sermons and discourses on several subjects
and occasions. 2 vol. 1723. 8°. *SC*.186.
[? MC.28: "Atterbury's Sermons:"]. See *CWC*.2217.

Atthill, William Lombe, ed. Documents relating to the
foundation and antiquities of the collegiate
church of Middleham, in the County of York. 1847.
8°. *SC*.15.

Aubert de Vertot D'Aubeuf, René. The history of the
Knights of Malta. 2 vol. 1728. fol. *SC*.61:
"History of the Knights of Malta, vol. 1, 8vo,
1770." [No two-volume edition of 1770 has been
found]. [? MC.66: "Hist: of Knights:"].

Auckland, Baron. See Eden, William.

Audiguier, Vital D'. A tragi-comicall history of our
times under the borrowed names of Lisander and
Calista. [Translated from the French ... by W.D.].
1635. fol. *SC*.675.

Audubon, John James. Ornithological biography; or, an account of the habits of the birds of the United States of America. 5 vol. Edinburgh, 1831-39. 8°. *SC*.90: "imp. 8vo, 1831."

d'Aulnoy, Countess. See La Mothe, Marie Catherine.

Aulus Gellius. See Gellius, Aulus.

Aungier, George James. Croniques de London, depuis l'an 44 Henry III jusqu' à l'an 17 Edward III. 1844. *SC*.15.

Aurelius Victor, Sextus. See Eutropius, Flavius.

Austin, Sarah. See Cousin, Victor.

Avison, Charles. As essay on musical expression. 3rd ed. 1775. 8°. *SC*.521. MC.34: "Essay on Music: Express:"

Ayloffe, Captain William. See Sedley, Sir Charles.

Ayscough, Samuel. See Shakespeare, William. Dramatic works.

B., P. A help to magistrates. 1700. 12°. [Wing: AU]. MC.39: "Help to Magistrates:"

B., R. See Beverley, Robert; Blackburne, Richard.

B.G., M. de. See Boisguilbert, Pierre Le Pesant de.

Bacon, Francis. See Montagu, Basil. Selections; Rawley, William.

————. The works of Francis Bacon, Lord Chancellor of England. A new edition, by Basil Montagu, Esq. 16 vol. 1825-36. 8°. LB.29: "1 Vol Ld Bacon." LB.50: "Bacon's Works Vol 1." See *LY*, 248 and 266 for WW's thanks to Montagu for Vols. 1-5. HL.MK.692: "Bacon's Works 16 vol."

————. The two bookes of Francis Bacon of the pro-
ficience and advancement of learning, divine and
humane. Oxford, 1633. 4°. *SC*.326: "1623."
MC.32: "Advancem: of Learning."

Bailey, Benjamin. The duties of the Christian ministry, with a view of the primitive and apostolical
church, and the danger of departing from its doctrine and discipline; a sermon. [? 1843]. 12°.
SC.187.

Bailey, Nathan. See Erasmus, Desiderius; Ovidius Naso,
Publius. Metamorphoses.

————. and Johann Anton Fahrenkrueger. Wörterbuch
der Englischen Sprache. Teutsch-Englisch, Englisch-
Teutsch. 2 vol. 1823. 8°. *SC*.327. MC.18:
"Bailey's Dicty: 2 Vol:" [? LB.27: "German Dicy."].

Baillie, Joanna. A collection of poems, chiefly manuscript, and from living authors. Edited ... by
Joanna Baillie. 1823. 8°. *SC*.686. LB.11.

Bain, Donald. Aera Astraea; or, the age of justice.
An ode to her ... Majesty Victoria, Queen of Great
Britain. Edinburgh, 1845. 8°. *SC*.459.

Baines, Edward, the Elder. History of the wars of the
French Revolution. 2 vol. 1817. 4°. *SC*.5.
[? LB.56: "History French Revolution:].

Baines, Edward, of Leeds. History, directory, and
gazeteer of the County Palatine of Lancaster. 2
vol. Liverpool, 1824. 8°. *SC*.91.

Baker, Sir Richard. See Guez, Jean Louis.

————. A chronicle of the kings of England from the
time of the Romans government unto the raigne of
our soveraigne Lord King Charles. 1653. fol.
SC.6. MC.59: "Chronicle of Kings of England."

Bale, John. A brefe chronycle, concernynge the ex-
aminacyon and death of the blessed martyr of
Christ syr John Oldecastell the Lorde Cobham.
Edited by John Blackbourne. 1729. 8°. *SC*.280.
MC.63: "Concerning Sir: J: Oldcastle:"

————. Kynge Johan: a play in two parts. Edited by
John Payne Collier. 1838. 8°. *SC*.15.

————. The pageant of popes, contayninge the lives
of all the Bishops of Rome, from the beginninge of
them to the yeare of Grace 1555 ... now Englished
... by I.S. [i.e. John Studley]. 1574. 4°.
SC.276. MC.62: "Pageant of Popes:"

[Ball, William]. The transcript; also the memorial,
and other poems. Private print [1853]. [*DAP*:
"An edition of 1855 gives the author's name"].
L: "*London*, 1855. 8°." *SC*.590: "*not published--*
n.d."

[Bandello, Matteo]. Certaine tragicall discourses
written oute of French and Latin, by Geffraie
Fenton, no lesse profitable then pleasant, and of
like necessitye to al degrees that take pleasure
in antiquityes or foreine reapports. [A translation of selected tales from [François de] Belleforest's version of Bandello]. 1567. 6.75 in.
[*CWC*:Ann; L]. *SC*.528: "4to." MC.21: "Tragicall
Discourses:"

Barbauld, Mrs. Anna Letitia. The works of Mrs. Barbauld; with memoirs, by Lucy Aikin. 2 vol. 1825.
8°. *SC*.328. LB.11.

Barbette, Paulus. [? Opera chirurgico-anatomica, ad
circularem sanguinis motum, aliaque recentiorum
inventa, accomodata. Lugdini, 1672. 12°.].
MC.36: "Barbette Opera Chyr: et Anatom:"

Barclay, John. Barclay his Argenis: or, the loves of
Poliarchus and Argenis: faithfully translated out
of Latine into English by Kingsmill Long. 1625.
fol. MC.91: "Barclay's Argenis:"

————. Argenis. Amstelodami, 1655. 12°. *SC*.329: "18mo." MC.8: "Barclaii Argenis:"

————. [? Euphormionis lusinini, sive satyricon, quadripartitum. Leydae, 1623. 12°.]. MC.8: "Barclaii Euphormio:" See *CN*, 3N 3276, 3728.

Barker, Edmund Henry. See Cicero, Marcus Tullius. Catilinarian orations.

————. I. The claims of Sir Philip Francis ... to the authorship of Junius' letters, disproved: II. Some enquiry into the claims of the late Charles Lloyd ... to the composition of them: III. Observations on the conduct, character, and style of the writings of the late Right Hon. Edmund Burke: IV. Extracts from the writings of several eminent philologists, on the laconic and Asiatic, the Attic and Rhodian styles of eloquence. 1828. 12°. [*NUC*]. *SC*.451.

————. Parriana; or, notices of the Rev. Samuel Parr. 2 vol. 1829. 8°. *SC*.145.

Barlow, J. Hume's history of England, with a continuation to the death of George II. by Dr Smollett, and a further continuation to the present time by J. Barlow. [WL.Ann: "Barlow's Continuation of Smollett. 5 vols. 1795. 12mo."]. MC.57: "Barlow's Continu: 5 Vol:". LB.29: "Barlow's D° [i.e. Continuation] &c." See Hume, David; Smollett, Tobias.

Barotti, Giovanni Andrea. See Ariosto, Ludovico.

Barrett, Charlotte. See Burney, Frances.

Barrett, afterwards Browning, Elizabeth Barrett. See Chaucer, Geoffrey.

————. Poems. 2 vol. 1844. 18cm. [NN.BC:Ann]. [WR]. LB.39.

————. Prometheus bound; translated from the Greek
of Aeschylus. And Miscellaneous poems by the
translator. 1833. 19cm. [NN.BC:Ann]. *SC*.623.
LB.26.

————. The seraphim, and other poems. 1838. 12°.
SC.460: "1832." LB.32.

Barrington, Daines. Observations on the more ancient
statutes, from Magna charta to the twenty-first
of James I. cap. xxvii. With an appendix, being
a proposal for new modelling the statutes. 3rd
ed. 1769. 27cm. [*NUC*]. [PSC.WWC.JB:Ann].
SC.7. MC.40: "Harrington [*sic*] on Stat:"

Barron, Richard. See Thomas, Sir Edmund.

Barton, Benjamin Smith. New views of the origin of
the tribes and nations of America. Philadelphia,
1797. 8°. *SC*.92: "1798."

Barton, Bernard. See Barton, Lucy.

*————. A bundle of poetical trifles, containing
a new-year offering for the Queen. *SC*.461: "(*with
Characteristic Autograph Presentation to the Poet
Laureate*)."

[————]. Poems: by an amateur. 1818. 4°. *SC*.666:
"8vo." MC.51: "Poems by an Amateur:"

[Barton, Lucy]. Selections from the poems and letters
of Bernard Barton. Ed. by his daughter [i.e. Lucy
Barton]. 1849. 19cm. "Memoir of Bernard Barton"
(signed E.F.G. [i.e. Edward Fitzgerald]). [*NUC*].
SC.544: "8vo, 1849." LB.46: "Bernard Barton's
Life 2 Vol." [No 2-vol. ed. has come to light].

————. New ed. 1853. 8°. [? LB.54: "B. Barton"].

Barton, William. Six centuries of select hymns and
spiritual songs, collected out of the Holy Bible.
1688. 12°. *SC*.199.

Bartram, William. Travels through North and South
   Carolina, Georgia, East and West Florida, the
   Cherokee Country, the Extensive Territories of the
   Muscogulges or Creek Confederacy, and the Country
   of the Chactaws. Containing an Account of the Soil
   and Natural Productions of Those Regions; together
   with Observations on the Manners of the Indians.
   2nd ed. in London. 1794. 8.625 in. [*CWC*].
   MC.71: "Bartrem's [*sic*] Travels:" See *CN*, 1N218.

Barwick, Peter. The life of the Reverend Dr. John
   Barwick, D.D. ... Translated into English by the
   Editor of the Latin Life [i.e. Hilkiah Bedford],
   with notes, and a brief account of the author; to
   which is added an appendix of letters. 1724. 8°.
   LB.13: "Dʳ Barwick."

Basnage, Jacques, Sieur de Beauval. The history of
   the Jews, from Jesus Christ to the present time
   ... Being a supplement and continuation of the
   History of Josephus ... Translated ... by Tho[mas]
   Taylor. 1708. fol. [? MC.62: "History of the
   Jews:"] [? LB.55: "Josephus"].

Bate, George. Elenchi motuum nuperorum in Anglia pars
   prima simul ac juris regii et parlamentarii brevis
   enarratio recognita et aucta 1660. Pars secunda:
   simul ac Regis effugii mirabilis e prelio Wigor-
   niae enarratio. 2 pt. 1661-63. 8°. *SC*.8. MC.59:
   "Elenchus Motu: Nuper:"

————. Elenc[h]us motuum nuperorum in Anglia or a
   short historical account of the rise and progress
   of the late troubles in England. In two parts,
   written in Latin by G.B. Motus compositi; or,
   the history of the composing the affairs of England by the restauration of K. Charles the Second.
   Written in Latin by T[homas] Skinner. Made
   English [by A. Lovel]. 3 pt. 1685. 8°. [WL:
   Ann: "Bates [*sic*]"]. *SC*.9: "Bates." MC.58:
   "Troubles in England."

Bauhinus, Casparus. [? Institutiones anatomicae cor-
   poris virilis et muliebris historiam exhibentes.

[Lyons,] 1604. 8°.]. MC.36: "Casparus Bauhinus:"
[Listed in a series of works on medicine].

Baxter, John, of Barkisland School, near Halifax. The
young Christian's cyclopaedia; or, a compendium of
Christian knowledge. Halifax, 1818. 12°. MC.25:
"Baxter's Cyclopaedia:"

Baxter, Richard. The catechizing of families; a teach-
er of householders how to teach their households.
[? 1683. 8°.]. MC.25: "Baxter's Catechising: John
[Wordsworth]."

————. Catholic unity. [? 1660. 8°]. [Ox]. *SC.*
189: "12mo." MC.25: "Catholic Unity:"

————. A holy commonwealth; or, political aphorisms,
opening the true principles of government.
[? 1659. 12°.]. [*NUC*]. *SC.*190: "8vo." MC.16/0:
"Holy Commonwealth:"

————. Reliquiae Baxterianae; or, Mr. Richard Baxter's narrative of the most memorable passages of
his life and times. Faithfully publish'd from his
own original MS. by Matthew Sylvester. 3 pt.
1696. fol. *SC.*188: "Baxteriani Reliquiae: The
Life of the Rev. Mr. Richard Baxter, written for
the most in 1644, with additions from 1665 to 1678,
by Matthew Sylvester (no title), folio." MC.65:
"Life of R^d Baxter:"

————. A treatise of conversion. London and Keder-
minster, 1658. 4°. *SC.*190. MC.25: "Baxter on
Conversion: John [Wordsworth]."

Baxterus, Gulielmus (Baxter, William). See Horatius
Flaccus, Quintus. Opera.

Bayreuth, Margravine of. See Frederica Sophia Wilhelmina.

Beale, Anne. Poems. 1842. 8°. *SC.*524.

Beattie, James. Poems on several subjects ... a new
    edition, corrected. 1766. 8°. *SC*.451a: "1765,
    4°."

Beatty, Charles. The journal of a two months tour;
    with a view of promoting religion among the fron-
    tier inhabitants of Pensylvania [*sic*], and of in-
    troducing Christianity among the Indians to the
    westward of the Allegh-geny mountains. To which
    are added, remarks on the language and customs of
    some particular tribes among the Indians. 1768.
    8°. [Another edition Edinburgh, 1798. 8°.].
    SC.92: "1758." [? MC.69: "Tour in America:"].

Beaumont, Charles. See Beaumont, Joseph.

Beaumont, Francis and John Fletcher. The dramatick
    works of Beaumont and Fletcher; collated with all
    the former editions and corrected; with notes,
    critical and explanatory, by various commenta-
    tors ... edited by George Colman, [the Elder].
    10 vol. 1778. 8°. *SC*.462: "*vol. 2 different
    ed., viz.* 1711." MC.44: "Beaumont & Fletcher: 10
    Vol:"

————. The works of Beaumont and Fletcher, with an
    introduction by G[eorge] Darley. 2 vol. 1840.
    8°. *SC*.463.

Beaumont, Joseph. Psyche, or love's mystery, in xxiv
    cantos: displaying the intercourse betwixt Christ,
    and the soul ... 2d ed., with corrections through-
    out, and four new cantos, never before printed.
    [Edited by Charles Beaumont]. Cambridge, 1702.
    fol. [*NUC*; *L*]. *SC*.464. MC.44: "Beaumont's
    Psyche:"

de Beaune, Florimond. See Descartes, René.

Bede, the Venerable, Saint. Ecclesiasticae historiae
    gentis Anglorum libri V ... Lovanii, 1566. 12°.
    SC.191. MC.60: "Venerabilis Beda:"

Bedford, Hilkiah.   See Barwick, Peter.

Bedingfield, Mrs. Bryan.   Long Hollow; a country tale.
    3 vol.   1829.   8°.   *SC*.465.   MC.88: "Long-hollow
    3 vols."   LB.10: "1st Long Hollow."

Beesley, Alfred.   Japheth; contemplation: and other
    pieces.   [Poems].   1834.   8°.   *SC*.460.

Begly, Connor.   [i.e. MacCurtin, Hugh, *pseud*.].   The
    English Irish dictionary.   A Bpairis [i.e. Paris],
    1732.   4°.   *SC*.370.   MC.16: "Irish Dictionary."

Behmen, Jakob.   See Böhme, Jakob.

Beilby, Ralph.   [? A general history of quadrupeds ...
    The figures engraved on wood by T[homas] Bewick.
    Newcastle upon Tyne, 1790.   8°.].   MC.75: "History
    of Quadrupeds:"

————.   [? History of British birds.   The figures
    engraved on wood by T. Bewick.   Vol. 1 containing
    the history and description of land birds [by R.
    Beilby].   Vol. 2 ... of water birds [by T. Bewick,
    revised by Henry Cotes].   2 vol.   Newcastle upon
    Tyne, 1797-1804.   8°.].   MC.76: "History of Brit:
    Birds:"

Bekker, Immanuel.   See Thucydides.

Belcher, Joseph.   See Huntley, afterwards Sigourney,
    Lydia.

[Beldam, Joseph].   Il pastore incantato; or, the en-
    chanted shepherd: a drama: Pompeii and other poems.
    By a Student of the Temple [i.e. J. Beldam].
    1823.   8°.   [*E*].   *SC*.548.

Bell, Andrew.   Elements of tuition ... 3 pts.   2 vol.
    1813-15.   8°.   *SC*.331: "Elements of Tuition, or
    the Application of the Madras system of Education
    to English Schools, vols. 2 and 3, 8vo, 1814-15,
    with Autograph Presentation, etc."   *SC*.332:

"Elements, etc., Another Copy." MC.82: "Bell. Elements of Tuit: 2 Cop:" LB.10: "Dr Bells Ed^n."

Bell, Sir Charles. The hand; its mechanism and vital endowments as evincing design. 2nd ed. 1833. 8°. [*EU*]. *SC*.194.

Bell, George. Descriptive and other miscellaneous pieces, in verse. Penrith, 1835. 6.5 in. [*CWC*]. *SC*.518: "Descriptions in Verse by Geo. Bell."

Bell, John. The poets of Great Britain complete from Chaucer to Churchill, 109 vol. Edinburg [*sic*], 1782-76-83. 12°. MC.43: "Bell's Poets: 109 Vol: with Johnson's Lives 4 Vol:" See Dryden, John; Milton, John.

Bell, Robert. See Southey, Robert. Lives of the British admirals.

La belle assemblée; or, Bell's court and fashionable magazine. 7 vol. 1806-10. 8°. MC.80: "La Belle Assemble [*sic*]: 5 Vol:"

Belleforest, François de. See Bandello, Matteo; Guicciardini, Lodovico.

*Belles-Lettres. [? *SC*.339: "two other books."] [? *SC*.543: "three other books"].

Bembo, Pietro. See Petrarca, Francesco.

Bennet, Georgiana. Ianthe; and other poems. 2nd ed. 1841. 17.5cm. [TxU.Wn:Ann]. *SC*.567.

————. The poetess, and other poems. 1844. 12°. *SC*.526.

Bennet, Thomas. Hebrew grammar. 1726. 8°. MC.17: "Bennet's Hebrew Grammar:" [? MC.18: "Hebrew Grammar:"]

*Bennett, George. Studio and other poems. 1846. *SC*.466.

Bennett, William. Narrative of a recent journey of
six weeks in Ireland, in connexion with the subject of supplying small seed to some of the remoter
districts; with current observations on the de-
pressed circumstances of the people, and the means
presented for the permanent improvement of their
social condition. 1847. 12°. *SC*.179: (*with
Autograph Presentation, etc.*)."

Bennoch, Francis. The storm, and other poems. 1841.
6.75 in. [*CWC*]. *SC*.469: "Frances Bennock ...
(*Presentation Copy from the Author*)."

Benson, Thomas. Vocabularium Anglo-Saxonicum, lexico
Gul. Somneri magna parte auctius. Oxoniae, 1701.
8°. MC.16: "Vocab: Anglo-Saxonic:"

Bentley, Richard. See Wotton, William.

————. The works of Richard Bentley ... collected
and edited by the Rev. Alexander Dyce. 3 vol.
1836–38. 8°. *SC*.334. LB.23.

————. Eight sermons preach'd at the Honourable
Robert Boyle's Lecture in the first year, MDCXCII
... the 5th ed. To which is now added a sermon
preach'd at the Publick-Commencement at Cambridge
July v. MDCXCVI., etc. Cambridge, 1724. 8°.
SC.186. MC.20: "Sent to Derwent, 1827"; MC.19:
"Bentley's Sermons." [? LB.23: "A folio & 2 Vols
of Bentley"].

Berkeley, George. [? Alciphron; or, the minute philosopher, in seven dialogues; containing an apology
for the Christian religion against free-thinkers.
2 vol. 1732. 8°.]. *SC*.258: "1775" [apparently 1
vol.]. MC.27: "Minute Philosopher:"

Bernard, Peter. Examples of the ancient sages; containing sententious fables; or, a lively description of the human passions, (chiefly of great men,)
and the virtues and vices which arise from them.
Collected out of the Eastern, Greek, and Latin

languages. [? London], 1761. 12°. [BB]. SC.46: 8vo."

Bernardine [Albizzeschi], of Siena, Saint. See Exemplis ac similitudinibus rerum.

Bernays, Adolphus. German poetical anthology; or, select pieces from the principal German poets; accompanied with notes ... and preceded by a historical sketch of German poetry. 2nd ed. 1831. 12°. SC.467.

Berquin, Arnaud. Le petit Grandisson; traduction libre du hollandais. [? 1810. 12°.]. [? Paris, 1821. 12°]. [BN]. SC.534: "1820."

Bersmanus, Gregorius. See Ovidius Naso, Publius. Fasti.

Betham, Matilda. The lay of Marie; a poem. 1816. 8°. SC.478. SC.504.

Beveridge, William. De linguarum orientalium. 1664. 8°. [NUC]. SC.372: "1644." MC.16: "On the Orient: Tongues:"

Beverley, Robert. The history and present state of Virginia. 2nd ed. rev. 1722. 8°. SC.92: "R.B." MC.61: "Hist: of Virginia: 2 Cop:" ["works" written above "Cop:"]. See Stith, William.

Bewick, Thomas. See Beilby, Ralph.

Bianchi, Vendramino. An account of Switzerland, and the Grisons; as also of the Valesians, Geneva, the Forest-towns, and their other allies ... made English from the Italian original. 1710. 8°. SC.163.

*Bible, Holy. SC.289: "Saint Jerome: Biblia cum Pleno, very early, black letter, no date."

*————. Latin. [CSJ:Ann: "imperfect, wants t. p. 16cm"]. *SC*.205: "8vo (*no title* [page])." MC.20: "Latin Bible:"

*————. *SC*.195: "Black letter." *SC*.197: "Black letter."

*————. *SC*.196: "Black letter. Printed 1552."

*————. MC.20: "Octavo Bible:--2 Cop:"

————. With arguments prefixed to the different books; and moral and theological observations at the end of every chapter: composed ... by Mr. [Jean Frédéric] Ostervald ... translated at the desire of ... the Society for Propagating Christian Knowledge. 2 vol. *C. Macfarquhar: Edinburgh*, 1770. 8°. [DD: Ostervald's Bible, fol.: "Edinburgh: Printed by Colin MacFarquhar" [date of publication torn off]. [This was the poet's father's Bible. Written on the fly leaf among births: "William, their Second Son, born 7th April 1770 at ten o'clock at night, baptized the 13th at Cockermouth and christen'd 18th Jan^ry 1772"]. MC.20: "Ostervald Bible:"

*————. MC.20: "Bible & Comm: Prayer: Qto:"

————. German. Biblia, Das ist: die ganze Heilige Schrift; altes und neues Testaments, nach der Deutschen Übersetzung D. Martin Luthers.... Lauenburg, 1774. [WL:Ann]. MC.97: "German Bible."

*————. New Testament. *SC*.205: "New Testament, in Greek, 18mo." *SC*.385: "Greek Testament, 18mo." MC.4: "Novum: Testam: Graec: 2 Vols:"

————. He kaine diatheke [in Greek]. Novum Testamentum; cum scholiis theologicis et philologicis. [By E[dward] V[alpy]. 3 vol. 1816. 8°. *SC*.306: "vol. 2."

*————. *SC*.249: "Bible, Testament."

Bickerstaff, Isaac. See Steele, Sir Richard.

Bickersteth, Edward Henry. Questions illustrating
    the thirty-nine articles of the Church of England;
    with proofs from Scripture. 1845. 12°. *SC*.198.

Bigsby, Robert. The miscellaneous poems and essays
    of Robert Bigsby. 1842. 8°. *SC*.468.

Bion and Moschus. Bionos kai Moschou ta leipsana [in
    Greek]. Illustrabat et emendabat G[ilbert] Wake-
    field. 1795. 4°. *SC*.556: "12mo." MC.1: "Bion
    & Moschus."

Biondi, Giovanni Francesco. Eromena; or, love and
    revenge ... now faithfully Englished, by Ja. Hay-
    ward. 1632. fol. *SC*.335. MC.88: "Love & Re-
    venge:"

Biondi, Johann Franz. See Biondi, Giovanni Francesco.

Biondo da Forli. See Blondus, Flavius.

Birch, Thomas. The life of ... Dr. John Tillotson,
    Lord Archbishop of Canterbury. Compiled chiefly
    from his original papers and letters. 1752. 8°.
    SC.303.

[Birch, Mrs. Walter]. Job; or, the Gospel preached
    to the patriarchs; being a paraphrase of the last
    ten chapters of the book of Job. By the widow of
    a clergyman. 1838. 8°. [*DAP*]. *SC*.255: *"with
    Autograph Letter from the Authoress*."

Bisse, Thomas. The beauty of holiness in the Common
    Prayer. 1744. 8°. *SC*.199. See STC entry.

Bizarres tomes, deux. *SC*.88.

Black, Charles Ingham. Juvenile poems. Dublin, 1843.
    8°. *SC*.469: "(*Presentation Copy from the Author*)."

Blackall, Offspring. Practical discourses on the
    Lord's Prayer: where the design, matter, and form

of it is explain'd. 1727. 8°. *SC*.223: "1717."
MC.24: "Blackall's Discourses/O."

Blackbourne, John. See Bale, John.

Blackburn, Richard. See Hobbes, Thomas.

Blackmore, Sir Richard. Prince Arthur; an heroick
poem, in ten books. 1695. fol. *SC*.470. MC.45:
"Prince Arthur:"

Blackstone, Sir William. Commentaries on the laws of
England. 3rd ed. 4 vol. Oxford, 1768-69. 4°.
[*NUC*]. *SC*.10. MC.40: "Blackstone's Comment: 4
Vol:"

Blake, William. [? Songs of innocence and of experience, showing the two contrary states of the
human soul. 1789,94. 8°.]. *SC*.523: "Songs of
innocence."

Blakesley, Joseph William. Conciones academicae; ten
sermons preached before the University of Cambridge. 1843. 8°. *SC*.247.

————. A life of Aristotle, including a critical
discussion of some questions of literary history
connected with his works. Cambridge, 1839.
8.625 in. [*CWC*:Ann]. *SC*.103: "1839."

Blamire, Susanna. The poetical works of Miss Susanna
Blamire ... collected by Henry Lonsdale ... With
a preface, memoir, and notes, by Patrick Maxwell.
Edinburgh, 1842. 8°. LB.58.

Blind bard of Cicestria. See Champion, Francis.

Blondel, François. The comparison of Pindar and
Horace ... Englished by Sir Edward Sherburne.
1696. 8°. *SC*.673. MC.93: "Comparison of Pindar
& Horace--from the Fr:"

Blondus, Flavius. Roma ristaurata, et Italia illustrata, di Biondo da Forli [Blondus, Flavius].

Tradotte in lingua volgare per L. Fanno. Venetia, 1543. 8°. *SC*.155: "1548."

Bloodworth, Emma. Thoughts suggested by a few bright names, and other poems. Sudbury, [1844]. 24°. *SC*.471.

Blount, Sir Thomas Pope. De re poetica; or, remarks upon poetry. With characters and censures of the most considerable poets, whether ancient or modern, extracted out of the best criticks. 1694. 4°. [Sir Geoffrey L. Keynes. *Bibliotheca Bibliographi; a Catalogue of the Library Formed by Geoffrey Keynes*. London, 1964, Item 812: Ann]. MC.81: "Blount's Rem: on Poetry:"

Boccaccio, Giovanni. MC.100: "Decamerone by Boccacio [*sic*]:"

[Bodenham, John]. Englands Helicon; or, the muses harmony. 1614. 8°. *SC*.629.

[————.] Politeuphuia. Wits commonwealth. [1640]. 13.5cm. [MA:Ann]. *SC*.543: "Wit's Commonwealth." MC.84: "Wit's Commonwealth:"   See Meres, Francis for the second part.

Böhme (or Behmen), Jakob. De signatura rerum; or, the signature of all things, showing the size and signification of the several forms and shapes in the creation, and what the beginning, ruin, and cure of everything is; it proceeds out of eternity into time, and again out of time into eternity, and compriseth all mysteries. Written in High Dutch, 1622. Translated by John Ellistone. 1651. 4°. *SC*.192. MC.32: "Signat: Rerum:"

————. J. Behmen's theosophick philosophy unfolded ... By Edward Taylor. 1691. 4°. *SC*.193. MC.32: "Taylor on Behmen's Philo:"

Bogan, Zachary. See Godwin, Thomas.

Boileau-Despréaux, Nicholas. Les oeuvres de M. Boileau-Despréaux, avec les éclaircissemens historiques. Nouvelle édition revue et corrigée
(par l'abbé Souchay). 3 tomes. Paris, 1768.
12°. *SC*.336. MC.102: "Boileau 3 [vol.]."

————. Oeuvres de Boileau Despréaux. a Paris. An x-
1801. 16°. (in Bibliothèque portative du
voyageur). [WL:Ann]. MC.100: "Oeuvres de Boileau."

Boisguilbert, Pierre Le Pesant de. See Dion Cassius.

Bombast von Hohenheim, Philipp Aureol Theophrast,
called Paracelsus. Paracelsus of the chymical
transmutation, genealogy and generation of metals
and minerals. 1657. 8°. *SC*.106. MC.30: "Paracelsus:"

Bond, John. See Persius Flaccus, Aulus.

[Bonell, Thomas]. The case of the orphan and creditors
of John Ayliffe, esq., for the opinion of the public. With an addenda of interesting queries ...
The whole ... authenticated from originals. 1761.
25cm. [*CWC*:Ann]. MC.84: "Case of the orphan &c:"

Boner, Charles. See Andersen, Hans Christian.

Bongars, Jacques. See Justinus.

Bonneval, Claude Aléxandre de, Count. Memoirs of the
Bashaw Count Bonneval written by himself, and col-
lected from his papers. 2 pt. 1750. 8°. [DD:
Ann]. MC.88: "Bonival's [*sic*] Memoirs:"

Bonney, Henry Kaye. See Middleton, Thomas Fanshawe.

Bonnycastle, John. [? An introduction to astronomy
in a series of letters from a preceptor to his
pupil in which the most useful and interesting
parts of the science are ... explained. 1786.
8°.]. MC.35: "Bonnycastle's Astronomy:"

The Book of Common Prayer. Cambridge: Baskerville,
1760. [DD: "Margaret Richardson" [probably MW's
maternal grandmother, Mrs. John Monkhouse (1717-
1788)]. Then: "Mary Wordsworth to Edward Quillinan Rydal Mt Janry 17th 1842."]. [? *Cambridge,*
1760, 8°. *Printed in double column. John
Baskerville*]. [? *Cambridge,* 1760, 8°. *Printed
in long lines, with a border to each page*].
[? MC.20: "Octavo comm: Prayer:"]

————. Welsh. 1683. fol. *SC*.418: "8vo." MC.98:
"Welsh Prayer:"

*Books, Miscellaneous. *SC*.286: "eleven other books."
SC.396 [probably 11]. *SC*.315 to 320: "Sundries,
omitted being otherwise named." [RP.QH shows
prices paid for each of these six lots].

Borgia, Stefano. See Exemplis ac similitudinibus
rerum.

Borough, Sir John. The soveraignty of the British
seas. Proved by records, history, and the muni-
cipall lawes of this kingdome. Written in the
yeare 1633. By the learned knight, Sr John
Boroughs [*sic*]. 1651. 13cm. [NNC.SC:Ann].
SC.44. MC.59: "Sovereignty of Brit: Seas."

Boswell, James. The journal of a tour to the Hebrides
with Samuel Johnson, LL.D. 6th ed. 1813. 8°.
SC.93. LB.17.

————. The life of Samuel Johnson, LL.D., with notes
by Malone. 4 vol. 1824. 23.5cm. [*NUC*]. *SC*.93.
LB.12.

Boufflers, Stanislas Jean de, Marquis. See Williams,
Helen Maria.

Bougainville, Louis Antoine de. Voyage autour du monde
par la frégate du roi la *Boudeuse* et la flûte
l'Étoile en 1766, 1767, 1768 et 1769. 2 vol.
Neuchâtel, 1773. 12°. [*BN*]. *SC*.534. MC.98:
"Voyage Auteur [*sic*] de [*sic*] Monde: 2 Vol:"

Bouhours, Dominique. The arts of logick and rhetorick,
    illustrated by examples taken out of the best
    authors ... interpreted and explain'd by ...
    Father Bouhours. To which are added parallel
    quotations out of the most eminent English authors
    in verse and prose. (Translated and paraphrased,
    from "La manière de bien penser" by John Oldmixon.)
    1728. 8°. *SC*.673: "Logic and Rhetoric, 8vo,
    1728." MC.12: "Bouhour's [*sic*] Logic:"

Bourne, Vincent. Poetical works, with his letters.
    2 vol. 1808. 12°. [Allibone]. MC.48: "Vincent
    Burn's [*sic*] Poet: Works 2 Vol:"

Bower, Archibald. See An universal history.

Bowle, John. See Cervantes Saavedra, Miguel de.

Bowles, afterwards Southey, Caroline. The birth-day;
    a poem, in three parts: to which are added, oc-
    casional verses. 1836. 8°. *SC*.526.

————. See Southey, Robert. The life of the Rev.
    Andrew Bell.

Bowles, William Lisle. The missionary; a poem. 2nd
    ed. 1815. 8°. *SC*.472: "12mo." *"with Valuable
    Presentation Note by the Author, and Autog. of
    the Laureate*." MC.50: "The Missionary:"

Boyer, Abel. See Salignac de la Mothe Fénelon,
    François de.

————. Dictionnaire royal, François et Anglois. La
    Haye, 1702. 4°. MC.16: "Buoyer's [*sic*] Fren:
    Dict\ :sup:`y`. Qto:"

————. The history of the reign of Queen Anne, di-
    gested into annals. 11 vol. 1703-1713. 8°.
    SC.3: "6 vol." MC.58: "Annals of Queen Anne:
    6 Vol:"

[Boyer, Jean Baptiste de, Marquis D'Argens]. The
    Chinese spy; or, emissary from the court of Pekin,

commissioned to examine into the present state of
Europe. Translated from the Chinese. 6 vol.
1765. 18cm. [*NUC*]. MC.62: "Chinese Spy: 6 Vol:"

Boyle, John, Earl of Cork and Orrery. See Carey,
Robert.

Boyle, Hon. Robert. Some motives and incentives to
the love of God, pathetically discours'd of in a
letter to a friend ... 1659. 8°. [*NUC*]. *SC*.223:
n.d. MC.29: "Boyle's Motives."

Bradford, John [Homely, Josias, *pseud*.]. Tales of the
moor. London, Newton-Abbot, 1841. 8°. *SC*.560.

Bradley, Richard Bladon. The portion of Jezreel: a
sacred drama. 2nd ed. 1843. 8°. *SC*.473.

Bramston, Sir John. The autobiography of Sir John
Bramston, K.B., of Skreens, in the hundred of
Chelmsford. 1845. 8°. *SC*.15.

Bray, Anna Eliza. See Stothard, afterwards Bray;
Colling, Mary Maria.

Braybrooke, Richard, Lord. See Pepys, Samuel.

Breton de la Martinière, Jean Baptiste Joseph. See
Lafontaine, August Heinrich Julius.

[? Bridel, Arleville. Chambaud's [Louis] exercises,
improved by Nicholson, rev., cor., and enlarged:
or, practical syntax of the French tongue: wherein
each rule is given separately ... By Arleville
Bridel, A.M. 1810. 16.5cm.]. [*NUC*]. MC.17:
"Syntax of the French Tong:"

*Briggs, John. Poems. Ulverstone, 1818. *SC*.516.

*————. Remains. 1825. 12mo. *SC*.572.

Brinsley, John. See Cicero, Marcus Tullius. The
first book of Tullies Offices.

The British annals of education; being the scholastic
    quarterly review. Edited by W[illiam] Martin.
    1844-45. 8°. *SC*.404: "a bundle."

*British guide to the making and managing of choice
    wines. 1813. 12mo. *SC*.173.

The British novelists. See Aikin, afterwards Barbauld,
    Anna Letitia.

[? Brittaine, George]. The confessions of Honor
    Delany. 1830. 12°. *SC*.471.

Brock, William John. Wayside verses. 1848. 12°.
    [Allibone]. *SC*.630.

Brockedon, William. Road-book from London to Naples.
    1835. 8°. [DD:Ann]. LB.25.

Brooke, Henry. The fool of quality; or, the history
    of Henry, Earl of Moreland. 4 vol. 1766. 12°.
    MC.88: "Fool of Quality 4 Vol:"

Brooks, Mrs. Maria (Gowen). Idomen; or, the Vale of
    Yumuri. By Maria del Occidente, *pseud*. New York,
    1843. 16cm. [*NUC*]. *SC*.560: "1846."

*Brown. *SC*.566: "Brown's Poems, 1826."

Brown, Abner William. Introits; or, collect hymns,
    adapted to the stated services of the Church of
    England; to which are added, a few hymns for the
    occasional services. 1845. 24°. *SC*.453 [n.d.].

Brown, Andrew. See the history of Glasgow.

Brown, John, M.D. The elements of medicine; or, a
    translation of the elementa medicinae Brunonis
    ... by the author of the original work. 2 vol.
    1788. 8°. [*EU*]. MC.36: "Brown's Elements of
    Med: 2nd Vol:"

[Brown, John, Vicar of Newcastle-upon-Tyne]. An es-
    timate of the manners and principles of the times.

By the author of Essays on the Characteristics
[Shaftesbury's], &c. [i.e. John Brown, Vicar of
Newcastle-upon-Tyne]. 2 vol. 1757,58. 8°. MC.
31: "Manners & Princip: 3 Vol:"

Brown, Robert, of Douglas, Isle of Man. Sermons on
various subjects. Wellington, Salop, 1818. 8°.
SC.255.

Brown, Thomas. See Erasmus, Desiderius. Twenty-two
select colloquies.

Browne, Charles Thomas. Irene; a poem. By Alexandre
de Comyn [Charles Thomas Browne]. 1844. 8°.
[*DAP*]. *SC*.548: "Irene, and Miscellaneous Poems
(not published) 1833."

*————. Poems, by A. Comyne. *SC*.617.

Browne, Edward, M.D., Son of Sir Thomas Browne. A
brief account of some travels in divers parts of
Europe, viz. Hungaria, Servia, Bulgaria, Macedonia,
Thessaly, Austria, Styria, Carinthia, Carniola,
and Friuli, through a great part of Germany and
the Low Countries. Through Marca Trevisana, and
Lombardy on both sides the Po. With some observations on the gold, silver, copper, quick-silver,
mines; and the baths and mineral-waters in those
parts. As also the description of many antiquities, habits, fortifications, and remarkable
places. The second edition [a reissue of], with
many additions. 1687. fol. [*L*; *TC*, II,213].
SC.167. [? MC.69: "Travels in Europe:"].

Browne, afterwards Hemans, Felicia Dorothea. See
Hughes, Mrs. Harriet.

————. Records of woman; with other poems. 1828.
12°. *SC*.553: "1838 (*Presentation Autograph*)."

————. Scenes and hymns of life, with other religious
poems. Edinburgh, 1834. 8°. *SC*.553: "(*Presentation Autograph*)."

————. Songs of the affections, with other poems. Edinburgh, 1830. 12°. [CSmH.ZZB.Ann]. *SC*.553: "*(Presentation Autograph)*." LB.11.

Browne, Moses. The works and rest of the Creation. 6th ed. Edinburgh, 1805. 12°. *SC*.586. MC.49: "The Works & Rest: of the Crea: by Moses Brown [*sic*]:"

Browne, Sir Thomas. Christian morals ... published from the original manuscript of the author, by J. Jeffery. Cambridge, 1716. 12°. MC.27: "Brown's [*sic*] Morals:" LB.29.

————. Hydriotaphia, urne-buriall, or a discourse of the sepulchrall urnes lately found in Norfolk. 1658. 8°. *SC*.338: "4to." MC.30: "Hydriotaphia:"

————. Pseudodoxia epidemica; or, enquiries into very many received tenents [*sic*] and commonly pre-sumed truths. 4th ed. 1658. 4°. *SC*.338.

————. Religio medici. 6th ed. ... Also observa-tions by Sir Kenelm Digby, now newly added. 1669. 8°. *SC*.339: "*(Autog. 'Wm. Wordsworth, given to him by Charles Lamb')*." [? MC.22: "Religio Medici"].

————. [Another copy]. 6th ed. 1669. 8°. [WR: "contains copious marginal and other MS. annota-tions by Coleridge, and has this inscription in-side the cover, 'Sara Hutchinson from S.T.C.'"]. [? MC.22: "Religio Medici"].

Browning, Elizabeth Barrett. See Barrett, afterwards Browning, Elizabeth.

Brownrig, Ralph. A sermon on the 5 of November. 1660. 12°. MC.21: "Brownrig's Sermon:"

Bruce, James. Travels to discover the source of the Nile, in the years 1768-73. 5 vol. Edinburgh, 1790. 4°. LB.15.

Bruce, John. See Hayward, Sir John.

————. Correspondence of Robert Dudley, Earl of
Leycester, during his government in the Low Countries ... Edited by John Bruce. 1844. 8°. *SC*.15.

————. Historie of the arrivall of Edward IV in
England and the finall recouerye of his kingdomes
from Henry VI. Edited by John Bruce. 1838. 8°.
SC.15.

————. Letters and papers of the Verney family down
to the end of the year 1639.... Edited by John
Bruce. 1853. 8°. *SC*.15.

————. Letters of Queen Elizabeth and King James VI
of Scotland.... Edited by John Bruce. 1849.
8°. *SC*.15: "1847."

————. Verney papers--notes of proceedings in the
Long Parliament, temp. Charles I, by Sir Ralph
Verney, Knight. Edited by John Bruce. 1845. 8°.
SC.15.

Bruce, Peter Henry. Memoirs of Peter Henry Bruce ...
containing an account of his travels in Germany,
Russia, Tartary, Turkey, the West Indies ... as
also several very interesting private anecdotes
of the Czar Peter I. of Russia. Dublin, 1783.
8°. *SC*.152. MC.66: "Bruce's Memoirs:" LB.7.

Brugière de Barante, Amable Guillaume Prosper, Baron.
Tableau de la littérature Française pendant le
dix-huitième siècle. Paris, Londres [printed],
1813. 8°. *SC*.52. MC.100: "Tablau [*sic*] de la
Litterature François [*sic*]:"

Brulart de Sillery, Stéphanie Félicité, Countess de
Genlis. Manuel du voyageur; or, the traveller's
pocket companion, consisting of familiar conversations in English, French, and Italian ... 7th ed.
enlarged by P[ietro] A. Cignani. [London,] 1816.
12°. *SC*.362: "Conversations in English, French,

and Italian, by De Genlis and Cignani." MC.97:
"Manuel du Voyageur:"

[Bruno, Raffaello del]. Ristretto delle cose più
notabili della città di Firenze. 5. impressione.
Firenze. 1745. 14cm. [*NUC*]. *SC*.156: "Ristretto
della citta di Firenze, 12mo ... 1745." MC.99:
"Ristretto."

Brutus, Joannes Michaelis (Bruto, Giovanni Michele).
See Cicero, Marcus Tullius. Orationum.

Bryan, Mrs. Mary. Sonnets and metrical tales. Bristol, 1815. 8°. *SC*.600. MC.50: "Poems by Mrs:
Bryan:"

Brydges, Sir Samuel Egerton. The anti-critic for
August, 1821, and March, 1822; containing liter-
ary, not political, criticisms, and opinions.
Geneva, 1822. 8°. [Mark L. Reed:Ann]. *SC*.342.

————. Arthur Fitz-Albini; a novel. 2nd ed. 2 vol.
1799. 12°. [DD:Ann]. *SC*.474. MC.88: "Arthur
Fitzalbin: 2 Vol:"

————. Bertram; a poetical tale. 2nd ed. 1816.
8°. *SC*.526. MC.52: "Bertram by Brydges:"

————. Cimelia: seu examen criticum librorum ex
diaries literaries lingua praecipue Gallica ab
anno 1665 usque ad annum 1792 scriptis selectum.
Genevae, 1823. 8°. *SC*.341: "*only* 75 *Copies
Printed, and those Distributed among the Author's
Friends*."

————. Gnomica; detached thoughts, sententious,
axiomatic, moral & critical, but especially with
reference to poetical faculties and habits.
Geneva, 1824. 8°. *SC*.342.

————. Mary de Clifford; a story. Interspersed
with many poems. 2nd ed. 1800. 12°. *SC*.557.
MC.88: "Mary de Clifford:"

————. Res literariae: bibliographical and critical,
for Oct. 1820 (for January 1821--for May 1821 to
February 1822). 3 vol. Naples, Rome, and Geneva,
1821,22. 8°. *SC*.341: "4 vols., *Presentation
Copy*."

————. The ruminator: containing a series of moral,
critical, and sentimental essays. [*L*; *CWC*:Ann].
SC.240: "2 vols., 12mo ... 1812." MC.79: "Ruminator 2 Vol:"

Buchanan, George. Opera omnia ... nunc primum in
unum collecta ... curante Thoma Ruddimanno.
Edinburgi, 1714-15. fol. [*BN*]. [? MC.1: Buch-
ananus"].

Buchanan, John Lanne. Travels in the Western Hebrides:
from 1782 to 1790. 1793. 8°. *SC*.163. MC.71:
"Buchanan's Travels in Heb:"

Bürger, Gottfried August. Gedichte. Herausgegeben
von Karl Reinhard. Erster theil. Göttingen,
1796. 12°. Zweiter theil. 1796. 12°. [Given
by Mrs. Dorothy Dickson in 1956 to Mr. Leo Wiener,
then custodian of the Wordsworth Museum, Grasmere.
Both volumes, when shown by Mr. Wiener to Chester
L. Shaver in 1959, were seen to have the bookplate
of WW2.] [? MC.99: "Gedichte: 2 Vols:"] See
EY, 233-4, 248.

Buffon, Count de. See Le Clerc, Georges Louis.

[? Bulstrode, Sir Richard]. Memoirs and reflections
upon the reign and government of King Charles the
I[st]. and K. Charles the IInd. containing an account
of several remarkable facts not mentioned by other
historians of those times: wherein the character
of the Royal Martyr, and of King Charles II are
vindicated from fanatical aspersions, *etc*. 1721.
8°. *SC*.9: "8vo ... (*no title*)."

Bulwer, afterwards Bulwer Lytton, Edward George Earle
Lytton, Baron Lytton. The last days of Pompeii.
3 vol. 1834. 12°. *SC*.477: "8vo."

─────. The Siamese twins; a satirical tale of the
times. With other poems. 1831. 8°. *SC*.478:
"*(with Autograph Presentation by the Author to the
'Illustrious Wordsworth')*."

Bunbury, Sir Henry Edward. The correspondence of Sir
Thomas Hanmer, Bart. with a memoir of his life.
To which are added other relicks of a gentleman's
[the Bunbury] family. Edited by Sir H. Bunbury.
1838. 8°. *SC*.123.

Bunyan, John. The life and death of Mr. Badman, pre-
sented to the world in a familiar dialogue between
Mr. Wiseman and Mr. Attentive. 1680. 12°.
SC.189. MC.22: "Life &c: of Mr: Badman:" LB.10.

─────. Le voyage du Chrétien vers l'éternité....
Traduit de l'anglois. Halle, 1752. 8°. *SC*.284:
"1722." MC.98: "Voyage du Chretien:"

Burder, Samuel. See Josephus, Flavius.

[Burgh, James]. Crito, or essays on various subjects
... 2 vol. 1766-67. 17cm. [NIC:Ann]. *SC*.400.

[─────]. Political disquisitions; or, an enquiry
into public errors, defects, and abuses.... 3
vol. 1774. 8.75cm. [*CWC*:Ann]. *SC*.59: "(*'From
Thomas de Quincey to William Wordsworth, Grasmere,
Friday, June 22nd, 1810,' in De Quincey's Autograph*.)" MC.40: "Polit: Disquisitions: 3 Vol:"

Burke, Edmund. The works of the Right Honourable
Edmund Burke. A new edition. [Edited until 1808
by Walker King, Bishop of Rochester, and Laurence
French; and afterwards by Walker King alone].
16 vol. 1803-27. 8°. LB.7: "5th vol Burke."
LB.58: "Vols. 3 & 6 of Burke's Works." HL.MK.54:
"Burke's Works 12 Vols. Imperf[t]."

Burn, James. See Nicolson, Joseph.

Burn, Richard. The justice of the peace and parish
officer. 10th ed. 4 vol. 1766. 8°. MC.40:
"Burn's Just: 4 Vol:"

Burnet, Gilbert. See Scougal, Henry.

————. An exposition of the thirty-nine articles of
the Church of England. [? 3rd ed. 1705. fol.].
[? 4th ed. 1720. fol.]. *SC*.201: "8vo. 1714
(*with Autographs of Sir R. Fleury, and W.W.*)."

————. History of his own time. (The life of the
author by the editor, T[homas] Burnet). 2 vol.
1724-34. fol. *SC*.12. MC.60: "Burnett's [*sic*]
History of his own times [*sic*]: 2 Vol:"

————. The history of the reformation of the Church
of England. 2nd ed. 2 vol. (or 3 vol.). 1681-
83, 1715. fol. *SC*.200: "vols. 2 and 3." MC.61:
"Burnett's [*sic*] Reformation 3 Vol: 1st: Vol:
wantȝ." LB.10.

————. Lives [of Sir M. Hale and the Earl of Roches-
ter], characters [taken from B.'s "History of his
own times"] and a sermon preached at the funeral
of the Hon. R. Boyle. Edited, with an introduction and notes, by J[ohn] Jebb. 1833. 8°.
SC.259.

————. The memoires of the lives and actions of
James and William, dukes of Hamilton and Castle-
herald. In which an account is given of the rise
and progress of the civil wars of Scotland ...
with many letters, instructions, and other papers,
written by King Charles the I. never before published. All drawn out of, or copied from the
originals. 1677. fol. *SC*.34. MC.63: "Mem of
Dukes of Hamilton &c:"

————. Travels through France, Italy, Germany, and
Switzerland. [? 1750. 17 cm.]. [*NUC*]. [? Edin-
burgh, 1752. 12°]. [*NUC*]. *SC*.94: "8vo, 1762."
MC.71: "Bp: Burnett's [*sic*] Travels:"

Burnet, Thomas. See Burnet, Gilbert. History of his
    own time.

————. The theory of the earth.... 3rd ed. 2 vol.
    1697. fol. *SC*.203. MC.34: "Theory of the Earth:"

————. A treatise concerning the state of departed
    souls, before, and at, and after the resurrection
    ... Translated by Mr. [John] Dennis. 1733. 8°.
    SC.202: "1633." MC.25: "Burnett [*sic*] on Dep:
    Souls:"

Burnett, George. Specimens of English prose writers,
    from the earliest times to the close of the seven-
    teenth century, with sketches biographical and
    literary. 3 vol. 1807. 8°. *SC*.428. MC.79:
    "Burnet's [*sic*] Specim: 3 Vol:"

Burney, Frances, Madame d'Arblay. Diary and letters
    of Madame d'Arblay. Edited by her niece [Char-
    lotte Barrett]. 7 vol. 1842-46. 8°. LB.29.

————. Evelina. 2 vol. 1810. 12°. [Vols. 38 and
    39 of The British Novelists]. *SC*.657. MC.87.
    LB.23.

Burns, James. See Wordsworth, William. Select pieces
    from the poems.

Burns, Robert. The works of Robert Burns; with an
    account of his life, and a criticism on his writ-
    ings. To which are prefixed, some observations
    on the character and condition of the Scottish
    peasantry. [By James Currie]. 4 vol. 1800.
    8°. *SC*.480. [? MC.48: "Burn's [*sic*] Poet: Works:"].

————. The poetical works of Robert Burns, including
    the pieces published in his correspondence and
    reliques, with his songs and fragments. To which
    is prefixed a sketch of his life [signed: A.C.,
    i.e. Alexander Chalmers]. London and Edinburgh,
    1813. 24°. [WL:Ann]. [? MC.48: "Burn's [*sic*]
    Poet: Works:"].

————. Poems, chiefly in the Scottish dialect. 2nd
ed. 2 vol. Edinburgh and London, 1793. 8°.
SC.479: "with MS. Marginal Glossary '*In the handwriting of my dear Sister, done long ago,*' Note
dated June 6th, 1847."

Burroughs, Sir John. See Borough, Sir John.

Burton, Edward. A description of the antiquities and
other curiosities of Rome. 2nd ed., with additions. 2 vol. 1828. 8°. LB.22.

Burton, Robert. See Lamb, Charles. John Woodvil.

————. The anatomy of melancholy.... 8th ed. 1676.
fol. [Ox]. *SC*.343. MC: "Anatomy of Melanch:
Fol:"

Busbequius, Angierius Gislenius [i.e. Busbecq, Ogier
Ghislain de]. Travels into Turkey, containing the
most accurate account of the Turks and neighbouring
nations, their manners, customs, religion, super-
stition, policy, riches, coins &c.... Translated
from the original Latin of A.G. Busbequius, with
memoirs of the illustrious author. 1744. 17cm.
[NIC:Ann]. *SC*.159. MC.70: "Travels into Turkey."

Busby, Richard. Grammatica Busbeiana auctior & emendatior, i.e. Rudimentum grammaticae graeco-latinae
metricum in usum nobilium puerorum in Schola Regia
Westmonasterii. 1702. 8°. *SC*.333: "(*Interleaved and copiously Annotated*)." MC.13: "Busbii
Rudim: Gram:"

Bush, James. The choice; or, lines on the Beatitudes
(in verse. With observations). 1841. 8°.
SC.291. LB.44.

[Busk, Hans]. The banquet; a poem in three cantos.
1819. 8°. *SC*.481. MC.51: "Banquet:"

[————]. The dessert; a poem. To which is added The
tea, by the author of The banquet. [Hans Busk.

With notes to each poem]. 1819. 8°. *SC*.481.
MC.51: "Tea:"

————. The lay of life; a poem. 1834. 8°. *SC*.590.

————. The vestriad; a poem. 1819. 8°. *SC*.481.
MC.51: "Vestriad:"

Butler, Samuel. The genuine remains in verse and
prose of Mr. Samuel Butler ... with notes by Robert
Thyer. 2 vol. 1759. 8°. *SC*.483. MC.46:
"Butler's Remains: 2 Vol:"

————. Hudibras. With large annotations by Zachary
Grey. 3 vol. 1770. 12°. *SC*.482. MC.47: "Hudibras: 3 Vol:"

Buxton, Charles. Memoirs of Sir Thomas Fowell Buxton,
Bart. With selections from his correspondence.
1848. 8°. LB.45.

Buxton, Sir Thomas Fowell. The African slave trade
and its remedy. 1840. 8°. *SC*.13.

Buxtorfius, Johannes. Lexicon hebraicum et chaldaicum ... Editio sexta. 1646. 8°. *SC*.344: "(*Autographs of S.T. Coleridge and W. Wordsworth*)."
MC.18: "Hebrew Lexicon: 2 Cop:"

[Byron, George Gordon Noel, Baron Byron]. Lara; a
tale. [By Lord Byron]. Jacqueline; a tale. [By
Samuel Rogers]. 1814. 8°. MC.51: "Lara:" LB.7.

————. The works of Lord Byron. 4 vol. 1830. 16°.
SC.484: "12mo, (*Wordsworth's Autograph in each
Vol.*)." LB.49: "2 vol of Byrons Poems."

Bysshe, Edward. The art of English poetry. 4th ed.
1710. 8°. [*LLA*]. *SC*.485. MC.81: "Bish's [*sic*]
Art of Poetry:"

C., A. See Chalmers, Alexander.

C., T.H.   See Townshend, Chauncy Hare.

Caesar, Caius Julius.   Caesaris Julii Commentariorum
    de bello Gallico libri VIII ... Venetiis, 1518,
    19. 8°. *SC*.14: "8vo, (no title);... 1508.
    (*With Presentation Autograph of* WALTER SAVAGE
    LANDOR.)." [*L* has an edition published at Lyons
    in 1508 but with a different title]. MC.2:
    "Caesar 2 Co:"

Callender, John.   An historical discourse, on the civil
    and religious affairs of the colony of Rhode-
    Island. By John Callender, M.A. With a memoir
    of the author; biographical notices of some of
    his distinguished contemporaries; and annotations
    and original documents illustrative of the history
    of Rhode-Island and Providence Plantations from
    the first settlement to the end of the first cen-
    tury. By Romeo Elton ... 3rd ed. Boston, New
    York, 1843. 22cm. [*NUC*]. *SC*.399: "The Early
    History of Rhode Island, *Boston*, *U.S.*, 1843."

Calvert, George Henry.   Count Julian; a tragedy.
    Baltimore, 1840. 19cm. [*NUC*]. *SC*.486: "8vo."

Calvin, Jean.   Institutio Christianae religionis ...
    Additi sunt nuper duo indices, ante ab Augustino
    Marlorato collecti. Genevae, 1569. 8°. *SC*.204:
    "*Genevae (Autographs of 'S.T. Coleridge' and 'W.
    Wordsworth*'). 1569." MC.24: "Calvinus de
    Christ: Relig:"

Cambridge prize poems: being a complete collection of
    the English poems which have obtained the Chan-
    cellor's gold medal in the University of Cambridge.
    1818. 8°. *SC*.525: "Cambridge Prize Poems, by C.
    Townsend, etc. etc., 8vo." HL.MK.281: "Camb Prize
    Poems 1818."

Camden, Marquis.   See Pratt, John Jeffreys.

The Camden miscellany. 3 vol. 1847, 1853, 1855. 8°.
    SC.15: "1851, 1853, 1855."

Campan, Jeanne Louise Henriette, Madame. [Title lacking]. LB.6: "M. Campan." ["M" under wax seal].

Campbell, John, LL.D. See An universal history.

————. The life of the celebrated Sir Francis Drake the first English circumnavigator. Together with the historical and genealogical account of Sir Francis Drake's family from Betham's Baronetage; and ... an account of the Richmond family of Highhead Castle. [Edited by Sir Thomas Trayton Drake]. Privately printed: London, 1828. 8°. *SC*.114: "(*Printed for Private Distribution only*), imp. 8vo, 1828."

Campbell, John, Minister of Kingsland Chapel. See Park, Mungo.

Campbell, Thomas. See Shakespeare, William. Dramatic works.

————. The poetical works of Thomas Campbell. [? 1837. 8°.]. [? 1839. 8°.]. *SC*.493: "12mo, 1836."

Camus, Nicolaus. See Terentius, Publius, Afer.

Canning, George. See the microcosm.

Cantelius, Petrus Josephus. See Justinus.

Canterus, Gulielmus. See Ovidius Naso, Publius. Metamorphoses.

Capel, Richard. Capel's remains. Being an useful appendix to his excellent treatise of tentations ... With a preface prefixed, wherein is contained an abridgement of the authors life, by his friend Valentine Marshall. 1658. 16°. [*NUC*]. *SC*.339: "Capel's Remains, 1658." MC.29: "Capels Treatise."

A captain of the British Navy. See A vocabulary of sea phrases.

Caraccioli, Louis Antoine de. See Clement XIV, Pope.

Card, Henry. A dissertation on the antiquities of
    the priory of Great Malvern in Worcestershire.
    1834. 4°. *SC*.95.

Carey, John. See Ainsworth, Robert.

Carey, Robert, Earl of Monmouth. Memoirs of the life
    of Robert Carey, Baron of Leppington and Earl of
    Monmouth. Written by himself, and now published
    from an original manuscript in the custody of John,
    Earl of Corke and Orrery [and edited by him].
    With some explanatory notes. 1759. 8°. *SC*.96.
    MC.66: "Life of Carey:"

*Cargill, R. Sermons on various subjects. 1844.
    SC.312.

Carleton, Captain George. The memoirs. of Cap. George
    Carleton ... who served in the two last wars
    against France and Spain ... Containing an account
    of the conduct of the Earl of Peterborough ...
    in which the genius, pride and barbarity of the
    Spaniards ... are set in a true light. 1743. 8°.
    SC.96. MC.64: "Mem: of Geo: Carleton:"

Carleton, William. The fawn of Spring-Vale, The clar-
    ionet, and other tales. 3 vol. Dublin, 1841.
    19cm. [NIC:Ann]. *SC*.487: "8vo, 1844." LB.56:
    Carletons Tales Vol 2."

Carlyle, Thomas. Chartism. 1840. 19.5cm. [*NUC*].
    SC.16: *"with Autog. of the late Laureate."*

Carnarvon, Earl of. See Herbert, H.J.G.

Carne, John. Letters from the East. 1826. 8°.
    SC.97. LB.12: "Cairns [*sic*] East."

Carpenter, Nathanael. Geography delineated forth in
    two bookes; containing the sphaericall and topical
    parts thereof. [? Oxford, 1625. 4°.]. MC.69:
    "Carpenter's Geography:"

Carrington, Nicholas Toms. The Teignmouth, Dawlish,
and Torquay guide; with an account of the sur-
rounding neighbourhood ... By N.T. Carrington and
others. Teignmouth, [? 1829]. 12°. *SC*.184.

Cartwright, Dr. Thomas. The diary of Dr. Thomas Cartwright, Bishop of Chester ... edited by the Rev.
Joseph Hunter. 1843. 8°. *SC*.15.

[? Carver, Jonathan. Travels through the interior
parts of North America, in the years 1766, 1767,
and 1768. 1768. 8°.]. *SC*.163: "Travels in North
America, vol. 1." LB.10: "Travels in N. Am: 2
vols." See Davis, John and Hall, Captain Basil.

Cary, Henry. Memoir of the Rev. Henry Francis Cary;
with his literary journal and letters by his son.
2 vol. 1847. 12°. [RPB.HLKC:Ann]. *SC*.98: "8vo."

Cary, Henry Francis. See Dante Alighieri.

Cary, Robert. See Carey, Robert.

Casaubonus, Isaacus. See Diogenes Laërtius; Strabo.

Castalio, Sebastianus. See Châteillon, Sebastien.

Casti, Giovanni Battista. Gli animali parlanti; poema
epico diviso in ventisei canti. 2 tom. 1803.
12°. *SC*.488: "2 tomes ... 8vo, 1813." MC.99:
"Animale [*sic*] Parlanti:"

A catalogue of a miscellaneous collection of old
books; forming vol. II. part II. of a catalogue
for 1818-19; to be sold by Longman, Hurst & Co.
[1819]. 8°. [? MC.16: "Longman's Catalogue:"].
[*L* also lists Longman's catalogues for 1820 and
1822].

*Catholici indices. MC.14: "Catholici: Indices:"

Cato, Marcus Porcius, the Elder and others. Scriptores de re rustica. 2 vol. Paris ... 1543.

6.5 in. [*CWC*:Ann]. *SC*.361: "De Re Rustica, M.
Catonis, etc. etc. ... *containing numerous MS.
Annotations and Observations by the late Poet
Laureate*, 2 vols., 4to, Parisiis ... 1543." LB.11:
"De Re Rustica." See *CN*, 1N815.

Cattley, H. See Mickiewicz, Adam.

Catullus, Caius Valerius. Catullus, Tibullus, Propertius, cum C. Galli (vel potius Maximiani) fragmentis. Serio castigati. Amstelaedami, 1686.
8°. *SC*.570: "1686 (*with Poet's Autog*. 1825)."
MC.2: "Catullus &c: 2 Cop:"

————. Catulli, Tibulli, et Propertii opera. Bir-
minghamiae, 1772, 4° and 12°. *SC*.669: "8vo." MC.2:
"Catullus &c: 2 Cop:"

*————. Catulli, Tibulli, et Propertii opera. 1816.
18°. *SC*.397. MC.2: "Catullus &c: 2 Cop:"

*————. Catulli, Tibulli, et Propertii carmina.
Neapoli, 1828. *SC*.556: "(*MS. Note of Purchase
at Florence*)."

Cave, William. Apostolici; or, the history of the
lives, acts, and martyrdoms of those who were
contemporary with, or immediately succeeded the
Apostles. 1716. fol. [Lowndes]. *SC*.106:
"(*Laureate's Autog., Rydal Mount*)." [? MC.60:
"History of Martyrdoms:"]

Caxton, William. See Lefèvre, Raoul.

Cazotte, Jacques. See Arabian tales.

Cebes of Thebes. See Epictetus.

Certain sermons or homilies, appointed to be read in
churches, in the time of Queen Elizabeth. 1635.
fol. *SC*.253. MC.28: "Sermons or Homilies--Queen
Eliz:" [? MC.20: "Certain Sermons:"] [? LB.63:
"Homilies."] See STC entry.

Cervantes Saavedra, Miguel de. Historia del famoso
cavallero Don Quixote de la Mancha ... Con anotaciones, indices y varias lecciones por el Reverendo D. Juan Bowle. 6 tom. Londres et Salisbury,
1781. 4°. *SC*.337: "2 tomes, 4to, 1781." MC.96:
"Historia del Famoso Caval: Don Quixote 2 Vol:"
SC.337: "*Anotaciones a la Historia de Don Quixote.
etc*.; Por el Reverendo D.J. Bowle ... 4to, 1682.
[? 1782]." MC.96: "Annotat: on do." LB.8: "3
vols Don Q."

————. The history of the valorous and witty knight-
errant Don Quixote of the Mancha. Translated into
English by Thomas Shelton and now printed verbatim
from the 4° ed. of 1620. 4 vol. 1740. 17cm.
[*NUC*]. [DD:Ann]. MC.88: "Don Quixote: 4 vol."
LB.9: "Don Quixote 4 vol."

————. Don Quixote, translated by Dr. [Tobias]
Smollett. In four volumes. [The novelist's maga-
zine, Vol. 8 (1782)]. LB.6: "1 vol Novelist's
Magazine Don Quixote."

Chalmers, Alexander. See Burns, Robert. The poetical
works.

Chalmers, George. See De Foe, Daniel. The life ...
of Robinson Crusoe.

Chalmers, Thomas. Lectures on the establishment and
extension of national churches. 2nd ed. Glasgow, 1838. 8°. *SC*.207. LB.60.

Chambaud, Louis. See Bridel, Arleville.

————. Fables choisies, à l'usage des personnes qui
commencent à apprendre la langue françoise.
[? 1751. 12°.]. MC.96: "Chambaud's Fables:"

Chamberlayne, Edward. Angliae notitia; or, the pre-
sent state of England. 1674. 12°. *SC*.367.
[? MC.60: "Angliae Notitia:"] [? MC.41: "Present
State of England by Chamberlain [*sic*]"].

————. Angliae notitia, sive praesens status Angliae
succincte enucleatus. [Abridged and translated
into Latin by Thomas Wood]. Oxonii, 1686. 12°.
SC.86: "Wood: Angliae Notitia, 1686 (*no title*)."
[? MC.60: "Angliae Notitia:"].

Chamberlayne, John. See Nieuwentijdt, Bernard.

Chamberlayne, William. Pharonnida; a heroick poem.
1659. 8°. *SC*.489 and *SC*.559. MC.50: "Pharonniday [*sic*] by Cham:"

Chambers, Robert. Scottish ballads, collected and
illustrated by Robert Chambers. Edinburgh, 1829.
8°. *SC*.489. LB.30.

Chambers, Robert, publisher. Cyclopaedia of English
literature. 2 vol. Edinburgh, 1844. 8°.
SC.345.

Chamisso de Boncourt, Louis Charles Adelaide de [called
Chamisso, Adelbert von]. The shadowless man; or,
the wonderful history of Peter Schlemihl. [1843].
16°. LB.32: "Shadowless Man."

Champion, Francis. The triumph of music; with other
poems. By the blind bard of Cicestria [Francis
Champion]. Chichester, 1841. 8°. [*DAP*].
SC.621.

Chandler, Richard. See Ward, Caesar.

Chandler, Samuel. The history of persecution ...
with ... remarks on Dr. Rogers's vindication.
1736. 20cm. [CSJ:Ann]. *SC*.201: "8vo." MC.59:
"History of Persecution:"

Le chansonnier des Grâces; avec la musique gravée des
airs nouveaux. 2 pt. Paris, 1809. 12°. *SC*.502:
"avec 30 Airs, Graveur, 1814."

Chapelain, Jean. See Southey, Robert. Joan of Arc.

Chapman, George. See Homer. The Iliad.

Chapman, Jane Frances. See Ingemann, Bernhard Severin.

Chapone, Hester. Letters on the improvement of the
mind, addressed to a young lady. 2 vol. [? 1773.
8°.]. MC.81: "Shapone's [*sic*] Letters for Imp:
2 Vol:"

Chappelow, Leonard. See Erpenius, Thomas.

Charles, Nicholas. The visitation of the county of
Huntingdon ... Edited by Sir Henry Ellis. 1849.
8°. *SC*.15.

[Charles I, King of England]. Eikon basilike; the
portraicture of His Sacred Maiestie in his solitude and sufferings. 1648. 8°. *SC*.99: "(no
title) 8 vo." MC.63: "Eikon Basilike [in Greek]."
[? LB.7: "Eicon Basilike"].

Charron, Pierre. Of wisdome, three bookes. Written
in French by Peter Charron ... Translated by Samson Lennard. [1651]. 7.375 in. [*CWC*:Ann].
SC.209: "another Copy, without the Explanation of
the Frontispiece." [? MC.31: "Charron"].
[? MC.36: "Of Wisdom"].

————. [Another edition]. *SC*.208: "(with the
curious Frontispiece and Explanation), small 4to
... 1670." [? MC.31: "Charron"]. [? MC.36: "Of
Wisdom"].

Châteillon, Sebastien [i.e. Castalio, Sebastianus].
Dialogorum sacrorum ad linguam simul & mores
puerorum formandos libri IIII. Edinburgi, 1700.
12°. [*NUC*]. *SC*.205. MC.26: "Sacred Dialog:"

Chatterton, Thomas. See Dix, John.

Chatto, William Andrew [Stephen Oliver, the Younger,
pseud.]. Rambles in Northumberland and on the
Scottish Border ... By S. Oliver. 1835. 8°.
SC.146: "12mo."

Chaucer, Geoffrey. See Todd, Henry John.

————. The poems of Geoffrey Chaucer modernized.
[Selections from The Canterbury tales and other
works, modernised in verse, by R.H. Horne, Thomas
Powell, W. Wordsworth, Leigh Hunt, E.B. Barrett,
and others. Preceded by a life of Chaucer by L.
Schmitz]. 1841. 8°. [*MR*]. [WL:Ann]. *SC*.493:
"12mo." LB.37.

Chaulieu, L'Abbé. See Anfrie de Chaulieu, Guillaume.

Chavis, Dom Denis. See Arabian tales.

Chelidon. See Derivations from the Welsh.

Chetwynd, John. Anthologia historica, containing
fourteen centuries of memorable passages and remarkable occurrents, collected out of the English,
Spanish, Imperial, and Jewish histories, and
several other authors and writers. 1674. 16cm.
[NIC:Ann]. *SC*.18.

Cheyne, George. Philosophical principles of natural
religion. 1705. 20cm. [IU:Ann]. *SC*.210.
[? MC.24: "Cheynes Nat: Relig:"] [? MC.26:
"Philosoph: Princip: of Relig:"].

————. Philosophical principles of religion, Natural
and revealed. 1753, 1733. 2 vol. in 1. 21cm.
[*NUC*]. *SC*.202: "8vo, 1753." [? MC.26: "Philosoph:
Princip: of Relig:]. [? MC.24: "Cheynes Nat:
Relig:"].

Child, Mrs. Lydia Maria (Francis). Philothea; a romance. Boston, 1836. 20cm. [*NUC*]. *SC*.454:
"(*with Authoress's Presentation Autograph*)." LB.23.

The Christian mother's magazine. Edited by Mrs. [Mary]
Milner. vol. 1, 2. 1844,1845. 8°. *SC*.212: "a
bundle."

*Christian saints. LB.33 [borrowed in late 1844 by
John Wordsworth].

Churchill, Awnsham and John. A collection of voyages
and travels, some now first published in English.
With a general preface [attributed by the publishers
to J. Locke] giving an account of the progress of
navigation from its first beginning. 3rd ed.
6 vol. 1744-46. fol. *SC*.172: "with Introductory
Discourse supposed to be written by the celebrated
Mr. Locke, 6 vols., folio, wanting vol. 4 ... 1744."

Cibber, Colley. An apology for the life of Colley
Cibber, comedian. With an historical view of the
stage during his own time. Written by himself.
1740. 4°. [WL:Ann: STC to SH "who lent this
book to her nephew Wm W Jr. on the last day he
saw her 1835"]. MC.66: "Life of Colley Cibber:"
LB.15.

*Cicero, Marcus Tullius. *SC*.348: "Cicero (*Latin*)."

*————. MC.2: "Ciceronis Cato Major:"

————. [? M. Tullii Ciceronis opera. cum indicibus
et variis lectionibus. (M. Tullii Ciceronis his-
toria ... per Franciscum Fabricium.--Desiderii
Jacotii Vandoperani de philosophorum doctrina ...
Clavis Ciceroniana [by J.A. Ernesti]. 10 tom.
Oxonii, 1783. 4°.]. MC.1: "Ciceronis Opera 10
Vol: Qto."

*————. MC.2/H[artley] C[oleridge]: "Ciceronis
Opera" [written in left margin].

————. M. Tullii Ciceronis de officiis libri tres
... ex recensione Joannis Georgii Graevii ...
Amstelodami, 1688. 8°. [*BN*]. [? *SC*.347: "8vo
... 1681"]. MC.2: "Cicero de Off: 3 Cop:"

————. M. Tullii Ciceronis de officiis libri tres.
1754. [WL:Ann]. MC.2: "Cicero de Off: 3 Cop:"

————. M. Tullii Ciceronis de officiis libri tres.
Notis illustravit, et ... emendavit Z[achary]
Pearce. Oxonii, 1803. 12°. *SC*.564: "ed. Pearce,
8vo, 1803." MC.2: "Cicero de Off: 3 Cop:"

————. The first book of Tullies Offices translated grammatically, and also according to the propriety of our English tongue [by John Brinsley] ... Done chiefly for the good of schools. 1616. 14.5cm. [CtY.BL:Ann]. MC.92: "First Book of Cicero's Off:"

————. Marci Tullii Ciceronis Epistolae ad familiares. A Dionysio Lambino Monstroliensi ex codibus manuscriptis emendatae. Eiusdem D. Lambini annotationes, seu emendationum rationes. Item Pauli Manutii annotationes braeuissimae, in margine adscriptae. 1575. 8°. *SC*.383: "a Lambini et Manutii ... 1575." [? MC.2: "Ciceronis Episto:"] [LB.27: "Ciceronis Epistolae. 1575"].

————. [? M. Tullii Ciceronis Epistolarum ad Quintum fratrem libri tres, et ad Brutum liber unus. ... Hagae Comitum, 1725. 8°.]. MC.2: "Ciceronis Episto: 4 Bks:"

————. The letters of M.T. Cicero to T.P. Atticus ... Translated ... with notes by William Heberden [the Younger]. 2 vol. 1825. 8°. *SC*.346: "to T.P. Cicero [*sic*]."

————. Orationum Marci Tvlli Ciceronis volvmen à Joann. Michäele Bruto [Giovanni Michele Bruto] emendatum. Accesserunt breues animadversiones ex doctissimorum hominum commentarijs quibus ita loci permulti explicantur, vt vulgo receptae lectionis vbique ratio habeatur. 1636. 13cm. [*NUC*]. *SC*.350: "Orationum M.T. Ciceronis a J.M. Bruto, emend., etc., vol. 2, 1664 ... *Autograph*." MC.2: "Ciceronis Orat: 2 Cop:"

————. The orations of M. Tullius Cicero, translated into English, with notes ... By W. Guthrie. Second edition ... revised ... with additional notes. 3 vol. 1745,52. 8°. *SC*.348: "vol. 1, 8vo, 1745." MC.91: "Guthrie's Cicero's Orat:"

————. Cicero's Catilinarian orations from the text of Ernesti, with notes by E.H. Barker. 1829.

12°. *SC*.579: "*(with Presentation Autog.).*" MC.2:
"Ciceronis Orat: 2 Cop:"

Cignani, Pietro A. See Brulart de Sillery, Stéphanie
Félicité, Countess de Genlis.

Cicogna, Strozzi. Palagio de gl'incanti, e della gran
meraviglie de gli Spiriti e di tutta la Natura;
divise in libri 45, e in 3 prospettive. Vicenza,
1605. 4°. [*L: "Only the first 4 books published"*]. *SC*.494: "8vo ... 1605."

A citizen of New York. See Hunt, Freeman.

Clarendon, Earl of. See Hyde, Edward.

Clarke, James. A survey of the lakes of Cumberland,
Westmoreland, and Lancashire; together with an
account historical, topographical, and descriptive of the adjacent country. 1789. fol. [WL:
Ann]. LB.30.

Clarke, John. See Nepos, Cornelius.

Clarke, Samuel. (1599-1683). See Life of Tamerlane.

————. A demonstration of the being and attributes
of God: more particularly in answer to Mr. Hobbs
[*sic*], Spinosa [*sic*], and their followers. Wherein the notion of liberty is stated and the possi-
bility and certainty of it proved in opposition
to necessity and fate; being the substance of 8
sermons, preached in the Cathedral-church of St.
Paul ... at the lecture founded by the Hon.
Robert Boyle ... 7th ed. revised. 1728. 19.5cm.
[OO.SC]. *SC*.309.

————. A letter to Mr. Dodwell; wherein all the
arguments in his epistolary discourse against the
immortality of the soul are particularly answered,
and the judgment of the Fathers concerning that
matter truly represented. 3rd ed. 1708. 7.5 in.
[*CWC*:Ann]. [Bound with the preceding are four

other pamphlets by Clarke on the same subjects,
and also William Higden, A defence of the view of
the English constitution with respect to the
sovereign authority of the prince, and the allegiance of the subject ... 1710. 7.5 in.]. *SC*.213:
"8vo ... 1708." MC.25: "Clarke's Letter to Dodwell:"

Clarke, Samuel. (1675-1729). See Rohault, Jacques.

Clarke, William Branwhite. Part the first; the River
Derwent and other poems. 1822. 8°. *SC*.504.

Clarkson, Thomas. Essay on the impolicy of the African slave-trade. 1788. 8°. *SC*.20: "*(with MS.
corrections in the handwriting of the Author)*."
MC.39: (*bis*): "Clarkson on the Slave Trade:"
[? LB.25: "Clarkson's Af."].

————. An essay on the slavery and commerce of the
human species, particularly the African; translated
from a Latin dissertation which was honoured with
the first prize in the University of Cambridge,
for the year 1785, with additions. 1786. 8°.
SC.20. MC.61: "Clarkson on Slavery:"

————. The history of the rise, progress, and accomplishment of the abolition of the African slave-
trade by the British Parliament. 2 vol. 1808.
21.5cm. [CtY.BL:Ann]. *SC*.21. MC.39 (*bis*):
"Clarkson on the Slave Trade:" [? LB.25: "Clarkson's Af."].

————. A portraiture of Quakerism, as taken from a
view of the moral education, discipline, peculiar
customs, religious principles, political and civil
oeconomy, and character, of the Society of Friends.
3 vol. 1806. 8°. *SC*.349: "vols. 2 and 3 ...
Presentation Autograph." MC.79: "Portrait: of
Quakerism: 3 Vol:"

————. Researches antediluvian, patriarchal, and
historical concerning the way in which men first

acquired their knowledge of God and religion.
1836. 8°. *SC*.229. LB.25.

————. Strictures on the Life of Wilberforce. 1838.
8°. *SC*.349: "*Presentation Autograph*." LB.24.

*Classics. *SC*.348: "*odd vols*. [probably 2]."

Claudianus, Claudius. [Poetical works]. [? Venetiis,
1642.] [*NUC*]. *SC*.347: "Claudius, 12mo, *Venetia*
... 1642." MC.2/H[artley] C[oleridge]: "Claudiani
opera" [written in left margin]. See *CN*, 3N3876.

Clayton, Robert. See Advice from a bishop.

Cleaveland, John. See Cleveland, John.

Clement, of Alexandria. Klementos Alexandreos Ta
heuriskomena [in Greek]. Clementis Alexandrini
opera graece et latine quae extant. Post accura-
tam D.V. Heinsii recensionem et breues additas
in fine emendationes, facta est. Lutetiae, 1629.
fol. [CSmH.ZZB:Ann]. *SC*.214. MC.2: "Clemens
Alexandr:"

Clement XIV, Pope. Interesting letters of Pope Clement
XIV (Ganganelli). To which are prefixed, anecdotes of his life. Translated from the French
edition published at Paris by Lottin, jun. 3 vol.
in 4. 1777. 18.5cm. (Vol. III has title: Interesting letters ... Likewise an original letter, in
answer to M. Voltaire's objections to the authenticity of Ganganelli's letters). [InU.WC:Ann].
(In Vol. I, in pencil, Wordsworth has written:
"These letters are attributed in the main to Louis
Antoine de Caraccioli a French author."). *SC*.215:
"4 vols., 8vo ... 1718 [*sic*]."

A clergyman. See Holworthy, Samuel; Watts, John.

Cleveland, John. J. Cleaveland revised: poems, orations, epistles, and other of his genuine incom-
parable pieces. 3rd ed. 1662. 8°. *SC*.506:
"12mo." MC.49: "Cleveland's Poems:"

Close, John. The book of the chronicles; or, winter
evening tales of Westmorland. Vol. 1 [*No more
published*]. Appleby, 1842. 12°. *SC*.157: "vol.
1, 1742 [*sic*]."

Close, William. See West, Thomas. The antiquities
of Furness.

A cloud of witnesses for the royal prerogatives of
Jesus Christ, or the last speeches and testimonies
of those who suffered for the truth in Scotland
since the year 1680 ... 10th ed. Glasgow, 1779.
8°. *SC*.219: "8vo, 1769 [*sic*]."

Cluverius, Philippus. Philippi Cluverii Introduc-
tionis in universam geographiam. Amstelodami,
1661. 12°. *SC*.101: "4to ... *Amsterdam*, 1661."
MC.14: "Cluverii Geograph:" *SC*.141: "P. Cluverii
Geographiae, 1674."

Cochrane, Captain Charles Stuart. Journal of a residence and travels in Colombia during the years
1823 and 1824. 2 vol. 1825. 8°. [*NUC*].
SC.174: "in Calcutta [*sic*], vol. 2, 8vo."

Cockings, George. War; an heroic poem, from the
taking of Minorca by the French; to the reduction
of the Havannah ... The second edition, to the
raising the siege of Quebec: With large amend-
ments and additions. By the author. (Britannia's
call, to her brave troops, and hardy tars [with
other poems]). Boston, 1762. 8°. *SC*.559: "by
George Coakings [*sic*]."

Coiffier de Verseux, Henri-Louis. Dictionnaire bio-
graphique et historique des hommes marquans de la
fin du dix-huitième siècle, et plus particulière-
ment de ceux qui ont figuré dans la Révolution
Française. Suivi d'un supplément et de quatre
tableaux des massacres et proscriptions. Rédigé
par une société de gens de lettres. 3 tom. 1800.
8°. *SC*.109: "3 tomes in 1."

Colby, Colonel Thomas. See Larcom, Sir Thomas Aiskew.

Cole, Thomas. The life of Hubert; a narrative, descriptive and didactic poem. Book the first ... to which are added some original and translated poems. 1795. 8°. *SC*.495. MC.49: "Cole's Life of Hubert:"

Coleridge, Derwent. See Coleridge, Hartley.

————. The scriptural character of the English Church, considered in a series of sermons; with notes and illustrations. 1839. 8°. *SC*.216.

Coleridge, Hartley. See Massinger, Philip; Ford, John.

————. Poems. Vol. I [Only 1 vol. published]. Leeds, London, 1833. 8°. [WL.HL]. *SC*.496: "1838 [*sic*]."

————. Poems; with a memoir of his life by his brother [Derwent Coleridge]. 2 vol. 1851. 8°. LB.51: "2 Vol Hartley Coleridge."

Coleridge, Henry Nelson. See Coleridge, Samuel Taylor. Confessions of an inquiring spirit; The literary remains.

————. Introductions to the study of the Greek classic poets. Part I. 1830. 12°. *SC*.356: "8vo."

————. Remarks on the Roman Catholic question. 1827. *SC*.217: "(*with Critical Observations in Mr. Wordsworth's Handwriting in Black-lead*)." [Perhaps identifiable with "The Roman Catholic Question--Ireland," *Quarterly Review*, Vol. 38, October, 1828, pp. 535-598. "Mr. Coleridge," says Allibone, "contributed to the Quarterly Review"].

Coleridge, Samuel Taylor. See Hurwitz, Hyman; Lloyd, Charles, The Younger; Schiller, Johann Christoph Friedrich; Southey, Robert. Omniana.

————. The poetical works of Coleridge, Shelley, and Keats. Complete in one volume. 3 pt. Paris, 1829. 8°. *SC*.497. LB.17.

————. The poetical works of S.T. Coleridge. 3 vol. [? 1829. 8°.]. [? 1834. 12°.]. LB.20: "1st Vol Coleridge [borrowed in 1835]."

————. Aids to reflection in the formation of a manly character, on the several grounds of prudence, morality, and religion; illustrated by select passages from our elder divines, especially from Archbishop Leighton. 1825. 8°. *SC*.218. LB.13: "Coleridge's Aids."

————. Biographia literaria. 2 vol. 1817. 8°. *SC*.351. MC.64: "Biographia Literaria:" LB.20: "Literaria Biographia [*sic*]."

————. Confessions of an inquiring spirit ... Edited from the author's MS. by H[enry] N[elson] Coleridge. 1840. 8°. *SC*.355: "12mo."

————. The friend; a literary, moral, and political weekly paper ... conducted by ... S.T. Coleridge. 1 June 1809-15 March 1810. 28 pt. Penrith, 1809, 10. 8°. *SC*.352: "*the original edition.*"

————. [Another edition]. 3 vol. 1818. 8°. *SC*.353.

————. The literary remains of Samuel Taylor Coleridge. Collected and edited by Henry Nelson Coleridge. 4 vol. 1836-39. 8°. [WL:Ann]. LB.25.

————. On the constitution of the Church and State, according to the idea of each; with aids towards a right judgment on the late Catholic Bill. 1830. 8°. *SC*.218.

————. Remorse; a tragedy. 1813. 8°. *SC*.352.

————. Specimens of the table talk of Samuel Taylor
Coleridge. 2 vol. 1835. 12°. *SC*.354. LB.19.

————. Sibylline leaves. A collection of poems.
1817. 23.5cm. [NIC:Ann]. *SC*.103. MC.53: "Coleridge's Sibyll: Leaves:" LB.11.

Coleridge, Sara. See Dobrizhoffer, Martin; de Mailles,
Jacques.

————. Phantasmion. 1837. 8°. LB.23.

A collection of plays by eminent hands. 4 vol. 1710.
12°. [? *SC*.619: "A Collection of Plays, 8vo."].

*Collection of the [? Minor] Latin poets. LB.11.
MC.7: "A Pocket vol: of the Minor Latin Poets
given by Anthony Harrison to S.T.C. taken by Hartley Coleridge Jay 2, 1829." See Poetae Latini
minores in STC Appendix.

A collection of the several statutes and parts of
statutes now in force, relating to high treason,
and misprision of high treason. 1709. 8°.
[? MC.41: "Statutes relating to High Treason"].

Collier, John Payne. See Bale, John. King Johan.

————, ed. The Egerton papers; a collection of public and private documents, chiefly illustrative
of the times of Elizabeth and James I. From the
original manuscripts, the property of the Right
Hon. Lord Francis Egerton, M.P. 1840. 8°. *SC*.15.

————. The poet's pilgrimage; an allegorical poem,
in four cantos. 1825. 4°. *SC*.498.

Colling, Mary Maria. Fables and other pieces in verse
... with some account of the author, in letters
to Robert Southey ... by Mrs. [Anna Eliza] Bray.
1831. 8°. *SC*.597. LB.22.

Collins, William. Odes on several descriptive and
allegoric subjects. 1747. 19cm. [NNMor:Ann].
SC.499: "4to, 1747, *the first edition*."

————. The poetical works of William Collins; with
the life of the author by Dr. [Samuel] Johnson;
observations on his writings by Dr. [John] Langhorne; and biographical and critical notes, by
the Rev. Alexander Dyce. London, Oxford, 1827.
19cm. [NjP:Ann]. *SC*.547.

Collins, William Wilkie. Memoirs of the life of William Collins [R.A.], with selections from his journals and correspondence. 2 vol. 1848. 12°.
[CSmH.ZZB:Ann]. *SC*.98. LB.44.

Colman, George, the Elder. See Beaumont, Francis.

———— and Bonnell Thornton. See Poems by eminent
ladies.

Comenius (or Commenius). See Komenský, Jan Amos.

Comes, Natalis. Natalis Comitis Mythologiae, siue
explicationis fabularum, libri decem ... nuper
ab ipso autore recogniti & locupletati. Eiusdem
libri iv de venatione ... Accessit G[eofredi]
Linocerij [Vivariensis] Musarum mythologia, &
anonymi obseruationum in totam de diis gentium
narrationem, libellus. Geneuae, 1651. 8°. pp.
1123. *SC*.389: "*Geneva*, 8vo, 1651, 1123 pp."
MC.12/0: "Natalis Comitis Mytholog:"

Comines, Philippe de. The historie of Philip de
Commines [*sic*]. [Translated from the French of
Thomas Danett]. The fourth edition corrected.
1674. fol. [DD:Ann]. MC.62: "Hist: of Philip
de Com:"

A companion by the way; or, a guide to the lakes in
Cumberland, Westmoreland, and Lancashire. London, Penrith, 1812. 12°. MC.72: "Companion by
the Way:"

[? Compleat sollicitor, performing his duty and teaching his clyent to run through and manage his own business as well in His Majesties Superiour Courts at Westminster as in the Mayor's Court, Court of Hustings, and other inferiour courts, both in the Citie of London and elsewhere. [? London], 1668. 24°]. [Wing]. MC.38: "Complete Solicitor:"

[Compton, Margaret, Marchioness of Northampton]. Irene. A poem in six cantos. Miscellaneous poems. 1833. 8°. *SC*.548: "Irene and Miscellaneous Poems (not published), 1833."

Compton, Spencer Joshua Alwyne, 2nd Marquis of Northampton. The tribute; a collection of miscellaneous unpublished poems, by various authors. Edited by Lord Northampton. 1837. 8°. *SC*.600.

Comyn, Alexandre de, *pseud*. See Browne, Charles Thomas.

*Concerning religions. MC.26: "Concernȷ Religions:"

Conciones et orationes ex historicis Latinis excerptae. Argumenta singulis praefixa sunt, quae causam cujusque et summam ex rei gestae occasione explicant. In usum Regiae Scholae Westmonasteriensis. Etonae, 1805. 16°. [*NUC*]. *SC*.40: "8vo, 1805."

Congreve, William. The works of Mr. Congreve: in two volumes ... The seventh edition. To which is prefixed, The life of the author. 2 vol. 1774. 17.5cm. [*NUC*]. [? *SC*.500: "Dramatic Works, with Life, etc., 2 vols., 1776"]. MC.83: "Congreve's Dram: Works:" LB.7: "2 Vol of Congreve."

Conington, John. See Aeschylus.

Conon Grammaticus. See Gale, Thomas.

Constable, John. See Leslie, Charles Robert.

Conti, Natale. See Comes, Natalis.

Conyers, Richard. See De morbis infantum.

Cook, Henry, Chevalier of the Order of SS. Maurizio e
    Lazaro. Pride; or, the heir of Craven. A tale of
    the fifteenth century, in six cantos. 1841. 22cm.
    [*NUC*]. *SC*.468.

Cook, Captain James. *SC*.104: "Two First Voyages round
    the World, 4 vols., 12mo, 1809." MC.70: "Cook's
    Voyages: 4 Vol:" [Probably Vols. 4,5,6, and 7 in
    Mavor, William Fordyce. General collections of
    voyages and travels from the discovery of America
    to the commencement of the nineteenth century.
    28 vol. 1809-10. 12mo.].

Cooke, James. See Hall, John. Select observations
    on English bodies.

[Cooper, Anthony Ashley, 3rd Earl of Shaftesbury].
    Characteristicks of men, manners, opinions, times.
    3rd ed. 3 vol. [London], 1723. 8°. *SC*.430.
    MC.34: "Shaftesbury's Charact:"

Cooper, E[dward]. Sermons chiefly designed to eluci-
    date some of the leading doctrines of the Gospel.
    1810. 8°. *SC*.298: "1820."

[Cooper, Mrs. Elizabeth and William Oldys]. The muses
    library; or, a series of English poetry, from the
    Saxons to the reign of King Charles II, containing
    the lives and characters of all the known writers
    in that interval, the names of their patrons, com-
    plete episodes, by way of specimens of the larger
    pieces, very near the intire [*sic*] works of some,
    and large quotations from others. Vol. I. [*only*].
    1737. 8°. *SC*.485: "vol. 1, 1787 [*sic*]." MC.46:
    "Muses' Library:"

Cooper, Thomas, the Chartist. The purgatory of sui-
    cides; a prison-rhyme in ten books. 1845. 8°.
    SC.501: "6 Nos., with most interesting *Presenta-
    tion Autograph* Letter from the Author, dated 7
    Park Place, Knightsbridge, Tuesday, November 2d,
    1847."

Corneille, Pierre. Les chefs-d'oeuvres de Pierre Cor-
neille, savoir: Le Cid, Horace, Cinna, Polyeucte,
Pompée, Rodogune, avec le jugement des savans à
la suite de chaque pièce. Nouvelle édition (par
J.-G. Dupré). Oxford, 1746. 8°. [*BN*]. *SC*.502.
MC.99: "Corneille:" LB.6.

Cornish, Thomas Harttree. The Thames; a descriptive
poem. 1842. 8°. *SC*.512.

Cornwall, Barry, *pseud*. See Procter, Bryan Waller.

Corpus poetarum Latinorum. See Maittaire, Michael.

Costa, Jerome à, *pseud*. See Simon, Richard.

Costanzo, Torquato. Bernardo Tasso, e poetesse del
secolo XVI. Venezia, 1787. 6.5 in. [*CWC*:Ann].
SC.584: "Costango [*sic*]." MC.97: "Constanzo [*sic*]:"

Coste, Pierre. See also Lafontaine, Jean de. Fables.

————. The life of Lewis of Bourbon, late Prince of
Condé ... digested into annals ... Done out of
French [of P. Coste, by N[ahum] Tate]. 1693. 8°.
MC.65: "Life of Conde [*sic*]:" LB.40: "Conde's
Life."

Cotes, Henry. See Beilby, Ralph.

Cottle, Amos Simon. See Edda, Poetic.

Cottle, Joseph. Early recollections, chiefly relating
to the late S.T. Coleridge, during his long residence in Bristol. 2 vol. 1837 [-39]. 8°.
[WL:Ann]. LB.22: "Cottles recollections of C."

————. Essays in reference to Socinianism. pt. 1.
London, Bristol, 1842. 12°. [*No more published*].
[CSmH.ZZB:Ann]. *SC*.307.

[————]. The fall of Cambria in twenty-four books
... [a poem]. 2 vol. 1808. 12°. *SC*.503: "3

[*sic*] vols., 1808." MC.46: "Fall of Cambria: 2 Vol:" See *The Monthly Review*, LVII, 279.

―――. Malvern Hills; a poem. 1798. 4°. *SC*.663: "(*with some MS. notes by Mr. Wordsworth*)."

―――. [Another edition]. With minor poems and essays. 4th ed. 2 vol. London, Bristol, 1829. 12°. *SC*.503: "2 vols. (title to 1st wanting), 1829."

―――. A new version of the Psalms. [? 1801]. [? 1805]. 8°. MC.45: "Cottle's version of Psalms:"

―――. Poems. 2nd ed. Bristol, London, 1796. 17cm. [*NUC*]. *SC*.503: "1796." MC.44: "Cottle's Poems:-- '96:"

―――. Reminiscences of Samuel Taylor Coleridge and Robert Southey. 1847. 8°. [DD: "From the Compiler. Mr Cottle, to M. Wordsworth July, 1850"]. LB.60.

[Cottle, Robert]. Romanism an apostate church. By Non Clericus [i.e. Robert Cottle]. 1852. 8°. [*DAP*]. *SC*.216.

Cotton, Charles. See Montaigne, Michel de.

―――. The genuine poetical works of Charles Cotton, Esq.; containing I. Scarronides ... II. Lucian burlesqu'd ... III. The wonders of the Peake ... The second edition, corrected. 1725. 12°. *SC*.506: "8vo." [? MC.44: "Cotton's Poems:"]

―――. Poems on several occasions. 1689. 8°. *SC*.505: "1686." [? MC.44: "Cotton's Poems:"]

―――. LB.10: "Cottons Poems Dr Bells Ed^n [i.e. John Bell's The poets of Great Britain, which see].

————. [? Scarronides; or Virgil travestie ... being the first book of Virgil's Aeneis in English burlesque. 1664. 8°.] MC.92: "Cotton's Virgil Travestie:"

*Coulton, Mrs. *SC*.581: "Poems by Mrs. Coulton [? 1844]."

A country vicar. The ax blunted, and prov'd to be no sharper than a wooden saw. In some remarks upon a late scurrilous pamphlet entituled, The ax laid to the root of Christian priestcraft. 2 pts. Worcester, 1745. 21.5cm. [*NUC*]. *SC*.311: "1745 ... 4to."

*County Itinerary. MC.70: "County Itinerary: 2 Vol:"

The court of Tuscany; a tragedy [in five acts, and in verse]. The heir of Innes; a tragedy [in five acts, and in verse]. 1822. 8°. *SC*.496.

Cousin, Victor. Report on the state of public instruction in Prussia, addressed to the Count Montalivet ... With plans of schoolhouses. Translated by Sarah Austin. 1834. 8°. *SC*.356.

Cove, Morgan. An essay on the revenues of the Church of England. 2nd ed. 1797. 8°. *SC*.207. MC.40/ JC/C. See STC entry.

Cowley, Abraham. The works of Mr. Abraham Cowley ... 5th ed. 1678. fol. *SC*.507. [? MC.46: Cowley's Works:"] [? MC.44/0: "Cowley's Poems:"]

————. The works of Mr. Abraham Cowley. 7th ed. 1681. fol. *SC*.508. [? MC.46: "Cowley's Works:"] [? MC.44/0: "Cowley's Poems:"]

Cowper, William. See Guyon, Jeanne Marie.

————. The works of William Cowper, comprising his poems, correspondence, and translations. With a life of the author by the editor, Robert Southey. 15 vol. 1835-37. 8°. [WL:Ann]. LB.20, LB.30.

————. Poems. 6th ed. 2 vol. 1794,95. 8°. *SC*. 509. [? MC.47: "Cowper's Poems: 2 Vol:"].

————. [? Poems. Edited by John Johnson. 3 vol. 1815. 12°.]. [Vol. 3 contains a number of new poems]. MC.47: "do [Cowper's poems] a third Vol:"

————. [? Poems, the early productions of William Cowper. Edited by James Croft. 1825. 16°.]. LB.41: "Cowper in one small volume."

[Coxe, Arthur Cleveland]. Athanasion. 2nd ed., with notes and corrections. Also, miscellaneous poems. By the author of "Christian ballads," &c. New York, 1842. 19.5cm. [*NUC*]. *SC*.568: "8vo, *New York*, 1842."

Coxe, Richard Charles. Poems; scriptural, classical, and miscellaneous. Newcastle, 1845. 8°. *SC*.568.

Coxe, William. Lettres de M. William Coxe à M.W. Melmoth sur l'état politique, civil, et naturel de la Suisse; traduits [*sic*] de l'Anglais, et augmentées des observations faites dans le même pays par le traducteur [i.e. Louis François Elizabeth Ramond de Carbonnières]. 2 tom. Paris, 1782. 8°. *SC*.105. MC.102: "Ramonds Translation of Cox's [*sic*] Swisserland [*sic*] 2 Vol." LB.11: "2 vol Raymonds Cox L."

Crabb, George. Elements of German and English conversation on familiar subjects ... Third edition, enlarged and improved. 1810. 12°. [? MC.18: "Elements of Germ: Convers:"].

————. Auswahl vorzüglicher stellen aus den besten deutschen schriftstellern zusammengetragen ... vierte vermehrte und verbesserte ausgabe. (Extracts from the best German authors, etc.) 1825. 12°. *SC*.358: "Extracts from the Book of [*sic*] German Authors, etc., 8vo, 1825."

Crabbe, George, the Elder. The poetical works of the Rev. George Crabbe; with his letters and journals, and his life, by his son [George Crabbe]. 8 vol. 1834. 8°. *SC*.510: "12 mo." LB.18.

————. Poems. 1807. 8°. *SC*.685. MC.47: "Crabbe's Poems:"

Crabbe, George, the Younger. See Crabbe, George, the Elder.

Crakanthorp (or Crakanthorpe), Richard. See also Ecclesiae Anglicanae.

————. Vigilius dormitans. Romes seer overseene: or, a treatise of the fift [*sic*] generall councell held at Constantinople, anno. 553, under Iustinian the Emperour, in the time of Pope Vigilivs. 1631. 29cm. [NIC:Ann]. MC.27: "Vigilius Dormitans:"

Cramer, John Anthony. See Nucius, Nicander.

Crawford, Earl of. See Lindsay, Alexander.

Creech, Thomas. See Horatius Flaccus, Quintus. The odes.

Croft, James. See Cowper, William. Poems.

Croker, Thomas Crofton, ed. Narratives illustrative of the contests in Ireland in 1641 and 1690. 1841. 22.5cm [*NUC*]. *SC*.15: "Conquests [*sic*]."

Cromwell, Thomas Kitson. The druid; a tragedy, in five acts. With notes on the antiquities and early history of Ireland. 1832. 8°. *SC*.468.

Crookshank, William. The history of the state and sufferings of the Church of Scotland, from the Restoration to the Revolution. 2 vol. 1749. 8°. *SC*.219. MC.61: "Crookshank's Hist: 2 Vol:"

Crossley, Thomas. Flowers of Ebor. London, Halifax, 1837. 12°. *SC*.616.

[Crouch, Nathaniel]. [? The secret history of the
four last monarchs of Great Britain: viz. James I.,
Charles I., Charles II., James II. To which is
added an appendix containing the later reign of
James the Second, from the time of his abdication
of England to this present January, 1691. With
particular remarks on his private actions in Ireland. 1691. 14.5cm.]. [Wing; *NUC*]. MC.60:
"Secret History:" See Kirkton, James.

Crowe, William. Lewesdon Hill; a poem. Oxford, 1788.
4°. LB.23.

Crucius, Jacobus. Jacobi Cruci[i] Suada delphica sive
orationes LXVIII varii argumenti studiosae juven-
tuti manuductio ad artem oratoriam. Editio nova
revisa & emendata. Amstelodami, 1709. 13.5cm.
[*NUC*]. [WL:Ann]. MC.10: "Suada Delphica."

Cudworth, Ralph, the Younger. The true intellectual
system of the universe: the first part; wherein
all the reason and philosophy of atheism is con-
futed; and its impossibility demonstrated. 1678.
fol. *SC*.220.

Culpepper, Nicholas. The English physician; or, an
astrologo-physical discourse of the vulgar herbs
of this nation. 1652. 12°. *SC*.106: "Culpepper,
N.: the English Physician, 8vo [n.p., n.d.]."
MC.36: "Culpep: English Phys:"

[? Cumberland ballads; containing Uncle Wully, Guid
strang yell, etc. n.p. 1809. 8°.]--[? Anderson,
Robert, of Carlisle. Ballads in the Cumberland
dialect ... with notes, and a glossary. Carlisle,
1805. 12°.]. MC.48: "Cumberland Ballads."

The Cumberland Magazine; or, Whitehaven monthly miscellany. Whitehaven, [? 1778-] 1781. [*NUC*].
SC.359: "*containing everything proper to dispense
to promote virtue, to help agreeable conversation*
etc. etc., 8vo, 1780."

Cunningham, Allan. The maid of Elvar; a poem, in
twelve parts. 1832. 12°. *SC*.588.

————. Sir Marmaduke Maxwell, a dramatic poem; the
   mermaid of Galloway; the legend of Richard Faulder;
   and twenty Scottish songs. 1822. 12°. *SC*.582.

Cunningham, Peter. Poems upon several occasions.
   1841. 4°. *SC*.512: "*(with Presentation Autograph)*, 8vo."

Currie, James. See Burns, Robert. The works.

Curterius, Johannes. See Hierocles.

Curtius Rufus, Quintus. Alexander Magnus. [Edited
   by M. Maittaire]. 1716. 12°. *SC*.410: "Q. Curtii
   Alex. Mag., 1716."

D., J. See Davies, John; Dodington, John. Urfé,
   Honoré d'.

D., W. See Audiguier, Vital D'.

Dacres, Edward. See Machiavelli, Niccolò.

Dafydd, ap Gwilym. Translations into English verse
   from the poems of Davyth ab Gwilym [by Maelog,
   i.e. Arthur James Johnes]. 1834. 12°. *SC*.623.

Dallas, Alexander Robert Charles. Felix Alvarez; or,
   manners in Spain, containing descriptive accounts
   of some of the prominent events of the late
   Peninsular War. 3 vol. 1818. 12°. *SC*.2. LB.16.

Dallington, Sir Robert. Aphorismes civill and mili-
   tarie amplified with authorities and exemplified
   with historie, out of the first quarterne of
   F[rancesco] Guicciardine. (A brief inference
   upon Guicciardine's digression, in the fourth
   part of the first quarterne of his Historie: for-
   bidden the impression and effaced out of the originall by the Inquisition). 1613. fol. *SC*.31.

Une dame de distinction. See Marmontel, Jean François.

Dana, Richard Henry. Poems and prose writings. Philadelphia, Boston, 1833. 19cm. [*NUC*]. *SC*.655.

Danett, Thomas. See Comines, Philippe de.

Daniel, Samuel. LB.8: "Daniel's Histy of England."
[Lent 3 Nov. 1825 and possibly STC's copy. See STC entry].

————. The poetical works of Mr. Samuel Daniel ...
to which is prefix'd memoirs of his life and writings. 2 vol. 1718. 8°. [WL:Ann]. MC.49:
"Daniels' [*sic*] Poems: 2 Vol:" LB.34.

*Danish grammar. MC.17: "Danish Gram:"

Dante Alighieri. [? The vision; or Hell, Purgatory,
and Paradise of Dante Alighieri. Translated by ... Henry F. Cary. 3 vol. 1814. 16°.]--[? 2nd ed. 3 vol. 1819. 8°.]. MC.46: "Carey's [*sic*]
Dante: 3 Vol:" LB.26. See *CN*, 1N165.

Darley, George. See Beaumont, Francis and John Fletcher.

————. Ethelstan; or, the Battle of Brunanburh. A
dramatic chronicle. In five acts. 1841. 8°.
SC.486.

————. Thomas à Becket. A dramatic chronicle. In
five acts. 1840. 8°. *SC*.486: "Ethelston [*sic*],
Dramatic Chronicle, and Thomas a Beckett [*sic*],
do., by George Darley (*with Presentation Autograph*), 1841."

Davenant, Sir William. The works of Sir W[illiam]
Davenant, consisting of those which were formerly printed, and those which he design'd for the press ... 3 pt. 1673. fol. [Paul F. Betz:Ann].
SC.513.

Davies, John, of Kidwelly. See Ross, Alexander; Vialart, Charles.

Davies, Sir John. The original, nature, amd immortality of the soul; a poem, with an introduction concerning humane [*sic*] knowledge. 3rd ed. 1715.
   12°. *SC*.559: "by Sir John Davis [*sic*], 1751 [*sic*]."

Davila, Enrico Caterina. Historia delle guerre civili
   di Francia ... nella quale si contengono le oper-
   ationi di quattro rè, Francesco II., Carlo IX.,
   Henrico III. e Henrico IV. cognominato il Grande.
   Venetia, 1646. 38cm. [*NUC*]. *SC*.23.

Davis, John, of Salisbury. Travels of four years and
   a half in the United States of America during
   1798-1802. London, Bristol, 1803. 8°. [*L*:Ann].
   LB.7: "Davis Travels." LB.10: "Davis's D⁰" [i.e.
   "Travels N. America"]. See Carver, Jonathan;
   Hall, Captain Basil.

Davy, John. Memoirs of the life of Sir Humphry Davy,
   Bart. 2 vol. 1836. 8°. [WL:Ann]. LB.20.

Day, Julia. Poems. [? 1847. 8°.]--[? Second series.
   [1849]. 8°.]. *SC*.567: [n.d.]. *SC*.514: "(with
   MS. corrections by the Authoress), 8vo."

Daye, Eliza. Poems on various subjects. Liverpool,
   1798. 8°. *SC*.548. MC.49: "Eliz: Day's [*sic*]
   Poems:"

Dearden, William. The star-seer; a poem, in five
   cantos. London, Halifax, 1837. 8°. *SC*.558.

Dee, Dr. John. The private diary of Dr. John Dee,
   and the catalogue of his library of manuscripts
   ... Edited by James Orchard Halliwell. 1842.
   8°. *SC*.15.

[? De Foe, Daniel. The family instructor. In three
   parts. 1715. 8°.]. MC.84: "Family Inst: Odd
   Vol:"

————. The life and adventures of Robinson Crusoe
... [With An account of the life of Daniel Defoe
selected from the life published by George
Chalmers]. 2 vol. 1804. 8°. *SC*.360.

————. [Another edition]. *SC*.515: "2 vols. [? Vols.
16 and 17 of The British novelists]. MC.87:
"Brit: Novelist:... Rob: Crusoe." 1810. 12°.

[————]. Memoirs of the Church of Scotland, in four
periods. With an appendix. 1717. 8°. *SC*.219.
[? MC.24: "Church of Scotland:"]

*De imitando Christo. MC.26: "De Imitando Christo:"
[? Thomas à Kempis. De imitatio Christi].

*Dejected soul's cure. MC.21: "Dejected Soul's Cure:"
"John [Wordsworth]."

Delille, Jacques Montanier, *called*. See Virgilius
Maro, Publius. Georgica.

————. Oeuvres de M. l'Abbé de Lille, contenant Les
géorgiques de Virgile, en vers françois, et Les
jardins, poème. 2 pt. 1788. 17cm. [*NUC*].
SC.502: "Oeuvres de M. l'Abbe [*sic*] de Lille [n.p.,
n.d.]." MC.99: "M: L'Abbe [*sic*] de Lille:"

*De morbis infantum. [? Wedelius, Georgius Wolfgangus.
De morbis infantum. Jenae, 1717. 4°]. [*BB*].——
[? Conyers, Richard. De morbis infantum disser-
tatio. 1748. 8°].——[? Harris, Walter. De morbis
acutis infantum. 1689. 8°.]. MC.36: "De Morbis
Infant:"

Demosthenes. See Aeschines.

————. All the orations of Demosthenes pronounced
to excite the Athenians against Philip, King of
Macedon ... Translated into English (with notes)
by Thomas Leland. Third edition, corrected. 3
vol. 1777. 8°. *SC*.107: "2 vols, 8vo ... 1777."

Denholm, James. See The history of Glasgow.

Dennis, John. See Burnet, Thomas.

De Quincey, Thomas. See Häring, Wilhelm.

*Derivations from the Welsh. [National Library of
    Wales: "London: E. Lumley, 1841. 35 p. 14cm.
    Signed 'Alethe, 1840.' Introduction is signed
    'Chelidon'"]. *SC*.412: "16mo, 1841, (*Present.
    Autog*.).'' Cf. More derivations from the Welsh.

Descartes, René. Geometria a Renato Des Cartes anno
    1637 gallice edita, postea autem una cum notis
    Florimondi de Beaune ... Editio tertia. 2 vol.
    Amstelodami, 1683. 4°. [*BN*]. *SC*.108.

————. Renati Des Cartes Principia philosophiae.
    Ultima editio cum optima collata, diligenter
    recognita & mendis expurgata. Amstelodami, 1677.
    21cm. [*NUC*]. *SC*.108.

*Description of plants. MC.76: "Descrip: of Plants."

*Descriptio poetarum. MC.2: "Descript: Poet: 2 Cop:"

Desprez, Louis. See Horatius Flaccus, Quintus. Opera.

De Vere, Sir Aubrey. See Hunt, afterwards De Vere,
    Sir Aubrey.

De Vere, Aubrey Thomas. The search after Prosperine,
    Recollections of Greece, and other poems. Oxford,
    1843 [? 1842]. 18cm. [*NUC*]. LB.29.

————. The Waldenses; or, the fall of Rora; a lyri-
    cal tale. With other poems. Oxford, 1842. 8°.
    LB.29.

Dewey, Orville. Discourses on various subjects. 2nd
    ed. New York, 1835. 21cm. [*NUC*]. *SC*.310.

*Dialogues in French and German. 1813. *SC*.358.

Dick, Andrew Coventry. Dissertation on church polity.
Edinburgh, London, 1835. 12°. *SC*.307: "by A.C.
Duck [*sic*]."

Dictionnaire de l'Académie Françoise ... corrigé et
augmenté par l'Académie elle-même. 5e éd. 2 tom.
Paris, 1814. 26.5cm. [*NUC*]. *SC*.363.

Dictionnaire françois, & portugais plus complet que
tous ceux qui ont paru jusqu'à present pour l'instruction de la jeunesse portugaise. Lisbonne,
1769. [n.s.]. [*NUC*]. *SC*.365: "imp. 8vo, *Lisbon*,
1769." MC.16/0: "French & Portug: Dicty."

Digby, Sir Kenelm. See also Browne, Sir Thomas.
Religio medici.

————. Two treatises, in the one of which, the nature
of bodies; in the other, the nature of mans soule;
is looked into: in way of discovery of the immortality of reasonable soules. 1665. 8°. *SC*.221:
"4to." MC.32/0: "On the Nature of Bodies:"

[Digby, Kenelm Henry]. The broad stone of honour: or,
rules for the gentlemen of England. (With alterations from the first edition [of 1822]). 1823.
12°. [WR: "1823, a presentation copy from the
author, with autograph of W. Wordsworth, an inscription in the handwriting of the author, and
the autograph of Dora Wordsworth"]. [DD: "William
Wordsworth Junr From his uncle Chr: Wordsworth
1823"]. LB.6: "Broad Stone."

[————]. The broad stone of honour: or, the true
sense and practice of chivalry. Bk. 1. Gode-
fridus. 1829. 12°. Bk. 2. Tancredus. 1828.
12°. [DD: "2 vols. London, 1829, 1828. W.W.
Jr."]. LB.10: "Tancredus." LB.28: "A Vol of
Broad Stone."

[————]. Catholic manners. Mores Catholici: or,
ages of faith. 11 bk. 1831-42. 8°. LB.32:
"2 vols Mores Catholici. 1827-1831." [No edition
beginning in 1827 has been found].

Diogenes Laërtius (or Laërtius Diogenes). Diogenis
  Laertii de vitis, dogmatis & apophthegmatis
  clarorum philosophorum, libri X. Hesychii ill.
  de iisdem philos. & de aliis scriptoribus, liber.
  Pythagoreorvm philosoph. fragmenta. Is. Casavboni
  notae ad lib. Diogenis multò auctiores & emen-
  datiores. Evnapii Sardiniani de vitis philosophorum & sophistarum liber, cui accesserunt eiusdem auctoris legationes. Omnia Graecè & Lat. ex
  editione postrema. Coloniae Allobrogum, 1616.
  [Ox:Ann]. *SC*.111.

Dion Cassius. Histoire de Dion-Cassius de Nice, abré-
  gée par Xiphilin, traduite de grec en français par
  M. de B.G. [i.e. Pierre Le Pesant de Boisguilbert].
  2 vol. Paris, 1674. 12°. [*BN*]. [*BU*]. *SC*.533:
  "tom. 1 ... 1692." [No edition of 1692 has come
  to light]. MC.100: "Histoire de Dion Cassius:"

A directory for the publique worship of God throughout
  the three kingdoms of England, Scotland, and Ireland. Together with an ordinance of Parliament
  for the taking away of the Book of Common-Prayer;
  and for establishing and observing of this present
  directory throughout the kingdom of England, and
  dominion of Wales. 1644 [1645]. 20.5cm. [*NUC*].
  MC.27: "Directory for Pub: Worship:"

*Discourses of all the religious orders which have
  been in the world unto this day. *SC*.222: "Imperfect, wanting great portion of the Discourse
  of France (*no title*), pp. 1234, folio."

D'Israeli, Isaac. Curiosities of literature. 10th
  ed., complete in 1 vol. 1838. 26cm. [*NUC*].
  [DD: "W.W. Jr."]. LB.25.

A divine of the University of Cambridge. See Smith,
  George.

Dix, afterwards Ross, John. The life of Thomas Chatterton, including his unpublished poems and correspondence. 1837. 8°. [DD: "William Wordsworth"]. LB.29.

Doane, George Washington. See Winslow, Benjamin
     Davis.

Dobrizhoffer (or Dobritzhofer), Martin. An account
     of the Abipones, an equestrian people of Paraguay.
     [Translated by Sara Coleridge]. From the Latin
     of Martin Dobrizhoffer, eighteen years a missionary
     in that country. 3 vol. 1822. 21.5cm. [ICN.
     RBC:Ann]. *SC*.112. LB.8.

Dobson, William. See Schleiermacher, Friedrich Ernst
     Daniel.

Dodington, John. See Vialart, Charles.

Dodwell, Henry, the Elder. A discourse concerning the
     one altar and the one priesthood insisted on by
     the ancients in their disputes against schism.
     Wherein the ground and solidity of that way of
     reasoning is explained, as also its applicableness
     to the case of our modern schismaticks, with par-
     ticular regard to some late treatises of M^r R.
     Baxter. 1683. 8°. *SC*.223. MC.23: "Discourse
     on the One Altar:"

Donatus, Aelius. See Terentius, Publius, Afer.

Donne, John. LXXX sermons preached by that learned
     and reverend divine, Iohn Donne, D^r in Divinity,
     late Deane of the cathedrall church of S. Paul's
     London. 1640. 35cm. [MH:Ann]. *SC*.224: "*Autog.*
     --'William Wordsworth, bought at Ashby de la
     Zouch, 1809')." MC.21: "Donne's Sermons:"

*————. Sermons by Donne, Hoadley, Atterbury, and
     others. *SC*.223: "1709."

Donovan, Edward. The natural history of British in-
     sects. 2 vol. in 1. 1792. 8°. [*MR*]. [Jonathan
     Wordsworth: Ann]. [? MC.75: "History of Insects:"]
     [? LB.9: "Insect Book"]. HL.MK.223: "Donovan's
     Brit. Insects."

Dorotheus, Saint, Bishop of Tyre, *pseud*. See Eusebius, Pamphili.

Douglas, Jonathan. Poems. Maryport, 1836. 8°. *SC*.516: "Douglas's (John) [*sic*]."

Douglas, Thomas, 5th Earl of Selkirk. Observations on the present state of the Highlands of Scotland, with a view of the causes and probable consequences of emigration. 2nd ed. Edinburgh, 1806. 8°. *SC*.1: "1816." MC.81: "Lord Selkirk's Observa:"

Downes, George. Letters from Continental countries. 2 vol. Dublin, 1832. 12°. *SC*.113: "8vo."

Downes, Joseph. The proud shepherd's tragedy; a scenic poem; edited by Joseph Downes. To which are added, Fragments of a correspondence, and Poems. Edinburgh, 1823. 8°. *SC*.517.

Doyle, Sir Francis Hastings Charles. Miscellaneous verses. 1840. 8°. *SC*.518: "12mo."

[D'Oyly, Thomas]. Poems, by Viator [*pseud*.]. 1843. 8°. *SC*.512. *SC*.617.

Drake, Sir Thomas Trayton. See Campbell, John.

*Drama. [? *SC*.664: "three others"]. [? *SC*.676: "three others"].

Drexelius, Hieremias. Aurifodina artium et scientiarum omnia excerpendi solertia. Omnibus litterarum amantibus monstrata. Ab Hieremia Drexelio. Antverpiae, 1641. 11.5cm. [TxU.Wn:Ann]. *SC*.141: "Annifodinae [*sic*], etc., 1641." MC.8: "Aurifodina."

————. Orbis Phaethon. Coloniae, 1634. 16°. *SC*.329. MC.13/0: "Drexelii Phaethon:"

Driver, Henry Austin. Harold de Burun, a semi-dramatic poem, in six scenes. 1835. 8°. *SC*.600.

Drummond, William. The most elegant and elabourate
    poems of that great court-wit, Mr. William Drummond.
    1659. 8°. *SC*.519: "(with curious MS. note by Mr.
    Wordsworth while at St. John's Coll., Cambridge)."
    MC.50: "Drummond's Poems:"   [? LB.19: "Drummonds
    Poems"].

Dryden, John. See Anderson, Robert, M.D. The works
    of the British poets, Vol. 6; Bell, John. The
    poets of Great Britain, Vols. 40-42; Juvenalis,
    Decimus Junius.

*————. *SC*.601: "Odd Volumes--Dryden, Pope, Virgil.
    etc. 12."

————. Poems on various occasions: and translations
    from several authors. By Mr. John Dryden. Now
    published in one volume. 1701. fol. *SC*.520:
    "('*From the Rev. Charles Townsend to William
    Wordsworth, in remembrance of a long and pleasant
    walk this day.--May 23rd, 1836.*')."

Du Bec-Crespin, Jean. See Life of Tamerlane.

*[? The Dublin magazine or general repository of
    philosophy, belles-lettres &c. 2 vol. Dublin
    [Jan.--Dec.] 1820]--[? The Dublin monthly maga-
    zine. Dublin, 1830. 8°.]. LB.18: "Dublin
    Mag." [Lent 3 Feb. 1834].

Du Bois, Edward. See Horatius Flaccus, Quintus. A
    poetical translation of the works of.

Dubois, Jean Antoine. Description of the character,
    manners, and customs of the people of India; and
    of their institutions, religious and civil.
    Translated from the French manuscript. 1817.
    11.25 in. [*CWC*:Ann]. *SC*.115.

Ducarel, Andrew Colté. See Newcome, William.

Du Chesne, André. Les antiquitéz et recherches des
    villes, chasteaux et places remarquables de toute

la France. Sixiesme édition. Paris, 1631. 8°.
SC.88. MC.98: "Les Antiquitez:"

Dufresnoy, Charles Alphonse. The art of painting ...
translated into English verse by William Mason ...
With annotations by Sir Joshua Reynolds. Lat. &
Eng. York, 1783. 4°. *SC*.521: "8vo."

Dugardus, Gulielmus (Dugard, William). See Lucian.

Dugdale, Sir William. The antient usage in bearing
of such ensigns of honour as are commonly call'd
arms. With a catalogue of the present nobility
of England. Second edition, corrected. Oxford,
1682. 15.5cm. [MH:Ann]. *SC*.367: "12mo." MC.40:
"Dugdale on Arms:"

Dunderdale, Robert. Redemption, and other poems.
Kirkby Lonsdale, 1834. 12°. *SC*.580: "Poems ...
1829."

Dunlop, John. See Irvine, William, M.D., the Elder.

Duperrier Dumouriez, General Charles François. An account of Portugal, as it appeared in 1766 ...
Printed at Lausanne in 1775. 1797. 12°. [*L*: "A
translation of the French work entitled 'État
présent du royaume de Portugal, *etc.*'"]. *SC*.94.
MC.69/0: "Acc. of Portugal:"

Dupleix, Scipion. La curiosité naturelle; redigée en
questions selon l'ordre alphabétique. Paris,
1606. 12°. *SC*.88: "La Curiosité Naturelle, etc."

Duppa, Richard. A brief account of the subversion
of the Papal Government, 1798. 3rd ed. 1807.
8°. *SC*.57. MC.62: "Subversion of Papal Gov:"

————. The life and literary works of Michel Angelo
Buonarotti. 1806. 4°. [? MC.65: "Life of
Michael Angelo:"]

Dupré, J.G. See Corneille, Pierre.

Durfee, Job. What cheer? or Roger Williams in banish-
    ment; a poem ... With a recommendatory preface,
    by the Revd Eustace Giles. Leeds, 1840. 12°.
    SC.460.

*Durham Cathedral. [? Englefield, Sir Henry Charles.
    Some account of the cathedral church of Durham,
    illustrative of the plans, elevations and sections
    of that building. 1801. fol. [*EU*]--[? [Hunter,
    Christopher]. Durham Cathedral as it was before
    the dissolution of the Monastry [*sic*]; containing
    an account of the rites, customs and ceremonies
    used therein ... together with the histories
    painted in the windows, (from a manuscript written
    by Prior Wassington); and an appendix of various
    antiquities. Durham, 1733. 12°.]. MC.60: "Dur-
    ham Cathedral:" [Classified as "History"].

Dwight, Timothy. The conquest of Canaan; a poem in
    eleven books. 1788. 12°. *SC*.559. MC.50: "Con-
    quest of Canaan:"

Dyce, Alexander. See Bentley, Richard; Collins,
    William; Greene, Robert; Middleton, Thomas; Peele,
    George; Webster, John.

————. Kemps nine daies wonder: performed in a
    daunce from London to Norwich. With an introduc-
    tion and notes by the Rev. Alexander Dyce. 1840.
    8°. *SC*.15.

————. Specimens of British poetesses; selected
    and chronologically arranged by Alexander Dyce.
    1825. 8°. *SC*.522.

————. Specimens of English sonnets, selected by
    Alexander Dyce. 1833. 8°. [DD: "William
    Wordsworth"]. LB.36: "Specimens of English Son-
    nets by Dyce."

Dyer, George. Academic unity: being the substance
    of a general dissertation contained in The privi-
    leges of the University of Cambridge, as translated

from the original Latin: with various additions
... With a preface giving some account of the
Dissenting colleges in the United Kingdom, and of
the London University. 1827. 23cm. [MA:Ann].
SC.207: "8vo."

―――. A dissertation on the theory and practice
of benevolence. 1795. 8°. *SC*.427. MC.30: "Theo:
& Pract: of Benevol:"

―――. History of the university and colleges of
Cambridge. 2 vol. 1814. 8°. *SC*.226: "2 vols.,
8vo ... 1811 [*sic*]." MC.60: "Dyer's Hist: of
Camb: 2 Vol:"

―――. Memoirs of the life and writings of Robert
Robinson. 1796. 8°. *SC*.303: "*Presentation
Autograph of the Author*." LB.58: "Memoirs of
Rob. Robinson by G. Dyer."

―――. Poems. 2 vol. 1802. 16°. *SC*.495: "(*Autog.
of Author, etc.*)." MC.45: "Dyer's Poems: 2 Vol:"

―――. The poet's fate; a poetical dialogue. 1797.
8°. *SC*.559: "The Poet's Taste [*sic*]." MC.45:
"Poet's Fate:"

―――. The privileges of the University of Cambridge,
together with additional observations on its history, antiquities, literature and biography. 2
vol. 1824. 8°. *SC*.225.

E., L.S. See Gathercole, Michael Augustus.

Eachard, Laurence. See Echard, Laurence.

Eastlake, Sir Charles L. See Kugler, Franz Theodor.

Ebert, Johann Arnold. J.A. Ebert's Episteln und
vermischte gedichte (Zweiter theil, nach des ver-
fassers tode mit einem grundrisse seines lebens

un charakters herausgegeben von J.J. Eschenburg).
2 Th. Hamburg, 1789-95. 8°. [WL:Ann]. MC.95:
"Ebert's Episteln:"

*Ecclesiae Anglicanae. [? Crakanthorp, Richard. De-
fensio Ecclesiae Anglicanae. 1625. 4°]--[? Gauden, John. Ecclesiae Anglicanae suspiria. 1659.
fol.]. MC.22: "Ecclesiae Anglicanae:"

Echard, Laurence. The gazetteer's: or, newsman's
interpreter: being a geographical index of all
the considerable cities, patriarchships, bishop-
ricks, universities, dukedoms, earldoms, and
such like in Europe. The 2d edition, corrected,
much enlarg'd, and improved. 1693. 15cm. [NUC].
SC.170: "1693 ... with the late Laureate's Autograph." MC.72: "Newsman's Interpreter:"

————. The history of England, from the first en-
trance of Julius Ceasar and the Romans (to the
conclusion of the reign of King James the Second,
and establishment of King William and Queen Mary).
Third edition, with additions. 2 vol. 1720.
fol. SC.27. MC.58: "Echard's Hist: of England:"

————. The Roman history, from the building of the
city, to the perfect settlement of the empire by
Augustus Caesar. The 5th ed., carefully revis'd;
and much improv'd. 4 vol. 1702-6. 19.5cm.
[NUC]. SC.26: "4 vols., 8vo ... 1702." MC.63:
"Echard's Rom: Hist: 4 Vol:" LB.7: "Roman History Vol 4th."

Edda, Poetic. Icelandic poetry; or, the Edda of
Saemund translated into English verse, by Amos
Simon Cottle. Bristol, 1797. 8°. SC.621.
MC.46/0: "Cottle's Iceland: Poet:"

[Eden, William, 1st Baron Auckland]. Principles of
penal law. 3rd ed. 1775. 24cm. [NUC]. SC.1.
MC.40: "Princip: of Penal Law."

Edmeston, James. Sonnets, chiefly sacred. Brighton,
    [n.d.]. 16cm. [*NUC*]. [Allibone: "Sonnets,
    1845"]. *SC*.523.

Edwards, John, D.D. A compleat history or survey of
    all the dispensations and methods of religion,
    from the beginning of the world to the consummation
    of all things. As represented in the Old and New
    Testament. In which the opinion of Dr. Spencer
    concerning the Jewish rites and sacrifices is
    examined and the certainty of the Christian reli-
    gion demonstrated against the cavils of the deists,
    &c. 2 vol. 1699. [n.s.] [*NUC*]. *SC*.213: "8vo,
    1699." MC.26: "Edwards on Religion:"

————. Exercitations ... on several important places
    in the writings of the Old and New Testament.
    1702. 8°. MC.27: "Edwards Exercitations:"

Edwards, John, Poet. The tour of the Dove, a poem;
    with occasional pieces. London, Derby, 1821.
    18.1cm. [Paul F. Betz:Ann]. *SC*.524.

Edwards, Samuel. The Copernican system: a poem.
    Cambridge, 1728. 4°. *SC*.129.

Edwards, Thomas. See Theocritus.

Egerton, Francis, Earl of Ellesmere. [? The pilgri-
    mage, and other poems. 1856. 24cm.] [*NUC*]--
    [? Translations from the German [of Schiller], and
    original poems. By Lord Francis Leveson-Gower
    [his earlier title]. 1824. 22.5cm.]. [*NUC*].
    SC.617: "Do. [Poems], by the Earl of Ellesmere."

Egerton, Sir Philip de Malpas Grey, ed. A commentary
    on the services and charges of William Lord Grey
    de Wilton. 1847. 4°. *SC*.15.

The eglantine; or, annual memorialist for 1839 (40).
    London, Nottingham, [1838,39]. 24°. *SC*.471.

Ellerton, John. See Lodge, afterwards Ellerton, John.

Ellesmere, Earl of. See Egerton, Francis.

Elliott, Ebenezer. Love, a poem, in three parts. To
    which is added, The giaour, a satirical poem.
    1823. 8°. SC.498: "Love, a Poem, and the Giaour,
    by E. Elliott, 1823."

————. The splendid village: Corn law rhymes; and
    other poems. 1833. 17cm. [NUC]. SC.526: "Corn
    Law Rhymes and other Poems, 12mo, 1833."

Elliott, Henry Venn. Psalms and hymns, for public,
    private, and social worship. 1835. 12°. SC.313.
    LB. 44.

Elliott, Mrs. Henry Venn. See Marshall, Julia Ann.

Ellis, Sir Henry. See Charles, Nicholas; Norden,
    John; Smyth, Richard; Vergil, Polydore.

————. Original letters of eminent literary men of
    the sixteenth, seventeenth, and eighteenth cen-
    turies; with notes, and illustrations by Sir Henry
    Ellis. 1843. 8°. SC.15.

————, ed. The pylgrymage of Sir Richard Guylforde
    to the Holy Land, A.D. 1506, from a copy believed
    to be unique, from the press of Richard Pynson.
    1851. 8°. SC.15.

Ellistone, John. See Böhme, Jakob.

*Eloisa and Abelard. MC.92: "Eloisa & Abelard:"
    [Classified under "Translations"; possibly an
    unidentified translation of Histoire d'Eloise et
    d'Abelard, La Haye, 1696. 12°.].

Elton, Romeo. See Callender, John.

Emerson, Ralph Waldo. Essays. 1841. 12°. SC.354.
    LB.40.

Emerson, William. See Fluxions.

Emmerich, Andrew. The culture of forests; with an appendix in which the state of the royal forests is considered, and a system proposed for their improvement. 1789. 8°. MC.75: "Culture of Forests:"

Encyclopaedia Britannica. 3rd ed. 18 vol. Edinburgh, 1797. 4°; 4th ed. 20 vol. Edinburgh, 1810. 4°. *SC*.369: "20 vols., 4to ... 1797."

The encyclopaedia of wit. [? 1801]. 12°. MC.84: "Encyclopoedia [*sic*] of Wit:"

England's black tribunall; set forth in the triall of K. Charles I. at the pretended Court of Justice ... Together with his majesties speech immediately before he was murdred [*sic*] on a scaffold ... Jan. 30, 1648. Also the severall dying speeches of the nobility and gentry ... put to death for their loyalty to their sovereign lord the king, from 1642 to 1658. 1660. 8°. *SC*.37. MC.60: "England's Black Tribun:"

Englefield, Sir Henry Charles. See Durham Cathedral.

An English vicar. See King, John Meyers.

Enoch, Frederick. Poems. London, Leamington, 1849. 12°. *SC*.567.

Ephemera, French. See Pamphlets, French.

Epictetus. Manuale, Cebetis Thebani tabula, Prodici Hercules et Theophrasti characteres ethici, graece et latine notis illustrati a Josepho Simpson. Oxford, 1739. 8°. *SC*.409. MC.2: "Epictetus: 2 Cop:"

Epigrammatum delectus ex omnibus tum veteribus tum recentioribus poetis ... decerptus ... [by Claude Lancelot]. Cum dissertatione [by Pierre Nicole] de vera pulchritudine ... Adjectae sunt elegantes sententiae ex antiquis poetis ... selectae. Parisiis, 1659. 8°. *SC*.668: "Epigrammatum Delectus, 8vo."

Erasmus, Desiderius. See Terentius Afer, Publius.

——————. All the familiar colloquies of D. Erasmus ...
rendered into English. By Nathan Bailey. 1725.
8°. *SC*.201. MC.93: "Familiar Colloquies of
Erasmus."

——————. Twenty-two select colloquies out of Erasmus
Roterdamus. By Sir Roger L'Estrange. To which
are added, seven more dialogues, with the life
of the author. By Mr. Tho. Brown. 1711. 19cm.
[NN.BC:Ann]. *SC*.201. MC.23: "L'Estrange's
Colloqu:"

——————. [? D. Erasmi Dialogus Ciceronianus, sive de
optimo genere dicendi. Lugundi Batavorum, 1643.
12°.]. MC.9: "Erasmi Ciceronianus:"

——————. Moriae encomium. Oxoniae, 1668. 12°.
SC.329. MC.9: "Erasmi Encomium:"

Ernesti, Johann August. See Cicero, Marcus Tullius.
Opera; Hederich, Benjamin; Tacitus, Publius Cornelius.

Erpenius, Thomas. Elementa linguae arabicae ex
Erpenii rudimentis ut plurimum desumpta; cujus
praxi grammaticae novam legendi praxin addidit L.
Chappelow. 1730. 8°. *SC*.372: "Chappelhow [*sic*],
Elementa Arabicae, 1730."

——————. Rudimenta linguae Arabicae. Lutetiae
Parisiorum, 1638. 8°. [*BN*]. *SC*.372: "Erpenii
Rudimenta Linguae Arabicae, 8vo, 1638 (*Auto-
graphs S.T.C. and W.W.*)." MC.17: "Erpenii Rudim:
Ling: Arab:"

Erskine, Thomas. Remarks on the internal evidence of
the truth of revealed religion. Third edition,
corrected and enlarged. Edinburgh, 1821. 12°.
SC.307.

Eschenburg, Johann Joachim. See Ebert, Johann Arnold.

Esménard, Joseph Alphonse. See Williams, Helen Maria.
    Recueil de poésies.

Estienne, Charles. See Stephanus, Carolus.

Estienne, Henri. See Stephanus, Henricus.

*Ethics. [? *SC*.286: "eleven other books [? of ethics]."

*L'étude. [? Gibbon, Edward. Essai sur l'étude de
    la littérature. 1761. 8°.]. MC.101: "L'Etude:"
    [Classified under "Modern Languages"].

Euagrius (Scholasticus). See Eusebius, Pamphili.

*Euclid. MC.35: "Euclid: 2 Cop:"

Eugene Francis, Prince of Savoy. The life ... of
    Prince Eugene. Second edition; with continuation
    of his actions, etc. 1707. 8°. [? *SC*.152: "Life
    and Actions of Prince Eugene of Savoy, to the time
    of his being made Governor of the Milanese, 8vo,
    1707"]. MC.65: "Life of Pr: Eugene:"

Eunapius Sardinianus. See Diogenes Laërtius.

Eusebius, Pamphili. The auncient ecclesiastical his-
    tories ... by Eusebius, Socrates, and Euagrius
    ... Whereunto is annexed Dorotheus, Bishop of
    Tyrus, of the lives and ends of the Prophets,
    Apostles, and 70 Disciples ... Translated ... by
    Meredith Hanmer. 1619. 28cm. [MA:Ann]. *SC*.243.
    MC.57: "Ancient Eccles: History [*sic*]:"

———. Historiae ecclesiasticae, scriptores Graeci
    ... Gr. and Lat. Ex interpretatione H. Valesii
    [Henri de Valois]. 3 vol. [Vol. I is Eusebius].
    Amstelodami, 1695. fol. [? *SC*.228: "Eusebius:
    Historicae Ecclesiasticae, Gr. et Lat. (*no title*),
    folio"]. [? LB.7: "Eusebius"].

Eutropius, Flavius. Eutropii breviarum historiae
    Romanae, ab urbe condita ad annum ejusdem urbis

DCCC.L. Accedit Sex. Aurelii Victoris de Romanis illustribus liber. Ad usum juventutis accommodata. Etonae, 1780. 17.5cm. [PSC.WWC.JB:Ann]. MC.2: "Eutropius 2 cop:"

Evans, John. See Owen, Charles.

Evans, Robert Wilson. The rectory of Valehead. 2nd ed. 1831. 16°. *SC*.304.

*Exemplis ac similitudinibus rerum Step. Borgia, Bernadine, Gregory, etc, 4to, black letter, no date. *SC*.373.

Faber, Basilius (Soranus). Basilii Fabri Sorani Thesavrus ervditionis scholasticae omnivm vsvi et disciplinis omnibvs accomodatvs [*sic*]. 2 vol. Francofurti et Lipsiae, 1749. 37.5cm. [*NUC*]. [WL:Ann]. MC.13 [where "scholasticae" appears as "Ecclesiast" although the work is listed among "Books illust: of the Classics"]. [For "Soranus" (i.e. Sorau in Brandenburg) see *BU, Suppl.*, 1837, Vol. 73, under "Faber, Basilius"]. See the STC entry.

*Faber, Frederick William. Colloquies on religion and religious education. *SC*.229: "8vo, cloth, 1837." [*DNB*: "On 6 Aug. 1837 he was ordained deacon ... Some tracts which he published at this period obtained an extensive circulation"].

————. Sights and thoughts in foreign churches and among foreign peoples. 1842. 8°. *SC*.229. LB.29.

————. Sir Lancelot. 1844. 8°. LB.54.

————. The Styrian lake, and other poems. 1842. 8°. [? LB.51: "Fabers Poems"].

————. Tracts on the church and her offices. 1840. 12°. [*NUC*]. *SC*.198.

Faber, George Stanley. [? A dissertation upon the prophecies that have been fulfilled, are now fulfilling, relative to the great period of 1260 years. 2nd ed. 2 vol. 1807. 8°.]--[? A general and connected view of the prophecies relative to the conversion ... and future glory of the Houses of Judah and Israel. 2 vol. 1808. 8°.]. LB.21: "Fabers Prophecies."

————. The origin of pagan idolatry ascertained from historical testimony and circumstantial evidence. 3 vol. 1816. 4°. *SC*.230.

Fabricius, Franciscus. See Cicero, Marcus Tullius. Opera.

Fahrenkrueger, Johann Anton. See Bailey, Nathan.

Fairfax, Edward. See Tasso, Torquato.

Falconer, Forbes. See Sa'dī.

Fanno, Lucio. See Blondus, Flavius.

[Fanshawe, Althea]. Thoughts on affectation; addressed chiefly to young people. 1805. 8°. MC.81: "On Affectation:"

Farish, Charles. The minstrels of Windermere; a poem. [1811]. 12°. *SC*.527: "1811." MC.48: "Farish's Minst: of Winder:"

Farrer, Henrietta Louisa. Tales of Kirkbeck; or the parish in the fells. 1848. 8°. [CSmH.ZZB:Ann]. LB.42.

Featley, Daniel. Katabaptistai kataptustoi [in Greek]. The dippers dipt; or, the Anabaptists duck'd and plung'd over head and ears, at a disputation in Southwark. 1647. 7.25 in. [*CWC*:Ann]. *SC*.231: "... *in Southwark*, 17th Oct. 1642, 4to, 1645." [*L*: "1645. 4°."].

Fénelon. See Salignac de la Mothe Fénelon, François de.

Fenton, Sir Geoffrey. See Bandello, Matteo.

Ferguson, Robert. The pipe of repose; or recollections of Eastern travel. 1849. 12°. LB.43: "Pipe of Repose."

————. The shadow of the pyramid: a series of sonnets. 1847. 18cm. [MA:Ann]. LB.39: "Shadow of the Pyramids."

————. Swiss men and Swiss mountains. [? 1851]. 8°. [Vol. 1 of The traveler's library, 25 vol. 1851-1856]. LB.57.

Fergusson, Robert. The poetical works of Robert Fergusson with the life of the author by David Irving. Glasgow, 1800. 12°. *SC*.529. MC.48: "Ferguson's [*sic*] Poems:"

Ferriar, John. An essay towards a theory of apparitions. London, Warrington, 1813. 8°. MC.32: "Ferriar on Apparit:"

[Field, Barron]. First fruits of Australian poetry. Sydney [? 1819. 4°; ? 2nd ed. 1823. 8°]. *SC*.622: "4to." [? LB.32: "Flowers of Australian poetry"].

Fielding, Henry. The works of Henry Fielding. MC.79: "Fielding's Works: 9 odd Vol:" [? DDSC.458: "Complete Works of Henry Fielding, edited by [Arthur] Murphy 1806 10 vols., full calf"].

————. The history of Tom Jones, a foundling. [? MC.79: "Fielding's Works: 9 odd Vol:"]. LB.23: "Tom Jones."

————. Joseph Andrews. *SC*.515. "Joseph Andrews, by Henry Fielding ... 12mo ... 1810." MC.87: "Brit: Novelist: 12 Vol ... Jos: Andrews. [Vol. 18, The British novelists, 1810, 12°.]." LB.23: "Joseph Andrews."

Filicaja, Vincenzo da. Opere. *SC*.530: "Opere di Vin-
cenzio [sic] da Filicaja, *in Prato*, 1793, 8vo,
sewed." [Brunet mentions an edition of Filicaja's
Poesie Toscane: "L'édition commune de *Prato*, 1793,
2 vol in-8, renferme quelques pièces de plus que
les précédentes."].

————. Poesie Toscane, edizione formata sopra quella
di Martini del 1707. Firenze, 1823. 8°. [Brunet].
SC.531.

[Finch, Anne, Countess of Winchelsea]. Miscellany
poems on several occasions, written by a lady
[i.e. Anne Finch]. 1713. 8°. MC.48: "Lady
Winchelsea's Poems:"

Fiorentino. See Francioscini, Lorenzo.

Fischerus, Johann Friedrich. See Weller, Jacob.

Fisher, Richard Trott. Three poems. I. Eleusinia;
or, the soul's progress; II. Nimrod, the first
tyrant; III. Sibylla Anglica. 2 vol. 1842.
21cm. [InU.WC:Ann]. *SC*.532: "(*with MS. Dedicatory Sonnet by the Author*)."

Fiston (or Phiston), William. See Le Fèvre, Raoul.

Fitzgerald, Edward. See Barton, Lucy.

Fletcher, Andrew, of Saltoun. The political works
of Andrew Fletcher. Glasgow, 1749. 12°. *SC*.46:
"8vo." MC.41: "Fletcher's Pol: Works:"

Fletcher, John. See Beaumont, Francis.

Fletcher, Miss S. Gabrielle and Augustina; or, virtue its own reward. A moral tale, translated
from the French by Miss S. Fletcher. Coventry,
1811. 12°. MC.88: "Gabrielle & Augustina:"

Florio, Giovanni (or John). See Montaigne, Michel de.

————. Vocabolario Italiano e Inglese, a dictionary,
Italian and English; formerly compiled by John
Florio ... now ... revised ... by G[iovanni]
Torriano. 1688. 36.5cm. [MH:Ann]. *SC*.444.

Florus, Lucius Annaeus. Rerum Romanorum libri quatuor,
annotationibus in usum studiosae juventutis, instar
commenta illustrati. Auctore Johanne Minellios
[*sic*]. 1706. nar. 16°. [*NUC*]. *SC*.410: "J. Min-
ellio, 1706." [? MC.7/·✕·: "L. Annaeus Florus"].
[? MC.3/·✕·: "Florus: 3 Cop:"

*Flowers of Australian Poetry. LB.32. See Field,
Barron.

*Fluxions. MC.35/0: "Fluxions." [? Emerson, William.
The doctrine of fluxions, not only explaining the
elements thereof, but also its application and use
in the several parts of mathematics and natural
philosophy. 1743. 21cm.]. [*NUC*]--[? Simpson,
Thomas. A new treatise of fluxions. 1737. 4°.].
[Lowndes].

Ford, John. See Massinger, Philip.

Ford, William, Curate of Wythburn, Keswick. A description of the scenery in the Lake District, intended
as a guide to strangers. Carlisle, 1839. 12°.
SC.181 [n.p., n.d.].

Forde, B. See Montagu, Basil.

Fordyce, James. Sermons to young women. 7th ed. 2
vol. 1771. 16°. *SC*.232: "2 vols., 12mo, 1775."
[Probably the 8th or 9th ed. as the 10th, according to *BN*, appeared in 1786 in 8°].

Forget me not: A Christmas and new year's present for
1825 (-47). [Ed. by Frederick Shoberl]. [1825-
47]. 12° and 8°. [*BUCP*]. LB.30. [Lent late in
1843].

Forli, Biondo da. See Blondus, Flavius.

The form and manner of making, ordaining, and conse-
crating of bishops, priests, and deacons, according
to the order of the Church of England. B[lack]
L[etter]. 1717. 4°. *SC*.253: "black letter, 4to
... 1748." LB.54.

Forster, Nathaniel. See Plato.

[Forster, Thomas]. The lay-man's lawyer; or, The
second part of the practice of the law: relating
to the punishments of offences ... with presidents
[*sic*] of indictments and warrants ... Also a discourse concerning pardons. 1654. 8°. [*NUC*].
MC.40: "Layman's Lawyer:"

Forsyth, Joseph. Remarks on antiquities, arts, and
letters during an excursion in Italy, in the years
1802 and 1803. 2nd ed. 1816. 8.875 in. [*CWC*:
Ann]. *SC*.535: "(*with Autograph Presentation by
Samuel Rogers*)."

Fosbroke, Thomas Dudley. The Wye tour; or, Gilpin on
the Wye, with picturesque additions, from [Francis]
Wheatley, [R.A.], [John] Price, &c. and archaeologi-
cal illustrations. By the Rev. Thomas Dudley
Fosbroke. 3rd ed. Ross, 1826. 18.5cm. [*NUC*].
SC.184: "Wye Tour, by J [*sic*].D. Fosbroke, 1826."

Foster, James. Discourses on all the principal branches
of natural religion and social virtue. 2 vol.
1749-52. 4°. *SC*.233. MC.23: "Foster's Discourses:" MC.23: "Foster on Nat: Relig:"

————. The usefulness, truth and excellency of the
Christian revelation. 1731. 8°. MC.28: "Foster's Christ: Revelation:"

Foulis, Henry. The history of the wicked plots and
conspiracies of our pretended saints: representing
the beginning, constitution and designs of the
Jesuite, with the conspiracies ... of some of the
Presbyterians proved by a series of examples.
1662. fol. *SC*.63: "1665 (*no title*). 'W.W.'"
MC.59: "History of Wicked Plots."

Foulkes, Peter. See Aeschines.

Fouqué. See La Motte Fouqué.

Fox, afterwards Vassall, Henry Richard, 3rd Baron
    Holland. Some account of the life and writings
    of L.F. de Vega Carpio. 1806. 8°. *SC*.130. MC.
    65: "Life of Lope Felix de Vega:"

Francioscini (or Franciosini), Lorenzo (Fiorentino).
    Vocabolario italiano e spagnolo non piu dato in
    luce ... composto da Lorenzo Franciosini Fioren-
    tino. 2 vol. in 1. Geneva, 1636. 17cm. [*CWC*:
    Ann; *NUC*]. *SC*.446: "8vo." [? MC.17: "Ital: &
    Span: Vocabulary:"]

Francis, Philip. See Horatius Flaccus, Quintus.
    Works.

Franklin, Benjamin. Essays and letters. 2 vol. in 1.
    13.5cm. [*NUC*]. MC.81: "Franklin's Essays:"

Fraser, Alexander. A verbatim report of the cause
    Doe Dem. Tatham v. Wright, tried at the Lancaster
    Lammas Assizes, 1834. 2 vol. Lancaster, 1834.
    8°. *SC*.76: "*(with Presentation Autograph of
    Admiral Tatham, the Plaintiff in the suit)*."

Frederica Sophia Wilhelmina [of Prussia], Consort of
    Frederick William, Margrave of Brandenburg-Bai-
    reuth. Memoirs ... written by herself. Trans-
    lated from the original French. 2 vol. 1812.
    8°. *SC*.130.

Freire de Andrade, Jacinto. The life of Dom John de
    Castro, the fourth Vice-Roy of India. By Jacinto
    Freire de Andrade written in Portuguese, and by
    Sir Peter Wyche translated into English. 1664.
    fol. *SC*.183. MC.66: "Life of Dom John:"

French, Laurence. See Burke, Edmund.

French, William and George Skinner. A new transla-
    tion of the Book of Psalms ... with explanatory

notes by William French and George Skinner. 1830.
8°. *SC*.234.

Frend, William. Evening amusements; or, the beauty
of the heavens displayed. In which several strik-
ing appearances to be observed ... in the heavens
during the year 1804 (-22) are described. 1806,
1805-22. 12°. [A periodical]. *SC*.117: "2 vols.,
1803-1809, ('*To Hartley Coleridge from his affectionate father, S.T. Coleridge, Feb., 1809*,' in
the autograph of S.T.C.)." MC.82: "Evening Amusements:" MC.84: "Evening Amusements:"

Frere, Right Hon. John Hookham. See Aristophanes;
The Microcosm.

[Friedel, Johann]. Eleonore [Countess], kein roman,
eine wahre geschichte in Briefen. 2 Th. Berlin,
Leipzig, 1780. 8°. *SC*.467. MC.96: "Eleonore:"

Friend, John. See Aeschines.

Fusseli, Johann Heinrich. See Winckelmann, Johann
Joachim.

Fuller, afterwards Ossoli, Sarah Margaret. Papers
on literature and art. 2 pt. 1846. 8°. *SC*.551:
"2 vol."

Fuller, Thomas. Good thoughts in worse times; consisting of personall meditations, Scripture observations, meditations on the times, meditations on
all kinds of prayers, occasionall meditations.
1647. 12°. MC.26: "Fuller's Meditations:"

————. The history of the Holy Warre. 2nd ed.
Cambridge, 1640. fol. *SC*.235. MC.59: "History
of Holy War:"

————. The history of the worthies of England. 4
pt. 1662. fol. LB.15: "Worthies of England."

G., R.P.   See Gillies, Robert Pierce.

Gale, Thomas.   Historiae poeticae scriptores antiqui.
Apollodorus Atheniensis, Ptolomaeus Hephaest[ioni]s,
Conon grammaticus, Parthenius Nicaensis, Antoninus Liberalis.   Graecè & Latinè.   Accessêre breves
notae & indices necessarij.   Parisiis, 1675.   18.5
cm.   [*NUC*; *L*; Brunet].   *SC*.687.

Galfridus, Frater.   Promptorium parvulorum sive cleri-
corum, lexicon Anglo-Latinum princeps, auctore
Fratre Galfrido Grammatico dicto ... Albertus
Way.   1843.   8°.   [*NUC*].   *SC*.15: "1853."

Galfridus, Monumetensis.   The British history, translated into English from the Latin of Jeffrey of
Monmouth.   With a large preface concerning the
authority of the history.   By Aaron Thompson.
1718.   8°.   *SC*.18: "1618."   MC.58: "British History:"

*Galinares, A.   *SC*.439: "Nouvelle Grammaire Universelle Espagnole et Françoise, par M.A. Galinares,
etc., 8vo, 1767."   MC.16/0: "Gram: Espagnole &
François [*sic*]:"

Galland, Antoine.   Les mille et une nuits; contes
Arabes, traduits en François.   [Brunet: "La
traduction des Milles et une nuits par Ant. Galland a paru la première fois à Paris, de 1704-
17, en 12 vol. in-12"].   *SC*.538: "Galland (M.):
Les Mille et une Nuits, Contes Arabes, Traduit
[*sic*] en François, 12 tomes, 12 mo ... 1729."

*Gallery guides, sundry.   *SC*.635 [apparently 5 vol.].

Galloway, William Brown.   The vow of the Gileadite.
A lyric narrative.   1842.   12°.   [Cambridge Univ.
Lib:Ann].   *SC*.524: "Gideonite."

Gallus, Cornelius.   See Catullus, Caius Valerius.

The game laws: or, a collection of the laws and
statutes made for the preservation of this king-

dom. 5th ed. 1714. 15.5cm. [Ox:Ann]. MC.38:
"Game Laws:"

Garbett, James. De rei critica praelectiones Oxonii
habitae. Oxonii, 1847. 8°. [*EU*]. *SC*.393.

[————]. De rei poetica idea, praelectiones quatuor.
Oxonii, 1843. 8°. *SC*.393.

Garnett, afterwards Godwin, Catherine Grace. The
night before the bridal, a Spanish tale. Sappho;
a dramatic sketch, and other poems. 1824. 8°.
SC.600.

————. The wanderer's legacy; a collection of poems.
1829. 8°. *SC*.541.

Gassend, Pierre. The mirrour of true nobility, being
the life of ... Nicolas Claude Fabricius ...
Englished by William Rand. 1657. 8°. *SC*.286:
"The Mirrour of True Nobility and Gentility."
MC.59: "Mirror of Gentility:"

Gastrell, Francis, Bishop of Chester. The Christian
institutes; or, the sincere word of God. Being
a plain and impartial account of the whole faith
and duty of a Christian. Collected out of the
writings of the Old and New Testament: digested
under proper heads and delivered in the words
of scripture. By ... Francis, late Lord Bishop
of Chester. 7th ed. 1748. 12°. [WL:Ann].
MC.25: "Christ: Institutes:"

[Gathercole, Michael Augustus]. Letters to a dissenting minister of the Congregational Independent
denomination, containing remarks on the principles of that sect, and the author's reasons for
leaving it and conforming to the Church of
England. By [Michae]L. [Augustu]S. [Gathercol]E.
[*DAB*: "The author has given the finials of his
name."]. [1834]. 8°. *SC*.313.

Gauden, John. See Ecclesiae Anglicanae.

Gaultier, Aloïsius Édouard Camille. Lectures graduées
  pour les enfans. 3 vol. 1798. 12°; second cours,
  en six volumes. 1800. 4°. MC.101: "Lectures
  Graduees: 6 Vol:"

*Gautier, J. *SC*.105: "Le Voyageur dans le Royaume
  des Pays Bas, etc. etc., par J. Gautier--*Bruxelles*,
  1827."

[? Gavin, Antonio. A master-key to Popery: containing ... a discovery of the most secret practices
  of the secular and regular Romish priests in their
  auricular confession. 2nd ed. 3 vol. 1725-26.
  12°.]. MC.25: "Key to Popery: 2 Vol:"

[? Gay, John. Fables. 2 vol. 1727-38. 4°.]. [*NUC*].
  MC.45: "Gay's Fables:"

*Gellius, Aulus. [? Noctes Atticae]. MC.1: "Aulus
  Gellius:"

A general description of all trades. 1747. 17cm.
  [MH:Ann]. *SC*.357: "Book of Trades, 1747." MC.66:
  "Gen: descript: of all Trades."

Genlis, Countess de. See Brulart de Sillery, Stéphanie
  Félicité.

A gentleman. See Jones, David; A trip to the Jubilee.

————. Secret memoirs of the life of the honourable
  Sir Cloudsley Shovel ... with a full account of
  all the naval battels since the Revolution ...
  By a gentleman ... several years under command
  of that admiral. 1708. 12°. MC.64: "Mem: of
  Sir: Clou: Shovel:"

[? The gentleman's magazine. LB.1: "2nd Vol Gent M"].
  [Entry unclear].

Geoffrey of Monmouth. See Galfridus, Monumetensis.

German Bible. See Bible, German.

*German dictionary. *SC*.374: "4to." LB.27: "German Dicy."

*German grammars, two. *SC*.374: "8vo." [? LB.27: "3 Grammars"]. [Entry follows "German Dicy"].

*German hymns. *SC*.467: "1742." MC.96: "German Hymns:" [? A collection of hymns of the Moravian Brethren, with a translation and a second collection, 1742]. [*LLA*].

Gerrond, John. The poetical and prose works, travels, and remarks of John Gerrond. Leith, 1815. 8°. [*E*]. *SC*.516: "Gerrard's [*sic*] Works, 1815." MC.54: "Gerronds. The [crossed out] *Swindler's Poems*."

Gesnerus, Joannes Matthias (Gesner, Johann Matthias). See Horatius Flaccus, Quintus. Opera.

Gibbon, Edward. See L'étude.

————. The history of the decline and fall of the Roman Empire. 12 vol. 1788-90. 8°. [*EU*]. *SC*.29. LB.38.

Gibson, Edmund. See Quintilianus, Marcus Fabius.

Gibson, John. See The history of Glasgow.

Gifford, William. See Massinger, Philip.

Gilbert, William. The hurricane: a theosophical and western eclogue. To which is subjoined a solitary effusion in a summer's evening. Bristol, 1796. 7.25 in. [*CWC*.594]. *SC*.516. MC.49: "Gilbert's Hurricane:" LB.41.

Giles, Eustace. See Durfee, Job.

[Gillies, Robert Pierce]. Childe Alarique; a poet's reverie, with other poems. [By R.P.G., i.e. Robert Pierre [*sic*] Gillies]. Edinburgh, 1814. 8°. *SC*.517. MC.49: "Gillie's [*sic*] Childe Alaric:"

[————]. Illustrations of a poetical character; in
six tales. With other poems ... [By Robert Pearce
[*sic*] Gillies]. 2nd ed. corrected and enlarged.
Edinburgh, 1816. 8°. *SC*.500. MC.51: "Illustrat:
of Poet: Char: by Gillies:" [MA: "Proof sheets,
apparently from the 1816 2d edition (no copy
available for examination), of three gatherings,
each mailed separately addressed to Wordsworth"].

[————]. Oswald; a metrical tale. Illustrative of
a poetical character. In four cantos. [By R.P.
Gillies]. Edinburgh, 1817. 4°. *SC*.498. MC.50:
"Oswald:"

*[————]. *SC*.663: "Poems, by R.P. Gillies, Esq.,
4to, (only ten Copies Printed), 1826:"

Gillman, James. The life of S.T. Coleridge. Vol. 1.
[No more published]. 1838. 24cm. [WL.DD.n.s.].
SC.103. LB.25.

————. Another copy. [CtY.BL:Ann].

Gilpin, William. [? Lectures on the catechism of the
Church of England. 1779. 8°.]. MC.28: "Gilpin's
Lectures:" LB.39: "Lectures on the Catechism."

————. Observations on the river Wye, and several
parts of South Wales ... relative chiefly to picturesque beauty; made in the summer of ... 1770.
2nd ed. 1789. 4°. *SC*.540: "8vo." MC.70: "Gilpin on Pictur: Beauty:" See Fosbroke, Thomas
Dudley.

————. Observations relative to picturesque beauty,
made in ... 1772, on several parts of England;
particularly the mountains and lakes of Cumberland
and Westmoreland. 2 vol. 1786. 8°. 2nd ed.
1788. 8°. [Lowndes]. *SC*.539: "1787, 8vo."
MC.70: "Gilpin on Pictur: Beauty: 2 Vol:"
[? LB.8].

Giovanni, M. See Gwinne, Matthew.

Gisborne, John.   Reflections; a poem, descriptive of
events and scenery connected with the different
months of the year.   1833.   8°.   *SC*.638.

Godwin, Catherine Grace.   See Garnett, afterwards
Godwin, Catherine Grace.

Godwin, Francis.   A catalogue of the bishops of England since the first planting of the Christian
religion on this island; with a briefe history of
their lives.   1615.   4°.   *SC*.236.   MC.21: "Catalogue of Bishops:"   [? LB.29: "Catalogue"].

Godwin (or Godwyn), Thomas.   Moses and Aaron; civil
and ecclesiastical rites used by the ancient
Hebrews.   5th ed.   1634.   4°.   [Bound with Godwyn,
Thomas.   Romanae historiae anthologia, 1642, and
Rous, Francis, Archaeologiae Atticae].   *SC*.237.

————.   [Another edition].   12th ed.   With additions
by Zachary Bogan.   1685.   4°.   *SC*.238.

————.   Romanae historiae anthologia recognita et
avcta.   An English exposition of the Romane antiquities, wherein many Romane and English offices
are paralleld, and divers obscure phrases explained.   For the use of Abingdon schools.   Revised
and enlarged by the author.   Oxford, 1623.   19cm.
[MH:Ann; *L*].   *SC*.67.   MC.12: "Roman: Histor: An-
tholog:"

————.   [Another edition].   Oxford, 1642.   4°.   *SC*.
237.   See Godwin, Thomas.   Moses and Aaron.

Goethe, Johann Wolfgang von.   Faustus; the bride of
Corinth; the first Walpurgis Night.   Translated
by John Anster.   1835.   8°.   [DD:Ann].   LB.20:
"Anster's Faust."

————.   [? LB.27: "Hermann & Dory"].   [MS. unclear.
Borrowed along with "German Dicy" and "3 Grammars"
sometime between 4 Oct. 1840 and 16 Apr. 1841 by
Frederick William Faber.   The most recent trans-

lation, entitled *Hermann and Dorothea*, was by
William Whewell in 1839].

Golding, Arthur. See Mornay, Philippe de; Ovidius
Naso, Publius. Metamorphosis.

Goldsmith, Oliver. The beauties of English poetry,
selected. 2 vol. 1767. 12°. *SC*.543: "1787,
8vo."

[————]. An history of England in a series of letters
from a nobleman to his son. [By Oliver Goldsmith].
2 vol. 1764. 12°. MC.58/JW [John Wordsworth]:
"Goldsmith's Hist: of England: 2 Co:"

[————]. The life of Richard Nash of Bath, Esq.;
extracted principally from his original papers.
1762. 8°. *SC*.143. MC.65: "Life of R: Nash:"

Goodwin, Thomas. The history of the reign of Henry
the Fifth, King of England. In nine books. 1704-
03. fol. *SC*.30: "History of the Reign of Edward
[*sic*] V...." MC.60: "History of Henry 5:"

Gordon, Alexander. The lives of Pope Alexander VI.
and his son Caesar Borgia; comprehending the wars
in the reigns of Charles VIII and Lewis XII.,
Kings of France, and the chief transactions and
revolutions in Italy from 1492 to ... 1506. With
an appendix of original pieces referred to in
the book. 1729. fol. *SC*.119: "from 1492 to
1516."

*Gordon, John. *SC*.239: "Gordon, John (Surgeon); The
Great Physician--the Connection of Diseases and
Remedies with the Truths of Revelation, 8vo, bds.,
1843."

Gordon, Pryse Lockhart. Belgium and Holland: with a
sketch of the revolution in ... 1830. 2 vol.
1834. 12°. *SC*.375: "... in the year 1838 ...
(*With presentation Autograph by the Author, Chel-
tenham, 1834, and a note in the late Laureate's*

handwriting: 'My dear Daughter and I became acquainted with this Gentleman at Brussels, where he showed great kindness to us both.'--W.W.)."

[Gore, Mrs. Catherine Grace]. Agathonia [a romance]. 1844. 12°. [*DAP*; *E*]. *SC*.634: "Agathonia, a Romance, 1844."

*Gostick, Joseph. *SC*.217: "The Church and the People, by Jos. Gostick, 8vo, 1844 (*Presentation Autograph*)."

Gottsched, Johann Christoph. Grammaire allemande, méthodique et raisonnée. Strasburg, 1786. 8°. [*E*]. *SC*.390. See STC entry. [? LB.27].

Gould, Hannah Flagg. Poems. Boston, 1832. 16°. *SC*.459: "12mo."

Gower, John. See Todd, Henry John.

Graecae grammatices rudimenta; in usum Regiae Scholae Etonensis. Etonae, 1788. 12°. MC.12: "Eton Greek Gram:"

Graevius, Joannes Georgius. See Cicero, Marcus Tullius. De officiis.

Graglia, C. [? Giuspanio]. An Italian and English pocket dictionary; in two parts. I. Italian and English. II. English and Italian, etc. 1787. 12°. [? LB.20: "Italian Gram: small Dicy do." MC.17: "Graglia's Ital: Dicty.--2 Cop:"

Graham, John. Geoffrey Rudel; or, the pilgrim of love. 1836. 8°. *SC*.569.

————. A vision of fair spirits; and other poems. 1834. 8°. *SC*.569.

Grahame, James. The birds of Scotland; with other poems. Edinburgh, 1806. 17.5cm. [MH:Ann]. MC.48: "Graham's [*sic*] Birds of Scotl^d:"

*Grammar, Dutch. *SC*.362: "Grammar of the Dutch Language. 1768." MC.17: "Dutch Gram:"

*Grammar, Flemish. *SC*.362: "Grammar of the Flemish Language, *Amst*., 1774." MC.17: "Grammaire Flammande:"

Grammar, Greek. See Graecae grammatices rudimenta; Westminster Greek Grammar.

Grant, Andrew. History of Brazil, comprising a geographical account of that country, together with a narrative of the most remarkable events which have occurred there since its discovery, etc. 1809. 8°. *SC*.159.

Grant, Mrs. Anne (MacVicker), of Laggan. See Grant, John Peter.

————. Letters from the mountains; being the real correspondence of a lady, between the years 1773 and 1803. 3 vol. 1806. 18cm. LB.37.

Grant, James Gregor. Madonna Pia: and other poems. 2 vol. 1848. 16°. [WL:Ann]. *SC*.544.

Grant, John Peter. Memoir and correspondence of Mrs. Grant [Mrs. Ann Grant] of Laggan ... edited by her son. 2nd ed. 3 vol. 1845. 19.5cm. [*NUC*]. *SC*.120. LB.51.

Grattan, Thomas Colley. Traits of travel; or, tales of men and cities. By the author of "Highways and Byways." 3 vol. 1829. 19.5cm. [CtY.BL:Ann]. LB.15.

Graves, John. The history of Cleveland, in the North Riding of the County of York. Carlisle, 1808. 4°. MC.71: "History of Cleveland:"

Gray, John. [? Translations of some odes and epistles of Horace, &c., and two original poems. Dundee, 1778. 8°.]. [*E*]. [? Poems. 1770. 8°.]. [*BB*]. MC.50: "Poems by J: Gray."

Gray, Thomas. The works of Thomas Gray, with memoirs
of his life and writings by William Mason. To which
are subjoined extracts, philological, poetical, and
critical from the author's original manuscripts,
selected and arranged by Thomas James Mathias. 2
vol. 1814. fol. *SC*.546: "... 4to ... *Autograph
Presentation, 'To William Wordsworth, from Samuel
Rogers,--January 27, 1836.'*"

————. MC.49: "Gray's Poems:"

————. The poems of Mr. Gray. To which are prefixed
memoirs of his life and writings by W[illiam]
Mason. 2 vol. Dublin, 1776. [n.s.]. [*NUC*].
SC.545: "with Memoirs of his Life and Writings,
by W. Mason ... 2 vols. 8vo ... 1776." MC.46:
"Mason's Gray: 2 Vol:"

Gray, Zachary. See Butler, Samuel.

Greatrex, Charles Butler. Leisure hours, a series of
early poems, revised, with additions. 2nd ed.
London; Liverpool, 1843. 7.25 in. [*CWC*:Ann].
SC.616: "... *with Presentation Autog.*"

Green, Joseph Henry. Vital dynamics; the Hunterian
oration ... 1840. 1840. 8°. *SC*.140: "*Presentation Autog.*"

Green, William. The tourist's new guide, containing a
description of the lakes, mountains, and scenery
in Cumberland, Westmorland, and Lancashire ...
being the result of observations made during a
residence of eighteen years in Ambleside and Keswick. 2 vol. Kendal, 1819. 22cm. [*NUC*].
SC.377. MC.71: "Greens Guide to the Lakes 2 Vol:"
MC.72: "Green's Guide:" LB.13.

Greene, George. A relation of several circumstances
which occurred in Lower Normandy, during the Revolution, and under the Governments of Robespierre
and the Directory, in 1789 to ... 1800, with the
confinement and sufferings of the author; together

with an account of ... the inhabitants ... of the Bocage. 1802. 8°. *SC*.163.

Greene, Robert. The dramatic works of Robert Greene, to which are added his poems. With some account of the author, and notes, by Alexander Dyce. 2 vol. 1831. 8°. *SC*.547: "12mo."

Gregory I., surnamed the Great, Pope. See Exemplis ac similitudinibus rerum.

Gregory, of Nazianzus, Saint, Patriarch of Constantin- ople. Opera, è graeco sermone in latinum uersa [Ex interpretatione Petri Mosellani ... Ruffini presbyteri ... Bilibaldi Pirckheymeri]. [? Lip- siae. ?1522]. 16cm. [*NUC*]. *SC*.240: "8vo ... 1522."

Gresset, Jean Baptiste Louis. Oeuvres de M. Gresset. Nouvelle édition revue, corrigée ... et donnée au public par l'auteur. 2 vol. Amsterdam, 1787. 12°. [*BN*]. *SC*.533. MC.99: "Oeuvres de Gresset: 2 Vol:"

[Greville, Charles Cavendish Fulke]. Past and present policy of England towards Ireland. [By Charles Cavendish Fulke Greville]. 1845. 8°. *SC*.57.

Grey, Anchitell. Debates of the House of Commons, from ... 1667 to ... 1694, collected by the Honble Anchitell Grey. 10 vol. 1769. 8°. *SC*.24: "1763." MC.39: "Gray's [*sic*] Parliamentary De- bates 10 Vol:"

Grey, Zachary. See Butler, Samuel.

Griffin, Gregory. See The microcosm.

Grimstone, Edward. See Acosta, Joseph de; Polybius.

Gronovius, Johann Friedrich. See Tacitus, Caius Cor- nelius. Opera.

Groot, Hugo de. See Grotius, Hugo.

Grotius, Hugo. See Tacitus, Publius Cornelius.

Guevara, Antonio de. The familiar epistles of Anthony
   of Guevara ... translated out of the Spanish
   tongue, by Edward Hellowes. 1577. 4°. *SC*.378.
   MC.83: "Guevara's Epistles:"

Guez, Jean Louis, Sieur de Balzac. Letters of Moun-
   sieur de Balzac 1, 2, 3, and 4th parts; translated
   out of French into English by S^r R[ichard] Baker,
   and others. Now collected into one volume. 1654.
   8°. [There is an engraved t.p. dated 1655].
   SC.432: "1755 [*sic*]." MC.93: "Baxter's [*sic*]
   translation of Balzac's Letters."

Guicciardini, Francesco. See Dallington, Sir Robert.

Guicciardini, Lodovico. L'hore di recreatione;...
   faictes Italiennes et Françoises [translated by
   François de Belleforest] pour l'utilité de ceux
   qui désirent apprendre les deux langues. Paris,
   1636. 12°. *SC*.379: "... a Paris, 1636, (*with
   Autographs of Thos. Hayward, the poet, and the late
   Poet Laureate*)." MC.98: "L'Hore de [*sic*] Recreat:"

*Guide books. *SC*.184: "Guide to the Lakes, by House-
   man; and three others."

*————. *SC*.121: "Guide Books, various, a bundle."

*Guide to German Language. [? The true guide to the
   German language in three parts. 1775]. [*BB*].
   MC.18: "Guide to Germ: Lang:"

*Guide to the City of Perth. [? A guide to the city
   of Perth and its environs; and to the principal
   tours through the county. Perth, 1812. 12°.].
   SC.118: "Guide to Perthshire." MC.70: "Guide to
   Perth:"

Guthrie, William. See Cicero, Marcus Tullius. The
   orations.

[Guyon, Jeanne Marie Bouvières de La Motte, Mme.].
Poems, translated from the French of Madame de la
Mothe Guion by the late W[illiam] Cowper; to which
are added some original poems not inserted in his
works. Newport-Pagnel, 1801. 12°. [*L*; *BN*].
SC.495. MC.45: "M: Guion's [*sic*] Poems by Cowp:"

Guzman, Juan de. See Virgilius Maro, Publius.
Georgica.

Gwinne (or Gwynne), Matthew. Nero. Tragedia nova [in
five acts and in verse] ... collecta e Tacito,
Suetonio, Dione, Seneca. Londini, 1639. 12°.
SC.397: "Nero, Tragaedia Nova, M. Giovanni, 1639."

H., G. See Stow, John.

H., W. See Hammond, William.

Haak, Theodore. The Dutch annotations upon the whole
Bible. 2 vol. 1567. fol. MC.23: "Haak's Annotat:--2 Vol:"

Habington, William. The historie of Edward the Fourth,
King of England. 1640. fol. *SC*.32. MC.59: "History of Edwd 4th:"

Haddon, James. Elements of algebra. 1850. 12°.
SC.117.

[Haering (or Häring), Wilhelm]. Walladmor: "freely
translated into German from the English of Sir
Walter Scott." And now freely translated from the
German [of Wilhelm Häring] into English. 2 vol.
1825. 12°. [*NUC*]. [DD:Ann]. *SC*.474: "Walladmor,
from the German, 2 vols., 12mo, 1825." LB.13.

Haining, Samuel. A historical sketch and descriptive
view of the Isle of Man; designed as a companion
to those who visit and make the tour of it. Douglas, 1822. 6.25 in. [*CWC*:Ann]. *SC*.179: "Guide
to the Isle of Man."

[Hake, Thomas Gordon]. The Piromides; a tragedy [in five acts and in verse]. 1839. 8°. *SC*.498.

Hale, Sir Matthew. The history of the common law of England. 4th ed. ... with notes, references, and some account of the life of the author, by Charles Runnington. 2 pt. 1779. 8°. *SC*.33. MC.40: "Hale's Hist: of Comm: Law."

―――――. The primitive origination of mankind, considered and examined according to the light of nature. 1677. 4°. *SC*.241: "fol."

[? Hall, Captain Basil, R.N. Travels in North America, 1827-28. 3 vol. Edinburgh, 1829. 8°.]. [*NUC*]. *SC*.163: "Travels in North America, vol. 1." LB.10: "Travels N. Am: 2 vols." See Carver, Jonathan; Davis, John.

Hall, John. Select observations on English bodies; or, cures both empericall [*sic*] and historicall, performed upon very eminent persons in desperate diseases. First, written in Latine by Mr. John Hall physician ... Now put into English ... by James Cooke practitioner in physick. 1657. 15cm. [*L*; *NUC*]. *SC*.106: "12mo." MC.75: "Select Observations:"

Hall, Joseph. See Montagu, Basil. Selections.

―――――. A recollection of such treatises as have been heretofore severally published and are now revised, corrected, augmented. With addition of some others not hitherto extant. Cambridge, 1615. 27cm. [DFo:Ann]. *SC*.242: "folio ... 1615."

Hall, Samuel Carter, ed. The amulet, or Christian and literary remembrancer. 11 vol. 1826-36. 12°. LB.9: "Amulet 2 vol [lent early in 1828]."

Hallam, Arthur Henry. Remains in verse and prose of Arthur Henry Hallam. [Edited, with a preface, by his father, Henry Hallam]. [London], 1834. 8°. [DD:Ann]. LB.49: "Remains of A.H.H."

Hallam, Henry.   See Hallam, Arthur Henry.

[Halleck, Fitz-Green].   Alnwick Castle, with other
    poems. New York, 1827. 22cm. [*NUC*]. *SC*.541.

Halliwell-Phillipps, James Orchard.   See also Dee, Dr.
    John; de Rishanger, William; Warkworth, John.

————. The Thornton romances; the Early English metri-
    cal romances of Perceval, Isumbras, Eglamour, and
    Degrevant ... Edited by James Orchard Halliwell.
    1844. 8°. *SC*.15.

Halyburton, Thomas.   Memoirs of the life of the Reverend
    Thomas Halyburton ... digested into four parts,
    whereof the first three were written with his own
    hand some years before his death, and the fourth is
    collected from his diary by another hand; to which
    is annex'd some account of his dying words by those
    who were witnesses to his death. Edinburgh, 1714.
    17cm. [*NUC*]. MC.64: "Mem: of Halyburton:"

Hamilton, Eliza Mary.   Poems. Dublin, 1838. 8°.
    SC.597: "*(with Autog. Dedication, etc.*)." LB.25:
    "Miss Hamiltons Poems."

Hamilton, Captain Thomas.   Men and manners in America.
    1833. 8°. LB.17: "America Mr Hamilton."

[Hamilton, William, of Gilbertfield].   A new edition
    [by W. Hamilton] of the life and heroick actions
    of ... Sir William Wallace. Glasgow, 1722. 8°.
    SC.489: "Life, etc., by [*sic*] Sir William Wallace,
    a Poem by W. Hamilton." MC.50: "Life of W͞m Wal-
    lace:"

Hamilton, Sir William Rowan.   On the argument of Abel,
    respecting the impossibility of expressing a root
    of any general equation above the fourth degree,
    by any finite combination of radicles and rational
    functions. [Transactions of the Royal Irish Aca-
    demy. Vol. 18, pt. 2, 1839]. [*NUC*]. *SC*.122:
    "4to, *Dublin*, 1848."

————. Supplement to an essay on the theory of systems of rays. [Transactions of the Royal Irish Academy, Vol. 16, 1830]. [*NUC*]. *SC*.122: "4to, 1838."

Hammond, Henry. A practical catechism. 13th ed. Whereunto is added the reasonableness of Christian religion by the same authour [*sic*]. 1691. 6.75 in. [*CWC*:Ann]. *SC*.213. MC.29: "Hammond's Practical Catech:" LB.6: "Hammonds Catechism."

[Hammond, William]. Poems. By W.H. 1655. 8°. [WL: Ann]. MC.49: "Poems by W:H: 1655."

Hankinson, Thomas Edwards. The ministry of angels. Cambridge, 1840. [*NUC*]. LB.27: "Hankinson's Ministry of Angels."

————. Poems. [Cambridge, 1827]. 8°. *SC*.617 [n.d.].

Hanmer, John, Baron Hanmer. Fra Cipolla, and other poems. 1839. 8°. *SC*.548.

————. Sonnets. 1840. 8°. *SC*.574.

Hanmer, Meredith. See Eusebius, Pamphili.

Hare, Augustus William. Sermons to a country congregation. 2 vol. 1836. 12°. *SC*.244. [? LB.21: "Hare's Sermons"].

Hare, Julius Charles. The mission of the comforter, and other sermons. With notes. 2 vol. 1846. 8°. *SC*.245. [? LB.40: "Hare's Sermons 1 Vol."].

————. Portions of the Psalms, in English verse, selected ... by Julius Charles Hare. 1839. 12°. *SC*.453 [n.d.].

————. Sermons preacht in Herstmonceux Church. 2 vol. London, Cambridge, 1841-49. 8°. *SC*.246: "Hare, Julius Caesar,[1] [[1]Read Julius Charles.-- Ed.]." [? LB.28: "Hare's Parochial Sermons"].

————. The victory of faith, and other sermons. Cambridge, 1840. 8°. *SC*.247. LB.28: "Hares Faith Sermons."

[———— and Augustus William Hare]. Guesses at truth, by two brothers. 2 vol. 1827. 17cm. [*NUC*]. [WL:Ann]. LB.8: "Guesses at Truth 1st vol. [lent September 5th, 1827]."

[————]. 2nd ed. 1st series. 1838. 18cm. [*NUC*]. LB.24: "Guesses at Truth 2^d Ed."

Hargrave, Francis, ed. A complete collection of state-trials, and proceedings for high treason ... 4th ed. 11 vol. (in 6). 1776-81. fol. [*EU*]. *SC*.35. MC.40: "State Trials: 11 Vol:"

Harington, Sir John. See Ariosto, Ludovico.

————. A briefe view of the state of the Church of England ... in Q. Elizabeth's and King James his reigne, to the yeere 1608. 1653. 12°. *SC*.249: "18mo."

Harness, William. The image of God in man. Four sermons preached before the University of Cambridge. 1841. 8°. *SC*.248.

————. Parochial sermons. 1837. 8°. *SC*.248: "1838."

[————]. Welcome & farewell, a tragedy. [1837]. 14.5cm. [*NUC*]. *SC*.567.

Harrington, James. The common-wealth of Oceana. 1656. fol. *SC*.36. MC.34/C: "Harrington's Oceana:" [A line has been drawn through the "C" and a "W" inserted between the "C" and the title]. MC.115s: "Oceana" [A line has been drawn through "Oceana"].

Harris, James. Hermes, or a philosophical inquiry concerning universal grammar. The second edition revised and corrected. 1765. 21cm. [MA:Ann]. *SC*.380: "8vo ... 1765."

Harris, John. Navigantium atque itinerantium bibliotheca: or, a compleat collection of voyages and
travels, consisting of above four hundred of the
most authentick writers. 2 vol. 1705. fol. [*CM*].
MC.71/JC: "Harris' Collection of Voy: 2 Vols."
LB.9: "Harris's Voyages 2 vol [lent 9 April 1828]."
See STC entry.

Harris, Walter. See De morbis infantum.

Harris, William. An historical and critical account
of the life and writings of Charles I., King of
Great Britain, after the manner of Mr. Bayle. 1758.
21.5cm. [NNMor:Ann]. *SC*.37: "8vo, 1758." MC.65:
"Life &c: of Charles I:" LB.6: "Harris Chas I."

*Harrison, Mrs. Leaves from the lake side. *SC*.523:
"*(with Presentation Autograph)*."

Harrison, Anthony. Poetical recreations. 2 vol. Penrith, London, 1806. 8°. *SC*.516. MC.46/1 JC:
"Harr: Poetical Recr: 2 cop:" See STC entry.

[? The Hastings guide. Containing a description of
that ancient town and port ... to which is added,
an account of the Cinque Ports, and a minute detail of the ... battle of Hastings. 5th ed.
Hastings, [? 1820]. 12°.]. *SC*.179: "Hastings
Guide."

Hastings, Sophia Frederica Christina Rawdon, Lady,
afterwards Stuart, Sophia Frederica Christina Rawdon Crichton, Marchioness of Bute. Poems by Lady
Flora Hastings, edited by her sister. Edinburgh,
1841. 8°. LB.44: "Lady F. Hastings Poems."

Hatfield, James. See James Hatfield.

Hawkesworth, John. Almoran and Hamet. [Vol. 26 of
The British novelists]. *SC*.515: "Almoran, etc.,
by Dr. Hawksworth [*sic*]." MC.87: "Almeron [*sic*].
--Ha." LB.55: "Brit. Novelist--26th V."

Hawkins, Sir John. See Walton, Izaak.

Hawkins, John Sidney. See Walton, Izaak.

Hawkshaw, Mrs. Ann. Dionysius the Areopagite: with other poems. London, Salford, 1842. 8°. *SC*.466.

Hay, Richard Augustine. Genealogie [*sic*] of the Sainte-claires of Rosslyn ... including the chartulary of Rosslyn. Edinburgh, 1835. 4°. *SC*.158: "4to (*printed for private distribution, Presentation Copy, with Autog.*) 1834 [*sic*]."

Haydn, Joseph. Dictionary of dates and universal reference, relating to all ages and nations. 2nd ed. 1844. 23cm. [MA:Ann]. *SC*.38: "8vo, 1844."

Haydon, Benjamin Robert. Lectures on painting and design. 2 vol. 1844-46. 8°. *SC*.551: "8vo, 1844 [presumably Vol. I only]."

Hayley, William. The poetical works of William Hayley. 3 vol. Dublin, 1785. 12°. *SC*.552: "3 vols., 8vo ... Dublin, 1785, *with MS. Notes, and Portrait by Holloway after Romney inserted.*" MC.47: "Hayley's Poet: Works: 3 Vol:"

Haynes, Henry W. The pleasures of poesy. A poem in two cantos ... 1846. 6.75 in. [*CWC*:Ann]. *SC*.527.

Hayward, Abraham. Some account of a journey across the Alps, in a letter to a friend. [1834]. 12°. [*L*: "Printed for private circulation"]. *SC*.164: "*Private Publication, with Autograph Presentation*)."

Hayward, James. See Biondi, Giovanni Francesco.

Hayward, Sir John. Annals of the first four years of the reign of Queen Elizabeth, by Sir John Hayward ... Ed. from a ms. in the Harleian collection, by John Bruce. 1840. 8°. *SC*.15.

[Haywood, Eliza]. The female Spectator. 4 vol. 1745. 8°. MC.79: "Female Spectator 4 Vol:"

Hearne, Samuel. A journey from Prince of Wales's Fort
in Hudson's Bay to the Northern Ocean, undertaken
... for the discovery of copper mines, a North West
passage, etc. in the years 1769-1772. 1795. 4°.
SC.124. LB.49: "Hearnes Voyages in the Northern
Ocean 4°."

[Heath, James]. Flagellum: or the life and death,
birth and burial of O. Cromwell the late usurper:
faithfully described. 1672. 16cm. [CSJ:Ann].
SC.37: "12mo, 1672." MC.65: "Life of Cromwell:"

Heaton, William. The flowers of Calder Vale: poems.
London, Halifax, 1847. 12°. *SC*.599: "Flowers of
Calder Vale;... Poems, by W. Heaton (*with MS. Let-
ter*), 1847."

Heavisides, Henry. The pleasures of home, and other
poems. 2nd ed. London, Stockton, 1840. 18cm.
[NIC:Ann]. *SC*.630.

Heber, Mrs. Amelia (Shipley). The life of Reginald
Heber by his widow, with selections from his correspondence, unpublished poems, and private papers;
together with a Journal of his tour in Norway,
Sweden, Russia, Hungary, and Germany, and a History
of the Cossacks. 2 vol. 1830. 4°. [*L*; *NUC*].
LB.16: "Hebers Life 1st vol."

Heber, Reginald. See Heber, Mrs. Amelia.

[————]. Palestine, a prize poem, recited in the
Theatre, Oxford, June 15, 1803. [Oxford, 1803].
23cm. [*NUC*]. LB.18: "Palestine."

Heberden, William, the Younger. See Cicero, Marcus
Tullius. The letters of M.T. Cicero to T.P.
Atticus.

Hederich, Benjamin. Graecum lexicon manuale ... cura
J.A. Ernesti, nunc iterum recensitum et ... auctum
a T. Morell. 1778, 4°. *SC*.381: "a [Patricii
[Samuel Patrick], Ernesti [Johann August Ernesti],
et Morell [Thomas Morell], 4to ... 1778."

[Hedge, Mary Ann]. The solace of an invalid. 1823.
   12°. [*L*: "A collection of essays"; *NUC*: "16.5cm
   ... A selection of prose and verse"]. *SC*.304:
   "1825."

Heinsius, Daniel. See Clement, of Alexandria.

Heinsius, Nicolaas. See Ovidius Naso, Publius. Opera.

The heir of Innes. See The court of Tuscany.

Hellowes, Edward. See Guevara, Antonio de.

[Helps, Sir Arthur]. The claims of labour; an essay
   on the duties of employers to the employed. 1844.
   8°. *SC*.269: "12mo."

Hemans, Felicia. See Browne, afterwards Hemans, Felicia
   Dorothea.

Henry, Matthew. [? The works of ... Matthew Henry,
   being a complete collection of all the discourses,
   sermons, and other tracts that were published by
   himself. Together with an account of his life and
   a sermon preach'd on the occasion of his death;
   both by W[illiam] Tong. 1726. fol.]. *SC*.309:
   "Sermons by Mat. Henry, and others, 1726."

Heraud, John Abraham. See Lalor, John.

[————]. The descent into Hell: a poem. 1830. 8°.
   [*EU*]. *SC*.555: "Heraud's (J.A.) Descent into Hell,
   a Poem (*with Autographs of the Poet and the Laureate*), 8vo, 1830."

————. 2nd ed. Revised and re-arranged. With an
   analysis and notes. To which are added Uriel, a
   fragment, and three odes. 1835. 12°. *SC*.623:
   "The Descent into Hell, Uriel, etc., by J.A.
   Heraud, 1835."

————. The judgement of the Flood. [A poem in twelve
   books]. 1834. 8°. *SC*.554: "4to (*with Autograph
   Presentation by the Author*), 1834."

Herbert, Edward, Baron Herbert of Cherbury. De religione gentilium, errorumque apud eos causis. Amstelaedami, 1700. 8°. *SC*.211. MC.27: "De Religione
Gentilium."

―――――. De veritate cui operi additi sunt duo alii
tractatus, de causis errorum; primus, De causis
errorum; alter, De religione laici. 2 pt. 1645.
4°. *SC*.250. MC.30/0: "Herbert de Veritate."

―――――. The life and reigne of King Henry the Eighth.
1683. 29.5cm. [MH:Ann]. *SC*.125: "folio, 1683."

Herbert, George. Herbert's remains; or, sundry pieces
of that sweet singer of the Temple, Mr. G.H. ... 3
pt. 1652. 12°. *SC*.180. MC.83: "Herbert's Remains:"

Herbert, Henry John George, 3rd Earl of Carnarvon.
Portugal and Gallicia, with a review of the social
and political state of the Basque Provinces; and a
few remarks on recent events in Spain. 2 vol.
1836. 8°. LB.32: "Portugal & Gallicia 2 vols."

Herbert, Sir Thomas. A relation of some yeares tra-
vaile, begunne anno 1626. into Afrique and the
greater Asia, especially the territories of the
Persian Monarchie, and some parts of the orientall
Indies ... of their religion, language, habit ...
and other matters concerning them. Together with
the proceedings and death of the three late am-
bassadors; Sir D[odmore] C[otton], Sir R[obert]
S[hirley] and the Persian Nogdi-Beg. 1634. fol.
SC.39. MC.71: "Herbert's Persian Monar:"

[Herd, David]. Antient and modern Scotish songs,
heroic ballads, &c. 2 vol. Edinburgh, 1791.
17.5cm. [*NUC*]. *SC*.455: "2 vols., 12mo ... 1791."
[? MC.48: "Scottish Songs: 2 Vol:"].

Herodian. Herodianou historion biblia e' [in Greek].
Herodiani Historiarum libri viii [Angelo Politiano
interprete, i.e. Angelus Politianus, i.e. Angelo

Ambrogini (Poliziano)] recogniti et notis illustrati. Oxoniae, 1678. 8°. [*BN*]. *SC*.40: "*with
numerous Notes in MS.*" MC.3: "Herodianus:"

Herodotus. The history of Herodotus translated from
the Greek by Isaac Littlebury. 3rd ed. 2 vol.
1737. 8°. *SC*.41. MC.91: "Littleburg's [*sic*]
Herodotus: 2 Vol:"

Herschel, Sir John Frederick William. A preliminary
discourse on the study of natural philosophy.
1831. [In Dionysius Lardner, The cabinet cyclopaedia, 133 vol., 1830–49, 8°.]. *SC*.126: "1835,
2 vols., 12mo (*Lardner's Cyclopaedia*)."

————. A treatise on astronomy. 1833. [This had
appeared in Dionysius Lardner, The cabinet cyclopaedia, 1830–49. 8°.]. *SC*.126: "1831."

Hervey, Thomas Kibble. Australia; with other poems.
2nd ed. 1825. 18.5cm. [MA:Ann]. *SC*.553: "by
T.K. Kervey [*sic*], 1825."

Hesiod. Hesiodi Ascraei quae extant ... Accedit ...
Pasoris Index ... studio C. Schrevelii. Gr. &
Lat. Cantabrigiae, 1672. 8°. *SC*.556: "*S.T.C &
W.W.*'." MC.3: "Hesiodus:"

Hesychius, of Miletus. See Diogenes Laërtius.

Hetherington, William Maxwell. Twelve dramatic sketches, founded on the pastoral poetry of Scotland.
Edinburgh, 1829. 18cm. [NIC:Ann]. *SC*.557: "8vo."

Heuzet, Jean. Selectae e profanis scriptoribus historiae, quibus admista sunt varia honeste vivendi
praecepta ex iisdem scriptoribus deprompta ...
[Auctore J. Heuzet]. Parisiis, 1727. 2 pt. in 1
vol. 12°. [*BN*]. MC.5: "Select: è Propha:"

Heylyn, Peter. Cosmographie in four bookes, containing the horographie and historie of the whole
world. 4 pt. 1652. fol. *SC*.128: "folio (*no
title*)." MC.69: "Heylin's [*sic*] Cosmogra:"

————. Cyprianus Anglicus; or, the history of the life and death of ... William [Laud] ... Archbishop of Canterbury ... Also the ecclesiastical history of ... England, Scotland and Ireland, from his first rising till his death. 1671. fol. *SC*.127. MC.65: "Cyprianus Anglic:"

Heyne, Christian Gottlob. See Pindar; Virgilius. Georgica.

*Heywood, _____. The shipwreck. MC.49: "Heywood's Shipwreck &c:"

*Heywood, Thomas. *SC*.625: "Divers Dramas, never before published, and a Miscellane of Sundrie Straines in Poetry, etc., by Thomas Heywood--(*title-page and a leaf of annotations wanting*)."

Hickes, George. Linguarum veterum sepentrionalium thesaurus grammatico-criticus et archaeologicus. 2 vol. Oxoniae, 1705. fol. *SC*.382: "3 vols., folio, *Oxon*., 1705." MC.18: "Hicks' [*sic*] Thesaurus: 3 Vol:" LB.55: "Lingu Vett. Sept."

Hierocles, of Alexandria. Hieroclis Philosophi commentarius in aurea Pythagoreorum carmina ... J. Curterio interprete. 2 vol. 1673. 8°. *SC*.383.

Hieronymus, Saint. Inventarivm primae [- tertiae] partis aepistolarvm sancti Hieronymi. 3 vol. [Lugduni, 1508]. 17cm. [NIC:Ann]. *SC*.288: "ST. JEROME: Epl' arii Divi Hieronomi, Doctoris alioquin Pfundissimi Necno Nostre Fidei Stabilimenti Solidissimi Codicilli, etc. etc., 2 vols., 8vo ... n.d. (*'W. Wordsworth from Walter Savage Landor,'--in the Handwriting of the Eminent Conversationist*)."

Higden, William. See Clarke, Samuel.

Higgins, William Mullinger. The earth; its physical condition and most remarkable phenomena. 1836. 8°. LB.23: "The Earth [lent in late 1837 or early 1838]."

Higginson, Edward. See Lalor, John.

Hill, John. A review of the works of the Royal Society
of London, containing animadversions, etc. 1751.
4°. [*EU*]. [CSmH.ZZB:Ann]. *SC*.129. MC.61: "Review of Royal Soc: of London:"

Hillhouse, James Abraham. Hadad, a dramatic poem.
New York, 1825. 8°. *SC*.558: "Haydad."

Hine, Joseph. See Wordsworth, William. Selections
from the poems.

*Hints. *SC*.11: "Hints, etc., 1830."

*History. MC.58: "History:"

*History of England. *SC*.42: "History of England, and
divers Elementary Historical Works [twelve volumes
in the lot]."

*The history of Glasgow. *SC*.118: "History of Glasgow."
MC.58: "History of Glasgow:" [? Gibson, John.
The history of Glasgow from the earliest accounts
to the present time. Glasgow, 1777. 8°.]--[?
Brown, Andrew. History of Glasgow; and of Pais-
ley, Greenock, and Port-Glasgow. 2 vol. Glasgow,
1795-7. 8°.]--[? Denholm, James. History of the
city of Glasgow and suburbs ... with a tour to
Loch Lomond, and the Falls of the Clyde. Glasgow,
1797. 12°].

*History of London. MC.59: "History of London: &c:
[line drawn through item]."

*History of Stirling. MC.70: "History of Sterling
[*sic*]:" [? A general history of Stirling, containing a description of the town, and origin of
the castle and burgh. Stirling, 1794. 12°.]--
[? The history of Stirling ... to which is added
a sketch of a tour to Callander and the Trossachs.
Stirling, 1812. 8°].

Hoadly, Benjamin. See Donne, John; A presbyter of the Church of England.

————. The measures of submission to the civil magistrate consider'd. In a defense of the doctrine delivered in a sermon [on Rom. xiii. 1] preach'd before the ... Lord Mayor ... Sept. 29, 1705. 4th ed. 1710. 8°. *SC*.251.

————. A sermon [on Rom. xiii. 1] preach'd before the election of the Lord Mayor, Sept. 29, 1705. 1705. 4°. MC.29: "Hoadley's [*sic*] Sermon."

————. Some considerations humbly offered to the ... Bishop of Exeter [Offspring Blackall], occasioned by his Lordship's sermon preached before her Majesty, March 8, 1708. 1709. 8°. MC.29: "Hoadley's [*sic*] Considerations."

Hobbes, Thomas. Tracts of Thomas Hobb's [*sic*] containing I. His life in Latine, part written by himself, since his death finished by Dr. R.B. [i.e. Richard Blackburne]. II. His considerations on his reputation, loyalty, manners, and religion. III. His whole Art of rhetorick, in English. VI. [*for* IV] His discourse by way of dialogue, concerning the common laws of England. V. Ten dialogues of natural philosophy. &c. 1681. 5 pts. in 1 vol. 17.5cm. [*NUC*]. *SC*.44: "Tracts, 12mo, 1681." MC.31: "Tracts of Tho: Hobbe's [*sic*]."

Hodgson, Joseph Stordy. Considerations on phrenology in connexion with an intellectual, moral, and religious education. 1839. 8°. *SC*.166. LB.53: "Hodgson on Phrenology."

Hogaeus, Gulielmus. Paraphrasis poetica in tria Johannis Miltoni ... poemata, viz. Paradisum amissum, Paradisum recuperatum, et Samsonem Agonisten. 1690. 8°. *SC*.610. MC.44: "Hogg's Parad: Lost:"

Hogan, John. Blarney; a descriptive poem. 1842. 8°. [*NUC*]. *SC*.612.

Hogg, James. The mountain bard; consisting of ballads
and songs founded on facts and legendary tales;
by James Hogg. [With an autobiography]. Edinburgh, 1807. 12°. *SC*.648. MC.51: "Hogg's Mount:
Bard:"

————. The Queen's wake: a legendary poem. Edinburgh, 1813. 8°. *SC*.648. MC.51: "Hogg's Queen's
Wake:"

Hogg, William. See Hogaeus, Gulielmus.

Holbach, Paul Heinrich Dietrich, Baron d'. Système
de la nature ou des lois du monde physique et du
monde moral, par M. Mirabaud [*pseud*.]. 2 vol.
1781. 8°. [*BN*]. *SC*.149. MC.100:"Systeme de la
Nature."

Holcroft, Thomas. See Trenck, Frederic, Baron.

Hole, Richard. Arthur; or, the northern enchantment,
a poetical romance. 1789. 8°. *SC*.559. MC.45:
"Hoole's [*sic*] Arthur:"

Holland, John. See Newsam, William Cartwright.

Holland, Lord. See Fox, afterwards Vassall, Henry
Richard.

Hollings, John. The state of human nature delineated.
As deliver'd in a Latin oration ... Translated
into English. 1734. 4°. *SC*.129: "E. Hollings."
MC.84: "State of Hum: Nat: &c:"

Holme, James. Mount Grace Abbey. A poem. [? 1843].
8°. *SC*.518: "[n.d.] (*with Presentation Autograph*)."

[Holworthy, Samuel]. Poems, by a clergyman. 1821.
8°. [*L*: "*With the autograph of William Wordsworth*"]. *SC*.638.

Holyday, Barten. See Juvenalis, Decimus Junius.

Homely, Josias, *pseud*. See Bradford, John.

Homer. See Statius, Publius Papinius.

*————. LB.17, LB.24: "Homer."

*————. *SC*.668: "Homer, imperfect." [? MC.3: "Homeri
Ilias: 2 Cop."].

————. The whole works of Homer; prince of poetts,
in his Iliads, and Odysses. Translated according
to the Greeke, by Geo. Chapman. 2 pt. *For Nathaniel Butter: London*, [1612]. fol. *SC*.490: "Chapman's (George) Translation of 'THE WHOLE works of
PRINCE OF POETS in his Iliads, and Odyssey, according to the Greeke' (with the Engraved Frontispiece by Hollar, and Portrait by Hole, so rarely
to be met with) at London--Printed for Nathaniel
Butter." MC.92: "Chapman's Homer:"

————. [Another edition]. 2 pt. [? 1616]. fol.
[MoSW.GNMC: "Samuel Taylor Coleridge's copy, with
his manuscript notes throughout the text. The
t.-p. bears Coleridge's signed autograph presentation inscription to Sarah Hutchinson, from whom it
subsequently passed into the library of William
Wordsworth." *SC*.491: "Chapman's Homer, Another
Copy, without the Frontispiece, but containing the
Engraved Dedication, on the back of which is
written thirteen lines by S.T. Coleridge, dated
Feb. 12, 1808, a comparison of Chapman with Ben
Jonson and Milton.--A long MS. criticism of Chapman's merits as a Translator, by the same eminent
writer, is also inserted within the cover." MC.
92/JC/C: "do--do [i.e. Chapman's Homer]." See STC
entry; *CN*, 2N3212; and *SHL*, p. 439, where SH re-
quests J.H. Green to return the volume to her in-
asmuch as it had been sent to STC by mistake.

*————. Ilias. *SC*.350: "(*no title*) ... *Autograph*."
[? MC.3: "Homeri Ilias: 2 Cop:"].

————. The Iliad of Homer, translated by William Sotheby. 2 vol. 1831. 8°. *SC*.659. [? LB.17: "Homer"]

————. A translation of the twenty-fourth book of the Iliad of Homer. [By Charles Lloyd, the Elder]. Birmingham, 1807. 8°. *SC*.580. MC.91: "Translation of 24 Book of Iliad:"

————. Homeri Odyssea, cum interpretatione lat. ad verbum, post alias omnes editiones repurgata plurimis erroribus ... partim ab Henr. Stephano, partim ab aliis. Adjecti sunt etiam Homerici centones--item, proverbialium Homeri versuum libellus. Editio postrema diligenter recognita per I.T.P. Cantabrigiae, 1664. 8°. [*L*; *NUC*]. *SC*.562: "Homeri Odyssea, Gr. et Lat., 8vo, *Cantab*., 1664." MC.3: "Homeri Odyssea: 2 Cop:"

————. A translation of the first seven books of the Odyssey of Homer. [By Charles Lloyd, the Elder]. Birmingham, 1810. 12°. [CaOTV.HD]. [*DNB*: "He also translated the first seven books of the 'Odyssey,' which appeared in 1810, Birmingham, 12mo."]. MC.91: "Lloyd's Odyssey:"

Homes, N. See Schickard, Wilhelm.

*Homilies. *SC*.223: "Homilies, etc., 1687." [? LB.64: "Homilies"]. See Certain sermons or homilies.

Hone, William. The table book. 1827. 9 in. [*CWC*. 728]. *SC*.384: "Hone, William: THE TABLE BOOK, 2 vols., 8vo, 1827."

————. The every-day book and Table book. 3 vol. 1826-27-28-39 [*sic*]. 8°. LB.13: "Hone's Everyday Book [lent 1 Feb. 1831]."

Hood, Edwin Paxton. Fragments of thought and composition. 1846. 17cm. [*NUC*]. *SC*.620.

Hook, Walter Farquhar. The Church and the Establishment; two plain sermons. 1834. 12°. *SC*.217: "(*Presentation Autograph*)."

————. [Another copy]. *SC*.255: "8vo."

————. Five sermons preached before the University of Oxford. Oxford, 1837. 8°. *SC*.254.

————. The last days of our Lord's ministry. A course of lectures. 1832. 8°. *SC*.254.

Hooke, Nathanael. See Solis y Ribadneyra, Antonio de.

Hooker, Richard. See Montagu, Basil. Selections.

————. The works of Mr. Richard Hooker, (that learned and judicious divine) in eight books of ecclesiastical polity, compleated out of his own manuscripts; never before published. 1666. 34.5cm. [*NUC*]. *SC*.256. MC.24: "Ecclesiast: Polity:"

Hoole, Charles. See Komenský, Jan Amos.

Hoole, John. See Scott, John; Tasso, Torquato.

Hope, Elizabeth. The immaterial system of man, contemplated in accordance with the beautiful and sublime, and in reference to a plan for general education. 2 vol. 1835. 12°. *SC*.269: "8vo."

Hope, F. See Wieland, Christoph Martin.

Horace. See Horatius Flaccus, Quintus.

Horam, the son of Asmar, *pseud*. See Ridley, James.

Horatius Flaccus, Quintus. See Gray, John.

*————. *SC*.644: "Horace, etc. etc." MC.3: "Horatius: 2 Cop:"

————. [? Q. Horatii Flacci opera: interpretatione et notis illustravit L. Desprez ... in usum ... Delphini. Parisiis, 1691. 4°]. *SC*.564: "Horatii Flacci Opera Delph., 8vo (*no title*)."

————. Q. Horatii Flacci opera; cum scholiis veteribus castigavit et notis illustravit Gulielmus

Baxterus. Varias lectiones et observationes addidit Jo. Matthias Gesnerus; quibus et suas adspersit Jo. Carolus Zeunius. Editio nova, priore emendatior. Glasguae, 1796. 8°. [*L*; *NUC*]. MC.3/H.C.: "Horatius Zeun:"

————. Horatius restitutus; or, the books of Horace arranged in chronological order according to the scheme of Dr. Bentley, from the text of his second edition in 1713 ... with a preliminary dissertation on the chronology and the localities of that poet. By James Tate. Cambridge, 1832. 8°. *SC*.563: "1831."

————. Eilhardi Lubini in Q. Horatii Flacci Poemata quae exstant omnia Paraphrasis scholastica nova. 10 pt. C. Reusner: Rostochii, 1599-98. 4°. [*L*]. [*NUC*: "10 pt. in iv. Rostochii, 1599-1600. Each part has a t.-p. with varying date"]. *SC*.562: "Eilhardi Lubini in Q. Horatii Flacci Poemata quae extant omnia, Paraphrasis Scholastica Nova, cura Chr. Reusneri." MC.3: "do [Horatius] Lubini."

————. The odes, satyrs, and epistles of Horace. Done into English [by Thomas Creech]. 1684. 8°. MC.92: "Creech's Horace:"

————. The works of Horace. Translated into English prose, for the use of those who are desirous of acquiring or recovering a competent knowledge of the Latin language. By C[hristopher] Smart. 2 vol. Dublin, 1772. 13.5cm. [Pembroke College Library, Cambridge: Vol. II only:Ann]. MC.3: "Horatius Smart: 1 Vol: 1 w⁸."

————. A poetical translation of the works of Horace, with the original text, and critical notes collected from his best Latin and French commentators. By Philip Francis. A new edition, with additional notes, by Edward Du Bois. 4 vol. 1807. 15cm. [NIC:Ann]. *SC*.536: "12mo." MC.3/1 H[artley] C[oleridge]: "Horatius Fran: 3 Vol: 1 w⁸."

————. The epistles of Horace; translated into English verse [by Charles Lloyd, the Elder]. Birmingham, 1812. 18cm. [NjP:Ann]. MC.92: "Lloyd's Epist: of Horace:"

Horne, Richard Hengist. See Chaucer.

————. Cosmo de' Medici; an historical tragedy [in five acts and in verse]. 1837. 8°. *SC*.486: "(*with Presentation Autograph and MS. Dedicatory Sonnet*)."

Horneck, Anthony. The great law of consideration. Eleventh edition, corrected. 1729. 8°. *SC*.213. MC.23: "Law of Consideration:" MC.25: "Law of Considerat:"

Horner, John. Buildings in the town and parish of Halifax. Drawn from nature and on stone by John Horner. Halifax, 1835. 42cm. [*NUC*]. *SC*.95: "*oblong folio*, lithog., 1835."

Horsley, Samuel. Nine sermons on the nature of the evidence by which the fact of our Lord's resurrection is established. To which is prefixed, A dissertation on the prophecies of the Messiah dispersed among the heathen by Samuel Horsley. 2nd ed. 1817. 8°. *SC*.312: "1827 [*sic*]."

[————]. On the prosodies of the Greek and Latin languages. 1796. 8°. MC.13: "On Prosod:"

Houghton, Lord. See Milnes, Richard Monckton.

Housman, John. A descriptive tour and guide to the lakes, caves, mountains ... in Cumberland, Westmoreland, Lancashire, and a part of the West Riding of Yorkshire. 2nd ed. Carlisle, 1802. 8°. *SC*.184 [n.d.].

Housman, Robert Fletcher. A collection of English sonnets. London, Lancaster, [1835]. 12°. *SC*. 565: "12mo ... 1835."

Howell, James. Familiar letters on important subjects, wrote from the year 1618 to 1650. 10th ed. Aberdeen, 1753. 17cm. [MH:Ann]. *SC*.432: "8vo." MC.82: "Howell's Letters:"

———. Instructions and directions for forreine travell ... With a new appendix for traveling into Turkey. 1650. 12°. *SC*.170: *"with the late Laureate's Autograph."* MC.70: "Howell's Instr: for Forn Travel:"

Howell, William. Medulla historiae Anglicanae. The ancient and present state of England: a compendious history of all its monarchs, from the time of Julius Caesar. 1679. 12°. *SC*.78: "8vo (*no title*)." MC.58: "Histor: Anglec [*sic*]:"

Howes, Edmund. See Stow, John.

Howie, James. Sketches of Britain. [In verse]. London, Glasgow, 1842. 8°. *SC*.665: "(*Presen. Autog*)."

Howitt, Mary. See Howitt, William.

———. The seven temptations. 1834. 8°. LB.28.

Howitt, Richard. Antediluvian sketches; and other poems. London, Thames Ditton, 1830. 8°. *SC*.518: "(with Dedicatory Stanzas in MS.)."

Howitt, William and Mary. The desolation of Eyam: The emigrant, a tale of the American woods: and other poems. 1827. 12°. [*L*; *NUC*]. *SC*.472: "(*with Autog*.)."

———. [Another copy]. *SC*.566: "1837 [*sic*]."

[Hoyle, Charles]. The pilgrim of the Hebrides, a lay of the North Countrie. By the author of "Three days at Killarney" [Charles Hoyle]. 1830. 8°. *SC*.621.

Hudson, John. See Longinus, Dionysius Cassius.

Hudson, John, of Kendal. A complete guide to the lakes, comprising minute directions for the tourist, with Mr. Wordsworth's description of the scenery of the country &c. and three letters upon the geology of the lake district, by the Rev. Professor [Adam] Sedgwick. Edited by the publishers. Kendal, Hudson and Nicholson; London. 1842. 19cm. [*NUC*]. *SC*.540: "interleaved, 12mo, 1842."

Hughes, Mrs. Harriet. The works of Mrs. Hemans; with a memoir of her life, by her sister [Harriet Hughes]. [With notes and portraits]. 7 vol. Edinburgh, London, 1839. 8°. LB.26: "Mrs Hemans Life [lent in October, 1839]."

Hughes, Terence McMahon. The Biliad, or, how to criticize; a satire [in verse], with The dirge of Repeal and other jeux d'esprit. 1846. 17.5cm. [*NUC*]. *SC*.599.

————. Iberia won; a poem descriptive of the Peninsular War; with impressions from recent visits to the battle-grounds and copious historical and illustrative notes. 1847. 12°. *SC*.568: "8vo."

Hulsius, Antonius. Antonii Hulsii ... Compendium lexici hebraici ... Editio 3^a ... Ultrajecti, 1674. 12°. [*BN*]. *SC*.385: "(*S.T.C.W.W.*)."

Hume, David. The history of England, from the invasion of Julius Caesar to the Revolution in 1688. A new edition, with the author's last corrections and improvements. To which is prefixed a short account of his life, written by himself. 13 vol. in 7. 1793-94. 14cm. [NIC:Ann]. *SC*.45: "13 vols., 1793." MC.57: "Hume's History of Eng: 13 Vol:" LB.29: "Hume Eng^d vol 13." For continuations see Smollett, Tobias and Barlow, J.

————. Political discourses. Edinburgh, 1752. 8°. *SC*.46: "8vo, 1782 [*sic*]."

Hume, George. Firstlings of fancy; or, poems on various subjects. Edinburgh. 8°. [*L*: "*With autograph of William Wordsworth*"]. *SC*.567: "12mo."

Hunt, afterwards De Vere, Sir Aubrey. The Duke of Mercia; an historical drama [in five acts and in verse]. The lamentations of Ireland and other poems. 1823. 8°. *SC*.504: "*(with Autograph Presentation).*" [? LB.29: "Sir Aubrey ... de Vere's Poems"].

————. A song of faith, Devout exercises and sonnets. 1842. 8°. [? LB.29: "Sir Aubrey ... de Vere's Poems"]. See *LY*, 409.

[Hunt, Freeman]. Letters about the Hudson River and its vicinity. Written in 1835 & 1836 ... By a citizen of New York [Freeman Hunt]. New York, Boston, 1836. 16cm. [*NUC*]. *SC*.174: "12mo, 1836."

Hunt, James Henry Leigh. See Chaucer.

————. The descent of liberty; a mask. 1815. 8°. *SC*.582: "*(with Presentation Autog, etc.).*" MC.51: "Hunts Desc: of Liberty:"

————. Imagination and fancy; or, selections from the English poets illustrative of those first requisites of their art; with markings of the best passages, critical notices of the writers, and an essay in answer to the question "What is Poetry?" 1844. 12°. LB.35: "Imag^n & Fancy."

————. A legend of Florence. A play, in five acts [and in verse]. 1840. 8°. *SC*.569.

————. The poetical works of Leigh Hunt. 1832. 8°. [WL:Ann]. LB.59: "Hunts Poems."

————. The reflector; a quarterly magazine on subjects of philosophy, politics, and the liberal arts. Conducted by the editor of The examiner [Leigh Hunt]. 2 vol. 1811. 21.5cm. [*NUC*].

SC.417: "2 vols., 8vo ... 1811." MC.79: "Reflector: 2 Vol:"

Hunter, Christopher. See Durham Cathedral.

Hunter, Joseph. See Cartwright, Thomas.

[————]. Who wrote Cavendish's Life of Wolsey? [By the Rev. Joseph Hunter]. 1814. 4°. *SC*.451.

————, ed. Ecclesiastical documents: viz. I A brief history of the bishoprick of Somerset from its foundation to the year 1174. II Charters from the library of Dr. Cox Macro. Now first published by the Rev. Joseph Hunter. 1840. 8°. *SC*.15.

Hunter, Thomas. Reflections critical and moral on the Letters of the late Earl of Chesterfield. 1776. 8°. *SC*.387. MC.81: "Hunter on Lord Chesterfield:"

Huntingford, George Isaac. See Moseley, William.

Huntington, Jedediah Vincent. Poems. New York, 1843. 12°. *SC*.568.

Huntley, afterwards Sigourney, Lydia. Letters to young ladies; [? with an introductory essay by Joseph Belcher. 1834. 16°]--[? new ed.; with two additional letters. 1841. 8°]. LB.30: "Letter [*sic*] to Young Ladies Mrs Sigourney [lent in autumn of 1843]."

————. Pocahontas, and other poems. New York, 1844. 12°. *SC*.581: "Poems by Mrs. Sigourney; by Mrs. Coulton; and by Thomas Powell, 1844."

[Hurd, Richard]. Moral and political dialogues; being the substance of several conversations between divers eminent persons of the past and present age ... now first published from the original MSS. With ... notes by the editor [Richard Hurd]. 1759. 8°. *SC*.427.

————. Moral and political dialogues with letters on chivalry and romance. 3rd ed. 3 vol. 1765. 8°. *SC*.386: "Discourses [*sic*]."

Hurwitz, Hyman. A Hebrew dirge, chaunted in the Great Synagogue, St. James' Place, Aldgate on the day of the funeral of the Princess Charlotte. With a translation in English verse by S.T. Coleridge. 1817. 8°. *SC*.257.

————. Vindiciae Hebraicae; or, a defence of the Hebrew Scriptures, as a vehicle of revealed religion: occasioned by the ... strictures ... of ... J. Bellamy; and in confutation of his attacks on all preceding translations. 1820. 8°. *SC*.257: "(*W. Wordsworth, Rydal Mount*)."

Hutcheson, Frances, the Elder. An inquiry into the original of our ideas of beauty and virtue. 1726. 8°. [*LLA*]. *SC*.387: "1726." MC.82: "Hutchinson [*sic*] on Beauty:"

Hutchinson, John. See Hutchinson, Mrs. Lucy.

Hutchinson, Mrs. Lucy. Memoirs of the life of Colonel [John] Hutchinson, Governor of Nottingham Castle and town ... with original anecdotes of many ... of his contemporaries, and a summary review of public affairs ... Published from the original manuscript by [Colonel] J[ohn] Hutchinson ... To which is prefixed The life of Mrs. [Lucy] Hutchinson written by herself, a fragment. 1806. 4°. LB.37: "Mrs Col Hutchinsons Memoirs." [Copy in *L* has MS. notes by STC].

Hutchinson, Thomas. See Xenophon.

Hutton, Mrs. Margaret. See Kugler, Franz Theodor.

Hyde, Edward, 1st Earl of Clarendon. The history of the rebellion and civil wars in England, begun in the year 1641. With the precedent passages, and actions, that contributed thereunto, and the happy end, and conclusion thereof by the King's blessed

Restoration, and return upon the 29th of May, in the year 1660. Written by the Right Honourable Earl of Clarendon. Oxford, 1705 [-06]. 3 vol. in 6. 22cm. [*NUC*]. *SC*.19: "vol. 1 (pts. I and II) and vol. 3 (pts. I and II) 4 vols. 1705, and 1706." MC.58: "Hist: of Rebellion: 3$^{rd}_{ll}$ & 5$^{th}_{ll}$ w$^{g}_{h}$." LB.58: "Two 1st vols of Clarendon's Hist. of the Rebellion."

————. The life of Edward Earl of Clarendon, Lord High Chancellor of England, and Chancellor of the University of Oxford. Containing, I. An account of the Chancellor's life from his birth to the Restoration. I. A continuation of the same and of his History of the Grand Rebellion, from the Restoration to his banishment in 1667. Written by himself. Printed from his original manuscripts, given to the University of Oxford by the heirs of the late Earl of Clarendon. 3 vol. Dublin, 1760. 21cm. [*NUC*]. [ICU: "Our set of the 1760 *Life* of Clarendon has separate title pages for each of the three volumes ... all dated 1759, while the general title page is dated 1760"]. *SC*.100: "3 vols., 8vo ... Dublin, 1759." MC.57: "Life of Lord Clarendon 3 vols." LB.6: "Clarendon's Life Vol I."

Hyginus, Caius Julius. Fabularum liber. Lugd[uni] Bat[avorum] et Amstel[odami], 1670. 12°. *SC*.570: "12mo ... *Lugd. Bat.*, 1670."

*Hymns for the sick and lonely by a Lady. *SC*.453.

I., R.H. See Thornton, Henry.

Ibbot, Benjamin. A course of sermons preach'd for the lecture founded by ... R[obert] Boyle ... in the years 1713 and 1714 ... To which is added a list of the ... persons who have preached the said lecture from its beginning. 1727. 8°. *SC*.251. MC.29: "Ibbott's [*sic*] Sermons."

Idrison. See Owen, afterwards Owen Pugh(e), William.

Ingelo, Nathaniel. Bentivolio and Urania. The second
    part. 1664. fol. [Ox]. *SC*.388: "1694." MC.88/
    0: "Bentivolio & Urania:"

Ingemann, Bernhard Severin. Waldemar, surnamed Seir;
    or, the victorious. Translated from the Danish
    ... by a lady [Miss Janes Frances Chapman]. 3 vol.
    1841. 12°. *SC*.695: "8vo ... (*from the Author*)."

Inglis, Sir Robert Harry. See Thornton, Henry.

————. On the Roman Catholic Question. Substances
    of two speeches delivered in the House of Commons
    on May 10, 1825, and May 9, 1828. London, Oxford,
    1828. 8°. *SC*.33.

An inquiry concerning faith. 1744. 8°. *SC*.199. MC.
    25: "Enquir: into Faith: John [Wordsworth]."

*Introduction to the game of chess. [? An easy intro-
    duction to the game of chess; containing one hundred
    examples of games, including the whole of Philli-
    dor's Analysis. 12°. 1813]. [*BB*]. *SC*.432:
    "Introduction to the Game of Chess, 8vo." MC.83:
    "Game of Chess:"

*Introduction to the grammar of the Latin tongue.
    SC.371: "1733." MC.13: "Introd: to Lat: Gram:"

*Introduction to the Latin tongue. MC.15: "Introduc-
    tion to the Latin Tongue:" cf. *SC*.371: "Introduc-
    tion to the Grammar of the Latin Tongue, 1733."

*Irish tour. LB.9: "Irish tour [lent Jan. 1828]."

Irvine, William, the Elder. Letters on Sicily. [? Edi-
    ted by John Dunlop]. 1813. 8°. *SC*.399.

Irving, David. See Fergusson, Robert.

Irving, Edward. For the oracles of God, four orations.
    For judgment to come, an argument, in nine parts.
    2nd ed. 1823. 8°. *SC*.234.

Isocrates. Ad Demonicum de officiis, ex interpretatione H[ieronymi] Wolfii. Parisiis, 1815. 12°. [*BN*].
SC.389: "*no title* ... small 4to."

————. Isocratis Orationes duae: 1. Ad Demonicum.
2. Ad Nicoclem. Editio secunda aucta et emendata.
Studio et opera G. Sylvani. Oxonii, 1677. 15cm.
[MA:Ann]. *SC*.350: "1677 ... *Autograph*." MC.4:
"Isocratis Orat: duae:"

Isola, Agostino. See Pieces of Italian poetry; Tasso,
Torquato. The Gerusalemme Liberata.

*Italian dictionary. MC.18: "Ital: Dicty:" [? Grag-
lia's]. [? LB.20].

*Italian grammar. MC.18: "Ital: Grammar." [? Grag-
lia's]. [? LB.20].

Jabet, George [Warwick, Eden, *pseud*.]. The poets'
pleasaunce; or garden of all sorts of pleasant
flowers, which our pleasant poets have, in past
time, for pastime, planted. 1847. 8°. LB.49:
"Poets' Plesance."

Jackson, William. Thirty letters on various subjects.
3rd ed., with ... additions. 1795. 8°. *SC*.158.

Jacob, Giles. A new law-dictionary. 1736. fol.
[*NUC*]. *SC*.391. MC.38: "Jacob's Law Dict.y:"

James, George Payne Rainsford. Adra, or the Peruvians;
the ruined city, etc. 1829. 8°. *SC*.597.

James Hatfield and the Beauty of Buttermere; a story
of modern times. 3 vol. 1841. 12°. *SC*.550:
"8vo." LB.39.

James the First, King of England. An apologie for the
oath of allegiance. (Triplici nodo triplex cuneus.
Against the two Breves of Pope Paulus Quintus, and

the late Letter of Cardinall Bellarmine to G. Black-
wel.) First set forth without a name; and now
acknowledged by the author ... James ... King of
Great Britain. Together with a Premonition of his
Majesties to all ... Monarches ... of Christendome.
1609. 4°. *SC*.47. MC.39: "K: James' Oath of
Alleg:"

[Jamieson, Robert]. The broken heart: a metrical tale
in three parts. 2nd ed. Edinburgh, 1833. 18cm.
[MA:Ann]. [*L*: "The Broken Heart: a metrical tale.
(The Vision of Feridoon, an Indian ballad.) *Edinburgh*, 1833. 12°"]. *SC*.524: "The Broken Heart,
1843 [*sic*]." LB.33: "Broken Heart."

Jebb, John. See Burnet, Gilbert; Phelan, William.

Jeffery, John. See Browne, Sir Thomas. Christian
morals.

Jenkins, David. Jenkinsius redivivus; or, the works
of ... Judge Jenkins, whilst a prisoner in the
Tower ... Wherein is plainly set forth, the just
power and prerogative of the King, the privilege
of Parliament, the liberty of the Subject, and
what is treason. 1681. 12°. *SC*.47. MC.39:
"Jenkinsius redivivus:"

Jerdan, William. Letters from James Earl of Perth,
Lord Chancellor of Scotland ... to his sister,
the Countess of Erroll, and other members of his
family. Edited by William Jerdan. 1845. 8°.
SC.15.

————. Rutland papers. Original documents illustrative of the courts and times of Henry VII. and
Henry VIII. Selected from the private archives of
his Grace the Duke of Rutland. By William Jerdan.
1842. 8°. *SC*.15.

Jerome, Saint. See Bible, Holy; Hieronymus, Saint.

Jewel, John. Apologia Ecclesiae Anglicanae. 1599.
12°. *SC*.191: "16mo." MC.27/0: "Apologia Ecclesias:
Anglic:"

Jewsbury, afterwards Fletcher, Maria Jane. Letters to
the young. 1828. 12°. LB.13.

————. Phantasmagoria; or sketches of life and literature. 2 vol. 1825. 8°. LB.8.

————. The three histories; the history of an enthus-
iast, the history of a nonchalant, the history of
a realist. 1830. 8°. LB.14.

*Jocelin, Sophia. *SC*.604: "My Dream Book, etc., by
Sophia Jocelin, 1847."

Jocelinus, de Brakelonda. Chronica Jocelini de Brakelonda, de rebus gestis Samsonis Abbatis monasterii
Sancti Edmundi. Edited by John Gage Rokewode.
1840. 8°. *SC*.15.

Johnes, Arthur James. See Dafydd, ap Gwilym.

Johns, Charles Alexander. Flora sacra; or, the knowledge of the works of nature conducive to the
knowledge of the God of Nature. [With specimens
of mosses]. 1840. 16°. *SC*.142.

Johnson, John. See Cowper, William. Poems.

[————]. The clergy-man's vade-mecum; or, an account
of the ancient and present Church of England. 5th
ed. 1723. 12°. [*NUC*]. *SC*.282. MC.22: "Clergyman's Vade Mecum 2 Cop:"

Johnson, Samuel, LL.D. See Collins, William; Savage,
Richard.

————. A dictionary of the English language. 8th
ed. 2 vol. 1786. 8°. *SC*.392. MC.18: "Johnson's Dicty: 2 Vols:"

[————]. A journey to the Western Islands of Scotland. [By Samuel Johnson]. 1775. 8°. MC.70: "Johnson's Journey to West: Islands:"

————. The lives of the most eminent English poets, with critical observations on their works. 4 vol. 1781. 8°. MC.43: "Bell's Poets: 109 Vol: with Johnson's Lives 4 Vol:" See Bell, John.

————. The rambler. 3 vol. 1824. 12°. *SC*.414. LB.55.

————. Rasselas. (Vol. 26 of The British novelists). *SC*.515. MC.87: "Rascilas [*sic*]." LB.55.

Johnson, Thomas. See Pufendorf, Samuel von, Baron.

Johnston, Charles. Sonnets, original and translated. 1823. 8°. *SC*.517.

Johnston, Nathaniel. The excellency of monarchical government, especially of the English monarchy; wherein is ... treated of the several benefits of kingly government and the inconvenience of commonwealths ... the several badges of sovereignty in general. 1686. fol. *SC*.48. MC.38: "Johnson [*sic*] on Monarch [*sic*] Gov:"

Johnstone, William. The table talker; or brief essays on society and literature. 2 vol. 1840. 16°. LB.55.

Joly, Marc Antoine. See Poquelin de Molière, Jean Baptiste.

[Jones, David]. A compleat history of Europe; or, a view of the affairs thereof, civil and military, from the beginning of the treaty of Nimeguen, 1676, to the end of the year, 1700. 3rd ed., corrected and enlarged. Written by a gentleman, who kept an exact journal of all transactions, for above these twenty years. 1701. 19.5cm. [*NUC*: "First published 1698, anonymously, bringing narrative

down to 1697 only. The 4th ed. 1705 forms v. 5
of the author's compleat history of Europe ... from
1600 to ... Queen Anne's death"]. *SC*.28: "A Complete History of Europe, from the beginning of the
Treaty of Nimeguen, 1676, to the end of the year
1700--17 vols., 8vo, calf, 1705." [But number of
vols. in this lot is given as "1"]. [? MC.57:
"History of Europe: 13 Vol:"].

[Jones, Ernest Charles]. The student of Padua. A domestic tragedy. [By Ernest Charles Jones]. In
five acts [and in verse]. [London], 1836. 12°.
SC.621.

Jones, John. Attempts in verse ... with some account
of the writer, written by himself, and an introductory essay on the lives and works of our uneducated
poets, by Robert Southey, Poet Laureate. 1831.
8°. [CSmH.ZZB:Ann]. *SC*.572. LB.23: "Uneducated
Poets."

Jonson, Ben. The works of Ben Jonson with a memoir
of his life and writings by Barry Cornwall [Bryan
Waller Procter]. 1838. 8°. *SC*.573.

Josephus, Flavius. The genuine works of Flavius
Josephus ... translated by William Whiston ...
with notes ... by Samuel Burder. 2 vol. 1812.
4°. *SC*.84: "n.d." [? LB.55: "Josephus"].

————. *SC*.291: "The Wars of the Jews, by Josephus,
2 vols., 1825." [? LB.55: "Josephus"].

Judkin, Thomas James. Church and home psalmody; being
a collection of Psalms from the Old and New Ver-
sions, and original hymns. 1831. 12°. *SC*.302.

*Jurisprudence. [? *SC*.16: "three other books, *each with
Autog. of the late Laureate*"]. [? *SC*.57: "three
other books"].

Justinus, the Historian. [? De historiis Philippicis,
et totius mundi originibus ... notis illustravit

P[etrus] J[osephus] Cantel[ius] ... in usum ...
Delphini. Huic editioni accessere J[acques] Bon-
garsii exceptiones chronologicae ad Justin histor-
ias accommodatae. 1750. 8°]. MC.4: "Justinus."

Juvenalis, Decimus Junius. D. Iun. Iuvenalis et Auli
Persii Flacci Satyrae, ex doct: virorum emendatio-
ne. Hagae-Comitum et Roterdami, 1683. 4.5 in.
[*CWC*:Ann]. [? MC.4: "Juvenalis"].

————. D.J. Juvenalis and A. Persius Flaccus translated and illustrated ... by Barten Holyday. Oxford, 1673. fol. *SC*.561. MC.91: "Holiday's [*sic*]
Juvenal:"

————. The Satires of D.J. Juvenalis. Translated
into English verse. By Mr. Dryden. And ... other
hands. Together with the Satires of Aulus Persius
Flaccus. Made English by Mr. Dryden ... To which
is prefix'd a discourse concerning the original
and progress of Satir ... Third ed. 1702. 8°.
SC.417. MC.91: "Dryden's Juvenal:"

K., B. See Keach, Benjamin.

[Kavanagh, Morgan Peter]. The reign of Lockrin, a
poem. (Present state of English literature. Notes
thereon). [By Morgan Peter Kavanagh]. 1839. 8°.
SC.524.

[Keach, Benjamin]. The glorious lover. A divine poem,
upon the adorable mystery of sinners redemption.
By B[enjamin] K[each], author of war with the Devil.
4th ed., with additions. 1696. 16°. *SC*.519:
"8vo." MC.54: "Glorious Lover--Sinner's Redem:"

Keats, John. See Coleridge, Samuel Taylor. The poetical works of Coleridge, Shelley, and Keats.

————. Poems. 1817. 19cm. [*NUC*]. [? MC.48: "Poems
by J: Keates [*sic*]:" [*MY*, II, 578 (WW to B.R.

Haydon, 16 Jan. 1820): "How is Keates [*sic*]"]. [WR:
"The first edition of Keats's 'Poems', 1817, is inscribed on the title 'To W. Wordsworth with the
author's sincere reverence'"]. [? LB.27: "Keats's
Poems"].

Keble, John. De poeticae vi medica; praelectiones
academicae Oxonii habitae annis 1832-1841. 2 vol.
Oxonii, 1844. 8°. *SC*.393. LB.50: "Praelectiones
Academicae 2 Vols."

[————]. Lyra innocentium; thoughts in verse on
Christian children, their ways and their privileges.
Oxford, 1846. 8°. [WL:Ann]. LB.39: "Lyra Inno-
centium."

The Keepsake. See Reynolds, Frederic Mansel.

Keith, Alexander. Evidence of the truth of the Christian religion, derived from the literal fulfilment
of prophecy. 10th ed. Edinburgh, 1833. 12°.
SC.234: "8vo."

Kelly, James. A complete collection of Scottish proverbs, explained and made intelligible to the English reader. 1721. 8°. MC.81: "Kelly's Proverbs:"

Kemble, John Mitchell. See Twysden, Sir Roger.

à Kempis, Thomas. De imitatione Christi. [Edition
not known]. LB.58. cf. MC.26: "De Imitando
Christo."

Kennedy, Rann and Charles Rann. See Virgilius Maro,
Publius.

Kenyon, John. Poems for the most part occasional.
1838. 8°. *SC*.595.

[————]. Rhymed plea for tolerance. In two dialogues.
With a prefatory dialogue. 1833. 17.5cm. [MA:
Ann]. *SC*.574: "sm 4to 1839."

Ker, John. Selectarum de lingua Latina observationum libri duo. Prior inscribitur Latine loquendi norma ... Posterior barbare, vitioseve loquendi consuetudinem investigat, patefacit, emendat. 2 pts. 1709, 08. 8°. [RPB.HLKC: "1708-09 [2 vols. in 1] ... presentation inscription from Hartley Coleridge to William Wordsworth"]. *SC*.365: "(*with MS. note, by H. Headley, Trin. Coll., Oxon.*), 1783, *and Autograph Presentation, 'Hartley Coleridge to William Wordsworth, May* 1827.'" [? MC.11: "Select: Observa: de Lingua Latina:"].

————. [Another copy]. *SC*.446: "Selectarium Lingue Latinum, 8vo, 1709." [? MC.11: "Select: Observa: de Lingua Latina:"].

Kidder, Daniel Parish. See Sketches of the Waldenses.

[King, John Meyers]. The parson's home; a poem. By an English vicar [John Meyers King]. 1849. 16°. *SC*.620.

King, Walker. See Burke, Edmund.

Kirby, William and William Spence. An introduction to entomology; or, elements of the natural history of insects. 4 vol. 1815-26. 8°. [DD:Ann]. MC.75: "Introduction to Entomol:" LB.15: "Kirby & Spence."

Kircher, Athanasius. Iter extaticum II qui et mundi subterranei prodromus dicitur, quo geoscomi opificium sive terrestris globi structura, una cum abditis in ea constitutis arcanioris naturae reconditoriis, per ficti raptus integumentum exponitur ... in 3 dialogos distinctum. Romae, 1657. 4°. [*BN*]. *SC*.263. MC.16: "Kircher: Prodromus:"

————. Principis christiani archetypon politicum, sive sapientia regnatrix, quam ... symbolicis obvelatim integumentis ... exponit Athanasius Kircherus. Amstelodami, 1672. 4°. [*BN*]. [Catalogue of T.D. Webster, Mere Manor, Diss, Norfolk, published Sept. 1959, Item 584: "sm 4to ... Amster-

dam, 1672 ... A note inside upper cover, initialed
W.P.R., states that the book was bought at the Rydal Mount Library sale. Worksworth's [*sic*] signature appears twice, on verso of end leaf and on
first page of text of dedication; Coleridge's
initials appear in top margin of portrait." (Information furnished by A.G. Lee, Librarian, St.
John's College, Cambridge)]. *SC*.262: "4to ...
Amsterdam, 1672." MC.34/C: "Christ: Architypon
[*sic*]."

Kirkby, John. The capacity and extent of the human
understanding exemplified in the extraordinary case
of Automathes, a young nobleman,... accidentally
left in his infancy upon a desolate island. 1745.
12°. *SC*.432: "Automata (by a native of Cumberland,
tutor of Gibbon the historian), no title." MC.88:
"Automathes:"

[? Kirkton, James. The secret and true history of the
Church of Scotland from the Restoration to the
year 1678 ... To which is added, an account of the
murder of Archbishop Sharp, by James Russell, an
actor therein. Edited from the MSS. by C[harles]
K[irkpatrick] Sharpe. Edinburgh, 1817. 4°].
MC.60: "Secret History:" See Crouch, Nathaniel.

Klauer-Klattowsky (or Klattovsky), Wilhelm. A comprehensive grammar of the German language ... in two
synoptical tables. [? 1843]. 2 folding tables in
case. 12°. [*NUC*]. *SC*.358: "A comprehensive grammar on a new plan, by W.K. Klattorsky [*sic*], in
pocket case."

————. The German manual for the young and for self-
tuition. 2 vol. 1845. 8°. LB.40: "German
Manuel [*sic*] 2 Vols. Klattowsky's."

*Der kleine Engländer, Englisch and Deutsch. Berlin,
1826. *SC*.362.

Knapton, James. See Bianchi, Vendramino.

The knickerbocker; or New York monthly magazine. Vols. 1-60. New York, 1833-62. 8°. *SC*.394: "vols. 7 & 8, ... 1836."

Knight, Charles. See The penny magazine.

————. Half-hours with the best authors; selected and arranged, with short biographical and critical notices, by Charles Knight. 4 vol. 1847-48. 8°. LB.44.

Knight, Paul Slade. Observations on the causes, symptoms and treatment of derangement of the mind ... With the particulars of the sensations and ideas of a gentleman during his mental alienation, written by himself during his convalescence. 1827. 8°. *SC*.140.

Knight, Richard Payne. An analytical inquiry into the principles of taste. 1806. 8°. See STC entry. .

Knowles, James Sheridan. The hunchback, a play in five acts, [chiefly in verse]. 1832. 8°; 2nd ed. 1832. 8°. *SC*.676: "1832."

[Knox, Vicesimus]. Elegant epistles; or, A copious collection of familiar and amusing letters, selected for the improvement of young persons, and for general entertainment, from Cicero, Pliny, Sydney ... and many others ... 1790. 23.5cm. *NUC*. *SC*.368. MC.80: "Elegant Epistles:"

[————]. Elegant extracts: or useful and entertaining pieces of poetry selected for the improvement of youth, etc. [c. 1770]. 8°. *SC*.619. MC.44: "Elegant Extracts: 2 Cop:" LB.36.

Knox, William. The lonely hearth, and other poems. North Shields, 1818. 12°. MC.48: "Knox' Lonely Hearth:"

Komenský, Jan Amos. Orbis Sensualium pictus ... J.A. Commenius's visible world ... translated into

English by C[harles] Hoole. 12th ed. 1777. 8°.
SC.170: "... *with the late Laureate's Autograph*."
MC.13: "Comenius's Visib: World:"

Krasinski, Henryk, Count. The Poles in the seventeenth
century. An historical novel. With a sketch of
the Polish Cossacks. 3 vol. 1843. 12°. *SC*.575.
[? LB: "History of the Poles 2 vol"].

Krasinski, Walerjan Skorobohaty, Count. Historical
sketch of the rise, progress, and decline of the
Reformation in Poland, and of the influence which
the Scriptural doctrines have exercised on that
country in literary, moral, and political respects.
2 vol. 1838-40. 8°. [RPB.HLKC:Ann]. *SC*.261.
[? LB: "History of the Poles 2 vol: "].

————. [Another copy]. *SC*.281.

Krummacher, Friedrich Wilhelm. Elisha; from the German. Revised by R[obert] F[rancis] Walker. [?
1838. 12°]. [? 1839, 8°]. *SC*.255. [n.d.].

Kugler, Franz Theodor. A hand-book of the history of
painting, from the age of Constantine the Great to
the present time. Translated from the German by a
lady [Mrs. Margaret Hutton]. In two parts. Part
I.--The Italian schools of painting. Edited, with
notes, by C.L. Eastlake. 1842. 20.5cm. [*NUC*; *L*].
[Paul F. Betz:Ann]. *SC*.535: "(*Autograph Presentation by the Editor*)." LB.35: "Eastlakes book upon
Painting."

Laborde, Alexander Louis Joseph de, Count. A view of
Spain; comprising a descriptive itinerary of each
province, and a general statistical account of the
country ... translated from the French of A. de L.
(Atlas). 5 vol. 1809. 8°. *SC*.131. MC.71: "La-
bourd's [*sic*] View of Spain 5 Vol: with Atlas:"
LB.7: "1st vol of Laborde & Map."

[La Curne de Sainte-Palaye, Jean Baptiste de]. Histoire littéraire des troubadours. [Edited by Claude François Xavier Millot]. 3 vol. Paris, 1774. 12°. *SC*.82: "8vo." MC.98: "Hist: des Troubadours:"

A lady. See Finch, Anne; Hutton, Mrs. Margaret; Hymns for the sick and lonely; Ingemann, Bernhard Severin; R., E.

Laet, Johannes de. See Smith, Sir Thomas.

Lafontaine, August Heinrich Julius. Les querelles de famille. Traduit de l'allemand par M. [Jean Baptiste Joseph] Breton [de la Martinière]. 2 vol. Paris, 1809. 17cm. [*NUC*]. *SC*.534: "3 tomes (*in one*), 1809." MC.100: "Quarelles [*sic*] de Famelle [*sic*]:"

Lafontaine, Jean de. Les amours de Psyché et de Cupidon, avec le Poëme d'Adonis. Paris, 1801. 16mo. [WL:Ann]. [In Bibliothèque portative du voyageur]. MC.100: "Amours Par la Fontaine:"

————. Contes et nouvelles en vers. 2 tomes. [? 1781. 12°]. *SC*.533: "2 tomes, 12mo [n.p., n.d.]." MC.98: "Contes et Nouvelles par M: de la Fontayne [*sic*] 2 Vol:"

————. Fables choisies, mise en vers; avec un nouveau commentaire par M. [Pierre] Coste. Paris, 1785. 24°. [Also, Lafontaine's Philémon et Baucis]. [*NUC*]. *SC*.533: "8vo, 1785 [n.p.]."

[Laing, David]. Early metrical tales; including The history of Sir Egeir, Sir Gryme, and Sir Gray-Steill. [Edited by David Laing]. Edinburgh, 1826. 8°. *SC*.429.

La Live d'Épinay, Louise F.P. de. [? Les conversations d'Émilie. 2 tom. Lausanne, 1784. 12°]--[? The conversations of Emily. Translated from the French. 2 vol. 1787]. LB.19: "2 vols of 'Emilie.'" See *EY*, p. 8, n. 1.

Lalor, John. Prize essays on the expediency and means of elevating the profession of the educator in society. By John Lalor, Esq., J.A. Heraud, Esq., Rev. E. Higginson, J. Simpson, Esq., Mrs. G.R. Porter. 1839. 12°. *SC*.356.

Lamb, Charles. The works of Charles Lamb. 2 vol. 1818. 8°. LB.9: "2 vols Lambs W^{rks}."

————. The works of Charles Lamb. With a sketch of his life by T.N. Talfourd. 3 vols. 1838. LB.28: "C Lamb with a sketch of his life--by T. Noon Talfourd 2 vols."

————. The adventures of Ulysses (In The juvenile library). [1808]. 12°. MC.83: "Lambs Advent: of Ulysses:"

————. Album verses, with a few others. 1830. 12°. *SC*.543 [n.p., n.d.].

[————]. Elia. Essays which have appeared under that signature in the London magazine. 1823. 8°. [CWW: signed "Wm Wordsworth"]. [? LB.30: "Elia Lambs"].

[————]. [Another copy]. [MB:Ann: "19cm. First edition, first issue"]. [? LB.30: Elia Lambs"].

————. Final memorials of Charles Lamb, consisting of his letters not before published ... By T.N. Talfourd. 2 vol. 1848. 12°. *SC*.578: "2 vols., 1838 [*sic*]." LB.43: "Talfourds Lamb 2 vols [lent in late 1848 or early 1849]."

————. John Woodvil; a tragedy [in five acts, and in prose and verse] ... To which are added, Fragments of Burton, the author of The anatomy of melancholy [purporting to be "extracted from a commonplace book, which belonged to Robert Burton," but really written by Charles Lamb]. 1802. 12°. *SC*.663. MC.52: "Lamb's John Woodville [*sic*]."

[————]. The last essays of Elia. Being a sequel to the essays published under that name. 1833. 19cm. [MB:Ann]. LB.18: "Elia 2^d vol [i.e. part; lent May 24, 1834, "Elia 1st p^t" having been lent on May 15]."

————. The letters of Charles Lamb, with a sketch of his life by Thomas Noon Talfourd. 2 vol. 1837. 8°. [WL:Ann]. *SC*.578. LB.22: "Lambs letters [lent in early August, 1837]."

————. The poetical works of Charles Lamb [with six poems by Mary Lamb]. A new edition. 1836. 8°. *SC*.577: "12mo."

————. The prose works of Charles Lamb. 3 vol. First collected edition. 1835. [*NUC*]. *SC*.577: "12mo." LB.22: "Lamb's prose Works 3 vols."

————. Specimens of English dramatic poets who lived about the time of Shakespeare. With notes. By Charles Lamb. 2 vol. [? 1835. 8°]--[? 1844. 14cm. *NUC*]. *SC*.576: "2 vols., 12mo, 1845 [*sic*]." MC.52: "do: [Lamb's] Spec: of Dram: [probably the one-volume edition of 1808, 8°, or that of 1813, 8°]."

————. A tale of Rosamund Gray and old blind Margaret. 1798. 12°. MC.88: "Lamb's Rosamund Gray:"

[———— and Mary]. Mrs. Leicester's school; or, the history of several young ladies, related by them-selves. 2nd ed. 1809. 17.5cm. [MB:Ann]. MC.88: "Mrs: Leicester's School:"

Lamb, Mary. See Lamb, Charles. The poetical works; Lamb, Charles and Mary.

Lambinus, Dionysius. See Cicero, Marcus Tullius. Epistolae.

La Mothe, Marie Catherine, Countess d'Aulnoy. Recueil des plus belles pièces des poëtes françois, tant

anciens que modernes, avec l'histoire de leur vie.
5 tomes. Paris, 1692. 8°. *SC*.633: "avec l'Histoire de leur Vies, par Mde. l'Anney [*sic*], 5
tomes, *Amsterdam*, 1692." [Brunet cites a reprint-
ing by G. Gallet at Amsterdam, 1692, 5 vol. 12°].
MC.102: "Recueil de Poetes 5 vol:"

La Motte Fouqué, Friedrich Heinrich Karl de, Baron.
Romantic fiction: select tales from the German of
De la Motte Fouqué and others. [? 1843]. 16°.
LB.33: "German Tales." LB.38: "Romantic Fiction
from the German."

————. The seasons: four romances from the German
(I. Undine II. The two captains. III. Aslauga's
knight. IV. Sintram). 4 pt. 1843. 8°. LB.35:
"The Seasons Fouqué."

————. Undine. A romance, translated from the German [of F.H.C. de la Motte Fouqué]. By G[eorge]
Soane. 1818. 20cm. [*NUC*]. LB.38: "Fouché's
[*sic*] Undine."

Lancaster, Joseph. Improvements in education, as it
respects the industrious classes of the community:
containing a short account of its present state,
hints towards its improvement and a detail of some
practical experiments conducive to that end. 1803.
8°. MC.83: "Lancaster on Education."

Lancelot, Claude. See Epigrammatum delectus.

[Landor, Walter Savage]. Gebir; a poem [by W.S. Lan-
dor] in seven books. 1798. 8°. *SC*.523: "Gebir
[n.p., n.d.] (*with Autographs of Sir Humphrey Davy
and W.W.*)."

————. Idyllia heroica decem: librum Phaleuciorum
unum partim jam primo partim iterum atq. tertio
edit Savagius Landor. Accedunt quaestiuncula cur
poetae Latini recentiores minus legantur. Pisis,
1820. 8°. *SC*.579: "8vo, printed for private distribution only, no date (*Presentation Autograph*)."

————. Imaginary conversations of literary men and statesmen. First series. 2 vol. 1824. 23 cm. [NN.BC:Ann]. *SC*.395: "*1st series*--2 vols., 8vo, 1824." LB.6: "Landor's Conversations."

————. Imaginary conversations of literary men and statesmen. Second series. 2 vol. 1829. 24cm. [NN.BC:Ann]. *SC*.395: "*2nd series*--2 vols., 1829." LB.19: "Landors Imgy Conversations 3 vols."

————. Pericles and Aspasia. 2 vol. 1836. 12°. LB.20: "W.S. Landors Aspasia 2 vols."

Landseer, John. Lectures on the art of engraving, delivered at the Royal Institution of Great Britain. 1807. 8°. *SC*.551. MC.75: "Landseer on Engraving:"

Langhorne, John. See Collins, William. Poetical works.

Languet, Hubert. H. Langueti ... Epistolae politicae et historicae, scriptae quondam ad ... P. Sydnaeum, equitem Anglum ... In quibus variae rerum suo aevo in Germania, Italia, Gallia ... aliisque orbis Christiani provinciis ... gestarum, narrationes, consilia, et eventus describuntur ... Nunc vero primum publicis typis divulgatae. Francofurti, 1633. 12°. *SC*.86.

Larcom, Sir Thomas Aiskew. Ordnance survey of the County of Londonderry. Colonel [Thomas, later Major General] Colby superintendent. Volume 1. (Memoir of the city and North Western Liberties of Londonderry. Parish of Templemore). [By Sir T.A.L.]. [*L: "This is the first volume of a series of local memoirs intended to accompany the Ordnance Survey of Ireland, and appears to have been the only one published"*]. *SC*.102: "4to, 1837."

Lardner, Dionysius. See Herschel, Sir John.

La Rue, Charles. See Ruaeus, Carolus.

*Latin exercises. MC.13: "Lat Exerc:"

Latin grammar. See A short introduction to grammar.

Lauder, William. An essay on Milton's use and imitation of the moderns in his Paradise lost. 1750. 8°. *SC*.610. MC.80: "Lawder [*sic*] on Milton."

Law, Edmund. See A learned hand.

Law, William. A serious call to a devout and holy life, adapted to the state and condition of all orders of Christians. [? 1729. 8°]. *SC*.223 [n.p., n.d.]. MC.27: "Law's Call:"

Lawrence, Mrs. Rose. Cameos from the antique; or, the cabinet of mythology. Selections illustrative of the mythology of Greece, and Italy for the use of children, and intended as a sequel to The poetical primer. Liverpool, 1831. 12°. *SC*.459: "1831."

————. Cameos from the antique. Second edition, revised. Liverpool, London, 1849. 12°. *SC*.473.

————. [? The last autumn at a favourite residence, with other poems ... 2nd ed., with many additions. 1829. 20cm.]. [*NUC*]. *SC*.548: "Poems by Mrs. Lawrence, 1839 [*sic*]."

————. The last autumn at a favourite residence. With other poems. [? 3rd ed.]. Liverpool, 1836. 12°. *SC*.580: "8vo, 1836."

————. Pictures, scriptural, and historical; or, the cabinet of history. With poetical selections, religious and moral ... for the use of children, intended as a sequel to The poetical primer. Liverpool, 1831. 12°. *SC*.665.

Layard, Sir Austen. Nineveh and its remains: with an account of a visit to the Chaldean Christians of Kurdistan. 2 vol. 1849. 8°. LB.46: "Layard's Nineveh."

A layman. See Peter, William.

A learned hand [i.e. Daniel Waterland]. A dissertation
upon the argument à priori, for proving the existence of a First Cause. By a learned hand. [Pub-
lished as an appendix to Edmund Law, An enquiry
into the ideas of space, time, immensity, and eter-
nity]. Cambridge, 1734. 8°. [L; DNB under
"Waterland, Daniel"]. [? MC.28/X/Southey: "Waterland's Dissertat:"].

A learned priest. See Simon, Richard.

Leatham, William Henry. Poems. London, Wakefield,
1840. 8°. SC.617 [n.p., n.d.].

*Lebanon; a poem. 1819. 12°. MC.50: "Lebanon:"

Le Clerc, Georges Louis, Count de Buffon. The system
of natural history ... abridged. 2 vol. [? Perth,
1791. 8°]--[? London, 1792. 8°]. MC.76: "Natural
History: 2 Vol:"

Lecteur François. See Murray, Lindley.

Lefèbvre de Saint-Marc, Charles Hugues. See Anfrie
de Chaulieu, Guillaume.

Lefèvre, Raoul. The ancient historie of the destruc-
tion of Troy. Divided into III. bookes ... Also
mentioning the rising and flourishing of divers
kings and kingdoms, with the decay and ouerthrow
of others ... Translated out of French into English
by W[illiam] Caxton. The 6th ed., now newly corr
[ected] and amended. [Edited by William Phiston].
1636. 18.5cm. [NUC]. SC.17: "4to ... black
letter, 1636."

Le Grice, Charles Valentine. [? Analysis of Paley's
Principles of moral and political philosophy.
Cambridge, 1796. 8°]--[? Indications of the Creator. Extracts, bearing upon theology, from the
history and philosophy of the inductive sciences.
1845. 12°]. LB.38: "Le Griceys Vol. 2 [lent 11
Feb. 1847]."

Leigh, Chandos, Baron Leigh. Poems, now first collected. 1839. 8°. *SC*.637: "1836 [*sic*]."

————. Thoughts at Whitsuntide, and other poems.
1842. 8°. *SC*.581.

Leighton, Robert. The whole works of ... Robert Leighton. To which is prefixed a life of the author
by J[ohn] N[orman] Pearson. New ed. 4 vol. 1825.
8°. [*EU*]. *SC*.264. LB.29: "Leighton's Works."

Leland, Thomas. See Demosthenes.

Lemprière, John. Bibliotheca classica; or, a classical
dictionary, containing a full account of all the
proper names mentioned in antient authors. 7th ed.
1809. 8°. *SC*.321. MC.14: "Lampriere's [*sic*]
Classical Dicty:"

————. [Another copy]. *SC*.449: "Lempriere's
Classical Dictionary (*imperfect*), 8vo." MC.14:
"Lampriere's [*sic*] Dicty:" [? WL:Ann: "A classical dictionary with front pages gone. Text begins
with AC, 'place of Arcadia,' etc."].

Lennard, Samson. See Charron, Pierre; Perrin, Jean
Paul.

Le Sage, Alain René. Histoire de Gil Blas de Santil-
lane. 4 tom. Paris, 1794. 8°. [*NUC*]. *SC*.643.
MC.97: "Histoire de Gil Blas: 4 Vol:" LB.8: "Gil
Blas French."

[Leslie, Charles]. The snake in the grass; or, Satan
transformed into an angel of light. Discovering
the deep and unsuspected subtilty which is couched
under the pretended simplicity of many of the
principal leaders of those people call'd Quakers.
1696. 8°. MC.22: "Snake in the Grass: 2 Cop:"

Leslie, Charles Robert. Memoirs of the life of John
Constable, R.A., composed chiefly of his letters.
1843. 4°. LB.49: "Memoirs of the Life of John
Constable [lent 5 Dec. 1850]."

L'Estrange, Hamon. The reign of King Charles: an history faithfully and impartially delivered and disposed into annals. 1655. 28.5cm. [*NUC*]. *SC*.49. MC.59: "History of Ki: Charles:"

L'Estrange, Roger. See Erasmus, Desiderius.

Leveson-Gower, Lord Francis. See Egerton, Francis.

Lewis, David. Miscellaneous poems by several hands. Published by D[avid] Lewis. 1726. 8°. *SC*.505: "published by D. Lewis, 8vo, 1776 [*sic*]." MC.48: "Lewis' Miscel: Poems:"

Lewis, Thomas Taylor, ed. Letters of the Lady Brilliana Harley, wife of Sir Robert Harley, of Brampton Bryan, Knight of the Bath. With introduction and notes by Thomas Taylor Lewis. 1854. 8°. *SC*.15.

Leyden, John. Scenes of infancy; descriptive of Teviotdale. Edinburgh, 1803. 12°. *SC*.582. MC.47: "Leyden's Scenes of Inf:"

[————]. Scotish descriptive poems; with some illustrations of Scotish literary antiquities. [Edited by J.L.]. Edinburgh, 1803. 8°. [*L: "With the autograph of William Wordsworth"*]. *SC*.529: "(*Presentation Autograph of D. [sic] L., the intimate friend of Sir Walter Scott*)."

Lickbarrow, Isabella. Poetical effusions. Kendal, 1814. 8°. MC.54: "Lickbarrow's Poet: Effu: 2 Co:"

Liddell, Henry Thomas, Earl of Ravensworth. The wizard of the North; the vampire bride; and other poems. Edinburgh, 1833. 8°. *SC*.569.

*Liederbuch. MC.99: "Leiderbuch [*sic*]:"

*Life of a private gentleman. MC.65: "Life of a Private Gent:"

[? The life of Tamerlane the Great; with his wars against the great Duke of Moso, the King of China,

Bajazet the great Turk ... [By Samuel Clarke].
1653. 4°]--[? The History of the life of Tamer-
lane the Great ... written in Arabic by Alhacen
... Translated ... from the French of J. du Bec
[By Lionel Vane]. 1750. 8°]. MC.65: "Life of
Tamerlane: G^r:"

The light-horse drill; describing the several evolu-
tions in a progressive series, from the first rudiments to the manoeuvres of the squadron ... designed for the use of the privates and officers of
the Volunteer Corps of Great Britain. 1799. 4°.
[*BB*]. MC.75: "Light Horse Drill:" See *The Monthly
Magazine*, Sept., 1798, p. 214.

Lille, Jacques de. See Delille, Jacques Montanier.

Limborch, Philippus van. Theologia Christiana. Editio
quinta ... Amstelaedami, 1730. fol. *SC*.265.

Lindsay, Alexander William Crawford, 25th Earl of Crawford and 8th Earl of Balcarres. Ballads, songs and
poems, translated from the German. Wigan, 1841.
4°. *SC*.583.

————. Lives of the Lindsays; or, a memoir of the
Houses of Crawford and Balcarres ... To which are
added, extracts from the official correspondence
of Alex., sixth Earl of Balcarres, during the
Maroon War; together with personal narratives by
his brothers, the Hon. Robert, Colin, James, John,
and Hugh Lindsay. 4 vol. Wigan, 1840. 8°. *SC*.
132: *"with Author's Presentation Autograph."*

————. Progression by antagonism: a theory, involving
considerations touching the present position,
duties and destiny of Great Britain. 1846. 8°.
SC.33.

————. Sketches of the history of Christian art.
3 vol. 1847. 8°. LB.38: "Lord Lindsay's Christian Art 3 Vols."

Lindsay, Sir Coutts. Alfred, a drama [in three acts and in verse]. 1845. 8°. *SC*.473.

Lindsay, Sir David. The warkis of the famous and worthie knight, Sir David Lyndsay of the Mont. Glasgow, 1754. 12°. *SC*.519: "8vo." MC.45: "Works of Sir: D: Lindsay:"

————. A dialogue betweene Experience and a Courtier, of the miserable estate of the worlde ... nowe newly corrected, and made perfit Englishe ... Hereunto are anexid certaine other pithy posys of woorkes, inuented by the said knight. [In verse]. 1566. 4°. [*L*: "*The running title of the 'Dialog' is 'The first (secund, thrid, fourt) buke of the Monarche'*"]. *SC*.50: "The Monarchie ... folio ... 1566." MC.44: "Lindsay's Monarch:"

Lindsay, Robert, of Pitscottie. The history of Scotland, from 21 February, 1436, to March, 1565 ... To which is added a continuation, by another hand, till August, 1604. Edinburgh, 1728. fol. *SC*.46 [n.p., n.d.]: "8vo." MC.61/X: "Lindsey's [*sic*] Hist: of Scotland:"

Lindsey, Theophilus. See Advice from a bishop.

Linocerius, Geofredus (Vivarius). See Comes, Natalis.

Linocier, Geoffroi. See Linocerius, Geofredus.

Lippi, Lorenzo. Il malmantile racquistato. Venezia, 1788. 18cm. [*NUC*]. *SC*.584: "8vo ... 1788." MC. 101: "Il Malmantile:"

Lipsius, Justus. See Tacitus, Publius Cornelius.

The literary annual register; or, records of literature, domestic and foreign. 2 vol. 1808. 8°. *SC*.416: "Records of Literature, etc. etc. a bundle."

*A little book. LB.55: "A little book."

Littlebury, Isaac. See Herodotus.

Littleton, Adam. Linguae Latinae liber dictionarius
    quadripartitus. A Latine dictionary in four parts.
    1678. 4°. MC.12: "Littleton's Lat: Dict^{y}:--2 Cop:"

Livingstone, David. Cambridge lectures; together with
    a prefatory letter by Professor [Adam] Sedgwick;
    edited, with introduction, life of Dr. Livingstone,
    notes, and appendix, by W[illiam] Monk. Cambridge,
    1858. 8°. LB.61: "Livingstons Lectures."

Livius, Titus. See Machiavelli, Niccolò.

————. *SC*.348: "Livy ... *odd volume*." [? MC.4: "Livii
    Histor: 2$^{nd}_{"}$ Vol:"]--[? MC.4: "Livius--1$^{st}_{"}$ Vol:
    ["Livy H.C." in left margin]"].

Lloyd, Charles, the Elder. See Homer. Iliad, Odyssey;
    Horatius Flaccus, Quintus. Epistles.

Lloyd, Charles, the Younger. See Alfieri, Vittorio.

————. Desultory thoughts in London; Titus and Gisip-
    pus; with other poems. 1821. 12°. *SC*.586. See
    Ca.OTV.HD.

————. The Duke d'Ormond, a tragedy [in five acts
    and in verse]; and Beritola, a tale [in verse].
    1822. 12°. *SC*.586: "*(Presentation Autog. and
    Notes by the Laureate)*."

————. Edmund Oliver. 2 vol. Bristol, 1798. 8°.
    SC.587. MC.88: "Edm$^{d}_{"}$ Oliver 2 Vol:" LB.16: "Edmund
    Oliver."

————. Nugae canorae. Poems ... Third edition, with
    additions [including a sonnet by S.T. Coleridge].
    L: "FEW MSS. NOTES [by S.T. Coleridge]." 1819.
    8°. *SC*.586: "Lloyd's (Charles) Poems, 1819."
    MC.54: "Lloyd's Poems: 1819:"

————. [Another edition]. 1823. 8°. *SC*.514.

—————. Poetical essays on the character of Pope, as a poet and moralist; and on the language and objects most fit for poetry. 1821. 12°. *SC*.566. See CaOTV.HD.

—————. LB.9: "Lloyds works 8 vols [not a collected edition, but presumably individual titles]."

Lloyd, David. State-worthies, during the reigns of ... Henry VIII, Edward VI ... Mary ... Elizabeth, James ... Charles I. 2nd ed., with additions. 1670. 8°. *SC*.177. MC.64: "State Worthies:"

Llwyd, Angharad. A history of the Island of Mona or Anglesey ... being the prize essay ... at the Royal Eisteddfod ... 1832. (A brief sketch of the Royal Eisteddvod held at Beaumaris ... 1832, selected from the Bangor and Chester papers). Ruthin, 1833. 4°. *SC*.133.

Locke, John. See Churchill, Awnsham.

—————. A letter to ... Edward [Stillingfleet] Ld Bishop of Worcester, concerning some passages relating to Mr. Locke's Essay of humane understanding; in a late discourse of his lordships, in vindication of the Trinity. 1697. 8°. *SC*.266. MC.31: "Locke to Bp: of Worcester:"

—————. Mr. Locke's Reply to the ... Bishop of Worcester's Answer to his Second letter. 1699. 8°. *SC*.266. MC.31: "Locke's Reply:"

[Lockhart, George]. Memoirs concerning the affairs of Scotland from Queen Anne's accession to the throne, to the commencement of the Union of the two kingdoms of Scotland and England in May 1707. 1714. 8°. *SC*.219. MC.63/X: "Memo: concern^g Scotl:"

Lockhart, John Gibson. Life of Robert Burns. London, Edinburgh, 1828. 8°. [? LB.36: "Life of Burns"].

————. Memoirs of the life of Sir Walter Scott, Bart. 7 vol. Edinburgh, 1837-8. 12°. [WL:Ann]. LB.22: "Scotts life 1st Vol [lent late in 1837]."

————. Life of Sir Walter Scott. 2nd ed. 10 vol. Edinburgh, 1839. 16°. *SC*.134: "12mo." LB.56: "Scotts life 9th vol & 10."

Lodge, afterwards Ellerton, John Lodge. The bridal of Salerno; a romance; with other poems and notes. 1845. 8°. *SC*.525. LB.38.

[Lofft, Capel, the Younger]. Ernest; or, political regeneration. [A poem]. 1839. 12°. *SC*.688: "12mo, 1679 [*sic*]." [*DNB*: "His next publication, likewise anonymous, was an epic poem in twelve books, 'Ernest,' dedicated to the memory of Milton, and printed for the author in 1839"].

de L'Oise. See Sallentin, Louis.

Long, Kingsmill. See Barclay, John.

Long, Roger. See Ockley, Simon.

Longfellow, Henry Wadsworth. Evangeline, a tale of Acadie. Boston, 1847. 19cm. [*NUC*]. *SC*.588.

————. Voices of the night. Cambridge [USA], 1839. 18.5cm. [*NUC*]. *SC*.553.

Longinus, Dionysius Cassius. Peri hypsous biblion [in Greek] ... liber de grandi sive sublimi orationis genere. Cum praefatione de vita et scriptis Longini, notis, indicibus, et variis lectionibus [by John Hudson]. Oxoniae, 1718. 8°. [? MC.4: "Longinus: Oxon:"].

————. Dionysii Longini De sublimitate commentarius, quem nova versione donavit, notis illustravit, et ... emendavit ... Z[achary] Pearce. Editio quarta. 1752. 8°. *SC*.211: "Z. Pearce, 1752." MC.4: "Longinus: Pearce:"

Longman's catalogue. See A catalogue.

Lonsdale, Henry. See Blamire, Susanna.

[Lordan, Christopher Legge]. Colloquies, desultory
    and diverse, but chiefly upon poetry and poets;
    between an elder, enthusiastic, and an apostle of
    the law. Romsey, 1843. 8°. *SC*.452: *"with Pre-
    sentation Autograph Letter)*."

Loredano, Antonio. See Tacitus, Publius Cornelius.
    Reflessioni.

Loredano, Giovanni Francesco, the Younger. Bizarrie
    academiche di Giovanni Francesco Loredano ... con
    altre compositioni del medesimo. Venetia, 1643.
    12°. [*BN*]. *SC*.441: "12mo, 1651 [n.p.]."

Lovel (or Lovell), Archibald. See Bate, George.

Lovett, Robert. Sermons on several important subjects
    connected with the Gospel of Jesus Christ. Paris,
    1832. 8°. *SC*.247.

[Lowe, Helen]. Zareefa, a tale, and other poems. By
    the author of "Cephalus and Procris" [Helen Lowe].
    1844. 17cm. [*NUC*]. *SC*.578: "Zareifa and other
    Poems, 1844."

Lowther, John, Viscount Lonsdale. [? Memoir of the
    reign of James II. [Edited, with a life of the
    author, by William Lowther, Earl of Lonsdale].
    York, 1808. 4°]. LB.41: "L.Wm Lowthers [? Mem-
    oir]."

Lowther, William, Earl of Lonsdale. See Lowther,
    John, Viscount Lonsdale.

The loyal servant. See Mailles, Jacques de.

Lubin, Eilhard. See Horatius Flaccus, Quintus.
    Poemata.

————. Clavis linguae Graecae. Amsterdam, 1647. 12°.
[*E*]. *SC*.350: "*Autograph*." MC.13: "Clavis Graec:
Ling:"

Lucanus, Marcus Annaeus. De bello civili libri decem.
Lugduni, 1546. 16°. *SC*.397. [? MC.4: "Lucanus:"].

————. Pharsalia, sive de bello civili libri decem.
Ad editionem Cortii fideliter expressi. Glasgow,
1785. 8°. [*MR*]. *SC*.531. [? MC.4: "Lucanus:"].

Lucian, of Samosata. Luciani ... Dialogorum selectorum
libri duo a G[ulielmo] Dugardo recogniti ... Gr. &
Lat. 1685. 12°. *SC*.397: "Luciani Samosatensis
Dialog. 1685." MC.4: "Lucian:"

Lucretius Carus, Titus. [? Titi Lucretii Cari De rerum
natura libri sex. 1813. 30cm.]. [*NUC*]. [WR: "A
copy of Lucretius 'De Rerum Natura,' 1813, is a
presentation one from Hartley Coleridge to Wordsworth, and has a MS. poem on the fly-leaf in the
handwriting of the former"]. MC.4: "Lucretius:"

Ludlow, Edmund. Memoirs of Edmund Ludlow, esq: lieu-
tenant general of the horse, commander in chief of
the forces in Ireland, one of the council of state,
and a member of the parliament which began on Nov.
3, 1640. With a collection of original papers,
serving to confirm and illustrate many important
passages contained in the Memoirs. To which is
now added, The case of Charles the First. With a
copious index. 3rd ed. 3 vol. Edinburgh, 1751.
17cm. [*NUC*]. *SC*.135. MC.64: "Ludlow's Mem: 3
Vol:"

Luther, Martin. See Bible, German.

*Lyrical pieces, Cambridge. See Townshend, Chauncey
Hare.

M., F.   See Meres, Francis.

M., G.   See Miege, Guy.

M., I.   See Southey, Robert.   Selections.

M., I.A.   See Merryweather, Mrs. I.A.

M., M.   See Montagu, M.

Mabbe, James.   See Alemán, Mateo.

M'Callum, Hugh and John.   An originall collection of
    the poems of Ossian, Orrann, Ulin, and other bards
    who flourished in the same age.   Collected and edi-
    ted by H. and J. M'Callum.   Montrose, 1816.   8°.
    SC.589.   MC.44: "Original Collection of the Poems
    of Ossian 1816."

MacConechy, James.   See Motherwell, William.

MacCurtin, Hugh, *pseud*.   See Begly, Connor.

M'Donald, Alexander.   A Galick and English vocabulary,
    with an appendix of the terms of divinity in the
    said language.   Edinburgh, 1741.   19cm.   [ICN.
    Bon:Ann].   *SC*.364.   MC.17: "Gal: & Eng: Vocab:"

*MacEwen, Andrew.   Zayda, and other poems.   1846.
    SC.460.

MacGill, Stevenson.   A collection of sacred transla-
    tions, paraphrases, and hymns.   Glasgow, 1813.
    12°.   MC.49: "Macgil: Hymns:"

Machiavelli, Niccolò.   Tvtte le opere di Nicolo Machia-
    velli ... divise già in V. parti ... Et di nuovo
    con somma accuratezza ristampate.   2 vol. in 1.
    [? Firenze], 1680.   24°.   [*NUC*].   *SC*.398: "Tutte
    le Opere, IV. Volumni, 12mo ... 1680."

————.   [? The history of Florence in eight books.
    Translated from the Italian.   2 vol.   Glasgow,

1761]. [*NUC*]. LB.8: "Hist^{ry} Florence 2 vol."
HL.MK.368: "Machiaveli's [*sic*] Florence 2 V."

————. Machiavels discourses upon the first decade
of T. Livius [books 1-3], translated out of the
Italian, with some marginall animadversions ... by
E[dward] D[acres]. 1636. 12°. *SC*.44.

Machyn, Henry. The diary of Henry Machyn, citizen and
merchant-taylor of London, from A.D. 1550 to A.D.
1563. Edited by John Gough Nichols. 1848. 8°.
SC.15.

Mackay, Charles. Legends of the Isles and other poems.
Edinburgh, 1845. 12°. *SC*.590: "(*Autog. Present.*)"

Mackenzie, Sir Alexander. Voyages from Montreal, on
the River St. Laurence, through the continent of
North America, to the Frozen and Pacific Oceans, in
the years 1789 and 1793. With a preliminary account
of the rise, progress and present state of the fur
trade of that country. 1801. 4°. *SC*.124: "in
1780 [*sic*]-1793."

Mackenzie, Henry. Julia de Roubigné. (Vol. 28 of The
British novelists). *SC*.515. MC.87. [Bound with
the following title].

————. The man of feeling. (Vol. 28 of The British
novelists). *SC*.515. MC.87.

————. Report of the committee of the Highland
Society of Scotland, appointed to inquire into the
nature and authenticity of the poems of Ossian.
Drawn up ... by Henry Mackenzie, its chairman.
With a copious appendix, containing documents on
which the report is founded. Edinburgh, 1805.
8°. *SC*.589. MC.44: "Rep: on Ossian's Poems:"

*Mackerstrom, _____. Magnetical and meteorological
observations, 1843-44, and 1846. Transactions of
the Royal Society of Edinburgh. Vols. 17, 18, 19.
SC.137.

[Mackinnon, William Alexander]. On the rise, progress, and present state of public opinion in Great Britain and other parts of the world. 1828. 8°. *SC*.275.

Mackintosh, Sir James. Vindiciae Gallicae. Defence of the French Revolution, and its English admirers, against the accusations of the Right Hon. E[dmund] Burke; including some strictures upon the late production of Mons. de Calonne. 4th ed. with additions. 1792. 22cm. [*NUC*]. *SC*.52: "8vo, 1792."

Mackintosh, Robert James. Memoirs of the life of ... Sir James Mackintosh. Edited [from his letters and journals] by his son [Robert James Mackintosh]. 2 vol. 1835. 8°. *SC*.136. LB.57: "Memoirs of Sir J. Mackintosh 1 & 2 Vols."

MacMullan, Mrs. Mary Anne. The wanderings of a goldfinch; or, characteristic sketches of the nineteenth century. 1816. 8°. MC.81: "Wandering's [*sic*] of a Goldfinch:"

MacNeile, Hugh. Lectures on the sympathies, sufferings, and resurrection of the Lord Jesus Christ. 2nd ed. 1843. 12°. *SC*.307.

Macpherson, James. The poems of Ossian. 2 vol. 1796. 8°. *SC*.603. [? MC.45: "Poems of Ossian: 2 Vol:"].

————. *SC*.628: "Poems of Ossian, 2 vols., Epistles, etc., 1813." [Lowndes cites an edition in 2 vol., Edinburgh, 1812, 8°]. [? MC.45: "Poems of Ossian: 2 Vol:"].

Macpherson, John. Edward the First; or, the tyrant's triumph: a drama [in five acts and in verse]. Edinburgh, 1844. 8°. *SC*.548.

McVickar, John. The professional years of J.H. Hobart, D.D. New York, 1836. 12°. *SC*.252. LB.22: "Bp Hobarts prof[1] years."

Maelog. See Dafydd, ap Gwilym.

*Magazines, sundry. *SC*.388 [probably five].

Magnenus, Joannes Chrysostomus. Democritus revivis-
cens, sive, de atomis. Addita est Democriti vita.
Papiae, 1646. 4°. *SC*.329: "1641 [*sic*]." MC.32:
"Democritus revivisc:"

[Mailles, Jacques de]. The right joyous and pleasant
history of the feats, gests, and prowesses of the
Chevalier Bayard the good knight without fear and
without reproach. By the Loyal Servant [Jacques
de Mailles]. [Translated from the French by Sara
Coleridge]. 2 vol. 1825. 8°. *SC*.130. LB.7:
"2d vol. of Bayard [lent November, 1825]."

Maittaire, Michael. See Curtis Rufus, Quintus; Terentius Afer, Publius.

[————]. Corpus omnium veterum poetarum latinorum,
tam prophanorum quam ecclesiasticorum; cum eorum,
quotquot reperiuntur, fragmentis. 2 vol. 1721.
37cm. [*NUC*]. [? MC.2: "Corpus Poetarum: 1st
Vol:"].

Malcolm, Sir John. Observations on the disturbances
in the Madras Army in 1809. 1812. 8°. MC.60:
"Malcolm's Observations:"

Malone, Edmond. See Boswell, James; Reynolds, Sir
Joshua.

Manchester, Earl of. See Montagu, Henry.

Mandosi, Prospero. Bibliotheca romana, seu Romanorum
scriptorum centuriae. 2 vol. Romae, 1682-1692.
4°. [*BN*]. [? MC.5: "Script: Roman:"].

Manning, Henry Edward, Archdeacon of Chichester. Sermons. 4 vol. 1842-50. 8°. LB.42: "Arch[n] Manning's Sermons."

Mant, Richard, Bishop of Down, Connor, and Dromore.
Church architecture considered, in relation to
the mind of the Church since and before the Reformation. In two addresses. Belfast, 1843. 8°.
[? LB.42: "Ch Architecture Part 1st [lent in mid-
1848]."

Mantell, Gideon Algernon. Thoughts on a pebble; or,
a first lesson in geology. 8th ed. 1849. 16°.
SC.142: "16mo."

Manutius, Paulus. See Cicero, Marcus Tullius. Epistolae.

Mapes, Walter. Gualteri Mapes De nugis curialium dis-
tinctiones quinque. Edited by Thomas Wright.
1850. 8°. *SC*.15.

————. The Latin poems commonly attributed to Walter
Mapes, collected and edited by Thomas Wright.
1841. 8°. *SC*.15.

*Maps--Pocket traveling companions--English and Contin-
ental--numerous, a bundle. *SC*.138.

Maria del Occidente. See Brooks, Mrs. Maria (Gowen).

Mariner, William. See Martin, John, M.D.

[? Marini, Marco. Tevat Noah [in Hebrew]. Arca Noe.
Thesaurus linguae sanctae novus. D. Marco Marino
... Auctore. 3 pts. in 1 vol. Venetiis, 1593.
fol.]. [*NUC*]. MC.17/0: "Epito: Thesauri Ling:
Sanct:"

Marinus, Marcus. See Marini, Marco.

Marloratus, Augustinus. See Calvin, Jean.

Marmontel, Jean François. Une semaine d'une maison
d'éducation de Londres, contenant des lectures
tirés des Incas de M. Marmontel ... par une dame
de distinction. Londres, 1797. 12°. MC.96/DW:
"Semaine D'une Maison D'Educatione [*sic*]."

Marsh-Caldwell, Mrs. Anne (Caldwell). Emilia Wyndham.
3 vol. 1846. 8°. [DD:Ann]. LB.37.

[Marshall, Julia Ann, afterwards Elliott, Mrs. Henry
Venn]. Poems on sacred subjects. 1832. 12°.
[*DAP*]. LB.37: "Julia Marshalls Poems."

Marshall, Valentine. See Capel, Richard.

[Marteilhe, Jean]. Mémoires d'un Protestant [Jean
Marteilhe], condamné aux galères de France pour
cause de religion; écrits par lui-même. Rotter-
dam, 1757. 8°. *SC*.284: "12mo." MC.99: "Mem: du
[*sic*] Protestant."

Martialis, Marcus Valerius. Epigrammaton libri XIIII.
Parisiis, 1528. 8°. *SC*.591: "(*Autog. 'William
Wordsworth, Presented by Walter Savage Landor'*)."
MC.4: "Martialis Epigram:"

Martin, Isaac. The tryal and sufferings of Mr Isaac
Martin, who was put into the Inquisition in Spain,
for the sake of the Protestant religion ... 2nd ed.
1724. 17cm. [*NUC*]. *SC*.96. MC.64: "Sufferings
of Is: Martin:"

Martin, John, M.D. An account of the natives of the
Tonga Islands, with an original grammar of their
language, compiled from the communications of
William Mariner. 2 vol. 1818. 8°. *SC*.399.
LB.13: "Mariners Voyage 2^d Vol."

Martin, John, Lexicographer. Nouveau dictionnaire de
poche Français-Allemand et Allemand-Français, rédigé par J. Martin. Troisième édition. Leipzig,
n.d. 13cm. [*NUC*]. [? *SC*.364: "Dictionnaire de
Poche François-Allemande [*sic*], etc., par Martin"].

Martin, Martin. A description of the Western Islands
of Scotland ... With a ... map ... To which is
added a brief description of the Isles of Orkney
and Shetland. 2nd ed., corrected. 1716. 8°.
SC.171. MC.71: "Martin's Westn Islands:"

————. A voyage to St. Kilda. The remotest of all the Hebrides, or Western Isles of Scotland ... 4th ed., corrected. 1753. 24cm. [CSJ:Ann]. MC.71: "Martin's St: Kilda:"

Martin, William. See The British annals of education.

Martineau, Harriet. Letters on mesmerism. 2nd ed. 1845. 16°. *SC*.166: "12mo." LB.32: "Mesmerism."

[————]. Life in the sick-room. Essays by an invalid [Harriet Martineau]. 1844. 12°. *SC*.268: "Life in the Sick Room [n.d.]." LB.30: "Life in Sick room."

[————]. [Another copy]. *SC*.268: "Essays by an Invalid, 1844."

Mason, William. See Dufresnoy, Charles Alphonse; Gray, Thomas.

————. Caractacus. A dramatic poem: written on the model of ancient Greek tragedy. 1759. 4°. [? MC.50: "Mason's Caractacus:"].

————. Odes. By Mr. Mason. Cambridge, London, 1756. 25.5cm. [*NUC*]. *SC*.451a: "1751 [*sic*]."

Massinger, Philip. The plays of Philip Massinger; with notes by William Gifford. 4 vol. 1805. 8°. *SC*.592. MC.44: "Plays of Massinger: 4 Vol:" LB. 20: "Massinger 4 vol."

———— and John Ford. The dramatic works of Massinger and Ford. With an introduction by Hartley Coleridge. 1840. 25cm. ... Added t.-p., engr. with vignette: dated 1839. [*NUC*]. *SC*.593: "imp. 8vo, 1839." LB.27: "Ford & Massinger."

[Mathews, Cornelius]. Wakondah; the master of life. A poem. New York, 1841. 20.5cm. [*NUC*]. *SC*.558: "4to."

Mathias, Thomas James. See Gray, Thomas.

Maude, Thomas. The school boy: a poem. 2nd ed. 1837.
8°. L: *"With the autograph of William Wordsworth."*
SC.567.

Maurice, John Frederick Denison. [? Introductory lectures [on theology], delivered at Queen's College
[London]. 1849. 16°]. LB.46: "Maurice's Lectures."

————. The Prayer-Book, considered especially in
reference to the Romish system ... nineteen sermons.
1849. 8°. LB.58: "Maurice on the Prayer Book."

Mavor, William Fordyce. See Cook, Captain James.

———— Historical account of the most celebrated
voyages, travels, and discoveries, from the time
of Columbus to the present period. 25 vol. 1796-
1801. 15cm. [*NUC*]. *SC*.139: "Collection of Voyages, Travels, and Discoveries, from the time of
Columbus to the present, 24 vols. [*sic*], 12mo--
wanting vols. 3, 6, and 7--1796, *with Engravings
and Illustrations after Richter, Ibbetson, etc.
etc.*" LB.10: "Maver's [*sic*] Travels 1--2."

Maximianus. See Gallus, Cornelius.

Maxwell, Patrick. See Blamire, Susanna.

Mead, Joseph. See Mede, Joseph.

Mead, Richard. A discourse of the plague. 9th ed.,
corrected and enlarged. 1744. 8°. *SC*.140. MC.
36: "Mead on the Plague:"

Mede, Joseph. Diatribae Pars IV. Discourses on sundry texts of Scripture; delivered upon several occasions ... And Dr. Mede his epistles in answer
of divers letters from learned men ... touching
some points of divinity ... As also, a short view
of the author's life and death. 1652. 4°. *SC*.311:
"Discourses upon Divers Texts of Scripture, by
Joseph Meade, D.D., with Life, etc., 4to, 1652."

Meel (or Meelius), Jan Willem van. Insignium virorum
epistolae selectae quae nunc primum prodeunt ex
bibliotheca J.G.M. Amstelaedami, 1701. 8°. *SC*.
211: "Epist. Selectae ex Meelii, 1701." MC.63:
"Epistolae Selectae:"

Mela, Pomponius. De situ orbis, [and other works by
P.M. etc.] [imperfect, wants t.p.] 16cm. [CSJ:Ann:
WW and STC]. *SC*.141: "Melae, Pomponii: De Situ
Orbis, etc. etc., 12mo ... (*no title*), *Lug. Bat.*
1646 (*Autographs of 'S.T. Coleridge' and 'W. Words-
worth'*)." [*L: "Lugd[uni] Batavorum*, 1646. 12°"].
[GW: "[Basle or Lyon c 1540]"]. MC.4: "Mela:"

*Memoirs. MC.64: "Memoirs:"

Meredith, Louisa Anne. See Twamley, Louisa Anne.

[Meres, Francis]. Wits common wealth. The second
part. A treasurie of divine, morall, and phyloso-
phicall similes, and sentences, generally vseful.
But more particularly published for the vse of
schools. By F[rancis] M[eres] Master of Arts of
both Vniversities. 1634. 13.5cm. [MA: "Bound with
this [i.e. Bodenham, John, Politeuphuia] and presumably also Wordsworth's, but without manuscript
indications"]. [? *SC*.543: "Wit's Commonwealth"].
MC.84: "Wit's Commonwealth."

Merewether, Francis. The case between the Church and
the Dissenters impartially and practically considered. 1827. 8°. *SC*.207.

[Merryweather, Mrs. I.A.]. The hermit of Eskdaleside,
with other poems. By I.A.M. [Mrs. I.A. Merry-
weather]. 2nd ed. Whitby, 1833. 12°. [*DAP*;
CWC.744]. *SC*.661 [n.p., n.d.].

Mickiewicz, Adam. Konrad Vallenrod; an historical
tale, from the Prussian, and Lithuanian annals:
translated from the Polish ... by H. Cattley.
1841. 8°. *SC*.525: "Conrad Valenrad, from the
Polish, by H. Catley [*sic*], 1841."

The microcosm; a periodical work. [No. 1–40; Nov. 6, 1786–July 30, 1787]. [By Gregory Griffin, of the College of Eton: inscribed to the Rev. Dr. Davies: i.e. by George Canning, John Smith, Robert Smith, John Hookham Frere, and others]. 3rd ed. 2 vol. Windsor, 1790, 1793. 19cm. [*DAP*; *L*]. [*CWC*:Ann]. *SC*.400: "2 vols., 1793."

Micyllus, Jacobus. See Ovidius Naso, Publius. Fasti.

Middleton, Charles S. Hours of recreation: a collection of poems. Written to the age of twenty-one. 1848. 16°. *SC*.527.

Middleton, Conyers. A letter from Rome, shewing an exact conformity between Popery and Paganism. 5th ed. 1742. 8°. *SC*.201.

Middleton, Thomas. The works of Thomas Middleton now first collected with some account of the author, and notes by Alexander Dyce. 5 vol. 1840. 8°. *SC*.594.

Middleton, Thomas Fanshawe. Sermons and charges ... with memoirs of his life, by Henry K. Bonney. 1824. 8°. LB.9.

[Miege, Guy]. A relation of three embassies from His Sacred Majestie Charles II. to the Great Duke of Muscovie, the King of Sweden, and the King of Denmark, performed by ... the Earle of Carlisle in the years 1663 & 1664. Written by an attendant on the embassies. [The "Epistle Dedicatory" subscribed G.M., i.e. G. Miege]. 1669. 8°. *SC*.78: "(*no title*)." MC.59: "Relation of 3 Embassies:"

Mignet, François Auguste Marie. Histoire de la Révolution Française. 2 tomes (in one). Bruxelles, 1833. 16°. *SC*.52: "12mo." [? LB.56: "History French Revolution"].

Miller, John, Brother of Gen. William Miller. Memoirs of General Miller, in the service of the Republic of Peru. 2 vol. 1828. 8°. *SC*.143.

[Miller, John]. Things after death; three chapters on
the intermediate state; with thoughts on family
burying places, and hints for epitaphs in country
church yards. 1848. 16°. *SC*.355. LB.53.

Miller, Philip and William Shaw. The practical gardener
... The whole compiled and arranged and the several
improvements and other original matter added, by
William Shaw. 1810. 21.5cm. [*NUC*]. *SC*.142:
"8vo." MC.75: "Practical Gardener:"

Millot, Abbé Claude François Xavier. See La Curne de
Sainte-Palaye, Jean Baptiste de.

Milner, Mrs. Mary. See The Christian mother's magazine.

Milnes, Richard Monckton, Baron Houghton. Memorials
of a residence on the Continent, and historical
poems. 1838. 8°. *SC*.595.

————. Memorials of a tour in some parts of Greece;
chiefly poetical. 1834. 8°. *SC*.600. LB.18:
"[? Millinses] book on Greece [lent after 2 May
1834]."

————. Palm leaves. [poems]. 1844. 8°. *SC*.616.
LB.33.

————. Poems of many years. 1838. 8°. *SC*.595.
LB.27: "Milnes Poems 2 Vols [lent after 4 October
1840]."

*Milton, _____. *SC*.644: "Milton's Glover."

Milton, John. See Hogaeus, Gulielmus (William Hogg);
Lauder, William; Shakespeare, William; Toland,
John.

————. A complete collection of the historical, political, and miscellaneous works of John Milton,
both English and Latin. With som [*sic*] papers
never before publish'd. To which is prefix'd the
life of the author [by John Toland]. 3 vol. Amsterdam, [London], 1698. fol. *SC*.401.

*————. MC.43: "Milton's Poems: 2 Vol:" [Perhaps one of the editions published by Jacob Tonson, with the title *Poetical Works*, 2 vol. 1705. 8° *et seq*.].

————. See Bell, John. The poets of Great Britain. Vols. 28-31. LB.24: "Milton--Bells." LB.29: "Milton Bells 4 Vols."

————. The poetical works of John Milton, from the text of the Rev. H.J. Todd, with a critical essay by J[ohn] Aikin. 4 vol. 1808. 12°. [Lowndes; *NUC*]. *SC*.455: "vols. 2, 3, 4, 12mo, 1808." [? LB. 1: "Poems Miltons"]. [? LB.9: "Milton 1 vol"].

————. The poetical works of John Milton, with notes of various authors. To which are added illustrations, and some accounts of the life and writings of Milton, by ... H[enry] J[ohn] Todd. Second edition, with considerable additions and with a verbal index to the whole of Milton's poetry. 7 vol. 1809. 8°. [DD: "Todd's edn. in 7 vols. 1809. Vol. 1 only: 'William Wordsworth from Samuel Rogers.' Verbal index to the poetry of Milton: 'William Wordsworth from Samuel Rogers'"]. LB.30: "Milton 4 vols Do Index."

————. Artis logicae plenior institutio, ad Petri Rami methodum concinnata. 1672. 12°. MC.13: "Milton's Logic:" [WR: "Other volumes which ... contain Wordsworth's autograph ... are ... Milton's Artes [*sic*] Logicae, 1672"].

————. The history of Britain, that part especially now call'd England, from the first traditional beginning, continu'd to the Norman Conquest. Collected out of the antientest and best authours by John Milton. 1670. 4°. MC.58: "Milton's Hist: of England:"

————. Paradise lost. A poem in twelve books. the author John Milton. 2nd ed. Revised and augmented by the same author. 1674. 8°. [WL:Ann]. MC.43: "Milton's Parad: Lost: 2nd Edit:"

————. Paradise lost ... translated into Welsh by
W[illiam] O[wen] Pughe ... Llundain, 1819. 22cm. [IU:
Ann]. *SC*.571: "Idrison ['*the Bardic name of W.
Owen Pughe*' (*L*)] Coll Gwynfa Cyfiethidd gan Idrison,
8vo, *Llundain*, 1819. The first translation of Mil-
ton's 'Paradise Lost' into Welsh."

Milton, M.S. The ocean bride: a tale of the sea. In
six cantons [*sic*] ... Edinburgh, 1834. 6.25 in.
[*NUC*]. *SC*.612.

Milward, Richard. See Selden, John.

[Mimpriss, Robert]. A harmony of the four Gospels arranged according to Greswell's Harmonia evangelica.
1833. 8°. *SC*.267.

Minellius, Jan (Jan Minell). See Florus, Lucius Annaeus; Ovidius Naso, Publius. Metamorphoseon.

Minois, Claudius. See Alciati, Andrea.

Minsheu, John. See Percyvall, Richard.

Mirabaud, Jean Baptiste de. See Holbach, Paul Heinrich Dietrich, Baron d'.

Misopappas, Philanax. See N., S.

The modern British drama. See Scott, Sir Walter.

Molesworth, Robert, Viscount. An account of Denmark as
it was in the year 1692. 1694. 8°. *SC*.150.
MC.62: "Account of Denmark:"

Molière. See Poquelin de Molière, Jean Baptiste.

Molinos, Miguel. The spiritual guide ... 2 pt. [Lon-
don], 1688. 8°. *SC*.284: "Molinos' Guide Spiri-
tuelle, 1688."

Monk, William. See Livingstone, David.

Monmouth, Earl of. See Carey, Robert.

Montagu, Basil. See Bacon, Francis.

————. An inquiry into the aspersions upon the late ordinary of Newgate (B. Forde), with some observations upon Newgate and upon the punishment of death. (Appendix. Hints for the improvement of the police ... by B. Forde). 2 pt. 1815. 4°. MC.38: "Montagu on Newgate:"

————. The opinions of different authors upon the punishment of death, selected by Basil Montagu. 2nd ed. 3 vol. 1812-1816. 8°. *SC*.53: "3 vols., 8vo ... 1809." MC.39: "Montagu on Punishment: of Death: 3 Vol:"

————. Selections from the works of Taylor, Hooker, Hall, and Lord Bacon; with an analysis of The advancement of learning. 1805. 8°. [? LB.12: "Montagu's Extracts"].

[————]. Some enquiries into the effects of fermented liquors. By a water drinker [Basil Montagu]. 3rd ed. 1841. 8°. *SC*.173: "8vo, 1841." MC.32: "Fermented Liquors:" [Perhaps a copy of the 1st ed., 1814. 8°].

————. Thoughts on the punishment of death for forgery. 1830. 12°. *SC*.16: *"with Autog. of the late Laureate*."

Montagu, Henry, Earl of Manchester. Manchester al mondo. Contemplatio mortis et immortalitatis. Fifth impression much enlarged. 1642. 12°. *SC*.199. MC.25: "On Death & Immortal:"

Montagu, M. See Schiller, Johann Christoph Friedrich von.

Montagu, Lady Mary Wortley. Letters of the Right Honourable Lady M--y W-----y M------e; written during her travels in Europe, Asia, and Africa, to persons of distinction, men of letters, &c. in different parts of Europe. Which contains, among

other curious relations, accounts of the policy
and manners of the Turks; drawn from sources that
have been inaccessible to other travellers. A new
edition. 3 vol. 1769. 12°. [*BN*]. *SC*.94.

*———. *SC*.432: "Letters of Lady M.W. Montague [*sic*],
complete in 1 vol., 18mo, 1825." [*L* lists The
works of Lady Mary Wortley Montagu. London, 1825.
12°].

Montaigne, Michel de. The essayes, or morall, politike,
and militairie discourses of Lo: Michaell de Montaigne ... Now done into English by ... John Florio.
1603. fol. *SC*.51. MC.38: "Montayne's [*sic*]
Essays:"

———. Essays of Michael Seigneur de Montaigne ...
New rendred into English by C[harles] Cotton, Esq.
2nd ed. 3 vol. 1693. 8°. *SC*.357: "vols. 1 and
3, 8vo, 1693." MC.80: "Montaign's [*sic*] Essays
3 Vol:"

*Montgomery, James. The loss of the locks, a poem.
SC.689: "*the two last pages MS., in the Autograph
of the Author, James Montgomery, Sheffield, Dec.
1799)."*

———. The wanderer of Switzerland, and other poems.
1806. 8°. *SC*.472: "(*with MS. Note, etc.*)." MC.52:
"Montgomery's Wand: of Switzerland:"

Montgomery, Robert. The Messiah. A poem. 1832. 12°;
5th ed. 1836. 8°. *SC*.597: "8vo. 1839 [*sic*]."

———. The omnipresence of the Deity; a poem. 1828.
8°. *SC*.555: "The Omnipotence [*sic*] of the Deity."

———. The omnipresence of the Deity. Thirteenth
edition ... enlarged. 1834. 12°. [WL:Ann]. LB.
45: "Omnipresence of the Deity [lent 24 Dec. 1849]."

The monthly chronicle; a national journal of politics,
literature, science, and art. 7 vol. 1838–41.
8°. *SC*.359: "vol. 1, 1838."

Monti, Vincenzo. Caius Gracchus, a tragedy. From the
Italian of Monti. [Liverpool], 1839. 21.5cm.
[*NUC*: "First ed. Inscribed presentation copy from
Dr. Vose"]. *SC*.676: "from the Italian of Monti,
by Dr. Vose (*with Presentation Autog., Liverpool*),
1839. [But DLC copy of limited ed., London, 1830,
23cm. has MS. note on fly-leaf reading "Translated
by Lord George William Russell." Perhaps a different translation]."

Moore, George, M.D. The power of the soul over the
body considered in relation to health and morals.
1845. 8°. *SC*.269: "12mo." LB.38: "Dr Moore's
2 Vols." LB.39: "Power of the Soul over the Body
by Dr Moore."

————. The use of the body in relation to the mind.
1846. 8°. *SC*.268. LB.38: "Dr Moore's 2 Vols."

Morant, Philip. The history of England, by way of
question and answer; revised and corrected, for
Thomas Astley. 1737. 4°. [*BB*]. [*DNB*: "12mo."].
MC.67: "Hist: of England--by Quest: & answer.--"
[? *SC*.46: "History of England, 1735"].

*More derivations from the Welsh. 1843. 12°. *SC*.412:
"(*Do*. [i.e. *Present. Autog.*])." See Derivations
from the Welsh.

More, Hannah. [? The works of Hannah More, including
several pieces never before published. 8 vol.
1801. 8°]. LB.20: "H. More 1st Vol."

[Morehead, Robert]. [? Poetical epistles and speci-
mens of translation. Edinburgh, 1813. 16.5cm.
[*NUC*.]--[? 2nd ed. Poetical epistles: and speci-
mens of poetical translation, particularly from
Petrarch and Dante. Edinburgh, 1814. 8°. [*EU*]].
[*BB*: "1819"]. MC.48: "Poet: Epist: & Translat:

Morelius, Gulielmus. Verborum Latinorum cum Graecis
Anglicisque coniunctorum locupletissimi commen-
tarii. 1583. fol. *SC*.402: "[n.d.], folio."

Morell, Sir Charles, *pseud.* See Ridley, James.

Morell, Thomas. See Ainsworth, Robert; Hederich, Benjamin.

————. Thesaurus Graecae poeseos; sive, lexicon Graeco-prosodiacum ... Cui praefigitur, de poesi, seu prosodia Graecorum tractatus. 2 pt. Etonae, 1762. 4°. [? MC.14: "Morel's [*sic*] Lexicon"]-- [? MC.13: "On Prosod:"].

*Morgan, A.M. The Christian commonwealth. 1845. imp. 4°. *SC*.270.

[Morgan, John Minter]. The revolt of the bees. 1826. 8°. [*DAP*]. *SC*.560: "(*Pres. Autog.*)."

Morley, George, Bishop of Worcester. The Bishop of Worcester's letter to a friend for vindication of himself from M^r [Richard] Baxter's calumny. 1662. 4°. *SC*.311.

Mornay, Philippe de. A worke concerning the trunesse [*sic*] of Christian religion ... The fourth time published. 1617. 8°. *SC*.271: "begun to be Translated into English by that Honourable Knight and Worthy Gentleman, Sir Philip Sidney Knight, and at his request finished by Arthur Golding, 4to ... 1617." MC.24: "Truenesse of Christ: Religion."

Morse, Jedidiah. The American geography; or, a view of the present situation of the United States of America. 2nd ed. 1792. 8°. *SC*.92. MC.71: "Morse's Amer: Geogra:"

Morton, James. The ancren riwle ... Edited and translated by James Morton. 1853. 8°. *SC*.15.

Moschus. See Bion.

[? Moseley, William. The most easy Greek exercises for the use of the lower forms ... or an introduction to Huntingford's Greek exercises. 1828. 12°]. MC.14: "Huntingford's Exercises:"

Mosellanus, Petrus. See Gregory of Nazianzus, Saint,
    Patriarch of Constantinople; Schade, Petrus
    (Mosellanus).

Motherwell, William. The poetical works of William
    Motherwell. Edited by James MacConechy. Second
    edition, enlarged. Glasgow, 1847. 8°. *SC*.598.
    [WL:Ann].

Moultrie, John. The dream of life, lays of the English
    Church, and other poems. 1843. 8°. [*CWC*:STC
    Family:Ann]. LB.40.

Moxon, Edward. The prospect, and other poems. 1826.
    12°. *SC*.599.

————. Sonnets. 2 pt. 1830-35. 8°. *SC*.600.

Muirhead, John Patrick. See Arago, Dominique; Watt,
    James.

[? Multum in parvo; or, some useful sayings in verse
    and prose, collected by a lover of virtue and
    goodness ... [John Pennyman]. 1687. 12°].
    [*NUC*]--[? Multum in parvo; or, the jubilee of
    jubilees. Being a description of the great mil-
    lenium ... With a description of the new heaven,
    the new earth, and the new Jerusalem. Birming-
    ham, 1732. 12°]. MC.27: "Multum in Parvo:"

Murdoch, Patrick. See Thomson, James.

Murphy, Arthur. See Fielding, Henry.

Murphy, James Cavanah. Travels in Portugal; through
    the provinces of Entre Douro e Minho, Beira, Estre-
    madura, and Alem-Tetjo, in the years 1789 and 1790,
    consisting of observations on the manners, customs,
    trade, public buildings, arts, antiquities, &c. of
    that kingdom. 1795. 11.75 in. [*CWC*:Ann]. *SC*.
    144: "4to, 1795."

Murray, Lindley. The English reader; or, pieces in
    prose and poetry selected from the best writers ...

by Lindley Murray. 1799. 12°. MC.84: "Murray's
Engl: Reader:"

————. Lecteur françois; ou, recueil de pièces, en
prose et en vers, tirées des meilleurs écrivains.
York, 1802. 12°. MC.18: "Lecteur François:"

Murray, Thomas Boyles. Lays of Christmas. 1847. 16°.
SC.523.

The Muses' pocket companion, a collection of poems,
by the most eminent modern authors. Dublin,
[? 1800]. 12°. MC.50: "Muses Pocket Comp:"

Myers, Frederick. Lectures on great men; with a preface by T.H. Tarlton. 2nd ed. 1856. 12°. *SC*.403:
"by J. [*sic*] H. Tarlton, 8vo, 1850 [*sic*]."

N., J.H. See Newman, John Henry.

N., N. See Wollaston, William.

N., S. Rawleigh redivivus; or, the life and death of
Anthony Earl of Shaftesbury ... By Philanax Misopappas. [The author's "Epistle Dedicatory" subscribed S.N.]. 2 pt. 1683. 8°. MC.65: "Rawleigh redivivus:"

Naigeon, Jacques André. See Racine, Jean.

Nalson, John. An impartial collection of the great
affairs of state, from the beginning of the Scotch
Rebellion in 1639, to the murther of King Charles
I ... wherein ... the whole series of the late
troubles in England, Scotland, and Ireland are
faithfully represented. 2 vol. 1682, 83. fol.
SC.54: "1816." MC.64: "Nalson's Collection:"

Narborough, Sir John. An account of several late
voyages and discoveries to the south and north
towards the Streights of Magellan, the South Seas,
... also towards Nova Zembla, Greenland or Spits-

berg ... by Sir J. Narborough, Captain J. Tasman,
Captain J. Wood, and F. Marten of Hamburgh. To
which are annexed a large introduction and supplement, giving an account of other navigations to
those regions. 1694. 8°. *SC*.171. MC.70: "Narborough and others' Acc^t of Voyages & Discov:"

*Narrative of London. MC.60: "Narrative of London:"

Nary, Cornelius. A new history of the world,... from
the creation to the birth of ... Jesus Christ: according to the computation of the Septuagint,...
with chronological tables. Dublin, 1720. fol.
MC.57: "Nary's Hist: of the World:"

*Nat Mag. LB.15: "Nat Mag [borrowed July 1832]." [?
The magazine of natural history. 9 vol. 1829-36.
8°]. [*L*]--[? The national magazine and general
review. I. 1826--May 1827]. [*BUCP*].

Nelson, Robert. A companion for the festivals and
fasts of the Church of England: with collects
and prayers for each solemnity. 36th ed. 1826.
8°. *SC*.272: "1836."

*Nepos, Cornelius. MC.2: "Cornelius Nepos: 3 Co:"

————. Vitae excellentium imperatorum cum versione
Anglica ... C. Nepos' lives of the excellent com-
manders. With an English translation ... by
J[ohn] Clarke. Lat. & Eng. 1723. 8°. MC.2:
"Cornelius Nepos: Clarke's:"

*Neue Hoog: Grammatik. MC.18: "Neue Hoog: Grammatik:"

Newcome, William. An historical view of the English
Biblical translations; the expediency of revising
by authority our present translation: and the
means of executing such a revision. (A list of
various editions of the Bible, and parts thereof,
in English, from the year 1526 to 1776 [with a
supplement by A[ndrew] C[oltée] Ducarel]). Dublin, 1792. 8°. *SC*.674: "by W. Newsom."

[Newman, John Henry]. The Cistercian saints of England. [Continued under the title of]: Lives of the English saints. [pts. 1, 2. Edited by J.H.N., i.e. John Henry Newman]. 15 pt. 1844-45. 8°. [*L: "The first two volumes only were issued under the editorship of Newman"*]. LB.33: "English Saints [lent after 14 June 1844]."

————. Parochial sermons. 6 vol. 1834-42. 8°. LB.29.

Newsam, William Cartwright. The poets of Yorkshire; comprising sketches of the lives, and specimens of the writings of those ... who have been ... connected with the county of York ... Commenced by ... W.C. Newsam; completed and published ... by J. Holland [i.e. John Holland, of Sheffield]. 1845. 8°. *SC*.355.

*New Testament. MC.20: "Octavo Testam."

Newton, Isaac. See Rohault, Jacques.

Nichol, John Pringle. The architecture of the heavens. 1850. 8°. *SC*.273. LB.46.

Nichols, John. Literary anecdotes of the eighteenth century. 9 vol. 1812-1815. 8°. [WL:Ann: "7 vols 1812-13"]. MC.79: "Nichols Literary anecdotes 7 Vol." MC.102: "Nichols Literary Anecdotes 7 Vol: [item crossed out]." LB.7.

Nichols, John Gough. See Machyn, Henry.

————. The chronicle of Calais, in the reigns of Henry VII. and Henry VIII. To the year 1540. Edited by John Gough Nichols. 1846. 8°. *SC*.15.

————. Chronicle of the Grey Friars of London. Edited by John Gough Nichols. 1852. 8°. *SC*.15.

————. The Chronicle of Queen Jane, and of two years of Queen Mary, and especially of the Rebellion of

Sir Thomas Wyat. Edited by John Gough Nichols.
1850. 8°. *SC*.15.

—————. Grants from the crown during the reign of
Edward the Fifth, from the original docketbook ms.
1854. 8°. *SC*.15: "1840."

Nicholson, Cornelius. Annals of Kendal; being a historical and descriptive account of Kendal and its
environs ... with biographical sketches of many
eminent personages connected with the town. Kendal, London, 1832. 8°. *SC*.684. [WL:Ann: "This
volume ... was part of lot 684 in the sale of the
Rydal Mount Library ... Gordon G. Wordsworth"].

Nicholson, William. See Nicolson, William.

Nicole. Pierre. See Epigrammatum Delectus.

Nicolson, Joseph and Richard Burn. The history and
antiquities of the counties of Westmorland and
Cumberland. 2 vol. 1777. 4°. [WL:Ann]. LB.28.

Nicolson, William, Archbishop of Cashel. The English
historical library; or, A short view and character
of most of the writers now extant, either in print
or manuscript; which may be serviceable to the
undertakers of a general history of this kingdom.
3 pts. in 1 vol. 1696-99. 18cm. [CtY.BL:Ann].
SC.55: "the three parts complete, 8vo, 1696 and
1699." MC.58: "Nicholson's [*sic*] Eng: Histor:
Libr:"

[—————]. Leges marchiarum, or border-laws: containing several original articles and treaties, made
and agreed upon by the commissioners of the re-
spective kings of England and Scotland, for the
better preservation of peace and commerce upon the
marches of both kingdoms: from the reign of Henry
III. to the Union of the two crowns, in K. James I.
With a preface, and an appendix of charters and
records, relating to the said treaties. By William, lord bishop of Carlile. [Later Archbishop

of Cashel]. 1705. 17.5cm. [*NUC*]. *SC*.11. MC.39:
"Border Laws:"

Nieuwentijdt, Bernard. The religious philosopher; or,
the right use of contemplating the works of the
Creator. I. In the wonderful structure of animal
bodies ... II. In the ... formation of the elements
... III. In the structure ... of the heavens ...
Designed for the conviction of atheists and infi-
dels ... translated ... by J[ohn] Chamberlayne.
3 vol. 1718, 19. 8°. *SC*.210. MC.24: "Religious
Philosopher:"

Nixon, Francis Russell. Lectures historical, doctrinal,
and practical on the catechism of the Church of
England. 1843. 8°. *SC*.274. LB.39.

A nobleman. See Goldsmith, Oliver.

Non clericus. See Cottle, Robert.

*Non-conformist's Champ. MC.21: "Non-conformist's
Champ:" "John."

Norden, John. Speculi Britanniae pars: an historical
and chorographical description of the county of
Essex, by John Norden. 1594. Edited by Sir Henry
Ellis. 1840. 8°. *SC*.15: "1830."

North, Christopher, *pseud*. See Wilson, John.

North, Sir Thomas. See Plutarch.

Northampton, Marquis of. See Compton, Spencer.

The novelist's magazine. 23 vol. Harrison & Co.,
1781-88. 22cm. [*NUC*]. *SC*.549: "Harrison's Novelist's Magazine, 21 vols., 8vo ... (*wanting vols*.
4, 10, 11, 14, 15, 19), 1786." [Vol. 4, The adventures of Gil Blas, Robinson Crusoe; Vol. 10-11,
Sir Charles Grandison; Vol. 14-15, Clarissa; Vol.
19, The expedition of Humphry Clinker, The history of Pompey the Little (Mr. Coventry), The

history of Ophelia (Miss Fielding), A thousand and
one quarters of hours (Gueulette; tr. by T. Floyd)].
[RP.QH: "Bought by Mr Wm Wordsworth"]. MC.87:
"Novelist's Magaz: 21 V:" LB.6.

Nucius, Nicander. The second book of the travels of
Nicander Nucius of Corcyra. Ed. from the original
Greek MS. in the Bodleian library, with an English
translation by the Rev. J[ohn] A[nthony] Cramer.
1841. 8°. *SC*.15.

Nugent, Thomas. The primitives of the Greek tongue
... also a treatise of prepositions and other un-
declinable particles, and an alphabetical collection of English words derived from the Greek ...
translated from the French of Messieurs de Port
Royal, with ... improvements by Thomas Nugent.
1773. 8°. MC.13: "Nugent's Primit:"

*Nuova guida di forastieri di Pozzuoli, Capri, Gaet.
1751. *SC*.156. MC.97: "Nova [*sic*] Guida:" [Author
uncertain, possibly Pompeo Sarnelli].

O., F. The Law-French dictionary. Eng, Fr. To which
is added the Law-Latin dictionary. Eng., Lat. ...
Collected out of the best authors by F.O. Corrected and enlarged. 1718. 8°. [*SM*]. *SC*.396:
"8vo ... 1718." MC.39: "Law French Dict͞y:"

O., W.C. See Oulton, Walley Chamberlain.

Obeah. See Poems on Obeah.

Ockland (or Ocland), Christopher. Anglorum praelia,
ab anno ... 1327 ... usque ad annum ... 1558.
Carmine summatim perstricta. 1580. 4°. MC.8:
"Anglorum Praelia:"

Ockley, Simon. The history of the Saracens. 3rd ed.
(An account [by Roger Long] of the Arabians ...
of the life of Mahomet, and of the Mahometan reli-

gion). 2 vol. Cambridge, 1757. 8°. *SC*.56. MC.
62: "Hist: of Saracens: 2 Vol:"

O'Dedy, U. A view of the laws of landed property in
Ireland, of the relation of landlords and tenants.
1812. 8°. MC.39: "Property in Ireland:"

Ogilvie, John. Poems on various subjects. To which
is prefix'd an essay on the lyric poetry of the
ancients; in two letters to Lord Deskfoord. 2 vol.
1769. 8°. MC.48: "Ogilvies Poems: 2 Vol:"

[Ogilvie, William]. An essay on the right of property
in land, with respect to its foundation in the law
of nature; its present establishment by the munici-
pal laws of Europe; and the regulations by which it
might be rendered more beneficial to the lower
ranks of mankind. [1781]. 8°. *SC*.1.

Ogle, Nathaniel. See Addison, Joseph. The spectator.

*Old English dictionary. MC.17: "Old Eng: Dicty."

Oldham, John. The works of Mr. John Oldham, together
with his remains. 1692. 8°. [Ox]. *SC*.602.
MC.15: "Oldham's Poems:"

Oldmixon, John. See Bouhours, Dominique.

[————]. Clarendon and Whitlock compar'd ... By the
author of The critical history of England [John
Oldmixon]. 1727. 8°. *SC*.451. MC.65: "Comparison
of Clarendon and Whitlock:"

Oldys, William. See Cooper, Mrs. Elizabeth.

Oliver, Stephen, the Younger. See Chatto, William
Andrew.

*On the Church. MC.26: "On the Church:"

An oration sacred to the imperial majesty of Anne,
Queen of Great Britain. 1707. 8°. MC.83: "Oration sacred to Q_{n}^{n} Anne:"

Ord, John Walker. England: a historical poem. 2 vol. 1834. 8°. *SC*.532.

An ordinance of the Lords and Commons for raising and maintaining of forces for defence of the Kingdom under the command of Sir T[homas] Fairfax. [15 Feb. 1645]. 1644. [o.s.]. 4°. *SC*.63: "and numerous others, 4to."

An ordinance of the Lords and Commons ... for the present setting ... of Presbyterial Government in the Church of England. [5 June 1646]. 1646 [1647]. 4°. *SC*.63: "and numerous others, 4to."

An ordinance of the Lords and Commons for the raising of 66,666£ 13s. 4d. by way of loane, for the better enabling of our brethren in Scotland, for our assistance. [27 Oct. 1643]. 1643. 4°. *SC*.63: "and numerous others, 4to."

Orford, Earl of. See Walpole, Horace.

Osborne, Francis. The works of Francis Osborne ... in four several tracts. 10th ed. 1701. 8°. *SC*.387. MC.40: "Osborne's Works:" MC.84: "Osborne's Works:"

————. Advice to a son. 6th ed. 2 pt. 1658. 12°. *SC*.170: *"with the late Laureate's Autograph."* MC.84: "Osborne's Adv: to Son:"

————. A miscellany of sundry essayes, paradoxes, and problematicall discourses, letters and characters; together with political deductions from the history of the Earl of Essex executed under Queen Elizabeth. 1659. 12°. *SC*.543. MC.84: "Osborne's Miscell:"

Osorius, Hieronymus (Osorio da Fonseca, Jeronimo). De gloria libri 5. Florentiae, 1552. 8°. MC.9: "Osorius de Gloria:"

Ossian. See Macpherson, James.

Ossoli, Sarah Margaret.   See Fuller, afterwards Ossoli,
Sarah Margaret.

Ostervald, Jean Frédéric.   See Bible, Holy.

O'Sullivan, John L.   Report in favor of the abolition
of punishment of death by law, made to the legisla-
ture of the State of New York.   April 14, 1841.
2nd ed.   New York, 1841.   *SC*.57.

[? Otley, Jonathan.   A concise description of the English Lakes and adjacent mountains.   2nd ed.   Keswick, 1825.   18.5cm.   [*L*: "front. (fold. map)"].
SC.179: "Otley's Pocket Map."   LB.27: "Ottey's
[*sic*] Guide."

Otway, Caesar.   Sketches in Ireland; descriptive of
interesting, and hitherto unnoticed districts in
the North and South.   Dublin, 1827.   8°.   *SC*.113.
LB.9: "Sketches in Ireland."

Oulton, Walley Chamberlain.   See Shakespeare, William.
Poems.

Ouseley, Thomas John.   Poems.   London, Shrewsbury,
1849.   15cm.   [*NUC*].   *SC*.604.

Ovidius Naso, Publius.   P. Ovidii Nasonis Operum quae
extant tomus III., quo continentur Fastorum lib.
vi., Tristium lib. v., De Ponton lib. iv., Dirae
in Ibin, Halieuticon fragmentum.   Ex postrema
J[acobi] Micylli recognitione, et recensione nova
G[regorii] Bersmani ... Editio tertia auctior.
Lipsiae, 1596.   8°.   *SC*.605.   LB.28: "Ovids Fasti."
[*L* lacks Vol. I (Heroidum epistolae, Amores, De
arte amandi, and De remedio amoris, "Omnia casti-
gatiora ex postrema Jac. Micylli recognitione et
recensione nova Gr. Bersmani, cum indicatione di-
versae scripturae et locor[um] quorund[um] explan-
atione") and Vol. II, "quo continentur Metamorphoseon libri xv, ex postrema Iacobi Micylli recognitione, et recensione nova Gregorii Bersmani, cum
eiusdem aliorumq[ue]; virorum doctissimorum nota-

tionibus: ac singvlarvm fabvlarum argvmentis, partim veteribus, partim recentibus. Editio tertia
aliquot locis auctior. Lipsiae, 1596. 16cm."
See *GBD*, III, 1238; Bersman, Gregor in *ADB*; and
NUC].

————. Opera. [CSJ:Ann: "Ovid. Opera. Tomus III
(only). 16mo. Amstelodami, 1717"]. *SC*.606:
"Ovidii Opera, in tres tomos diviso [*sic*], 18mo,
Amsterdam, 1717." [*L*: "Operum P. Ovidii Nasoni
editio nova. Accurante N. Heinsio. 3 tom. *Amstelodami*, 1717. 24°"].

————. Electa ex Ovidio, et Tibullo, in usum Regiae
Scholae Etonensis. Editio altera recensita et in
gratiam rudiorum notis aucta. 1787. 18cm. [*AWC*:
Ann]. MC.3: "Electa ex Ovidio."

————. Metamorphoseon series compendiosa. Ex Gul
[ielmi] Canteri novis lectionibus. [P. Ovidii
Nasonis Opera, tom. 1 1715. 12°]. *SC*.605: "1772
[*sic*] (*with Autographs of John Tweddell and W.
Wordsworth, given to him by John Tweddell, who
died at Athens*)." MC.5: "Ovidii Metam: 4 Cop:"
[? LB.30: "Ovid Met^s 1 vol."].

————. Minellius Anglicanus; sive Metamorphoseon
libri xv, cum arg. notisque Minellianis, Anglice
redditis studio N[athan] Bailey. Editio secunda.
1733. 8°. [*NUC*]. *SC*.607. MC.5: "Ovidii Metam:
4 Cop:"

————. The xv. books of P. Ovidius Naso, entituled
Metamorphosis, translated oute of Latin into
English meeter, by Arthur Golding. 1593. 4°.
SC.542. MC.91: "Golding's Ovid:"

————. Ovid's Metamorphosis englished [in verse] by
G(eorge) S(andys). 1626. fol. *SC*.642. MC.91:
"Sandy's [*sic*] Ovid:"

————. P. Ovidii Nasonis De tristibus libri v. 1728.
12°. *SC*.347: "8vo." MC.5: "Ovidii Tristia [*bis*]:"

————. [? Ovid's Tristia. Containing five bookes of
mournfull elegies ... Translated in English [in
verse] by W[ye] Saltonstall. 1633. 8°]. [*DAP*]—
[? Ovid's Tristia. Containing five books of mourn-
ful elegies ... Newly translated into English by
T.P. 1713. 12°]. MC.92: "Ovid's Tristia:"

[Owen, Charles]. Some account of the life and writings
of Mr James Owen, Minister of the Gospel in Salop.
[Edited by J. Evans, D.D.]. 1709. 8°. MC.65:
"Life of James Owen:"

Owen, Robert. An address delivered to the inhabitants
of New Lanark ... at the opening of the new institution established for the formation of character.
2nd ed. 1816. 8°. *SC*.404.

————. A new view of society; or, essays on the principle of the formation of the human character.
2nd ed. 1816. 8°. *SC*.275. MC.80: "Owen's New
View of Soc^y:" LB.30: "On the Formation of Character."

Owen, afterwards Owen Pugh, William. See Milton, John.
Paradise Lost.

————. Geiriadur Cymraeg a Saesoneg. An abridgement
of the Welsh and English dictionary by W. Owen.
1806. 12°. *SC*.412: "8vo, 1826 [*sic*] (*Autog. 'W.
Wordsworth, from Robert Jones.'"*)

Oxendon, Charles. Sermons on the seven penitential
psalms. [? London], 1838. 12°. *SC*.198. LB.25:
"Oxendons Sermons."

*Oxford guide. *SC*.179: "Oxford Guide." [? The Oxford
University and city guide. Oxford, 1818. 8°]—
[? The new Oxford guide; or, companion through the
University. Oxford, 1759. 8°].

*Oxford prize poems. MC.51: "Oxford Prize Poems:" [Cf.
SC.624: "Prize Poems—twenty, various—(tied and
labelled by Mrs. W.) a bundle"].

P., I.T. See Homer. Odyssea.

P., T. See Ovidius Naso, Publius. Tristia.

*Pamphlets and ephemera--French, a bundle. *SC*.405

*Pamphlets on slavery. *SC*.80: "Pamphlets on Slavery,
   etc ... *two bundles*."

*Pamphlets, poetical various, a bundle. *SC*.609.

*Pamphlets, religious, miscellaneous, a bundle. *SC*.278.

*Pamphlets, chiefly theological, a bundle. *SC*.277.
   MC.22: "Pamphlets [? theological]."

*Pamphlets, [? theological] "numerous other 4to."
   SC.311.

Paracelsus. See Bombast von Hohenheim, Philipp.

The parent's high commission, 1843. 8°. *SC*.301.

Pareus, Daniel. See Quintilianus, Marcus Fabius.

Park, Andrew. The royal visit. Glasgow, 1842. 8°.
   SC.604.

Park, Sir James Allen. Memoirs of William Stevens,
   Esq., Treasurer of Queen Anne's Bounty. 4th ed.
   1825. 18cm. [*NUC*]. *SC*.252.

Park, Mungo. Travels in the interior of Africa, in
   the years 1795, 1796, 1797, also in 1805 and 1806;
   ... Compiled from his original works, and other
   authentic sources, by John Campbell. Edinburgh,
   1816. 12°. *SC*.174.

Parker, Samuel. A demonstration of the divine authority of the law of nature, and of the Christian
   religion. 1681. 8°. *SC*.279: "4to." MC.30/0:
   "Divine Authority:"

Parkhurst, John. A Greek and English lexicon to the New Testament ... To this work is prefixed a plain and easy Greek grammar. 1769. 8°.

Parkinson, Richard. The old church clock. 1843. 12°. LB.32.

————. Poems sacred and miscellaneous. 1832. 12°. *SC*.588.

Parliamentary abstracts; containing the substance of all important papers laid before the two Houses of Parliament during the session of 1825 (-1826). 2 vol. 1826,27. 8°. *SC*.58.

Parliamentary history and review, containing reports of the proceedings of the two Houses of Parliament during the session of 1825: 6 Geo. IV. With critical remarks on the principal measures of the session. 1826. 8°. [*EU*]. *SC*.58. LB.10.

*Parliamentary papers and abstracts. 1826. 8°. *SC*. 58. [Probably identifiable as Parliamentary abstracts, *supra*].

[Parry, Charles Henry]. Ellen Parry [Eleanor Matilda Maria Parry, 1822-1840]. [Bath, ? 1841]. 17cm. [*NUC*]. LB.35: "Ellen Parry's Memoir."

————. A memoir of Peregrine Bertie eleventh Lord Willoughby de Eresby, commander in chief of Queen Elizabeth's forces in the Low Countries and in France. By a descendant in the fourth generation. (On oeconomy, an address to his son by the author of the memoir). [Edited by Charles Henry Parry]. 1838. 8°. *SC*.123.

Parson, William and William White. History, directory, and gazetteer, of the counties of Durham and Northumberland. 2 vol. Newcastle, 1827,28. 12°. *SC*.146: "8vo ... 1827."

Parthenius, Nicaensis. See Gale, Thomas.

Pasley, Sir Charles William. Essay on the military policy and institutions of the British Empire. 1810. 8°. MC.39: "Military Policy."

Pasor, Georgius. See Hesiod.

————. Manuale Graecarum vocum N. Testamenti. [? Lugd[uni] Batavorum, 1634. 12°]. *SC*.205: "(*no title*" [n.p., n.d.]. MC.13: "Pasor's Manual:"

[Pasquin, Antoine Claude]. Voyages historiques et littéraires en Italie pendant les années 1826, 1827 et 1828. Par M. Valery [*pseud*.]. Bruxelles, 1835. 8°. *SC*.169.

Pastoral charges. See Sermons.

Paterculus. See Velleius Paterculus, Caius.

Paterson, Daniel. A new and accurate description of all the direct and the principal cross roads in Britain. 1771. 8°. *SC*.181: [n.d.]. MC.69: "Roads in Britain:"

Paterson, James. A complete commentary, with etymological, critical and classical notes, on Milton's Paradise Lost. 1744. 12°. *SC*.610. MC.80: "Patterson's [*sic*] Commty on Paradise Lost:" LB.63.

Paton, Allan Park. Poems. Second series. 1848. 12°. *SC*.459.

Patrick, Samuel. See Hederich, Benjamin.

Patrick, Simon. Mensa mystica: or, a discourse concerning the sacrament of the Lord's Supper. 1660. 8°. MC.23/0: "Mensa Mystica:"

Pausanias. The description of Greece: translated ... with notes. [By Thomas Taylor]. 3 vol. 1794. 8°. *SC*.147. MC.92/C: "Pausanias' History of Greece:"

Payne, Joseph. Studies in English poetry ... New ed.
1846. 8°. *SC*.598: "1845."

Peabody, Elizabeth Palmer. Aesthetic papers. [A maga-
zine]. Edited by Elizabeth Palmer Peabody. Boston,
1849. 8°. *SC*.403.

————. Record of a school: exemplifying the general
principle of spiritual culture. [Taught by A.B.
Alcott]. Boston, New York, Philadelphia, 1835.
12°. [*NUC*]. *SC*.313.

Pearce, Zachary. See Cicero, Marcus Tullius. De officiis; Longinus, Dionysius Cassius.

Pearson, John Norman. See Leighton, Robert.

Peel, Edmund. The Christian pilgrim, a poem of Palestine. [? 1830]. 8°. *SC*.636.

————. The conquerors of Lahore. An ode; with other
odes and sonnets. By the author of "The Christian
Pilgrim." 1846. 16°. [*L* (under "Lahore")]. [Al-
libone: "18mo."]. *SC*.581: "The Conquest [*sic*] of
Lahore, an ode, 1846."

————. The fair island; a poem. 1851. 8°. *SC*.527.

————. Judge not, a poem, on Christian charity.
(Minor poems, odes, etc.). 2 vol. 1834. 12°.
SC.612.

Peele, George. The works of George Peele: now first
collected. With some account of his writings and
notes: by the Rev. Alexander Dyce. 3 vol. 1828
[Vols. I-II]-1839 [Vol. III]. 19cm. [DFo.AC:Ann].
SC.613: "3 vols., 8vo, 1829-1839."

Peers, Charles. Christ's lamentation over Jerusalem;
a Seatonian prize poem. Cambridge, 1805. 4°.
MC.51: "Jerusalem: Prize Poem:"

Pellico, Silvio. Esther of Engaddi. A tragedy [in five acts and in verse]. From the Italian of Silvio Pellico. [1836]. 8°. *SC*.632.

Penfold, Jane Wallas. Madeira flowers, fruits and ferns. A selection of the botanical productions of that island, foreign and indigenous, drawn and coloured from nature by J.W. Penfold. 1845. fol. [DD:Ann]. LB.39: "Maldeira [or Maldura]."

The penny magazine. First and second series. [Edited by Charles Knight]. 14 vol. 1832-45. fol. *SC*. 406: "both series." LB.16.

Pennyman, John. See Multum in parvo.

Pepys, Samuel. Memoirs of Samuel Pepys. Comprising his diary from 1659 to 1669, deciphered by the Rev. J. Smith, from the original short-hand MS. in the Pepysian Library, and a selection from his private correspondence. Edited by Richard, Lord Braybrooke. 2nd ed. 5 vol. 1828. 8°. *SC*.148.

Percival, Edward. See Percival, Thomas.

Percival, Thomas. The works, literary, moral, and medical of Thomas Percival ... To which are prefixed, memoirs of his life and writings [by Edward Percival] and a selection from his literary correspondence. A new edition. 4 vol. 1807. 8°. *SC*.407.

[Percy, Thomas]. Reliques of ancient English poetry consisting of old heroic ballads, songs, and other pieces of our earlier poets, together with some few of later date. 4th ed. 3 vol. 1794. 16.8cm. [MH:Ann; *L*]. *SC*.614: "*(with MS. Note, bought at Hamburgh, 1798, by William Wordsworth)*"]. MC.47: "Percy's Reliques: 3 Vol:"

Percyvall, Richard. A dictionarie in Spanish and English, first published ... by R. Percivale ... now enlarged ... by J[ohn] Minsheu. 1623. fol. *SC*. 366. MC.16: "Minsheu's Span: Dicty:"

*Perfect peace, 1846. *SC*.307.

*Periodicals, miscellaneous. *SC*.116: "a bundle."

Perkins, Charles Callahan. Eight melodies dedicated
   to my sister. Huit mélodies dédiées à ma soeur
   ... 9 plates ... For voice and piano; English
   and French words. Paris, [184-]. [Includes Ode
   to a skylark (Wordsworth)]. [*NUC*]. *SC*.615: "Perkins' (C.L.). Eight Melodies, *with nine pictorial
   Illustrations after Francia* [Francesco Raibolini
   called Il Francia [*DNB*]] *beautifully lithographed,
   4to, with Presentation Autog.*"

Perrault, Charles. [Contes des fées]. Histoires ou
   contes du temps passé. Paris, 1698. 12°. MC.97:
   "Perrault's Contes:"

[Perrault, Nicholas]. The Jesuits morals. Collected
   by a doctor of the Colledge of Sorbon in Paris.
   [By Nicholas Perrault]. 1670. fol. *SC*.260.
   MC.28: "Jesuits Morals:"

Perrin, Jean Baptiste. Fables amusantes; avec une table
   générale et particulière des mots et de leur signification en Anglois. 1771. 12°. MC.101: "Perrin's Fables Amusantes:"

Perrin, Jean Paul. Luthers fore-runners; or, a cloud
   witnesses, deposing for the Protestant faith.
   Gathered together in the historie of the Waldenses ... faithfully collected ... by I.P. P[errin]
   L[ion], translated out of French by S[amson] Lennard. 1624. 4°. *SC*.236. MC.24: "Luther's
   Forerunners:"

Perrot d'Ablancourt, Nicholas. See Tacitus, Publius
   Cornelius.

Persius Flaccus, Aulus. See Juvenalis, Decimus
   Junius.

———. A. Persii Flacci satyrae sex. cum posthumis
   commentariis, Johannis Bond. Parisiis, 1644.

8°. *SC*.397: "London, 1684." MC.5: "Persius:--
Bond."

A person of honor. See An account of some matters relating to the Long Parliament.

Peter, William. See Schiller, Johann Christoph Friedrich von.

————. Sacred songs, being an attempted paraphrase
of some portions of Scripture, with other poems.
By a layman [William Peter]. A new edition. 1834.
12°. *SC*.636.

Pétis de la Croix, François. Les milles & un jour.
Contes persans. Traduits en françois par m. Pétis
de la Croix. 5 vol. Amsterdam, 1712-26. [n.s.].
[*NUC*]. *SC*.511: "5 tomes, 12mo, *Amsterdam*, 1726."

————. The thousand and one days: Persian tales ...
translated from the French by M^r [Ambrose] Philips. [Philips' translation is the second of
two titles in Vol. 13 (1783) of the Novelist's
magazine]. LB.13: "Persian Tales."

Petrarca, Francesco. Il Petrarca con dichiarationi
non più stampate insieme con annotationi ... di
... Bembo ... e più una conserva di tutte le sue
rime ridotte sotto le cinque lettere vocali [by
Luca Antonio Ridolfi]. Venetia, 1564. 12°.
SC.379.

Pettitt, Edward. The visions of government, wherein
the antimonarchical principles and practices of
all fanatical Commonwealths-men and Jesuitical
politicians are ... exposed. 1684. 8°. MC.38:
"Visions of Govern:"

Phaedrus. Fabularum AEsopiarum libri quinque. [1765].
[PSC.WWC.JB:Ann]. MC.5: "Phaedrus: Cop:"

Phelan, Margaret. See Phelan, William.

Phelan, William. The remains of William Phelan. [Edited by Margaret Phelan]. With a biographical memoir by John [Jebb], Bishop of Limerick. 2 vol. 1832. 8°. *SC*.280.

Philips, Ambrose. See Pétis de la Croix, François.

*Phillips, [? John ? Katherine]. Poems. MC.50: "Phillips' Poems:"

Philippson, Joannes, Sleidanus. De quatuor summis imperiis, Babylonico, Persico, Graeco, et Romano, libri tres. Amstaelodami, 1705. 16°. *SC*.410. MC.9: "Sleiden de Monar:"

Phipps, E. [? Hon. Edmund]. The Fergusons; or, woman's love and the world's favour. [By E. Phipps]. 2 vol. 1839. 8°. [*E*]. *SC*.487. LB.36.

Phiston (or Fiston), William. See Lefèvre, Raoul.

*Physical science. [? *SC*.129: "three others"].

*Pieces of Italian poetry. [? Isola, Agostino. Pieces selected from the Italian poets ... and translated into English verse by some gentlemen of the University. Cambridge, 1778. 8°. 2nd ed. Cambridge, 1784. 8°]. MC.46: "Pieces of Ital: Poetry:"

*Pilgrim, Edward Trapp. [? Poetical trifles. 1785. 8°; 2nd ed. 1813. 8°]--[? Poetical scraps, on various subjects, serious and comic. Exeter, 1837. 8°]. *SC*.617: "Pilgrim's [E. Trapp, Esq.) Poems (*with Present. Autog. by 'an old Pilgrim'*)."

*Pindar. *SC*.348: "odd vol."

————. Carmina, cum lectionis varietate et adnotationibus, iterum curavit Chr. Gottl. Heyne ... 5 pts. in 4 vol. Gottingae, 1798-99. 8°. [*BN*]. *SC*.618: "3 vols. (in 4)." MC.5: "4 vol."

Pirckheimer, Bilibaldus. See Gregory, of Nazianzus,
Saint, Patriarch of Constantinople.

Plato. The Cratylus, Phaedo, Parmenides, and Timaeus
of Plato, translated from the Greek by Thomas
Taylor. With notes on the Cratylus, and an explanatory introduction to each dialogue. 1793. 8°.
[WL.Ann]. *SC*.408.

————. Dialogi V. Recensuit notisque illustravit N.
Forster. Oxonii, 1745. 8°; ed. 3a. Oxonii,
1765. 8°. *SC*.409: "1752."

*Plays. MC.47: "Plays: 1 Vol:"

Plinius Caecilius Secundus, Caius. Epistolarum libri
x. et panegyricus. Accedunt variantes lectiones.
Lugd.-Batavorum, 1640. 12°. [*BN*]. *SC*.410. MC.
5: "Plinii Epist: 2 Cop:" "1. H[artley] C[ole-
ridge]."

Plumptre, Anne. A narrative of a three years' residence in France, principally in the southern
departments, from ... 1802 to 1805; including
some ... particulars respecting the early life of
the French emperor. 3 vol. 1810. 8°. MC.69:
"Plumptree's [*sic*] Residence in France 3 Vol:"

Plutarch. The lives of the noble Grecians and Romans,
compared together, by that grave learned philosopher & historiographer Plutarch of Chaeronea.
Tr. out of Greek into French, by James Amiot
[Jacques Amyot] ... and out of French into English,
by Sir Thomas North, knight ... and now in this
edition are further added, The lives of several
eminent persons, translated out of ... Andrew
Thevet. Cambridge, London, 1606. 35.5cm. [CtY.
BL:Ann]. *SC*.77. MC.64: "Plutarch's Lives:"

Pocket traveling companions. See Maps.

*Poems. [? *SC*.461: "19 various." ? *SC*.471: "eight
other books." ? *SC*.523: "six other" [RP.QH:

"pamphlets"]. ? *SC*.616: "two other books." ? *SC*.
617: "and others [probably 14]." ? *SC*.622: "four
others--various--4to." ? *SC*.661: "twelve other
Poetical productions by various authors." ? *SC*.
677: "Three others"].

*Poems. *SC*.524: "Poems, 1816."

Poems by eminent ladies: particularly Mrs Barber, Miss
Behn, Miss Carter, Lady Chudleigh, Mrs Cockburn,
Mrs Grierson, Mrs Jones, Mrs Killigrew, Mrs Lea-
por, Mrs Madan, Mrs Masters, Lady M.W. Montague,
Mrs Monk, Dutchess of Newcastle, Mrs K. Philips, M^rs
Pilkington, Mrs Rowe, Lady Winchelsea. [? Edited
by George Colman, the Elder, and Bonnell Thornton].
2 vol. 1755. 12°. *SC*.500. MC.49: "Poems by
Em: Ladies: 2 Vol:" LB.13.

*Poems on Obeah. MC.47: "Poems on Obeah &c:"

Poetae Latini minores. LB.11: "Col^n Latin poets H.
Coleridge 1830/March 21/returned." See STC entry.

*Poetical extracts. *SC*.619: "Poetical Extracts, 8vo,
calf, 1791."

Poiret, Jean Louis Marie. Travels through Barbary,
in a series of letters, written from the ancient
Numidia in the years 1785 and 1786, and containing
an account of the customs and manners of the Moors
and Bedouin Arabs. [1791]. 12°. MC.70: "Travels
through Barbary:"

*Polemical Divinity. [? *SC*.217: "six others"].

Poliziano, Angelo Ambrogini. See Herodian.

Polybius. The history of Polybius ... the five first
bookes entire; with all the parcels of the subsequent bookes unto the eighteenth according to the
Greeke originall ... Translated by Edward Grime-
ston. 1634. fol. *SC*.60. MC.92: "History of
Polybius."

Pomey, François Antoine. See Tooke, Andrew.

Ponsonby, Mrs. Catherine. Lays of the Lakes, and other poems of description and reflection. Glasgow, 1850. 12°. *SC*.620.

Poole, Matthew. The nullity of the Romish faith; or, a blow at the root of the Romish Church, being an examination of that fundamental doctrine of the Church of Rome concerning the Churches infallibility ... together with an appendix tending to the demonstration of the solidity of the Protestant faith. 2nd ed. Oxford, 1667. 8°. [*L*: *"With the autograph of William Wordsworth, the Poet"*]. *SC*. 282. MC.22: "Roman Faith:"

Pope, Alexander. See Montagu, Lady Mary Wortley.

*———. *SC*.601: "Odd Volumes--Dryden, Pope, Virgil, etc. 12." HL.MK.167: "4 Odd Vols. Pope."

Poquelin de Molière, Jean Baptiste. Chefs-d'oeuvre de Molière. Paris, 1787-88. 12°. [*BN*]. *SC*.502: "2 tomes ... 1787." [? MC.96: "Moliere: 3 Vol:"]. [? LB.52: "Oeuvres de Molière"].

———. Oeuvres. Nouvelle ed. [Par Marc Antoine Joly]. 8 vol. Paris, 1770. 12°. [*BN*]. *SC*. 596: "7 tomes." [? MC.96: "Moliere: 3 Vol:"]. [? LB.52: "Oeuvres de Molière"].

Porter, Mrs. George Richardson (Sarah). See Lalor, John.

Port Royal, Messieurs de. See Nugent, Thomas.

Potter, John. Archaeologia Graeca. New ed. [Evidently the 10th]. 2 vol. 1795. 8°. *SC*.61: "vol. 1, 8vo ... 1808."

Powell, Thomas. See Chaucer, Geoffrey.

————. The blind wife; or, the student of Bonn. A tragic romance. 1843. 8°. *SC*.514: "*(with Presentation Autograph)*."

————. [Another copy]. *SC*.664.

————. The confessions of the ideal, and other poems. 1844. 18cm. [NIC.Ann]. *SC*.599.

————. The Count de Foix. A tale of the olden time. [In verse]. 1842. 8°. *SC*.621.

————. [Another copy]. *SC*.632.

————. [Another copy]. *SC*.686.

————. Poems. 1842. 18cm. [TxU.Wn:Ann]. *SC*.612. *SC*.637.

————. Poems. 1845. 16°. [L: "*A different collection from the preceding*"]. *SC*.581: "1844 [*sic*]."

Pratt, John Jeffreys, Marquis of Camden. See Wordsworth, Christopher, Bishop of Lincoln. Ode performed in the Senate House, Cambridge.

*Prayer. [? *SC*.302: "three other books"].

Prentis, Stephen. Le Grand-Bey; or, the tomb of Chateaubriand. [Included as of 1849 in his Opuscula, Dinan, 1853, 4°, but cited in *DNB* as a separate publication. 1849]. [*NUC*; *L*]. *SC*.622: "1849."

————. Translations from the French. Dinan, 1848. 4°. [Included in his Opuscula]. *SC*.622.

————. A tribute to May. [In verse]. Dinan, 1849. 4°. *SC*.622: "*(with Pres. Autog.)*, 1848."

————. Winter flowers. [Dinan], 1849. [Included in his Opuscula]. *SC*.622: "4to *(Pres. Autog.)*."

————. The wreck of the Roscommon. [A poem]. Dinan, London, 1844. 8°. [L: *"With the autograph of William Wordsworth"*]. *SC*.632.

————. Tintern. Stonehenge. "Oh! think of me at times!" [In verse]. Dinan, London, 1843. 8°. *SC*.512.

A presbyter of the Church of England. Mr. [Benjamin] Hoadly's Measures of submission to the civil magistrate, enquired into, and disprov'd. By a presbyter of the Church of England. 1711. 19cm. [NIC. Ann]. MC.29: [? "On Hoadley's [*sic*] Measures of Subm:"].

Prescott, Thomas. Sermons, doctrinal, miscellaneous, and occasional. Glasgow, 1848. 16°. *SC*.187.

Price, Sir Uvedale. An essay on the modern pronunciation of the Greek and Latin languages. Oxford, 1827. 8°. *SC*.411: *"with Wordsworth's Autog. and MS. Notes in reference to divers errata (probably) in the Author's handwriting."*

Prideaux, Humphrey. Ecclesiastical tracts formerly published. 1716. 8°. *SC*.213.

————. The Old and New Testament connected in the history of the Jews and neighboring nations. 11th ed. 4 vol. 1749. *SC*.283.

————. The original and right of tithes for the maintenance of the ministry in a Christian church truly stated. 2 pt. 1710. 8°. *SC*.190. MC.40: "Prideau's Right of Tithes:"

Pringle, Thomas. The poetical works of Thomas Pringle. With a sketch of his life by Leitch Ritchie. 1838. 8°. *SC*.623: "1828."

Prior, Sir James. The country house and other poems. 1846. 8°. [*E*]. *SC*.630.

*Prize poems. *SC*.624: "twenty, various."

Proceedings of the Association for Promoting the Dis-
    covery of the Interior Parts of Africa. 2 vol.
    1790, 1802. 4°. [*L*: "*Vol. 2 has a second title
    reading: African Researches*"]. *SC*.20 [apparently
    a single volume]: "8vo, 1791; *with Autographs of
    Coleridge and Wordsworth*." MC.72: "Proceed: of
    African Associat:"

Proceedings of the Royal Society of Edinburgh. [Vol.
    1--Dec. 1832]. Edinburgh, 1845. 21.5cm.--26.5cm.
    [*NUC*]. *SC*.116: "sundry numbers."

Procopius, of Caesarea. Procopii Caesariensis de rebus
    Gothorum, Persarum, ac Vandalorum libri vii, una
    cum aliis mediorum temporum historicis, quorum cat-
    alogum sequens indicabit pagina. His omnibus ac-
    cessit rerum copiosissimus index. Basiliae, 1531.
    13.25 in. [*CWC*:Ann]. *SC*.62: "folio, *Basilae* [*sic*],
    1531." MC.5: "Procopius:---Fol:" MC.18: "Proco-
    pius."

Procter, Bryan Waller [Cornwall, Barry, *pseud*.]. See
    Jonson, Ben.

————. Dramatic scenes and other poems. 2nd ed.
    1820. [Ian Jack:Ann]. [? LB.39: "Dramatic Scenes
    1 vol."].

————. English songs, and other small poems. 1832.
    12°. *SC*.526.

————. Marcian Colonna, an Italian tale, with three
    dramatic scenes and other poems. 1820. 8°. *SC*.
    504. See CaOTV.HD. [? LB.39: "Dramatic Scenes 1
    vol."].

Prodicus of Ceos. See Epictetus.

Propertius, Sextus. LB.29: "A small colection [*sic*]
    Propertius &c." See Catullus, Caius Valerius.

Prout, Samuel. Facsimiles of sketches made in Flanders and Germany, and drawn on stone. [1833]. 55cm. [*NUC*; *L*]. LB.54: "Prout's Belgium Views &c &c, large Folio."

*Proverbs. MC.83: "Proverbs: &c:"

Prynne, William. A legall vindication of the liberties of England against illegall taxes and pretended acts of Parliament lately enforced on the people. 1649. 4°. *SC*.63. MC.38/C: "Vindicat: of Libert:"

Psalmanazar, George. See An universal history.

————. An historical and geographical description of Formosa ... giving an account of the religion customs, manners, &c of the inhabitants. 1704. 8°. *SC*.159.

Ptolemaeus Hephaestionis. See Gale, Thomas.

Pufendorf, Samuel von, Baron. De officio hominis et civis juxta legem naturalem libri duo. Editio secunda ... emendatior. Selectis variorum notis ... illustravit, indicemque rerum subjunxit Thomas Johnson. 1737. 8°. *SC*.149.

Pugh, William O. See Owen, afterwards Owen Pugh, William.

Purchas, Samuel. Purchas his pilgrimage; or, relations of the world and the religions observed in all ages. 3rd ed., much enlarged. 1617. fol. *SC*.285. MC. 23: "Purchas' Pilgrimage:"

Pythagoras. See Diogenes Laërtius.

Quarles, Francis. Divine poems: containing the history
    of Jonah, Ester [*sic*], Job, Sampson. 1642. 8°.
    SC.625: "12mo." MC.50: "Divine Poems:"

————. Enchiridion: containing institutions, divine
    [contemplative. practicall, Moral [ethicall. oe-
    conomicall. political. Written by Fra: Quarles.
    1658. 12.5cm. [*NUC*]. *SC*.180: "12mo."

Quillinan, Edward. The conspirators, or the romance
    of military life. 3 vol. 1841. 12°. [DD:Ann].
    LB.30: "Conspirators 3 Vols."

Quintilianus, Marcus Fabius. M. Fabii Quinctiliani
    De institutione oratoria libri duodecim, cum dupli-
    ci indice. Ex tribus codicibus MSS. et octo im-
    pressis emendavit, atque lectiones variantes adje-
    cit E[dmundus] Gibson ... Accedunt Emendationum
    specimen, et Tribunus Marianus, declamatio, nunc
    primum ex codice MS. edita. Oxoniae, 1693. 4°.
    SC.413. MC.5: "Quintilianus Qto:"

————. M. Fabii Quintiliani Institutionum oratoriarum
    libri xii; summa diligentia ad fidem vetustissi-
    morum codicum recogniti ac restituti; nunc huic
    editioni adiecit Fabianarum notarum spicilegium
    subcisivum Daniel Pareus, Phil. F.; accesserunt
    etiam Quintilianorum declamationes; cum indice ac-
    curatissimo. Genevae, 1641. 17.5cm. [*NUC*].
    SC.389. MC.5: "Quintilianus: duodo:"

R., E. Geography and history selected by a lady for
    the use of her own children. [The preface is
    signed, E.R.]. 1790. 12°. MC.71: "Geogr: & Hist:
    by a Lady:"

R., S. See Rogers, Samuel.

Rabelais, François. Rabelais moderne; ou les oeuvres
    de Maître François Rabelais, M.D. 6 tomes (in 7).
    Amsterdam, 1752. 12°. [*L*: "*Tom. 4 and 5 are each*

in two parts"]. *SC*.626: "6 tomes (in 7), 12mo, *Amst.*, 1752." *SC*.534: "tome 4, 1752." LB.20: "Rabelais 1st vol English--D° D° French."

————. The works of Francis Rabelais. Translated from the French, and illustrated with explanatory notes, by M. [Jacob] Le Du Chat and others. 4 vol. 1784. 12°. *SC*.627: "8vo." LB.20: "Rabelais 1st vol English."

Racine, Jean. Oeuvres de Jean Racine [avec la notice de J[acques] A[ndré] Naigeon]. 4 vol. Paris, an X--1802. 32°. (in Bibliothèque portative du voyageur). [*BN*]. [WL:Ann: "Tome premier ... Tome deuxième 16mo."]. MC.100: "Oeuvres de Jean Racine 3 Vol:"

Radcliffe, Mrs. Ann. See Ward, afterwards Radcliffe, Ann.

Raffald, Elizabeth. The experienced English house-keeper, for the use and ease of ladies, house-keep-ers, cooks, &c ... consisting of near 800 original receipts, most of which never appeared in print. Manchester, 1769. 8°. MC.76: "Raffald's Cookery: Mrs. Luff's."

Ragg, Thomas. Heber, Records of the poor, Lays from the prophets, and other poems. 2nd ed. 1841. 12°. *SC*.466: "J. [*sic*] Ragg."

————. The martyr of Verulam, and other poems. 2nd ed. 1835. 12°. *SC*.514.

————. Sketches from life, Lyrics from the Pentateuch, and other poems. 1837. 12°. *SC*.599.

[Raine, James]. A brief account of Durham Cathedral. Newcastle, 1833. 8°. *SC*.11.

Ramond de Carbonnières, Louis François Elizabeth, trans. See Coxe, William.

Ramsay, Allan. The evergreen, being a collection of Scots poems, wrote by the ingenious before 1600. 2 vol. Glasgow, 1824. 14cm. [*NUC*]. *SC*.628. LB.10: "2 vols Evergreen."

Rand, William. See Gassend, Pierre.

Randolph, Robert. See Randolph, Thomas.

Randolph, Thomas. Poems, with the Muses looking-glass, and Amyntas. The fifth edition corrected. [Edited by Robert Randolph]. Oxford, 1668. 8°. *SC*. 629: "12mo, *Oxford*, 1688 [*sic*]." MC.45: "Randolph's Poems:" MC.47: "Randolph's Poems:"

Rapin, René. Reflections on Aristotle's treatise of poesie, containing the necessary, rational, and universal rules for epick, dramatick, and the other sorts of poetry. With reflections on the works of the ancient and modern poets. [Translated by Thomas Rymer]. 1674. 8°. *SC*.602. MC.81: "Rapin's Reflect: on Arist:"

[Rastell, John, printer]. Les termes de la ley; or, certaine difficult and obscure words, and termes of the common lawes of this realme expanded. 1671. 16°. *SC*.85: "8vo, 1671." MC.38: "Law Terms:"

Rauthmell, Richard. Antiquitates Bremetonacenses; or, the Roman antiquities of Overborough; wherein Overborough is proved to be the Bremetonacae of Antonius. 1746. 4°; Antiquitates Bremetonacenses ... reprinted from the original edition of 1746; with additions. Kirkby Lonsdale, 1824. 4°. *SC*. 157: "The Roman Antiquities of Overborough, by R. Rauthmell, 8vo, 1814 [*sic*]." [? MC.12: "Roman Antiquit:"].

Rawley, William. Resuscitatio, or bringing into ... light several pieces of the works of F[rancis] Bacon. 3rd ed. 1671. fol. *SC*.415. MC.38: "Resuscitatio:"

Ray, John. Observations, topographical, moral, and
   physiological; made in a journey through part of
   the Low-Countries, Germany, Italy, and France;
   with a catalogue of plants not native of England,
   found spontaneously growing in those parts, and
   their virtues ... Whereunto is added A brief account of Francis Willughby [*sic*] Esq. his voyage
   through a great part of Spain. 1673. 8°. *SC*.150.
   MC.72: "Ray's Observations."

Reade, John Edmund. Catiline; or, the Roman conspir-
   acy; an historical drama [in five acts and in
   verse]. 1839. 8°. *SC*.632: "*(Private Publication,
   with Autog. Presen.)*".

————. The deluge; a drama, in twelve scenes. [With
   other poems]. 1839. *SC*.664.

————. Italy: a poem in six parts, with historical
   and classical notes. 1838. 8.625 in. [*CWC*: Ann].
   SC.631: "8vo, 1838." LB.24: "Itaty [*sic*]: Poem
   [lent in mid-1838]."

————. A record of the Pyramids; a drama, in ten
   scenes [and in verse]. (Miscellaneous poems).
   1842. 8°. *SC*.632: "*(Presen. Autog.)*."

————. Revelations of life; and other poems. 1849.
   16°. [NIC:Ann; *L*]. *SC*.630: "16mo."

————. Sacred poems, from subjects in the Old Testament. (Miscellaneous poems). 1843. 8°. *SC*.632:
   "*(with Presen. Autog.)*."

Records of literature. See The literary annual register.

Reece, Richard. A practical dictionary of domestic
   medicine. With a popular description of anatomy,
   physiology ... surgery. 1808. 8°. *SC*.151.

Reed, Henry Hope. Lectures on English history and
   tragic poetry, as illustrated by Shakespeare.

[Ed. William Bradford Reed]. 1856. 8°. LB.59:
"Mr Reed's 2nd Vol. [lent after 5 June 1856]."
See article on Henry Reed in *DAB*.

Reed, Sampson. Observations on the growth of the mind.
Boston, 1829. 12°. [DD:Ann]. LB.11: "Sampson
Reed Growth of Mind."

Reed, William Bradford. See Reed, Henry Hope.

Reeve, Clara. The old English baron. (Vol. 22 of The
British novelists). *SC*.515. MC.87.

Reinhard, Karl. See Bürger, Gottfried August.

Relph, Josiah. A miscellany of poems, consisting of
original poems, translations, pastorals in the
Cumberland dialect, familiar epistles, fables,
songs, and epigrams ... with a pref[ace] and a
glossary. Glasgow, 1747. 19cm. [*NUC*; *L*]. LB.41:
"Relph's Poems."

The remorse of Orestes, King of Argos, Lacedemon, My-
cenae, and Sicyon, son of Agamemnon. 1841. 8°.
SC.623.

Rennie, James. See Walton, Izaak.

Reresby, Sir John. The memoirs of Sir John Reresby
... containing several private and remarkable
transactions from the Restoration to the Revolution inclusively. 1735. 8°. *SC*.152.

Reynolds, Edward. A treatise of the passions and
faculties of the soule of man. With the several
dignities and corruptions thereunto belonging.
1647. 18.5cm. [MH:Ann]. [Ox: "1647. 4°"].
SC.221. MC.32: "Treat: of the Passions:"

Reynolds, Frederic Mansell, ed. The keepsake. 1828-
1835. 8°. LB.12 [probably the 1829 volume, to
which WW contributed. See *CWC*.500].

Reynolds, Sir Joshua. See Dufresnoy, Charles Alphonse.

————. The works of Sir Joshua Reynolds, knight ...
containing his Discourses, Idlers, A journey to
Flanders and Holland, and his commentary on Du
Fresnoy's Art of painting; printed from his revised
copies, (with his last corrections and additions.)
... To which is prefixed An account of the life
and writings of the author by Edmond Malone, esq.
... The 3rd ed. corrected. 3 vol. 1801. 22cm.
[*NUC*]. [DD:Ann]. MC.79: "Sir Jos: Reynold's [*sic*]
Works: 3 Vol:" LB.11: "Reynolds 3 Vols."

Rhodes, E. Peak scenery; or, excursions in Derbyshire.
1824. 8°. [*L: "The plates do not accompany this
edition of the letterpress"*]. *SC*.634: "8vo, 1824."

Richards, Thomas. Antiquae linguae britannicae thesaurus; being a British, or Welsh-English dictionary. To which is prefix'd a Welsh grammar with
all the rules in English. [Also] a large collection of British proverbs. Bristol, [1751]. [n.s.]
[*NUC*]. *SC*.418: "8vo ... 1751."

Richardson, Charles. A new dictionary of the English
language. 2 vol. 1836. 4°. *SC*.419. LB.49:
"Richardson's Dictionary 2 Vols."

Richardson, Jonathan, the Elder and the Younger. Explanatory notes and remarks on Milton's Paradise
lost. By Jonathan Richardson, father and son.
With the life of the author, and a discourse on
the poem, by J. Richardson, Sen. 1734. 8°.
[WL:n.s.]. *SC*.165. MC.80: "Richardson on Milton:"

Richardson, Samuel. Clarissa Harlowe. (Vol. 14-15 of
The novelist's magazine). LB.9: "Clarissa H 2
Vols."

————. The history of Sir Charles Grandison. (Vol.
10-11 of The novelist's magazine). LB: "Sir C.
Grandison."

————. [? Pamela; oder die belohnte tugend. Aus der
6. vermehrten Englischen aufl[age] in das Teutsche
übersetzt und mit kupfern gezieret. 4 vol. Leip-
sig [*sic*], 1750. 18cm.]. [*NUC*]. *SC*.608: "Pamela,
in German, 4 vols. 8vo, 1750." MC.99: "Pamela 4
Vol:"

Richardson, William. Anecdotes of the Russian Empire,
in a series of letters written ... from St. Peters-
burgh. 1784. 8°. *SC*.171.

Richer, François. Causes célèbres et intéressantes;
avec les jugemens qui les ont decidées. 22 tomes.
Amsterdam, 1772-1788. 17cm. [*NUC*]. *SC*.65: "20
tomes, 12mo ... *Amsterdam*, 1772-1787."

Rickman, William Charles. Biographical memoir of John
Rickman, Esq., F.R.S. 1841. 4°. *SC*.153: "(*Printed for Private Distribution only*)."

[Ridley, James]. The tales of the Genii; or the de-
lightful lessons of Horam, the son of Asmar. Faithfully translated from the Persian manuscript ...
by Sir Charles Morell [i.e. James Ridley]. [The
first item in Vol. 3 (1781) of Harrison's The
novelist's magazine]. LB.15: "Tales of Genii."
[For Ridley's authorship see the article about
him in *DNB*].

Ridley, Mark. A short treatise of magneticall bodies
and motions. 1613. 4°. *SC*.154. MC.33: "Treatise on Mag: Bodies:"

Ridolfi, Luca Antonio. See Petrarca, Francesco.

Rio, Alexis François. De la poésie chrétienne dans
son principe, dans sa matière et dans ses formes;
par A.-F. Rio. Forme de l'art, peinture. [2 par-
tie]. Paris, 1836. 22.5cm. [Published before
the first part, which was issued in 1841, with
title: De l'art chrétien]. [*NUC*]. [*BN*: "2° par-
tie. Paris, 1836. 8°"]. *SC*.635: "8vo ... 1837."

————. La petite Chouannerie ou histoire d'un col-
lége breton sous l'Empire. Londres, Paris, 1842.
8°. [DD:Ann]. *SC*.168: "*(with some Pencilled
Notes by the Poet W.).*"

Rishanger, William de. The chronicle of William de
Rishanger, of the Barons' War, the miracles of
Simon de Montfort. Edited by James Orchard Halli-
well-Phillips. 1840. 8°. *SC*.15.

Ritchie, Leitch. See Pringle, Thomas.

[Ritson, Joseph]. Ancient songs, from the time of
King Henry the Third to the Revolution. [Collec-
ted and published, with observations on the ancient
English minstrels, a dissertation on the songs and
music of the ancient English, notes and a glossary
by J. Ritson]. 1790. 8°. [WL:Ann]. [PL: "After
the date on the title page there has been added
by hand & in ink the figure 'II,' attempting therefore to turn the imprint date from 'M DCC XC' to
'M DCC XCII'"]. MC.44: "Anc^t: Songs from Henry
III to Revolut:"

[————]. Pieces of ancient popular poetry; from authentic manuscripts and old printed copies. [Edi-
ted by J. Ritson]. 1791. 8°. [WL:Ann]. MC.44:
"Ancient Pop: Poetry:" [? LB.41: "Rittsons [*sic*]
Ballads"].

[————]. Scotish song. [A collection of Scotch
songs, with the airs. Edited, with an historical
essay and notes, by Joseph Ritson]. 2 vol. 1794.
12°. [? MC.48: "Scottish Songs: 2 Vols:", which
may represent David Herd. Ancient and modern Scottish songs, heroic ballads, &c. 2nd ed. 2 vol.
Edinburgh, 1791. 12°, *SC*.455, which see]. LB.32:
"Scotish Songs, Vol 1."

[————]. A select collection of English songs.
[Edited, with an historical essay on national song,
by J. Ritson]. 3 vol. 1783. 8°. [*L: "Vol. 3
contains the musical notes"*]. [WL:Ann]. MC.47:

"Ritson's Songs: 3 Vol:" LB.41: "English Songs 2 vols 1783."

Roberts, George. See Yonge, Walter.

Roberts, Mrs. Martyn. The spiritual creation, or soul's new birth. A poem. 1843. 8°. *SC*.636. LB.30: "Mrs Roberts [lent in 1843]."

Roberts, William Isaac. Poems and letters ... by William Isaac Roberts. With some account of his life. 1811. 8°. *SC*.522.

Robertson, Frederick William. Sermons preached at Trinity Chapel, Brighton. First series. 1855. 8°; second series. 1855. 8°. LB.61: "Robertson's Sermons *1st & 2nd* 1st Vol. [lent 25 Nov. 1858]."

Robertson, Rev. Joseph, of Edinburgh. The traveller's guide through Scotland and its' [*sic*] islands. 3rd ed. Edinburgh, 1806. [n.s.]. [*NUC*]. [*BB*: "1806. 8°"]. [WL:Ann]. *SC*.181. MC.70: "Guide through Scotland."

Robertson, Patrick, Lord. Sonnets, reflective and descriptive; and other poems. Edinburgh, 1849. 8°. *SC*.367.

Robertson, William, Lexicographer. Thesaurus linguae sanctae compendiose scil. contractus, plane tamen reseratus, pleneque explicatus: sive concordantiale lexicon Hebraeo-Latino-Biblicum ... una cum concordantiis Hebraicis. 1680. 4°. MC.12: "Robertson's Thesaurus:" [Possibly also MC.17/0: "Epito: Thesauri Ling: Sanct:"].

Robertson, William, D.D. The works of William Robertson ... to which is prefixed an account of his life and writings, by Dugald Stewart. 1831. 8°. *SC*.420.

————. The history of America ... In which is included the posthumous volume. 4 vol. Alston, 1809. 12°. *SC*.66: "8vo."

Robinson, Henry Crabb. Exposure of misrepresentations contained in the preface to The correspondence of William Wilberforce. 1840. 21cm. [NIC:Ann]. *SC*.349.

[Robinson, John]. An account of Sweden; together with an extract of the history of that kingdom. [By John Robinson, Bishop of London]. 1694. 8°. *SC*.78: "Account of Sweden, 1694." MC.61: "Account of Sweden."

Robson, John. Three early English metrical romances with an introduction and glossary. Edited by John Robson, Esq. 1842. 8°. *SC*.15.

Roche, Regina Maria. Contrast. 3 vol. 1828. 12°. *SC*.465. LB.15.

[Rogers, _____, Translator]. The case of seduction against the Rev. Abbé Claudius des Rues, for committing rapes upon 133 virgins; translated from the French, by Mr. Rogers. 1726. 8°. [*BB*]. MC. 38: "Case of Seduction:"

Rogers, Samuel. See Byron, George Gordon Noel, Baron Byron.

————. Italy, a poem. Part the first. 1822. 15.9cm. [Paul F. Betz:Ann]. LB.6: "Italy by Saml Rogers 12mo [returned 25 Aug. 1824]."

————. Italy, a poem. 1830. 21cm. [*NUC*]. [WL: "William Wordsworth Jr. from his aunt D.W. November 4th, 1835"]. [? LB.12: "SR's Italy [lent 14 Feb. 1831]"].

————. [Another copy]. [Richard Wordsworth: "From the author" and the autograph of John Wordsworth (either the son or the grandson of WW)]. [? LB. 12: "SR's Italy [lent 14 Feb. 1831]"].

————. Italy, a poem. Paris, 1840. 12°. *SC*.569: "1840."

————. The pleasures of memory. 6th ed. 1794. 8°. [WL:Ann]. MC.51: "Pleas: of Memo:"

————. The pleasures of memory, with other poems. 1839. 12°. [Lowndes]. *SC*.569.

————. Poems. 1812. 8°. MC.47: "Rogers' Poems: 1812:" MC.51: "Roger's [*sic*] Poems: 1812:"

————. Poems. 1816. 8°. MC.51: "Rogers' Poems: 1816:"

Rogerson, John Bolton. Rhyme, romance, and revery. 1840. 8°. *SC*.638: "Revelry [*sic*]."

————. A voice from the town, and other poems. 1842. 12°. *SC*.460.

————. The wandering angel, and other poems. 1844. 8°. *SC*.466.

Rohault, Jacques. J. Rohaulti Physica. Latine vertit, recensuit, et adnotationibus ex ... I. Newtoni philosophia maximam partem haustis, amplificavit ... S. Clarke.... Editio quarta, in qua annotationes sunt ... auctiores, additaeque octo tabulae aeri incisae. 1718. 8°. *SC*.154.

Rokewoode, John Gage. See Jocelinus.

Rosa, Salvatore. [? Satire di Salvatore Rosa, con le note d'Anton Maria Salvini e d'altri, ed alcune notizi appartenenti alla vita dell'autore. Ed. 3, corretta ed accresciuta. Amsterdam, 1790. 14cm.]. [*NUC*]. *SC*.570: "18mo, Amst ... *n.d.*"

Roscoe, Mrs. Henry. See Sandbach, Margaret.

Rose, Hugh James. The commission and consequent duties of the clergy; in a series of discourses preached before the University of Cambridge, in April, 1826. London, Cambridge, 1828. 8°. *SC*.248: "by H.J. Rouse [*sic*]."

————. Eight sermons preached before the University
of Cambridge ... To which is added a reprint of a
sermon [on Eccl. iii. 2] preached before the university on Commencement Sunday 1826. Cambridge,
1831. 8°. *SC*.248: "1830."

Ross, Alexander. Pansebeia [in Greek]; or, a view of
all religions in the world ... Second edition. To
which are annexed, the lives, actions and ends of
certain notorious hereticks (translated out of the
Latine by J. Davies). 2 pt. 1655. 8°. *SC*.287.
MC.26: "View of Religions: 2 Cop:"

Ross, John. See Dix, afterwards Ross, John.

Rossignol, Céphas. Dieu et famille, poésies, par
Céphas Rossignol. Paris, 1840. 8°. [*BN*]. *SC*.
641.

Rossini, Pietro, the Elder. Il Mercurio errante delle
grandezze di Roma ... di Pietro Rossini. 7th ed.
2 pt. in 1 vol. Roma, 1750. 12°, pl. [*BN*]. *SC*.
156: "8vo ... *numerous Etchings by Piranesi and
others*, 44." MC.96/X/WW/C ["C" crossed out]:"
MC.112s: "Mercurio Errante:"

Rous, Francis, the Younger. Archaeologiae Atticae
libri septem. Seaven books of the Attick antiquities. Containing the description of the citties
glory, government ... their religion. Third edition much enlarged. Oxford, 1649. 4°. *SC*.237.
See Godwin, Thomas. Moses and Aaron.

Rousseau, Jean Jacques. Les confessions, suivies des
rêveries du promeneur solitaire. 2 tom. Genève,
1782. 12°. *SC*.639: "2 tomes, 8vo ... *Genève*,
1782." [*BN*: "Genève, 1782. 2 vol. in-8°"].

————. Du contrat social, ou principes du droit
politique, par J.-J. Rousseau. Amsterdam, 1762.
8°. MC.98: "Du Contrat Socio [*sic*]:"

————. Émile, ou de l'éducation. Par J.J. Rousseau,
citoyen de Genève. 4 vol. in 2. Francfort, 1762.

17.5cm. [*NUC*]. *SC*.639: "2 tomes, 8vo ... *a Franckfort*, 1762." MC.99: "Emile, 2 Vol:"

Rowe, Nicholas. [? The dramatick works of Nicholas Rowe. 2 vol. 1720. 12°]. LB.10: "Rowes Dr Works 2 vols."

Ruaeus, Carolus. See Virgilius. Opera.

[Rubbi, Andrea, ed.]. Lirici misti del secolo XVII. Venezia, 1789. 18cm. (Tom. 41 in Parnaso Italiano, ed. Andrea Rubbi, 56 tom. Venezia, 1784-1791. 8°.) *SC*.584: "8vo, 1789." MC.98: "Lyrici [*sic*] misti:"

Ruddiman, Thomas. See Buchanan, George.

*Rudiments of the Italian tongue. 1781. 8°. *SC*.390: "(MS. Note by MRS. WORDSWORTH--*'This book was much valued as belonging to my dear husband when he studied the language at Cambridge, M.W.--1850')*." [Possibly a translation of Domenico Soresi. I rudimenti della lingua Italiana. Milano, 1756. 8°. See Bartolommeo Gamba da Bassano, *Serie Dei Testi di Lingua*, Venezia, 1839, p. 656].

Rufinus, Tyrannus. See Gregory, of Nazianzus, Saint, Patriarch of Constantinople.

Runnington, Charles. See Hale, Sir Matthew.

[Ruskin, John]. Modern painters: their superiority in the art of landscape painting ... [Vol. 1.]. By a graduate of Oxford [John Ruskin]. 1843. 8°. [*L*: "No more was published of this edition"]. 2nd ed. [Vol. 1]. 1844. 8°. *SC*.640: "2 vols., 8vo, 1843-46, *not uniform in size*."

Russell, James. See Kirkton, James.

Ryan, John. A disclosure of the principles, designs, and machinations of the Popish revolutionary faction of Ireland. London, Dublin, Bristol, 1838. 8°. *SC*.33.

————. The history and antiquities of the County of Carlow. Dublin, 1833. 8°. *SC*.157. LB.35: "History of [*sic*] Antiquities of Carlow by John Ryan."

Ryder, Henry Dudley. The Angelicon: a gallery of sonnets, on the divine attributes, and the passions, the graces and the virtues. 1840. 13cm. [*NUC*]. *SC*.471.

Rymer, Thomas. See Rapin, René.

Ryves, Browne (or Bruno). Mercurius rusticus: or, the countries complaint of the barbarous outrages committed by the sectaries of this late flourishing kingdom. Together with a brief chronology of the battels, sieges, conflicts, and other most remarkable passages, from the beginnings of this unnatural war, to the 25th of March, 1646. 4 vol. in 1. 1685. 7 in. [*CWC*:Ann]. *SC*.9: "8vo ... 1685." MC.59: "Mercur: Rusticus:"

S., I. See Studley, John.

[? S., J. Great Britain's glory: being the history of King Arthur, with the adventures of the Knights of the Round Table. [The preface is signed J.S.]. [? 1680]. 4°]. [*NUC*: "[169- ?].".]. MC.88: "History of King Arthur:"

*Sacred hours. *SC*.249: "vol. 2."

Sa'dī. The saint and the sinner, a tale from the Bostan of Sa'dī translated and accompanied by the original Persian, the various readings of twelve mss., and notes, by Forbes Falconer. 1839. 8°. [*NUC*]. *SC*.372.

————. Selections from the Bostân of Sâdi. Intended for the use of students of the Persian language. By F[orbes] Falconer. 1838. 12°. *SC*.372.

Sadler, _____, of Chippenham. Wanley Penson; or, the
melancholy man. 3 vol. 1792. [*DAP*]. *SC*.682:
"3 vols., 8vo ... 1792." LB.16: "Wanly [*sic*] Penson." See *N&Q*, Jan. 1964, p. 16.

Saemund, See Edda, Poetic.

[Saint German, Christopher]. Doctor and student; or,
dialogues between a doctor of divinity and a student in the laws of England ... To which is now
added an account of the author. [London], 1721.
12°. *SC*.170: "1721 ... *with the late Laureate's
Autograph*." MC.38: "Doctor & Student:"

Saint-Marc, M. de. See Lefèbvre de Saint-Marc, Charles
Hugues.

Saint-Pierre, Jacques Henri Bernardin de. [? Pablo y
Virginia por Jacobo Bernardino Enrique de Saint
Pierre. Traducción castellana. Madrid, 1798.
[n.s.]. [*NUC*]. MC.97: "Pablo y Virginia:"

————. Paolo e Virginia. 2 vol. Firenze, 1795.
13cm. [*AWC*:Ann]. [? LB.20: "1st Vol of Paul &
Virgine"].

————. A voyage to the Isle of France, the Isle of
Bourbon and the Cape of Good Hope; with observations and reflections upon nature and mankind.
Translated from the French. To which is added
some account of the author. 1800. 8°. *SC*.163:
"2 vols., 8vo, 1800."

Sale, George. See An universal history.

Salignac de la Mothe Fénelon, François de, Archbishop
of Cambrai. A demonstration of the existence,
wisdom, and omnipotence of God ... Translated
from the French [By A. Boyer]. 1713. 12°. MC.
29: "Abp. Cambrai's Existance [*sic*] &c: of God."

————. Suite de quatrième livre de "l'Odyssée" d'Ho-
mère, ou les avantures [*sic*] de Télémaque, fils

d'Ulysse. Paris, 1699. 12°. [*BN*]. MC.100:
"Aventures de Telemaque:" LB.17: "Telemaque."

Salkeld, Samuel. Pleasures of home, and other poems.
Shrewsbury, London [ca. 1815]. 23cm. [*NUC*].
SC.572.

Sallentin, Louis [*alias* de l'Oise]. L'improvisateur
français. 21 tom. Paris, 1804-06. 12°. *SC*.585:
"20 tomes, 8vo, 1804." MC.95: "Improvisateur Fran-
cais [*sic*] 21 Vol:"

*Sallustius Crispus, Caius. MC.6: "Sallustius: 2 Cop:"

Saltonstall, Wye. See Ovidius Naso, Publius. Tristia.

Salvini, Anton Maria. See Rosa, Salvatore.

Sanchez de las Brozas, Francesco. Francisci Sanctii
Brocensis ... Comment. in And. Alciati Emblemata,
nunc denuo ... recognita. Lugduni, 1573. 8°.
SC.322. [? MC.10: "Alciati Emblemata"].

Sandbach, Margaret (Mrs. Henry Roscoe). Poems. 1840.
8°. *SC*.496.

Sanderson, Robert. De juramento. Seven lectures concerning the obligation of promissory oathes. Read
publickly at the Divinity School at Oxford. Translated into English by his late Majesties speciall
command, and afterwards revised and approved under
his Majesties own hand. 1655. 8°. MC.30: "Sanderson de Juramen:"

————. Logicae artis compendium. Secunda hac editione ... duplici appendice auctum. 2 pt. Oxoniae, 1618. 8°. MC.13/JC/O: "Sanderson's Logic
(logicae Art:)."

Sanderson, Thomas. See Anderson, Robert, of Carlisle.
The poetical works.

Sandford, Daniel. Remains of the late Right Reverend
Daniel Sandford including extracts from his diary

and correspondence, and a selection from his un-
published sermons. With a memoir, by the Rev.
John Sandford. 2 vol. Edinburgh, 1830. 23.5cm.
[*NUC*]. *SC*.303: "2 vols., 8vo, 1820 [*sic*]."

Sandford, John. See Sandford, Daniel.

Sandoval, Prudencio de. The civil wars of Spain, in
the beginning of the reign of Charles the 5^t, Emperor of Germanie, and King of that nation. Written originally in the Spanish-tongue, by Prudencio
de Sandoval, doctor of divinity, and abbat of the
monasterie of St Isidro el Real, in Valladolid,
of the Order of St Bennet, historiographer roial
to Philip the Third; never yet translated, now put
into English by Captain J[ames] W[adsworth]. 1652.
27.5cm. [*NUC*]. *SC*.68: "folio ... 1672 [*sic*]."

Sandys, George. See Ovidius Naso, Publius. Metamorphoses.

Sarnelli, Pompeo. See Nuova guida.

Sarrasin, Jean François. Les oeuvres de Mr. Sarrasin,
contenant les traitez suivans: la conspiration de
Valstein contre l'empereur; s'il faut qu'un jeune
homme soit amoureux, dialogue; la vie de Pomponius
Atticus. 2 parties en 1 vol. Paris, 1694. 12°.
[*BN*]. *SC*.534: "1694." MC.101: "Les Oeuvres de
Sarasin [*sic*]:"

The Saturday magazine; published under the direction
of the Committee of General Literature and Education appointed by the Society for Promoting Christian Knowledge. 25 vols. [1832]-44. 8°. *SC*.
422: "from the commencement in 1834 [*sic*], to the
discontinuance in 1844, 24 vols. in 12 [*sic*]."
[? LB.16: "Sat Penny Mag [lent after Oct. 1832]"].
Cf. The penny magazine.

Saturday night; comprising a review of new publications, biography, essays on literature, the arts
and sciences, anecdotes, topographical descriptions.
2 vol. 1824. 8°. LB.54: "Saturday Night."

[Saumaise, Claude de]. Defensio regia pro Carolo I.
ad serenissimum Magnae Brittaniae Regem Carolum II.
[Leyden], 1649. 12°. MC.39: "Defensio Regia pro
Carolo: 1:"

Savage, Richard. [? The poetical works of Richard
Savage. With a life of the author, by Dr. [Samuel]
Johnson. Cooke's ed., n.d., n.s.]. [*NUC*]. *SC*.
644. MC.47: "Savage."

Savoy, Prince Eugene of. See Eugene Francis, Prince
of Savoy.

Sayer, W. Sayer's History of Westmoreland, containing
the substance of all the remarkable events recorded
by Burn and Nicolson, together with a variety of
... information from ancient MSS. Vol. 1 (*No more
published*). Kendal, 1847. 8°. *SC*.157: "vol. 1,
1847."

Sayers, Frank. Disquisitions metaphysical and literary. 1793. 8°. MC.83/X: "Sayers' Disquis:"

Scaliger, Joseph Juste. Josephi Scaligeri ... Opus
de emendatione temporum, castigatius et auctius
... Item veterum Graecorum fragmenta selecta ...
cum notis ejusdem Scaligeri. Lugduni Batavorum,
1598. fol. *SC*.69. MC.31: "Scaliger de Emend:
Temp:"

Scaliger, Julius Caesar. Viri clarissimi de causis
linguae Latinae libri tredecim. Heidelberg, 1584.
8°. [PSC.WWC.JB:Ann]. *SC*.424: "8vo ... 1584."

————. Julii Caesaris Scaligeri Exotericarum exerci-
tationum liber quintus decimus, de subtilitate, ad
Hieronymum Cardanum. Lugduni, 1615. 8°. [*BN*].
SC.423. MC.31/C: "Scaliger de Subtilit:" MC.37/
JC: "Jul: Caes: Scaliger de subtilitate."

Scapula, Joannes. Lexicon Graecolatinum novum, in quo ex
primitivorum et simplicium fontibus derivata atque
composita ordine ... dialectorum omnium a Jacobo

Zwinguo [*for* Zwingero] ... in ... tabulas compendiose redactarum. Genevae, 1628. 34cm. [*NUC*].
SC.425: "folio ... *Geneva, 1688* [*sic*]. '*This edition of Scapula is the next in value to the Elzevir edition, 1653* [*for* 1652], *which is by some
considered the best edition. The present value of
this edition is from seven to nine guineas ...
March, 1817.*'--Note in MR. WORDSWORTH'S HANDWRIT-
ING." MC.14/H.C.: "Scapula." See STC entry.

Scarron, Paul. Le romant comique. Paris, 1651. 8°.
[*L*: "*With an engraved titlepage, dated* 1652]. *SC*.
533: "1652." MC.96: "Le Romant: Comique:"

Schade, Carl Benjamin. Neues Englisch-Deutsches und
Deutsch-Englisches Taschenwörterbuch ... A new
pocket dictionary. 2 pt. London, Leipzig, 1797.
12°. MC.17: "Schade's Germ: Dicty:" [? LB.27:
"German Dicy"].

Schade, Petrus (Mosellanus). See Mosellanus, Petrus.

Schickard, Wilhelm. W. Schickardi Horologium Hebraeum, sive consilium, quomodo sancta lingua spacio
XXIV. horarum a totidem collegis, seu eorundem
semisse sufficienter apprehendi queat, septies com-
probatum et impressum ... quum prius ... emendatum ... annotationculis elucidatum, et lexici
compendium ... exauctum fuisset a N.H. (Oxoniensi)
... [i.e. ? N. Homes]. (Rota Hebraea pro facili-
tate conjugandi pridem inventa ... a W. Schickardo
... Nunc recusa denuo). 2 pt. 1639. 8°. MC.17:
"Horolog: Hebraeum:" MC.17: "Horolog: Ebraeum:
[another copy]."

Schiller, Johann Christoph Friedrich von. The Piccolomini, or the first part of Wallenstein, a drama
in five acts. Translated from the German of Frederick Schiller by S.T. Coleridge. 1800. 8°.
The death of Wallenstein. A tragedy in five acts.
Translated ... by S.T. Coleridge. (2 vols. in 1).
1800. 8°. [WL:Ann: WW from STC with many notes
by STC]. *SC*.351: "Piccolomini, Wallenstein, etc.,

1800." MC.53: "Coleridge's Wallenstein 2 Co:"
See STC entry.

————. The song of the bell; and other poems; translated from the German [by M.M., i.e. M. Montagu].
1839. 8°. *SC*.504.

————. William Tell ... From the German of Schiller,
with notes and illustrations, by William Peter.
Heidelberg, 1839. 8°. *SC*.616.

————. See Leveson-Gower, Lord Francis. Translations.

Schindler, Valentin. Lexicon pentaglotton, Hebraicum,
Chaldaicum, Syriacum, Talmudico-Rabbinicum, et
Arabicum. Hanoviae, 1612. fol. *SC*.426. MC.14/0:
"Pentaglotton:"

Schleiermacher, Friedrich Ernst Daniel. Schleiermacher's Introductions to the Dialogues of Plato.
Translated from the German by William Dobson. Cambridge, 1836. 22cm. [*NUC*]. *SC*.408.

Schmitz, Leonhard. See Chaucer, Geoffrey.

Schrevelius, Cornelius. See Hesiod.

Scott, David Wardlaw. Dora Marcelli, the last of her
race. A poem. Edinburgh, 1843. 8°. *SC*.473:
"Marcilla [*sic*]."

Scott, John, of Amwell. Critical essays on some of
the poems of several English poets. With an account of the life and writings of the author, by
M^r [John] Hoole. 1785. 8°. *SC*.427. MC.82:
"Scot's [*sic*] Crit: Essays:"

Scott, John, Editor of *The Champion* (newspaper). The
house of mourning, a poem; with some smaller
pieces. 1817. 8°. *SC*.512.

————. Paris revisited in 1815 by way of Brussels,
including a walk over the field of battle at

Waterloo. 1816. 8°. *SC*.70. MC.69: "Paris revisited:" LB.13: "Paris Revisited."

————. A visit to Paris in 1814; being a review of
the moral, political, intellectual and social condition of the French capital. 1815. 8°. *SC*.70:
"8vo [n.d.]."

Scott, Jonathan. See The Arabian nights.

Scott, Sir Walter. See Häring, Wilhelm.

[————]. The ancient British drama. 3 vol. 1810.
8°. [Jonathan Wordsworth:Ann]. *SC*.475: "2 vols."
MC.44: "Anc^t: Brit: Drama: 3 Vol:" [? LB.18:
"British Drama"]. For Scott's editorship see
Lowndes and Margaret Ball, *Sir Walter Scott As a
Critic of Literature*, pp. 52, 151-2.

————. Ballads and lyric pieces. Edinburgh, 1806.
8°. *SC*.648. MC.54: "Scot's [*sic*] Ballads &c:"

————. The lay of the last minstrel, a poem. 1805.
4°. *SC*.648. MC.54: "Scot's [*sic*] Lay of Last
Minst:"

————. The Lord of the Isles, a poem in six cantos.
Edinburgh, 1815. 4°. *SC*.649: *"with Autog. 'W.
Wordsworth, from Walter Scott.'* [RP.QH: *'Not* Sir
W.S.'s autograph']." MC.54: "Scot's Lord of the
Isles:"

————. Marmion; a tale of Flodden Field. Edinburgh,
1808. 29cm. [NN.BC. "1st ed.: Fly-leaf inscribed
'From the author' in unknown hand; title-page inscribed 'Walter Scott esq. W. Wordsworth' in
Mary Wordsworth's (?) hand"]. *SC*.647: "4to, 1808,
with Autog. 'Walter Scott to W. Wordsworth.' [RP.
QH: 'Not Sir W.S.'s autograph']." MC.54: "Scot's
[*sic*] Marmion: 2 Cop:"

————. [Another edition]. Edinburgh, 1808. 8°.
[WL:Ann:2nd ed. 1808]. MC.54: "8vo:"

————. Minstrelsy of the Scottish Border. 3 vol. Kelso, Edinburgh, 1802,03. 8°. *SC*.646. MC.49: "Minstrelsy of Scot: Border:"

————. The modern British drama. 5 vol. 1811. 8°. *SC*.476. MC.44: "Mod: Brit: Drama: 5 Vol:" LB.53: "(Mod^n Drama 4th Vol)."

[————]. Trial of Duncan Terig alias Clerk, and Alexander Bane Macdonald, for the murder of Arthur Davis, Sergeant in General Guises Regiment of Foot, June, A.D. M.DCC.LIV. [Edited by Sir Walter Scott]. Edinburgh, 1831. 4°. [A Bannatyne Club publication]. *SC*.81.

————. Waverley novels. [? 41 vol. Edinburgh, 1823-33. 15.5cm. [*NUC*: "v.[39-41] Introductions, and notes and illustrations to the novels, tales, and romances of the author of Waverley ... 1833"]. *SC*.645: "Waverley Novels, vols. 1 to 10 (the Author's last edition), with Notes, etc."

[Scougal, Henry]. The life of God in the soul of man; or, the nature and excellency of the Christian religion ... In two letters. [By H. Scougal. With a preface by Gilbert Burnet, Bishop of Salisbury]. 1677. 8°. MC.25: "Burnett's [*sic*] Life of God:"

Secker, Thomas, Archbishop of Canterbury. [? Nine sermons ... on the occasion of the late war and rebellion. 1758. 8°]--[? Fourteen sermons preached on several occasions. 1766. 8°]--[? Six sermons on the liturgy of the Church of England. Cork, 1784. 12°]. LB.63: "Archbishop Secker's Sermons."

Sedgwick, Adam. See Hudson, John; Livingstone, David.

————. A discourse on the studies of the University [of Cambridge]. London, Cambridge, 1833. 8°. *SC*.207.

Sedgwick, Catherine Maria. Letters from abroad to kindred at home. 2 vols. New York, 1841. 12°. *SC*.328. LB.43: "Miss Sedgwicks letters Vol. 1."

Sedley, Sir Charles. The poetical works of the Honourable Sir Charles Sedley Baronet, and his speeches in Parliament, with large additions never before made publick. Published from the original ms. by Capt. [William] Ayloffe, a near relation of the authors. With a new miscellany of poems by several of the most eminent hands, and a compleat collection of all the most remarkable speeches in both houses of Parliament; discovering the principles of all parties and factions; the conduct of our chief ministers, the management of publick affairs, and the maxims of the government from the year 1641 to the happy union of Great Britain. By several lords and commoners. Viz. the dukes of Albemarle and others. 1707. 21cm. [NIC:Ann: "The Miscellany of poems ... is lacking. A compleat collection of ... speeches ... has separate t.p. and paging"]. *SC*.485: "Poetical Works of Sir Charles Sedley, 1707."

Selden, John. The historie of tithes. That is, the practice of payment of them. [London], 1618. 4°. *SC*.236. See STC entry.

————. Table-talk: being the discourses of John Selden, Esq.; or his sence [*sic*] of various matters of weight and high consequence relating especially to religion and state [ed. Richard Milward]. 1689. 4°. LB.21: "Selden's John Table Talk."

Selkirk, Earl of. See Douglas, Thomas.

Seneca, Lucius Annaeus. L. Annei Senecae Cordubensis. Tragoediae X. Basiliae, 1563. 8°. [WL:Ann]. MC.6: "Senecae Tragoe:--3 Cop: 1 H[artley] C[oleridge]."

*Sermons, pastoral charges, etc. etc. *SC*.290: "nearly 100. a bundle."

Seward, Anna. [? Louisa, a poetical novel, in four
epistles. 4th ed. Lichfield, 1784. 27cm. (Bound
with this are her:) Elegy [on Captain Cook. 4th
ed. Lichfield], 1784; Monody on Major André [2nd
ed. Lichfield], 1781, and Poem to the memory of
Lady Miller, 1782]. [*NUC*]. MC.50: "Louisa: Cap:
Cook:and Maj: Andrews [evidently bound together]."

Sewel, Willem. A compendious guide to the Low-Dutch
language; containing the most necessary and essential grammar-rules ... Korte wegwyzer de Nederduy-
tsche taal ... by Willem Sewel. 3rd ed., corr.
and enl. 3 pts. in 1 vol. Amsterdam, 1760. 12cm.
[*NUC*]. *SC*.362: "Guide to the Dutch Language, by
W. Sewel, *Amst.*, 1706 [*sic*]." MC.17: "Dutch Gram:"

Shadwell, Thomas. The dramatick works of Thomas Shadwell. 4 vol. 1720. 12°. *SC*.650: "4 vols., 8vo,
1720, *with ... Autog. of the elder Coleridge.*"
MC.81/JC/H: "Shadwell's Plays: 4 Vol:" LB.41: "3
vols of Shadwell."

Shaftesbury, Earl of. See Cooper, Anthony Ashley.

Shakespeare, William. See Milton, John. The sonnets
of Shakespeare and Milton.

————. The works of Shakespeare. With corrections
and illustrations from various commentators. 10
vol. Edinburgh, 1767. 12°. *SC*.651: "10 vols.,
8vo (wanting vol. 10), 1767." MC.43: "Shakspeare
[*sic*]: 10 Vol:"

————. Shakespeare's dramatic works; with explanatory notes. A new edition. To which is now added, a copious index to the remarkable passages
and words, by the Rev. S[amuel] Ayscough. 3 vol.
1790. 8°. [DD:Ann]. MC.43: "Stockdale's
Shakespeare: 2 Vol:" [Ayscough's work was a supplement to Stockdale's ed. of 1790 in two volumes].
See *CN*, 2N3145.

————. The dramatic works of William Shakespeare. With remarks on his life and writings by Thomas Campbell. 1838. 8°. *SC*.652.

————. The plays of William Shakespeare, complete, in eight volumes. 8 vol. 1796. 8°. *SC*.654.

————. Poems, by William Shakespeare. With illustrative remarks, original and select. To which is prefixed a sketch of the author's life. [Edited by W.C.O., i.e. Walley Chamberlain Oulton]. 2 vol. 1804. 8°. *SC*.653: "Shakespeare's Poems, with Illustrative Remarks, Life, etc., 9 [*sic*] vols., 12mo [*sic*], 1804." MC.43: "Shakspeare's [*sic*] Poems: 2 Vol:"

*————. *SC*.644: "Shakespeare's Poems." MC.43: "Shakspeare's [*sic*] Poems:"

————. The sonnets of Shakespeare and Milton. 1830. 17cm. [NN.BC:Ann]. LB.36: "Sonnets of Shakespeare & Milton."

Sharp, James. See Young, Arthur.

[Sharp, Richard]. Epistles in verse. [By Richard Sharp]. 1828. 8°. *SC*.597: "Epistles in Verse, 1828."

————. Letters and essays in prose and verse. 1834. 8°. *SC*.655: "Sharp's (Richard) Essays and Letters [*sic*] in prose and verse, 8vo, 1834." LB.18: "Sharpe's [*sic*] Book [lent 21 May 1834]."

Sharpe, Charles Kirkpatrick. See Kirkton, James.

[Shaw, Peter]. The tablet, or picture of real life. 1762. 8°. [*NUC*]. *SC*.357. MC.82: "Tablet of Real Life:"

Shaw, William. See Miller, Philip.

Shelley, Mary Godwin. See Shelley, Percy Bysshe.

————. Rambles in Germany and Italy in 1840, 1842,
    and 1843. 2 vol. 1844. 7.5 in. [*CWC*:Ann]. LB.
    33: "1st Vol Mrs Shellys [*sic*] Rambles."

Shelley, Percy Bysshe. See Coleridge, Samuel Taylor.
    The poetical works of Coleridge, Shelley, and
    Keats.

————. Essays, letters from abroad, translations,
    and fragments; edited by Mrs. Shelley. 2 vol.
    1840. 12°. *SC*.655: "8vo." LB.28: "Shelleys Let-
    ters."

————. The poetical works of Percy Bysshe Shelley.
    Edited by Mrs. Shelley. 4 vol. 1839. 12°. [DD:
    Ann:WW2]. LB.26: "Shelley's Poems 1st Vol. [lent
    October, 1839]."

Shelton, Thomas. See Cervantes Saavedra, Miguel de.

Shelvocke, George. See An universal history.

————. A voyage round the world by the way of the
    Great South Sea, performed in the years 1719-1722.
    1726. 8°. *SC*.159. MC.71: "Shelvock's [*sic*]
    Voyage:" LB.15: "Shelvokes [*sic*] Voy." See *CWC*.
    583.

Shenstone, William. Essays on men and manners. 1787.
    22cm. (Vol. 8 of [James] Harrison's British Clas-
    sicks). [*NUC*]. MC.80: "Shenstone's Essays:"

Shepherd, William, Unitarian Minister. Paris in eight-
    een hundred and two and eighteen hundred and four-
    teen. 1814. 8°. *SC*.70.

Sheppard, John. Thoughts chiefly designed as a pre-
    parative or persuasive to private devotion. 1824.
    12°. *SC*.187. LB.45: "Shepherd's [*sic*] thoughts."

Sheppard, William. The covrt-keepers gvide; or, a
plaine and familiar treatise, needfull and usefull
for the helpe of many that are imployed in the
keeping of law dayes, or courts baron. Wherein
is largely and plainly opened the jurisdiction of
these courts, with the learning of mannors, copy-
holds, rents, herriots and other services and ad-
vantages belonging unto mannors, to the great pro-
fit of lords of mannors, and owners of these courts.
1649. 14.5cm. [*NUC*]. MC.39: "Court Keeper's
Guide:"

Sherburne, Sir Edward. See Blondel, François.

Sheridan, Richard Brinsley. The rivals. [In Scott,
Sir Walter. The modern British drama. 5 vol.
1811. 8°. Vol. 4]. LB.53: "Sheridan's Rivals
(Mod^n Drama 4th Vol)."

[? Sherlock, William. A practical discourse concerning
a future judgement. 1692. 8°]. MC.27: "Discourse
on Fut: Judgm:"

Shoberl, Frederick. See Forget me not.

A short introduction to grammar; for the use of the
lower forms in the King's School at Westminster.
1759. 8°. MC.12: "Westmin: Lat: Gram: Low^r:
Form:"

Shovel, Sir Cloudesley. See A gentleman.

Sidney, Sir Philip. See Mornay, Philippe de.

——. The Countess of Pembroke's Arcadia. [? 3rd
ed. 1593. fol.]. *SC*.656: "[title wanting] folio." MC.88: "Countess of Pembroke's Arcadia:"

Sigfusson, Saemund. See Edda, Poetic.

Sigourney, Mrs. See Huntley, afterwards Sigourney,
Lydia.

[Simon, Richard]. The history of the original and progress of ecclesiastical revenues ... Written in French. By a learned priest [Jerome à Costa, i.e. Richard Simon] and now done into English. 1685. 8°. *SC*.282. MC.40: "Hist of Ecclesiast: Rev:"

Simonde de Sismondi, Jean Charles Leonard. A history of the Italian republics; being a view of the origin, progress, and fall of Italian freedom. 1832. 8°. (In Lardner's Cabinet cyclopaedia, 1832, Vol. 14, 17cm). [*L*; *NUC*]. [? LB.40: "Repblcs Italy [lent in Feb. 1848]"].

Simpson, Bolton. See Xenophon.

Simpson, James. See Lalor, John.

Simpson, Joseph. See Epictetus.

Simpson, The Rev. Joseph. See Sympson, Joseph.

Simpson, Thomas. See Fluxions.

[Sinclair, Arthur]. The decameron of the West. A series of tales. Edinburgh, 1839. 12°. [*L*; *NUC*]. LB.30: "Decameron of the West."

Sinner, Jean Rodolphe. Voyage historique et littéraire dans la Suisse occidentale. Nouvelle édition augmentée. 2 tom. En Suisse, 1787. 8°. *SC*.105: "2 tomes ... 1787." MC.100: "Voyage dans la Suisse 2 Vol:"

Sketches of the Waldenses. [Edited by Daniel Parish Kidder]. London, Philadelphia, New York, 1846. 15.5cm. [*L*; *NUC*]. *SC*.164: "Sketches of the Waldenses, 12mo."

Skinner, George. See French, William.

Skinner, Thomas. See Bate, George.

Skurray, Francis. A metrical version of the Book of
   Psalms, composed for private meditation or public worship. 1843. 12°. *SC*.291.

————. Sermons on public subjects and occasions. 2
   vol. Bath, London, 1817[-32]. 12°. *SC*.291:
   "12mo, 1817."

————. The shepherd's garland, composed of gatherings during leisure hours, from ways of pleasant-
   ness. London, Warminster, [1832]. 8°. *SC*.504.

*Slavery. ? *SC*.20: "three others [? books]."

Sleidanus. See Philippson, Joannes.

Small, James Grindlay. The Highlands, Scottish mar-
   tyrs, and other poems. Edinburgh, 1843. 12°.
   SC.460: *"with Embellishments and Autograph Note
   by the Author."*

Smart, Alexander. Rambling rhymes. New edn. enlgd.
   Edinburgh, 1845. 12°. [*EU*]. [MH:Ann: "Mont-
   rose, 1845. 16.8cm."]. *SC*.620: "1845."

Smart, Christopher. See Horatius Flaccus, Quintus.
   Works.

Smith, Mrs. Charlotte. Elegiac sonnets, and other
   essays. Fifth edition, with additional sonnets
   and other poems. 2 vol. 1789-97. 16°. [*DNB*:
   "Fifth edition, 1789 [reissued with a second
   volume ... under the title of 'Elegiac Sonnets
   and other poems,' in 1797]"]. [WL:Ann: "1789"].
   MC.48: "C: Smith's Sonnets:"

Smith, Eaglesfield. Poetical works. 2nd ed. 2 vol.
   1822. 12°. [*NUC*; Allibone]. *SC*.558: "2 vols.,
   1822."

[Smith, George]. An epistolary dissertation addressed
   to the clergy of Middlesex. Wherein the doctrine
   of St. Austin concerning the Christian Sacrifice

is set in a true light: by way of a reply to Dr.
[Daniel] Waterland's late charge to them. By a
divine of the University of Cambridge. 1739. 8°.
MC.28/x Southey: "Waterlands' Dissertat:"

Smith, John. See The microcosm.

Smith, John, of Southwark. The mysterie of rhetorique
   unvailed, wherein above 130 of the tropes and figures are severally derived from the Greek into
   English together with lively definitions and variety of Latin, English, Scriptural examples ...
   Conducing very much to the right understanding of
   the sense of the letter of Scripture. 1657 [1656].
   8°. MC.14: "Mystery of Rhetor: unv^{d}."

Smith, P. See Willet, Andrew.

Smith, Robert. See The microcosm.

Smith, Sir Thomas. De republica Anglorum libri tres.
   Quibus accesserunt chorographica illius descriptio,
   aliique politici tractatus. [Edited by Johannes
   de Laet]. Editio ultima prioribus auctior. Lug
   [duni] Batavor[um], 1641. 16°. *SC*.86: "*Lugd.
   Bat. Elzevir*, 1641."

Smith, Thomas Southwood. Illustrations of the divine
   government. Fourth edition. 1826. 12°. *SC*.
   272. LB.24: "Divine Government."

————. The philosophy of health; or, an exposition
   of the physical and mental constitution of man.
   2 vol. 1835-37. 12°. *SC*.239: "2 vols., 12mo
   ... 1836." [*NUC*: "1836-38. 16cm."]. LB.32:
   "Philosophy of Health 2 vols."

Smollett, Tobias. See Cervantes Saavedra, Miguel de.

————. The expedition of Humphrey Clinker. (Vols.
   30 and 31 of The British novelists.) *SC*.657:
   "2 vols. 1810. 12°." MC.87: "Brit: Novelist:
   12 Vol:" ["Hump: Clinker" is Item 4].

————. Hume's [David] history of England, with a continuation to the death of George II. by Dr Smollett.
7 vol. 1794. 12°. *SC*.45: [7 vol.]. MC.57:
"Smollet's [*sic*] Continu: 7 Vol:" LB.29: "Smollet's
[*sic*] contin. &c 6." See Hume, David.

Smyth, Richard. The obituary of Richard Smyth of the
Poultry Compter, London: being a catalogue of all
such persons as he knew in their life: extending
from A.D. 1627 to A.D. 1674. Edited by Sir Henry
Ellis. 1849. 8°. [*NUC*]. *SC*.15.

Smyth, William Henry. Descriptive catalogue of a
cabinet of Roman Imperial large brass medals. Bedford, 1836. 4°. *SC*.431: "4to, Bedford, 1834."

Snelgrave, William. A new account of some parts of
Guinea and the slave trade. 1734. 8°. *SC*.94.
MC.62: "Account of Guinea:"

Sneyd, Charlotte Augusta. A relation; or, rather, a
true account of the Island of England; with sundry
particulars of the people and of the royal revenues
under King Henry VII., about the year 1500. From
the Italian, with notes ... by Charlotte Augusta
Sneyd. 1847. 8°. *SC*.15.

Snow, Joseph. Lyra memorialis. Original epitaphs and
churchyard thoughts in verse. By Joseph Snow.
With an essay, by William Wordsworth. Reprinted
by his permission. A new edition, remodelled and
enlarged. 1847. 16°. [WL:Ann]. LB.50: "Lyra
Memorialis [lent 6 Feb. 1851]."

Snow, Robert. Memorials of a tour on the Continent;
to which are added miscellaneous poems. 1845.
7.625 in. [*CWC*:Ann]. LB.35.

————. Poems on miscellaneous subjects; with a preface and notes. 1843. 8°. *SC*.580.

Soane, George. See La Motte Fouqué, Friedrich Heinrich
Karl de, Baron.

Soave, Giovanni Francesco. See Virgilius Maro, Publius. Georgica.

Socrates (Scholasticus). See Eusebius, Pamphili.

The soldier's guide: being an essay offer'd to all of that profession. Authoris'd by many late examples, especially in the late wars between France and Holland; containing divers observations upon several remarkable accidents, which happened in those wars. 1686. 15cm. [*NUC*]. MC.84: "Soldier's Guide:"

Solis y Ribadneyra (or Rivadneyra), Antonio de. The history of the conquest of Mexico by the Spaniards. Translated into English from the original Spanish of Don Antonio de Solis ... By Thomas Townsend ... The whole translation revised and corrected by Nathanael Hooke. 2 vol. 1738. 20.5cm. [NNMor: Ann]. *SC*.56. MC.61: "Hist: of Conq: of Mexico:" LB.9: "Conquest of Mexico 2 vols."

Somnerus, Gulielmus. See Benson, Thomas.

*Sophocles. MC.5: "Sophocles." LB.58: "Sophocles."

Soresi, Domenico. See Rudiments of the Italian tongue.

Sotheby, William. See Homer; Virgilius Maro, Publius. Georgica.

―――――. Orestes; a tragedy in five acts [and in verse]. London, Bristol, 1802. 4°. *SC*.663: "4to, large paper, 1802." [? LB.12: "Sothebys play"].

―――――. Saul; a poem, in two parts. 1807. 4°. *SC*.658. MC.52: "Sotheby's Saul:"

―――――. Tragedies ... The death of Darnley. Ivan. Zamorin and Zama. The confession. Orestes. 1814. 8°. *SC*.658. MC.52: "Sotheby's Tragedies:" LB.12.

Souchay, l'abbé. See Boileau-Despréaux, Nicholas.

South, Robert. Maxims, sayings, explications of Scripture phrases, descriptions and characters, extracted from the writings of ... Dr. R[obert] South.
1717. 8°. MC.26: "South's Maxims:"

————. Twelve sermons preached upon several occasions.
4th ed. 6 vol. 1727. 8°. [*BN*]. *SC*.295: "6
vols., 8vo ... 1727." LB.12: "South 1 vol."

Southey, Charles Cuthbert. See Southey, Robert. The
life of the Rev. Andrew Bell.

————. The life and correspondence of Robert Southey;
edited by his son [i.e. Charles Cuthbert Southey].
6 vol. 1849-50. 8°. LB.45.

Southey, Robert. See The annual anthology; Cowper,
William; Jones, John.

————. All for love; and The pilgrim to Compostella.
1829. 18.5cm. [NN.BC:Ann]. *SC*.660. LB.16.

————. The book of the Church. 2nd ed. 2 vol.
1824. 8°. [WL:Ann]. *SC*.292. [? MC.57: "Southey's
His^{ry} of the Church of Eng^d 2 vol:"]. LB.6.

————. Carmen triumphale, for the commencement of the
year 1814. Carmina aulica, written in 1814 on the
arrival of the allied sovereigns in England. 2nd
ed. 1821. 12°. *SC*.495: "(*with Autographs of
Southey and Wordsworth*)."

————. Common place book; edited by his son-in-law
J[ohn] W[ood] Warter. 4 vol. 1849-51. 8°.
[WL (Vol. 1):Ann]. LB.50: "1 vol."

————. The curse of Kehama. 1810. 4°. [WL:Ann].
MC.53: "Southey's Kahama [*sic*]:" LB.23.

[————]. The doctor. 7 vol. 1834-47. 20cm. [Vols.
1-5 published anonymously, 1834-38; vols. 6-7 ed.
by John Wood Warter]. [*DLC*]. [WL:Ann]. [WR: "The
five volumes of Southey's 'Doctor' were presented

by the author, and two of the volumes contain Wordsworth's autograph"]. LB.17 (Vol. 1), 27 (Vol. 5),
37 (Vol. 6).

————. Essays moral and political ... now first collected. 2 vol. 1832. 8°. [WL:Ann]. LB.15.

————. The expedition of Orsua; and the crimes of
Aguirre. 1821. *SC*.355. LB.16.

————. History of Brazil. 3 vol. 1810-19. 4°.
SC.73: "vol. 3." MC.61: "Southey's Hist^y of Brazil: 3 Vol."

————. History of the Peninsular War. 3 vol. 1823-
32. 17.5cm. [NjP:Ann]. *SC*.71. LB.6.

————. Joan of Arc, an epic poem. Bristol, 1796.
4°. [WL.PL: "No inscription--but includes Coleridge's notes"]. MC.53: "2 Cop:" "1 JC [i.e.
STC's]." See *CN*, 3N4166.

————. Joan of Arc. (Analysis of La Pucelle ou la
France délivrée by [Jean] Chapelain.) 3rd ed.
2 vol. 1806. 8°. [WL:Ann]. LB.16: "Joan of Arc
2 D° [i.e. vols.]."

————. The lay of the laureate. Carmen nuptiale.
[on the marriage of the Princess Charlotte]. 1816.
12°. *SC*.661. MC.53: "Southey's Lay of the Lau:"
LB.16.

————. Letters written during a short residence in
Spain and Portugal. 3rd ed. 2 vol. 1808. 12°.
[Lowndes]. *SC*.432: "vol. i., 1808." MC.80:
"Southey's Letters in Spain &c: odd Vol:"

————. The life of Nelson. 2 vol. 1813. 8°. MC.
66: "Southey's Life of Nelson 2 Vol:" LB.7.

————. The life of the Rev. Andrew Bell ... Comprising
the history of the rise and progress of the system
of mutual tuition. The first volume by Robert

Southey ... edited by Mrs. Southey [born Caroline Bowles]. The last two by his son, the Rev. Charles Cuthbert Southey. 3 vol. 1844. 22.5cm. [NNC. SC:Ann]. *SC*.293.

————. The life of Wesley; and the rise and progress of Methodism. 2 vol. 1820. 8°. *SC*.294. LB.10.

————. Lives of the British admirals, with an introductory view of the naval history of England. 5 vol. 1833-40. 8°. (In Dionysius Lardner. The cabinet cyclopaedia. Vols. 68-72. The fifth volume, according to Lowndes, is by Robert Bell). *SC*.72: "4 vols., 12mo ... (*Lardner's Cab. Cyclo.*)." LB.17.

————. Madoc. 1805. 4°. [WL:Ann]. MC.53: "Southey's Madoc:" LB.11.

————. The minor poems of Robert Southey. 3 vol. 1815. 12°. *SC*.660. MC.53: "Southey's Minor Poems: 3 Vol:" LB.16.

[———— and Samuel Taylor Coleridge]. Omniana; or, horae otiosiores. 2 vol. 1812. 18cm. [CtY.BL: Ann]. *SC*.340. MC.80: "Southey's Omniana:" LB.42.

[————]. The origin, nature, and object of the new system of education. [On the work of Andrew Bell and Joseph Lancaster]. 1812. 8°. LB.16: "New System of Edu[n]."

————. [? The poetical works ... complete in one volume. Paris, 1829. 8°]. LB.12: "Vol of Southey."

————. The poetical works. 10 vol. 1837-38. 8°. LB.22: "1st/2d Vol Southeys Poet[l] W."

————. The poet's pilgrimage to Waterloo. 1816. 12°. [WL:Ann. Bound with Southey's A tale of Paraguay]. MC.53: "Southey's Pilgrimage:" LB.16.

————. Roderick, the last of the Goths. 1814. 4°. [WL:Ann]. MC.53: "Southey's Roderick:" LB.9.

————. Selections from the poems of Robert Southey
... chiefly for the use of schools. [Edited by
I.M.]. 1831. 12°. [WL:Ann:WW2]. *SC*.557: "8vo."

————. Sir Thomas More; or, colloquies on the progress and prospects of society. 2 vol. 1829. 8°.
SC.433. LB.16.

————. Specimens of the later English poets, with
preliminary notices. 3 vol. 1807. 8°. *SC*.662.
MC.53/JC/H[artley]: "Southey's Specimens."

————. A tale of Paraguay. 1825. 12°. [WL:Ann].
LB.7.

————. Thalaba the destroyer. 2nd ed. 2 vol. 1809.
8°. [WL.PL: "There are 2 vols in WL both the gift
of Dorothy Dickson. Vol I 'William Wordsworth
from the Author'"]. MC.53: "Southey's Thalaba: 2
Vol:" LB.11.

————. Vindiciae Ecclesiae Anglicanae. Letters to
Charles Butler, Esq. comprising essays on the
Romish religion and vindicating "The Book of the
Church." 1826. 8°. [RPB.HLKC:Ann]. *SC*.292.
LB.41. See CaOTV.HD.

————. A vision of judgment. 1821. 4°. *SC*.663:
"(*with Presen. Autog. 'To William Wordsworth from
Robert Southey, 14th March, 1821*')." LB.16.

Southey, Mrs. Robert (born Caroline Bowles). See
Southey, Robert. The life of the Rev. Andrew Bell.

Sparrow, Anthony. A rationale, or practical exposition of the Book of Common-Prayer ... 7th ed.
1725. 16°. [*NUC*]. *SC*.232. MC.26: "On Common
Prayer:"

Spence, Joseph. A guide to classical learning; or,
Polymetis abridged ... by N[icholas] Tindal. 5th
ed. 1786. 12°. *SC*.673: "1796, 8vo." MC.14:
"Tyndal's [*sic*] Polymetis:"

Spence, William. See Kirby, William.

————. Tracts on political economy: viz. 1. Britain
    independent of commerce; 2. Agriculture the source
    of wealth; 3. The objections against the Corn Bill
    refuted; 4. Speech on the East India trade. 1822.
    8°. *SC*.1.

Spencer, John. Dissertatio de Urim & Thummin in Deu-
    teron. C.33, v. 8. Cantabrigiae, 1669. 8°.
    SC.385. MC.25: "De Urim et Thummin:"

Spenser, Edmund. The poetical works of Edmund Spen-
    ser ... from the text of J. Upton. With a pre-
    face by J[ohn] Aikin. 6 vol. 1802. 8°. [DD:
    Ann]. MC.43: "Spencer [*sic*]. 6 Vol:" LB.11:
    "Spenser 6 vols."

[Sprat, Thomas]. A true account of the horrid con-
    spiracy against the late King [Charles II.], his
    present Majesty [James II.], and the government:
    as it was order'd to be published by His late
    Majesty. 1685. 32cm. [*NUC*]. *SC*.22.

Staël-Holstein, afterwards Rocca, Anne Louise Germaine
    de, Baroness. Corinne; ou, l'Italie. [? Nou-
    velle édition. 3 vol. Londres, 1809. 18cm.].
    [*NUC*]. MC.98: "Corine [*sic*]--3 Vol:" LB.6: "M^e
    de Stael."

Stanfield, James Field. The Guinea voyage, a poem.
    1789. 4°. MC.46: "Guinea Voyage:" LB.41: "Gui-
    nea Voyage."

Stanley, Arthur Penrhyn. The life and correspondence
    of Thomas Arnold, D.D., late head master of Rugby
    School. 2 vol. 1844. 8°. LB.46: "Dr Arnold's
    Life."

————. Sinai and Palestine, in connection with their
    history. 1856. 8°. [DD:Ann:MW]. LB.59.

Stapleton, Thomas. Chronicon Petroburgense. Edited
    by Thomas Stapleton. 1849. 8°. *SC*.15.

————. De antiquis legibus liber. Cronica Maiorum
et Vicecomitum Londoniarum ... Thoma Stapleton.
Ed. 1846. 8°. *SC*.15.

————. Plumpton correspondence. A series of letters,
chiefly domestic, written in the reigns of Edward
IV. Richard III. Henry VII. and Henry VIII. Edited by Thomas Stapleton. 1839. 8°. *SC*.15.

Starkey, Digby Pilot. Judas; a tragic mystery. Dublin, 1843. 8°. *SC*.664.

————. Theoria. Dublin, 1847. 16°. *SC*.599: "by
T. [*sic*] B. [*sic*] Starkey."

*Statius, Publius Papinius. MC.5: "Statii Sylvae
[written in left margin: 'Statius &c H[artley]
C[oleridge]']."

*————. *SC*.436: "Statius, Apolodorus [*sic*], Homer,
etc. etc., Gr. et Lat. (*with Autographs of Coleridge
and Wordsworth*)."

Steele, Sir Richard. See Addison, Joseph.

————. The Christian hero: an argument proving that
no principles but those of religion are sufficient
to make a great man. 1701. 8°. *SC*.249 [n.d.].
MC.25: "Christian Hero:"

[———— and Joseph Addison]. The tatler. By Isaac
Bickerstaff [Sir Richard Steele, Joseph Addison,
and others]. 4 vol. 1710-11. 8°. [? MC.79:
"Tatler:--4 Vol:"].

Stephanius, Stephen Hansen. Nomenclatoris Latino-
Danici minoris libri IV in usum scholarum Daniae
et Norvegiae conscripti et in lucem edita a Steph.
Johs. Stephanio, nunc denuo una cum locupletiori
appendice emendatius recensiti et notis quanti-
tatam pronunciationis, declinationum, generum et
numerorum accuratius aucti. Hauniae. u. A. --
Nomenclatoris Latino-Danici pars altera, quae

verba omnium conjugationum, ordine alphabetico, ex-
hibet. In usum scholarum Daniae et Norvegiae.
Hafniae. 1638.--Sorae. 1654. [H. Ehrencron-Mül-
ler, *Forfatter-lexicon omfattende Danmark, Norge
og Island Indtil* 1814. 12 vol. København, 1924-
35, VIII (1930), 35]. *SC*.437: "1654;... Ditto
pars altera, etc., cum Indice, etc., 8vo." MC.16:
"Nomenclator Lat:= Danic:"

Stephanus, Carolus. Dictionarium historicum, geo-
graphicum, poeticum ... gentium, hominum, deorum,
gentilium, regionum, locorum ... hac editione auctius et locupletius redditum. I. Stoer: [Genevae],
1603. 4°; another edition, Genevae, 1662. 4°.
SC.110: "4to, *Genevae*, Stoer--(Date torn off the
Title-page)." MC.11: "Diction: Histor: Geog: Poet:"
LB.30: "Dictio Hist Geog^r."

Stephanus, Henricus. See Homer. Odyssea.

Stephens, George. Gertrude and Beatrice; or, the Queen
of Hungary. A historical tragedy, in five acts [in
verse]. 1839. 8°. *SC*.486: "*(Presentation Autograph)*."

————. The manuscripts of Erdély: a romance. 3 vol.
1835. 8°. *SC*.438: "3 vols., 8vo, 1836."

[Stephens, James]. The crisis of the sugar colonies;
or, an enquiry into the objects and probable effects of the French expedition to the West Indies;
and their connection with the colonial interests
of the British Empire. To which are subjoined,
sketches of a plan for settling the vacant lands of
Trinidada. In four letters to the Right Hon.
Henry Addington. 1802. 8°. MC.61: "Crisis of
the Sugar: Colon:"

Sterling, John. Poems. 1839. 12°. [PSC.WWC.JB:Ann].
SC.638: "Stirling [*sic*]."

Stevenson, Alan. Account of the Skerryvore Lighthouse,
with notes on the illumination of lighthouses.

Edinburgh, 1848. 4°. *SC*.161: *"interesting Auto-graph Presentation by the Author."* LB.46:"Stevensons Lighthouses."

Stevenson, Seth William. A tour in France, Savoy, Northern Italy, Switzerland, Germany, and the Netherlands, in the summer of 1825. London, Norwich, 1827. 8°. *SC*.162: "with Observations on the scenery of the Necker [*sic*] and the Rhine, 2 vols., 1827." [Erroneously ascribed to "Seth A. [*sic*] Stevenson"].

Stewart, Dugald. See Robertson, William.

Stewart, Thomas. The Constantiniad, a poem. Book I. 1845. 8°. *SC*.512.

Stillingfleet, Edward, Bishop of Worcester. The Bishop of Worcester's charge to the clergy of his diocese, in his primary visitation. 1691. 4°. *SC*. 311: "1690." MC.29: "Bp: of Worcester's charge sermon &c: &c:"

————. Irenicum, a weapon-salve for the Churches wounds; or, the divine right of particular forms of church government, discussed and examined. Second edition, with an appendix concerning the power of excommunication in a Christian church. 1662. 4°. *SC*.297: "4to ... 1662." MC.22: "Weapon Salve:"

————. Origines sacrae, or a rational account of the grounds of Christian faith. 7th ed. Cambridge, 1702. fol. *SC*.296.

————. A second discourse in vindication of the Protestant grounds of faith, against the pretence of infallibility in the Roman Church. 1673. 8°. MC.24: "Stillingfleet's Vindication of Protest: Faith:" ["John" [John Wordsworth] written in left margin].

Stith, William. The history of the first discovery and settlement of Virginia. Williamsburg, 1747.

8°. *SC*.92: "by W. Smith [*sic*]." [? MC.61: "Hist: of Virginia: 2 Cop:"]. [Two titles? See Beverley, Robert].

Story, Robert, of Wark. The magic fountain, with other poems. 1829. 12°. *SC*.500.

Stothard, afterwards Bray, Anna Eliza. See Colling, Mary Maria.

Stow, John. The abridgement of the English chronicle ... augmented with ... many ... antiquities, and continued ... unto the end of ... 1610. By E[dmund] H[owes]. 1611. 8°. *SC*.74: "unto the end of the yeare 1610, by G. [*sic*] H., Gentleman, sm. 4to ... 1611." MC.59: "Eng: Chronicle:"

————. A survey of London. [? 1598. 4°]. MC.59: "Survey of London:"

Strabo. Strabonis rerum geographicarum libri XVII., I[saacus] Casaubonus recensuit ... emendavit ac commentariis illustravit ... Accessit & tabula orbis totius descriptionem complectens. Adjecta est etiam G[ulielmi] Xylandri ... Latina versio, cum ... indicibus. Gr. & Lat. [Geneva], 1587. fol. *SC*.160: "Isaacus Causaubonus [*sic*] recensuit, etc., adest [*sic*] etiam Gul. Xylandri, etc. folio [n.p., n.d.]." MC.6: "Strabo: Fol:" LB.17: "Strabo."

Strong, Charles. Sonnets. 1835. 8°. *SC*.588.

————. Specimens of sonnets from the most celebrated Italian poets: with translations by C.S. 1827. 8°. *SC*.588.

*Strype, E.H. Poems. *SC*.686: "4to, 1845."

A student of the Temple. See Beldam, Joseph.

Studley, John. See Bale, John.

*Suckling, Sir John. Poems. *SC*.602: "*no title*)."
    MC.46: "Sucklin's [*sic*] Poems:"

*Suetonius Tranquillus, Caius. MC.6: "Suetonius."
    ["H.C." [i.e. Hartley Coleridge] written in left
    margin].

Sumner, John Bird. A practical exposition of the Gos-
    pel according to St. John. 2nd ed. 1835. 12°.
    SC.299. [? MC.28: "St John Gospel"].

————. A practical exposition of the Gospel of St.
    Luke, in the form of lectures [with the text], in-
    tended to assist the practice of domestic instruc-
    tion and devotion. 3rd ed. 1833. 8°. *SC*.299.

————. A practical exposition of the Gospels of St.
    Matthew and St. Mark. 1831. 12°. *SC*.298.

*Sundries. *SC*.315 to *SC*.320: "omitted being otherwise
    named."

*Swedish and English grammar. *SC*.439. MC.17: "Swedish
    Gramm:"

Swift, Jonathan. See Temple, Sir William. Works.

————. The works of Dr. Jonathan Swift. With the
    author's life and character. 13 vol. Edinburgh,
    1768. 17.5cm. [TxU.An:Ann: Vol. V only]. *SC*.
    440: "13 vols., 8vo ... *Edinburgh* (wanting vol. i),
    1768." MC.79: "Swifts Works: 13 Vol: 1st: w$_{\text{ii}}^{\text{g}}$"
    [? LB.11: "Tale of a Tub"]. [WR: "A copy of Swift's
    'Gulliver's Travels' ... contains a long critical
    MS. note by S.T. Coleridge"]. [This note, amount-
    ing to 89 lines of commentary, is in the University
    of Texas volume: i.e. Vol. 5 (*Gulliver's Travels*)].

Swinton, John. See An universal history.

Sylvanus, Georgius. See Isocrates.

Sylvester, Matthew. See Baxter, Richard. Reliquiae.

Symington, Andrew James. Harebell chimes; or, summer
memories and musings [poems]. 1849. 12°. *SC*.665:
"*(with MS. Notes, etc.) Edin*., 1849."

[Sympson, Joseph]. The beauties of spring; a poem.
1785. 27cm. [*DLC*; Christopher Wordsworth. *Memoirs of William Wordsworth*. 2 vol. Boston, 1851.
I, 179]. MC.46: "Beauties of Spring:"

————. Science revived; or the vision of Alfred.
1802. 4°. [MBAt]. *SC*.666. MC.46: "Simpson's
[*sic*] Vision of Alfred:"

Synopsis communium locorum. Oxoniae, 1700. 8°.
[Wing]. MC.10: "Synopsis commu: Locorum:"

Tacitus, Caius Cornelius. C. Corn. Tacitus ex J. Lip-
sii editione cum not. et emend. H. Grotii. Amstelodami, 1649. 12°. [Graesse]. *SC*.410: "Tacitus
(Elzevir), 1649." MC.6: "Tacitus: Elzeverii:"

————. C. Cornelii Taciti Opera quae extant omnia,
ad editionem optimam Joh. Fre. Gronovii ... expressa. 2 vol. Glascuae, 1743. 12°. [*BN*].
[CSJ:Ann: "Opera extant omnia. Ad editionem optimam Joh. Fre. Gronovii accurate expressa. Tomus
I. 17cm. Glasguae, 1743"]. MC.6: "Tacitus: 1st
Vol:--2 Cop:"

————. [? Opera ex recensione J[ohann] A[ugust] Ernesti. 2 tom. Lipsiae, 1752. 8°]. MC.6: "Tacitus: Ernesti:--3 Cop:"

————. Oeuvres de Tacite, traduits en français, avec
des remarques par [Nicholas] Perrot d'Ablancourt.
2 tom. Amsterdam, 1670. 8°. [Graesse]. *SC*.75.
MC.91: "Dablancourt's [*sic*] Tacit:"

*————. *SC*.441: "Reflessioni [*sic*] Morali, di C.C.
Tacito, di Ant. Loredano, 12mo, *Venetia*, 1572."

Taggart, Cynthia. Poems. (Memoir of William Taggart, written by himself.) Providence [R.I.], 1834. 8°. [*L*: "*With the autograph of William Wordsworth*"]. *SC*.621: "1824."

Taggart, William. See Taggart, Cynthia.

Talfourd, Sir Thomas Noon. See Lamb, Charles. Final Memorials; Letters; Works.

————. The Athenian captive. A tragedy [in five acts and in verse]. 1838. 8°. *SC*.486: "(*Presentation Autograph*.)" LB.25.

————. Glencoe; or, the fate of the Macdonalds. A tragedy, in five acts [and in verse]. 2nd ed. 1840. 8°. *SC*.676: "(*with Presentation Autog*.)."

————. Recollections of a first visit to the Alps, in August and September, 1841. [? 1842]. 12°. *SC*.164: "(*with Autograph Presentation of the learned Author, and MS. Sonnet on the Reception of the Poet Wordsworth at Oxford*)."

————. Three speeches delivered (18th May, 1837, 25 April, 1838, and 28th February, 1839) in the House of Commons in favour of a measure for an extension of copyright. 1840. 8°. *SC*.16: "*with Autog. of the late Laureate*."

Tarlton, Thomas Henry. See Myers, Frederick.

Tasso, Bernardo. Le lettere di M. Bernardo Tasso ... Venetia. 1570. 8°. *SC*.441: "1591." MC.97: "Le Lettere de [*sic*] Tasso:" See Costanzo, Torquato.

Tasso, Torquato. The Gerusalemme liberata of Tasso: with explanatory notes on the syntax in obscure passages, and references to the author's imitations of the ancient classics. To which is prefixed a compendious analysis of metre. By A[gostino] Isola. 2 vol. Cambridge, 1786. 8°. *SC*.

667: "(*with MS. Notes by Mr. Wordsworth*)." See STC entry.

——. Godfrey of Bulloigne; or, the recoverie of Jerusalem; done into English heroicall verse by E[dward] Fairfax, gent. 4th ed. 1749. 8°. *SC*. 417: "Fairfax's Tasso, 1749." LB.37: "Fairfax's Tasso." See STC entry and App. I.

——. Rinaldo, a poem, in xii. books; tr. from the Italian of Torquato Tasso. By John Hoole ... 1792. 22cm. [*L*; *DLC*]. MC.50: "Rinaldo:"

Tate, James. See Horatius Flaccus, Quintus. Horatius Restitutus.

Tate, Nahum. See Coste, Pierre.

Taylor, Edward. See Böhme, Jakob.

Taylor, Sir Henry. Edwin the fair; an historical drama. 1842. 8°. [DD:Ann]. LB.28.

——. The eve of the Conquest, and other poems. 1847. 16°. *SC*.581.

——. The statesman. 1836. 8°. *SC*.355.

[Taylor, Isaac]. Fanaticism. 1833. 8°. *SC*.227. LB.15.

[——]. Home education. By the author of Natural History of Enthusiasm. [Isaac Taylor]. 1838. 8°; 2nd ed. 1838. 8°. *SC*.268: "1838."

[——]. Natural history of enthusiasm. [By Isaac Taylor]. 7th ed. 1834. 8°. *SC*.227.

[——]. Physical theory of another life. By the author of Natural history of enthusiasm. [Isaac Taylor]. 1836. 8°. *SC*.227.

[——]. Saturday-evening, by the author of the Natural history of enthusiasm [Isaac Taylor].

1832. 8°; "Fourth thousand." 1834. 8°. *SC*.227: "1834."

[————]. Spiritual despotism by the author of Natural history of enthusiasm [Isaac Taylor]. 1835. 8°; 2nd ed. 1835. 8°. *SC*.227: "1835."

Taylor, Jeremy. See Montagu, Basil. Selections.

————. A dissuasive from Popery to the people of Ireland. 3rd ed., revised and corrected by the author. 1664. 8°. [*L*: *"With the autograph of William Wordsworth"*]. *SC*.282: "12mo." MC.23/JC: "Taylor on Popery." See STC entry.

————. Eniautos [in Greek]: a course of sermons for all the Sundays of the year. Third edition, enlarged. [? 1668,67]. fol. [*E*]. *SC*.300: "1688, fol." MC.21: "Taylor's Sermons:"

————. The rule and exercises of holy living ... 23rd ed. 1719. [With this is bound his The rule and exercises of holy dying. 23rd ed. 1719]. [00]. [DD: "Holy Living and Holy Dying, London, 1717. [Specially bound by Fred Westley: 'The Binding of this Volume Presented by Permission to Mrs. William Wordsworth as a Memorial of Two Visits to Rydal Mount. By Fred. Westley. Augt 11 & 18. 1845'"]. [The DD copy is presumably the 22nd ed.]. LB.41: "Taylor's H Liv^g & Dying [lent 25 June 1848]."

————. Theologia eklektike [in Greek]. A discourse of the liberty of prophesying. 2nd ed., corrected. 1702. 8°. *SC*.202. MC.23: "Taylor's Liberty of Prophesy^g."

————. The worthy communicant; or, a discourse of the nature, effects, and blessings consequent to the worthy receiving of the Lord's Supper. 1674. 8°. [*L*: "MS. Notes [by S.T. Coleridge]"]. *SC*.251: "1678." [Lowndes: "With an additional Sermon ... 1678, 8vo"]. MC.23: "Taylor's Worthy Communic:"

Taylor, John, Author of "Monsieur Tonson." Poems on
     various subjects. 2 vol. 1827. 8°. *SC*.580.

Taylor, John Edward. Michael Angelo, considered as a
     philosophic poet; with translations. 1840. 8°.
     SC.551.

Taylor, Thomas. See Basnage, Jacques, Sieur de Beau-
     val; Pausanias; Plato.

*MC.80: "Temple's Essays:" [? Temple, Sir William.
     Essays. 2 vol. 1821. 8°. (In the British prose
     writers. Vol. 4. 1819. 8°.)]--[? Temple, Laun-
     celot, *pseud*. [i.e. Armstrong, John]. Sketches;
     or essays on various subjects. 1758. 8°].

Temple, Launcelot. See Armstrong, John.

Temple, Sir William. The works of Sir William Temple,
     Bar^t ... To which is prefix'd some account of the
     life and writings of the author [by Jonathan Swift].
     A new edition. 4 vol. 1757. 8°. *SC*.442: "His
     Works and Life, 4 vols., 8vo ... 1759."

————. An introduction to the history of England.
     1695. 8°. *SC*.367: "(*Autog*.)." MC.66: "Introduc-
     tion to Hist: of England."

[————]. Memoirs of what past in Christendom from
     the war begun in 1672 ... to the peace concluded
     in 1679. [By Sir William Tenple]. 1692. 8°.
     SC.44. MC.64: "Memoirs: 1672--'79:"

————. Miscellanea. 3rd ed. 1691. 8°. *SC*.443:
     "1791 [*sic*]."

————. Observations upon the United Provinces of the
     Netherlands. 1673. 8°. *SC*.150. MC.69: "Sir W.
     Temple's Observations on the United Provinces."

Tennyson, Alfred, Lord. Poems. By Alfred Tennyson.
     In two volumes. 1842. 8°. LB.1: "2 Vols Tenny-
     sons Poems."

Terentius, Publius, Afer. Terentius; in singulas
scenas argumenta, fere ex Aelii Donati commentariis, transcripta. Versuum genera per Erasmum
Roterod. Lutetiae, 1551. 8°. SC.669. MC.6:
"Terentius: Lutet:" [? LB.58: "Terence"].

—————. P. Terentii ... Comoediae sex. Interpretatione et notis illustravit N[icolaus] Camus ... In
usum Delphini. (Prolegomena Terentiana). Parisiis, 1675. 4°. MC.6: "Terentius: Delph:"

—————. Publii Terentii ... Comoediae sex. [Edited
by Michael Maittaire]. 1729. 12°. [L; GBD].
SC.668: "Comoediae Sex, 8vo, 1729."

Thelwall, Algernon Sydney. Letters to a friend whose
mind had been harassed by many objections against
the Church of England. 1835. 8°. LB.19: "Thel-
walls Letters."

Theocritus. Selecta quaedam Theocriti Idyllia. Recensuit ... Thomas Edwards. Cantabrigiae, 1779. 8°.
SC.670: "cur. J. [sic] Edwards, S.T.P., Cantab.,
1779."

*Theology. [? SC.199: "six other books"]. [? SC.232:
"two other books"]. [? SC.232: "two other bks."].

Theophrastus. See Epictetus.

Thevet, Andrew. See Plutarch.

Thicknesse, Philip. Useful hints to those who make
the tour of France, in a series of letters written
from that kingdom. 2nd ed., corrected. 1770.
12°. SC.78: "8vo."

Thirlwall, Connop. A history of Greece. 8 vol.
(Lardner's Cabinet Cyclopaedia). 1835-44. 12°.
SC.79. LB.37.

Thomas, Sir Edmund. A short view of the conduct of
the English clergy, so far as relates to civil

affairs, from the Conquest to the Revolution. 1737. 8°. (In Barron, Richard. The pillars of priestcraft and orthodoxy shaken. 2 vol. 1752. 12°. I, 1). [Woodward, I, 211]. *SC*.1. MC.28: "View of Clergy &c:"

Thompson, Aaron. See Galfridus, Monumetensis.

Thoms, William John. Anecdotes and traditions, illustrative of early English history and literature, derived from MS. sources. Edited by William J. Thoms. 1839. 8°. *SC*.15: "Arundel [*sic*] Traditions." LB.41: "Anecdotes & Traditions."

Thomson, Henry. The Lord's table; being forty addresses to communicants, and two sermons for the morning and evening of a communion sabbath. Edinburgh, 1839. 8°. *SC*.301: "Penrith, 12mo."

Thomson, James. The works of James Thomson. With his last corrections and improvements ... With the life of the author by P[atrick] Murdoch. 3 vol. 1768. 8°. *SC*.672: "1763-1768." [? MC.47: "Thomson Poet: Works 2 Vol:"].

————. The seasons, a hymn, a poem to the memory of Sir Isaac Newton, and Britannia, a poem. 5 pt. 1730. 8°. *SC*.671: "This appears to be the second edition of 'The Seasons' collectively--the first having been published in quarto in the same year ... R[obert] S[outhey]." MC.47: "Thomson's Seasons: 1730."

Thornton, Bonnell. See Colman, George, the Elder.

Thornton, Henry. Family prayers. [Edited by R.H.I., i.e. Sir Robert Harry Inglis]. 1834. 8°. *SC*. 247: "Henry Thomson [*sic*]."

————. [Another edition]. 1839. 12°. *SC*.302.

Thucydides. The history of the Peloponnesian War ... The text according to [Immanuel] Bekker's edition,

with some alterations ... With notes by Thomas
Arnold. 3 vol. Oxford, [1830] 1832-35. 8°.
LB.18.

Thyer, Robert. See Butler, Samuel.

Tibullus, Albius. See Catullus, Caius Valerius;
Ovidius Naso, Publius. Electa.

Tillotson, John. [? Sixteen sermons preached on several subjects and occasions. 14 vol. 1695-1704.
8°]. MC.21: "Tillotson's Sermons: 4th Vol:"

Timberlake, Henry. The memoirs of Lieut. H. Timberlake
(who accompanied the three Cherokee Indians to
England in the year 1762) containing whatever he
observed remarkable ... during his travels to and
from that nation ... also the principal occurren-
ces during their residence in London. 1765. 8°.
SC.143: "1745." MC.63: "Timberlake's memoirs:"

Tindal, Nicholas. See Spence, Joseph.

Todd, Henry John. See Milton, John. The poetical
works.

————. Illustrations of the lives and writings of
Gower and Chaucer, collected from authentic documents. 1810. 8°. *SC*.674.

Todd, James Henthorn. See Wycliffe, John.

Toland, John. See Milton, John. A complete collection.

[————]. Amyntor; or a defence of Milton's life.
Containing I. A general apology for all writings
of that kind. II. A catalogue of books attributed
in the primitive times to Jesus Christ, his apostles, and other eminent persons: With several important remarks ... relating to the Canon of Scripture. III. A complete history of the book inti-
tul'd, Icon Basilike, proving Dr Gauden, and not
King Charles the First to be the author of it:

With an answer to all the facts alledg'd by M^r
Wagstaf to the contrary; and to the exceptions
made against my Lord Anglesey's memorandum, D^r
Walker's book or Mrs Gauden's narrative, which
last piece is now the first time publish'd at
large. [By J.T., i.e. John Toland]. 1699. 8°.
SC.165. MC.64: "Amyntor:"

[————]. The life of John Milton. 1698. fol. *SC.*
165 [n.d.]. MC.65: "Toland's Life of Milton:"

Tong, William. See Henry, Matthew.

Tooke, Andrew. See Walker, William.

————. The pantheon, representing the fabulous histories of the heathen gods and most illustrious
heroes; translated from the Pantheum mithicum of
... François Antoine Pomey. 1698. 8°. *SC*.170:
"with the late Laureate's Autograph. [n.d.]."
MC.14: "Tooke's Pantheon:" LB.53.

*Topography. *SC*.118: "four other Topographical works."

Torriano, Giovanni. See Florio, Giovanni.

*Tour in America. MC.69: "Tour in America:" See
Beatty, Charles.

Townsend, Charles. Winchester, and a few other compo-
sitions in prose and verse. Winchester, 1835. 4°.
SC.498.

Townsend, Chauncy Hare. See Townshend, Chauncy Hare.

Townsend, Thomas. See Solis y Ribadneyra, Antonio de.

Townshend, Chauncy Hare. See Cambridge Prize Poems.

[————]. A descriptive tour in Scotland; by T.H.C.
[Chauncy Hare Townshend]. Bruxelles, 1840. 8°.
SC.113: "A Descriptive Tour in Scotland, by T.H.C.,
12mo.--*Bruxelles*, 1840." LB.40.

————. Facts in mesmerism, with reasons for a dispassionate inquiry into it. 1840. 8°. *SC*.166: "(*with Presentation Autograph*)." LB.32.

Transtagano, Antonio Vieira. See Vieira, Antonio.

Trapp, Joseph. Praelectiones poeticae in schola naturalis philosophiae Oxon. habitae ... Volumen primum. Oxonii, 1711. 8°. *SC*.670. MC.11: "Praelect: Poeticae: Trap [*sic*]:"

Trebicka or Trembicka, Françoise, Mme. Mémoires d'une Polonaise pour servir à l'histoire de la Pologne depuis 1764 jusqu'à 1830. 2 tom. Paris, 1841. 8°. *SC*.168.

————. [Another copy]. *SC*.641.

Trench, Richard Chenevix. Genoveva; a poem. 1842. 8°. *SC*.677.

[————]. Poems. [By R.C. Trench]. [Privately printed]. [? 1841]. 12°. [*L: "With a MS. note from the Author to William Wordsworth, together with the autograph of the latter"*]. *SC*.514: "Poems--not published--*with Autograph Letter, etc., by the Rev. Author, R.C. Trench.*" [? LB: "Trenchs [*sic*] Poems"].

————. Sabbation; Honor Neale, and other poems. 1838. 12°. *SC*.526.

————. The story of Justin Martyr, and other poems. 1835. 12°. *SC*.553.

Trenck, Frederic, Baron. The life of Baron Frederic Trenck, containing his adventures ... during ten years imprisonment at the fortress of Magdeburg ... Also, anecdotes historical, political and personal. Translated from the German by Thomas Holcroft. Boston, 1792. 12°. *SC*.587: "Holcroft's Life of Baron Trenck:" LB.16: "Trenk Memoirs."

*Trials and charges. *SC*.80: "Trials and charges in Courts of Law, etc. etc.—a bundle tied and labelled by Mrs. Wordsworth (*with presentation Autographs of numerous authors*)."

[? A trip to the Jubilee; by a gentleman who was at the late grand one at Rome, containing a diverting account of the most remarkable, &c. 1750. 8°]. MC.82: "Trip: to the Jubilee:"

Tristram, Thomas. See Vida, Marcus Hieronymus.

Tryon, Thomas. Tryon's letters, domestick and foreign, occasionally distributed in subjects, viz., philosophical, theological, and moral. 1700. 8°. MC.33: "Tryon's Letters:"

[Tupper, Martin Farquhar]. Probabilities; an aid to faith, by the author of Proverbial philosophy [M.F. Tupper]. 1847. 16°. *SC*.304: *"with Presentation Autograph."*

[————]. A thousand lines: now first offered to the world we live in. [By M.F. Tupper]. 1845. 12°. *SC*.677.

Turner, Robert. See Paracelsus.

Turner, William. A compleat history of the most remarkable providences, both of judgment and mercy, which have hapned [*sic*] in this present age. 1697. fol. *SC*.305. MC.23: "History of Provid:"

Turnley, Joseph. The spirit of the Vatican, illustrated by historical and dramatic sketches during the reign of Henry the Second. 1845. 8°. *SC*.574. LB.34.

Twamley, afterwards Meredith, Louisa Anne. Poems ... with original illustrations, drawn and etched by the authoress. 1835. 12°. *SC*.595: " ... *Present. Autog. by the Authoress.*"

*Twenty-four original sonnets, 1816. *SC*.498.

Twining, Henri. Voyage en Norwège et en Suède. Paris, 1836. *SC*.168.

Twysden, Sir Roger. Certaine considerations upon the government of England. By Sir Roger Twysden, kt. and bart. [Edited by John Mitchell Kemble]. 1849. 8°. *SC*.15.

Tymms, Samuel. Wills and inventories from the registers of the Commissary of Bury St. Edmund's and the Archdeacon of Sudbury. Edited by Samuel Tymms. 1850. 4°. *SC*.15: "ed. Samuel Tymons [*sic*]."

The universal gazetteer. [? 1760]. [*BB*]. [Paul F. Betz:Ann: "[Title page missing]. 21.4cm"]. *SC*. 181: "(*no title*), 8vo." MC.70: "Universal Gazetteer."

An universal history, from the earliest account of time to the present: compiled from original authors [by G. Sale, G. Psalmanazar, A. Bower, G. Shelvocke, J. Campbell, J. Swinton, etc.] and illustrated with maps, cuts, notes, etc. 60 vol. 1779-84. 8°. *SC*.83: "Universal History, from the Earliest Account of Time to the present, vols. I. to XI., 8vo ... 1799 [*sic*]." MC.57: "Universal History:--11 Vol:"

Upton, John. See Spenser, Edmund.

Urfé, Honoré d'. Astrea, a romance written in French by ... Honoré d'Urfé and translated by a person of quality. [With a preface signed J.D.]. 3 vol. 1657, 58. fol. *SC*.678. MC.88: "Astrea."

Valerius Maximus, Caius. Valerii Maximi Dictorum factorumque memorabilium exempla. Lugduni, 1534. 8°. *SC*.445: "*Lugd* ... 8vo ... 1540." [? MC.6: "Valerius Max:"].

————. Valerii Maximi Dictorum factorumque memorabilium Libri IX. Amstelodami, typis L. Elzevirii,
sumptibus societatis, 1650. 12cm. [*DLC*]. *SC*.410:
Libri IX, (ELZEVIR), 1650." [? MC.6: "Valerius
Max:"].

Valery, M. See Pasquin, Antoine Claude.

Valois, Henry de. See Eusebius, Pamphili.

Valpy, Edward. See Bible, Holy; New Testament, Greek.

Vandoperanus, Desiderius Jacotius. See Cicero, Marcus
Tullius. Opera.

Vane, Lionel. See Life of Tamerlane.

[Varennes, Claude de]. Le voyage de France, dressé
pour l'instruction et commodité tant des François
que des étrangers. [By Claude de Varennes].
Paris, 1639. 8°. [? MC.101: "Voyage de France:"].

*Velleius Paterculus, Marcus (or Caius). MC.5: "Pater-
culus: 2 Cop:"

Venn, Henry. The life and a selection of the letters
of ... Rev. Henry Venn ... author of "The Complete
Duty of Man" ... The memoir ... by ... John Venn.
1834. 8°. LB.20: "Venn's Life."

Venn, John. See Venn, Henry.

Vergil, Polydore. Polydore Vergil's English history,
from an early translation preserved among the MSS.
of the old Royal Library in the British Museum.
Vol. I containing the first eight books, comprising the period prior to the Norman Conquest. Edited by Sir Henry Ellis, K.H. 1846. 8°. *SC*.15.
LB.41.

————. Three books of Polydore Vergil's English history, comprising the reigns of Henry VI., Edward
IV., and Richard III. From an early translation,

preserved among the MSS. of the old Royal Library
in the British Museum. Edited by Sir Henry Ellis,
K.H. 1844. 8°. *SC*.15. LB.41.

Vialart, Charles. The history of the government of
France under the administration of the great Ar-
mand du Plessis, Cardinall and Duke of Richlieu
[*sic*] ... Translated out of French [of Charles
Vialart] by J.D. Esq. [? John Davies. ? John
Dodington]. 1657. fol. [*L*; *DLC*]. *SC*.64: "folio
... 1744." [? MC.63: "Hist. of France:"].

Viator. See D'Oyly, Thomas.

Victor, Sextus Aurelius. See Eutropius.

Vida, Marcus Hieronymus. Poematum ... pars prima, continens de arte poetica libros tres, et epistolam
ad J.M. Gibertum ... Edidit T[homas] Tristram.
Oxonii, 1722. 8°. *SC*.679: "(*Autographs of S.T.
Coleridge and W.W.*)." MC.6: "Vida:"

Vieira (or Vieyra) Transtagano, Antonio. A new Portu-
guese grammar in four parts ... The second edition.
1777. 8°. [*BN*]. [WL:Ann]. MC.16/0: "Transtagano's Portu: Gram."

[Vincent, Thomas]. God's terrible voice in the City:
wherein you have I. The sound of the voice, in the
narration of two late dreadful judgments of plague
and fire, inflicted by the Lord upon the city of
London; the former in the year 1665, the latter in
... 1666. II. The interpretation of the voice ...
By T[homas] V[incent]. [London], 1667. 8°.
SC.232. MC.25: "God's Voice in the City:"

Virgilius Maro, Publius. Publii Virgilii Maronis
opera interpretatione et notis illustravit C.
Ruaeus ... ad usum Delphini ... Parisiis, 1675.
4°. MC.6: "Virgilius: Delph:"

————. P. Virgilii Maronis Opera: emendabat et
notulis illustrabat G[ilbertus] Wakefield. 2 vol.

1796. 8°. MC.7: "Virgilius: Wakefield: 2 Cop:"
LB.34: "Virgilius (Wakefield) 2 vols."

————. [Eclogues, Georgics, and Aeneid. Title-page
missing]. 6.375 in. [*CWC*:Ann]. *SC*.347: "Virgil
(*imperfect*)." [? MC.6: "Virgilius: duodo:"].
[? LB.30: "An old Virgil ... 1 vol."].

————. The works of Virgil translated [into English
blank verse]. The first four Pastorals, the Georgics, and the first four Aeneids by Rann Kennedy.
The last six Pastorals, and the last eight Aeneids,
by Charles Rann Kennedy. 2 vol. 1849. 8°. *SC*.
681.

————. Aeneis. [? LB.30: "Aeneis 1 vol."].

————. Aeneis. MC.91: "Virgil's Aeneis: [classified
as a translation]."

————. Virgil's Bucolics. Translated by F[rancis]
Wrangham. Scarborough, 1815. 8°. MC.92: "Wrangham's Trans: of Bucol:"

————. The Georgics of Virgil translated by W[illiam]
Sotheby. [In verse. With the text]. Lat. and
Eng. 2nd ed. 1815. 8°. *SC*.658. MC.92: "Sothe-
by's Trans: of Georgics:"

————. Georgica Publii Virgilii Maronis hexaglotta.
1827. 43.5cm. [Heyne's text, with Spanish translation by Juan de Guzmán, German by Johann Heinrich Voss, English by William Sotheby, Italian by
Giovanni Francesco Soave, and French by Jacques
Montanier, called Delille; edited by William Sothe-
by]. [*DLC*; *L*]. [*DLC*: "Presentation copy to William Wordsworth, Esq., from William Sotheby. June
10th 1828"]. *SC*.680: "elephant 4to, 1827--'*To
William Wordsworth from W. Sotheby, June 10th,
1828.*'"

————. *SC*.601: "Odd Volumes--Dryden, Pope, Virgil,
etc. 12."

A vocabulary of sea phrases and terms of art used in
seamanship and naval architecture. In two parts.
I. English and French. II. French and English ...
By a captain of the British Navy. 2 vol. 1799.
12°. *SC*.170: "1799 ... *with the late Laureate's*
Autograph."

*A voice from the dormitory. *SC*.523: "A Voice from
the Dormitory."

Voltaire, See Arouet de Voltaire.

Vose, Dr. See Monti, Vincenzo.

Voss, Johann Heinrich. See Virgilius Maro, Publius.
Georgica.

Vossius, Gerardus Joannes. Latina grammatica ... in
usum scholarum adornata. Editio 3ª. Amstelodami,
1639. 8°. [*BN*]. MC.12: "Vossius' Lat: Gram:"

*Voyages and travels. MC.70: "Voyages & Travels 3
Vol:"

Wade, Thomas. Mundi et cordis: de rebus sempiternis
et temporariis: carmina. Poems and sonnets. 1835.
8 in. [*CWC*:Ann]. *SC*.597: "8vo, 1835."

*Wadsworth, Charles. Duties individual and national.
[? Philadelphia], 1844. 8°. *SC*.217: "by Charles
Wordsworth [*sic*], D.D., 8vo, 1844 (*Presentation*
Autog.)." [Presumably Charles Wadsworth, D.D., a
Presbyterian minister, of Philadelphia. See Alli-
bone].

Wadsworth, Captain James. See Sandoval, Prudencio de.

Wakefield, Gilbertus. See Bion; Virgilius Maro, Publius. Opera.

Walker, George. Select specimens of English poetry,
from the reign of Elizabeth to the present time.
London, Leeds, 1827. 8°. *SC*.429.

————. Select specimens of English prose, from the
reign of Elizabeth to the present time. With an
Introduction. London, Leeds, 1827. 19cm. [*AWC*:
Ann]. *SC*.429.

Walker, Robert Francis. See Krummacher, Friedrich
Wilhelm.

Walker, William. A treatise of English particles;
shewing much of the variety of their significations
and uses in English, and how to render them into
Latine ... fifteenth edition ... corrected by
A[ndrew] Tooke. 1720. 8°. *SC*.371. MC.18:
"Treatise of English Part:"

[Wallace, Robert]. Various prospects of mankind, nature, and Providence. 1761. 8°. *SC*.258. MC.81:
"Wallace's Prospects:"

Waller, Edmund. Poems. 7th ed. With several additions never before printed. 1705. 8°. *SC*.602.
MC.45: "Waller's Poems:"

Walpole, Horace, fourth Earl of Orford. The castle of
Otranto. (Vol. 22 of The British novelists).
SC.515. MC.87.

Walters, Hannah. See Walters, John.

Walters, John. An English-Welsh dictionary. 3rd ed.
[With a dissertation on the Welsh language by the
same author: and a dedicatory epistle by Hannah
Walters]. 2 vol. Denbigh, 1828. 8°. *SC*.447.

Walton, Izaak. The lives of Donne, Wotton, Hooker,
Herbert, and Sanderson. 1827. 16°. *SC*.252:
"1828. [n.s.]." LB.21: "Waltons Lives."

———— and Charles Cotton. The complete angler ...
with the lives of the authors, and notes ... by
Sir John Hawkins. [Edited by J[ohn] S[idney] Haw-
kins]. 6th ed. 1797. 12°. [*L*; Richard Words-
worth:Ann]. [? MC.75: "Complete Angler:"].

————. [Another edition]. [DD:Ann: "7th ed. 1808."
[? MC.76: Comp: Angler: 2 Cop:]. [? LB.24: "Complete Angler"].

————. [Another edition]. Edited by James Rennie.
Edinburgh, 1833. 8°. [WL:Ann].

Warburton, William. The alliance between church and
state: or, the necessity and equity of an established religion and a test-law demonstrated, from
the essence and end of civil society, upon the fundamental principles of the law of nature and nations. In three books. The 2nd ed., corr. and
improved. 1741. 21cm. [CtY.BL:Ann]. *SC*.190:
"8vo ... 1741." MC.41: "Warburton's Alliance:"

Ward, afterwards Radcliffe, Ann. The romance of the
forest. (Vols. 43 and 44 of The British novelists).
SC.657: "2 vols., 1810. [12mo]." MC.87. LB.9.

Ward, Caesar and Richard Chandler. The history and proceedings of the House of Commons from the Restoration to the present time ... collected from the
best authorities. [The dedication is signed by C.
Ward and R. Chandler].... Together with a large
appendix, containing exact lists of every Parliament, the names of the Speakers, etc. 14 vol.
1742-44. 8°. *SC*.43. [? MC.39: "Parliam" Debates:
14 Vol:"].

Warkworth, John. A chronicle of the first thirteen
years of the reign of King Edward the Fourth, by
John Warkworth. Edited by James Orchard Halliwell-
Phillipps. 1839. 8°. *SC*.15.

Warner, Ferdinando. See advice from a bishop.

Warter, John Wood. See Southey, Robert. Common place
  book; The doctor.

Warwick, Eden, *pseud*. See Jabet, George.

Warwick, Sir Philip. Memoires of the reigne of Charles
  I. with a continuation to the happy restauration of
  King Charles II. Published from the original manu-
  script. 1701. 8°. MC.64: "Warwick's Memo:"

Wassington, Prior. See Durham Cathedral.

A water drinker. See Montagu, Basil.

Waterland, Daniel. See A learned hand.

————. Eight sermons ... in defense of the divinity
  of Our Lord Jesus Christ. Cambridge, 1720. 8°.
  SC.213: "Waterland's Moyer-Lecture Sermons in Defence of the Divinity of Christ, 8vo, 1720." MC.
  29: "Waterland's Sermons."

Waterton, Charles. Wanderings in South America, the
  North-West of the United States, and the Antilles,
  in 1812, 1816, 1820, and 1824. With original instructions for the preservation of birds &c. for
  cabinets of natural history. 2nd ed. 1828. 8°.
  SC.174. LB.17: "Waterton [MS. unclear]."

Watson, Richard. An apology for the Bible, in a series
  of letters addressed to Thomas Paine, author of
  ... "The age of reason, part the second, being an
  investigation of true and of fabulous theology."
  ... A new ed. 1819. 18cm. [*DLC*]. *SC*.307: "8vo,
  1829." MC.23: "Watson's Apology:"

Watt, James. Correspondence of the late James Watt on
  his discovery of the theory of the composition of
  water ... Edited by James Patrick Muirhead. 1846.
  8°. [*EU*]. *SC*.89: "4to." LB.43: "Watts Correspondence."

[Watts, John]. Meditations and prayers selected from
the Holy Scriptures, the liturgy, and pious tracts
... By a clergyman [John Watts]. 2nd ed. 1816.
8°. [? MC.22: "Watt's [*sic*] Meditat:"

Way, Albert. See Galfridus, Frater.

Webb, Daniel. An inquiry into the beauties of painting.
2nd ed. 1761. 8°. [*L*]. [PSC.WWC.JB:Ann]. *SC*.
521: "12mo, 1741." MC.81: "Webb's Beauties of
Painting:"

Webb, John. A roll of the household expenses of Richard de Swinfield, Bishop of Hereford, during part
of the years 1289 and 1290. 1854-55. 8°. *SC*.15:
"2 vols. 1844 and 1845."

Weber, Friedrich A. New complete pocket dictionary of
the English and German languages. London, Leipzig,
1838. 8°. *SC*.448: "8vo, 1838, sewed." [? MC.27:
"German Dicy."].

Webster, John. The works of John Webster; now first
collected, with some account of the author, and
notes. By ... A[lexander] Dyce. 4 vol. 1830.
8°. [RPB.RBC:Ann]. *SC*.683: "5 vols." LB.15: "2
Vols Webster."

Wedelius, Georgius Wolfgangus. See De morbis infantum.

Weller, Jacob. Grammatica Graeca nova. Curavit hanc
novam editionem et praefatus est J.F. Fischerus.
Lipsiae, 1781. 8°. *SC*.449: "J.G. [*sic*] Fischerus."

Wells, Edward. Harmonia grammaticalis; or, a view of
the agreement between the Latin and Greek tongues,
as to the declining of words. 1611 [1711]. 8°.
[Date corrected in *L*]. *SC*.333: "8vo ... 1611."
MC.14: "Harmon Grammat:"

Welwood, James. Memoirs of the most material transactions in England, for the last hundred years, pre-

ceding the Revolution in 1688. 6th ed. 1718.
12°. [*L*; Lowndes]. [MH:Ann: "16.3cm."]. *SC*.135.
MC.63: "Welwood's Memoirs:"

Wendeborn, Gebhardt F.A. An introduction to German
    grammar. 1797. 8°. *SC*.362: "Wenderborn's [*sic*]."
    MC.18: "Introduc: to Germ: Gram:" [? LB.27: "3
    [German] Grammars"].

West, Thomas. The antiquities of Furness; or, an ac-
    count of the Royal Abbey of St. Mary in the Vale of
    Nightshade near Dalton in Furness ... with addi-
    tions by W[illiam] Close. Ulverston, 1805. 8°.
    SC.175. MC.71: "West's Antiq: of Furness:"

[————]. A guide to the lakes in Cumberland, West-
    morland, and Lancashire. By the author of The
    antiquities of Furness. 9th ed. Kendal, London,
    1807. 23cm. [NN.BC:Ann]. *SC*.175: "*Kendal*, 1807."
    MC.175: "West's Guide to the Lakes:"

West, William. Symboleography. Which may be termed,
    the art, or description, of instruments and presi-
    dents [*sic*]. Collected by William West ... Aug-
    mented with diuers new presidents not heretofore
    printed. 2 vol. in 1. 1632, 27. 22cm. [*L*; *DLC*].
    SC.85: "4to, 1622 [*sic*]."

*Westminster Greek grammar. [? Graecae grammaticae
    compendium [for the use of Westminster School].
    1721. 8°]. MC.11: "Westminster Greek Gram:"

Whewell, William. See Goethe, Johann Wolfgang von.
    Hermann und Dorothea.

————. Architectural notes on German churches. A
    new edition. To which is now added, notes written
    during an architectural tour in Picardy and Nor-
    mandy. Cambridge, 1835. 8°. *SC*.684. LB.38:
    "Whewell's Archi[l] Notes."

————. Astronomy and general physics considered with
    reference to natural theology. 1833. 8°. [*LLA*].
    SC.194. [? LB.41: "Whewells Astronomy"].

————. [Another edition]. 1837. 12°. *SC*.356. [?
LB.41: "Whewells Astronomy"].

————. The elements of morality, including polity.
2 vol. 1845. 8°. *SC*.308: "*Presentation Autograph of Author*."

————. On the principles of English university education. 1837. 8°. *SC*.207.

Whiston, William. See Josephus, Flavius.

Whitby, Daniel. A discourse of the necessity and usefulness of the Christian revelation; by reason of
the corruptions of the principles of natural religion among Jews and Heathens. 1705. 8°. *SC*.309.
MC.29: "Whitby's Discourse."

————. Ethices compendium, in usum academicae juventutis. Auctius ... quarto editum. 1724. 8°.
SC.211. MC.29: "Whitby's Ethics:"

White, Hugh. Meditations and addresses chiefly on the
subject of prayer ... Second edition, corrected.
Dublin, 1835. 8°. *SC*.310: "12mo, 1845."

White, William. See Parson, William.

[Whitelocke, Bulstrode]. Monarchy asserted, to be the
best, most ancient and legall form of government,
in a conference had at Whitehall [11 Apr.–8 May,
1657]; with Oliver late Lord Protector and a Committee of Parliament. [By Bulstrode Whitelocke].
1660. 8°. *SC*.36. MC.39: "Monarchy Asserted:"

Whytehead, Thomas. Poems. 1842. 8°. LB.51: "Whytehead's Poems."

The widow of a clergyman. See Birch, Mrs. Walter.

Wieland, Christoph Martin. Gandalin; or, love for
love. A poem. Translated from the German ... by
F. Hope. London, Nottingham, 1838. 12°. *SC*.612:
"Gandala [*sic*], or, Love for Love, 1838."

*————. Oberon. [*L*: "Oberon ... Neue und verbesserte
Ausgabe. [The preface signed: 'W.,' i.e. C.M. Wie-
land]. Reuttlingen, 1791. 8°"]. *SC*.467: "Oberon,
1792." MC.101: "Oberon:--Germ:"

Wilberforce, Robert Isaac. The five empires; an out-
line of ancient history. (Vol. 12, The English-
man's library). 1840. 12°. *SC*.355. LB.45: "Wil-
berforces 5 Empires."

Wilberforce, William. A practical view of the prevailing religious system of professed Christians, in
the higher and middle classes in this country con-
trasted with real Christianity. 12th ed. 1817.
8°. [WL.DW:Ann]. MC.22: "Wilberforce on Christianity:"

Wilde, J. Original pieces, songs, etc. Edinburgh,
1816. 12°. [*EU*]. *SC*.628: "Wilde's Songs, etc.
1816."

Wilkins, John, Bishop of Chester. A discourse concerning the gift of prayer ... Whereunto may be added,
Ecclesiastes: or, a discourse concerning the gift
of preaching. 1690. 8°. [*L*: *"Not containing the*
'Ecclesiastes'"]. *SC*.202: "8vo, 1690."

Wilks, Samuel Charles. Rose-buds rescued, and presented to my children. 1835. 8°. *SC*.612: "Rescued
Rosebuds [*sic*] ... 1835."

Willet, Andrew. Hexapla in Genesin, that is, a six-
fold commentary upon Genesis. 1605. fol. [? MC.
22: "Willet's Hexapla in Genesis [*sic*]:"].

[————]. Hexapla in Leviticum; that is a six-fold
commentarie upon the third Booke of Moses, called
Leviticus. [By A[ndrew] Willet] ... Perused and
finished by P. S[mith]. 1631. fol. [? MC.22:
"Willet's Hexapla in Levitic:"].

Williams, Helen Maria. Letters containing a sketch
of the politics of France from the thirty-first of
May 1793 till the twenty-eighth of July 1794. 2

vol. 1795. 12°. *SC*.2. MC.81: "Willam's [*sic*]
Letters 2 Vol:" [? LB.14: "Miss Williams"]. LB.
36: "Miss Williams Letters."

————. Poems on various subjects. With introductory
remarks on the present state of science and literature in France. 1823. 8°. *SC*.685: "('*Sent to me
by the Author from Paris--W.W.*')."

————. Recueil de poésies, extraites des ouvrages
d' H.M.W.; traduites de l'Anglais par M. S[tanis-
las Jean] de Boufflers, et par M. [Joseph Alphonse]
Esménard. Paris, 1808. 8°. *SC*.531.

[Williams, Nathaniel]. Imago saeculi: the image of
the age represented in four characters. To which
is added a pindarique elegie on ... Dr Willis.
2nd ed. Oxford, 1683. 8°. [? MC.54: "Williams'
Imago Saeculi:"].

Williams, Thomas Walter. A compendious digest of the
statute law, comprising the substance and effect
of all the public acts of Parliament in force,
from Magna charta, in the ninth year of King Henry
III. to the twenty-seventh year of His present
Majesty King George III. inclusive. The 2nd ed.,
cor., enl., and considerably improved. 1788.
21cm. [*DLC*]. *SC*.85: "8vo ... 1788." MC.40:
"Williams' Digest:"

Willis, Thomas, M.D. De anima brutorum quae hominis
vitalis ac sensitiva est, exercitationes duae:
prior physiologica ... altera pathologica. 2 pt.
1672. 8°. [? MC.33/JC/O: "De Anim: Brutorum:"].
See STC entry.

Willymott, William. The peculiar use and signification of certain words in the Latin tongue. [?
3rd ed.]. 1713. [? 8°]. *SC*.371: "1713." MC.11:
"Peculiar Use &c:--Lat: Tong:"

Wilson, Alexander. Specimen of modern printing types
cast at the letter foundry Alex. Wilson & Son, at

Glasgow, 1833. [Daniel Berkeley Updike. *Printing Types*. Cambridge (U.S.A.). 1937. p. 193: "A similar quarto specimen was issued in the same year by the Edinburgh branch house of Wilsons & Sinclair"]. *SC*.450: "Wilson: Specimens of Modern Printing Types cast at the Foundry of Messrs. Wilson and Sinclair, 4to ... 1832 [*sic*]."

Wilson, Edward. Sermons for Sunday evenings. 1832. 20.5cm. [MA:Ann]. *SC*.198.

Wilson, James. A voyage round the coasts of Scotland and the Isles. 2 vol. Edinburgh, 1842. 12°. *SC*.176: "8vo."

Wilson, John, Recorder of Londonderry. A discourse of monarchy, more particularly, of the imperial crowns of England, Scotland, and Ireland ... With a close from the whole, as it relates to the succession of His Royal Highness, James Duke of York. 1684. 8°. *SC*.367. MC.41: "Discourse of Monarchy."

Wilson, John [Christopher North, *pseud*.]. The city of the plague [a dramatic piece in three acts and in verse], and other poems. Edinburgh, 1816. 8°. *SC*.686. MC.54: "Wilson's City of Plague:"

————. The isle of palms, and other poems. Edinburgh, 1812. 8°. *SC*.685. MC.54: "Wilson's Isle of Palms:"

Winchelsea, Countess of. See Finch, Anne.

Winckelmann, Johann Joachim. Reflections on the painting and sculpture of the Greeks; with instructions for the connoisseur, and an essay on grace in works of art, translated from the German of the Abbé Winkelmann ... by H. Fusseli. 1765. 8°. [? MC. 81: "Winkleman's [*sic*] Reflect:"

Wingfield, George. Solitude, a poem; with other poems. 1842. 12°. *SC*.558: "8vo."

Winslow, Benjamin Davis. The true catholic churchman
in his life and death; the sermons and poetical
remains of Benjamin Davis Winslow ... with ...
notes by George Washington Doane. Oxford, 1842.
8°. *SC*.252. LB.30: "Winslow's Remains."

Winstanley, William. England's worthies: select lives
of the most eminent persons from Constantine the
Great to the death of Oliver Cromwell late Protec-
tor. 1684. 8°. *SC*.177: "from Constantine the
Great down to these times, 8vo ... 1684." MC.66:
"Winstanley's Worthies:"

Winterbottom, Thomas. An account of the native Afri-
cans in the neighbourhood of Sierra Leone; to which
is added an account of the present state of medicine among them. 2 vol. 1803. 22.5cm. MC.69/0:
"Winterbottom on Nat: Afr:"

Winterton, Ralph. Wintertonii poetae minores Graeci.
Cantabrigiae, 1700. 12°. [Wing]. *SC*.687: "8vo,
Cantab., 1700." [? MC.5: "Poetae Minor: Graeci:"].
LB.30: "Poetae Minores Graeci."

[Wirgman, George]. The Christian examiner, an exposition of the basis of Christianity, developing the
operation of the Spirit Incarnate, or Divinity,
in human nature through the reasoning soul of man.
By the author of "An essay on man [i.e. George
Wirgman]." no. 1-7. 1838-41. 8°. [L; *DAP*].
SC.212: "Christian Examiner, etc. etc. *a bundle*."

Wither, George. Britains remembrancer, containing a
narration of the plague lately past; a declaration
of the mischiefs present, and a prediction of
judgments to come, if repentance prevent not. [In
verse]. [London], 1628. 12°. [L]. [MH:Ann].
SC.688. MC.49: "Brit: Remembran:"

Withering, William. An arrangement of British plants.
3rd ed. 4 vol. 1796. 8°. [WL:Ann]. *SC*.178.
MC.75: "Withering's Brit: Plants 4 vol:" LB.32:
"1st 2d Vols Withering."

Witherspoon, John. A practical treatise on regenera-
    tion. 1789. 12°. [Lowndes]. *SC*.301: "1789."

Wit's commonwealth. See Bodenham, John; Meres, Fran-
    cis.

Wit's recreations, augmented, with ingenious conceites
    for the wittie and merry medecines for the melan-
    cholie. 1641. 8°. *SC*.611: "12mo, 1641." MC.46:
    "Wits Recreation: 1641."

Wolff (or Wolf), Christian, Baron von. [? LB.11:
    "Wolfe [lent 1 June 1829]"]. See STC entry.

Wolfius, Hieronymus. See Isocrates.

[Wollaston, William]. The religion of nature delinea-
    ted. [Signed: N.N., i.e. William Wollaston].
    1724. 4°. *SC*.129. [? MC.24: "Relig: of Nature:"].

Wollstonecraft, afterwards Godwin, Mary. Letters writ-
    ten during a short residence in Sweden, Norway, and
    Denmark. 2nd ed. 1802. 17cm. [*AWC*:Ann]. *SC*.78:
    "Mary Woolstonecraft [*sic*]." MC.69: "Letters from
    Sweden &c:"

Wood, Captain George, 82nd Regiment. The subaltern
    officer. A narrative. 1825. LB.13: "Subaltern
    Officer."

Wood, John. Account of the Edinburgh Sessional School,
    and the other parochial institutions for education
    established in that city in ... 1812, with stric-
    tures on education in general. Third edition,
    with additions. Edinburgh, 1830. 12°. *SC*.117.

Wood, Thomas. See Chamberlayne, Edward.

Woodfall, William. The law of landlord and tenant.
    [2nd ed.]. 1804. [*SM*, III, 250]. *SC*.85: "8vo,
    1804." MC.40: "Woodford's [*sic*] Landlord & Ten:"

Wordsworth, Charles, D.D. See Wadsworth, Charles.

Wordsworth, Charles. Christian boyhood at a public
school; a collection of sermons and lectures delivered at Winchester College. 2 vol. 1846. 8°.
LB.35: "Charles Sermons [lent 19 March 1846]."

—————. Communion in prayer; or, the duty of the congregation in public worship: three sermons. 1843.
8°. *SC*.302.

Wordsworth, Christopher, Master of Trinity. [? Christian institutes: a series of discourses and tracts
selected from the writings of the most eminent
divines of the English Church. 4 vol. 1836. 8°].
[Lowndes; *DNB*]--[? Christian institutes: a series
of discourses and tracts selected, arranged ...
and illustrated with notes, by Christopher Wordsworth. 4 vol. 1837. 8°]. LB.23: "Chris: Ins:
3d Vol." LB.23: "Christian Institutes 1st Vol."
[Both borrowed after 12 Nov. 1837].

—————. Ecclesiastical biography; or, lives of eminent men, connected with the history of religion
in England: from the commencement of the Reformation to the Revolution: selected and illustrated
with notes by Christopher Wordsworth. 6 vol.
[? 1810. 8°]--[? 2nd ed. 1818. 8°]. MC.64:
"Wordsworth's Ecclesiast[1]: Biography 6 Vol:" LB.
7: "Wordsworths Ecclesiastical Biography."

—————. The ecclesiastical commission and the universities; a letter to a friend. 1837. 8°. LB.22:
"Dr Ws Pamphlet Ch Affairs [lent after 13 Nov.
1837]."

—————. King Charles the First, the author of Icôn
Basilikè further proved, in a letter to His Grace,
the Archbishop of Canterbury, in reply to the objections of Dr. Lingard, Mr. Todd, Mr. Broughton,
the Edinburgh Review, and Mr. Hallam. 1828.
8.75 in. [*CWC*:Ann]. *SC*.99: "8vo, 1828, *with
Autographs of the Author and the late Laureate,
his Brother.*" *SC*.349: "8vo, 1828, *Presentation
Autograph.*"

————. Sermons on various subjects. 2 vol. 1818.
8°. MC.21: "Wordsworth's Sermons: 2 Vol:" LB.7:
"Wordsworth's Sermons 2 Vol^s."

————. Who wrote "Eikon Basilike"? Considered and
answered. 1824. 8°. *SC*.451. LB.6: "Wordsworths
Icon [returned 20 Dec. 1824]."

Wordsworth, Christopher, Bishop of Lincoln. Athens
and Attica; journal of a residence there. 1836.
8°. [DD:Ann]. LB.20: "Chri^s: Athens & Attica
[lent 5 Nov. 1836]."

[————]. Church principles and church measures: a
letter to Lord John Manners. With remarks on a
work entitled "Past and present policy of England
toward Ireland." By the author of "Maynooth, the
crown, and the country" [i.e. Christopher Wordsworth, Bishop of Lincoln]. 1845. 8°. LB.36:
"Church principles & measure[s] [lent soon after
30 June 1846]."

————. Diary in France; mainly on topics concerning
education and the Church. 1845. 12°. LB.36:
"Diary in France [lent 30 June 1846]."

————. Is the Church of Rome the Babylon of the
Book of Revelation? An essay, partly derived from
the author's Lectures on the Apocalypse. 3rd ed.
1856. 8°. *SC*.313.

————. Lectures on the Apocalypse: critical, exposi-
tory, and practical ... being the Hulsean Lectures
for 1848. 1848. 8°. LB.51: "Wordsworth on the
Apocalypse."

————. Letters to M. [Jules] Gondon ... on the de-
structive character of the Church of Rome, both
in religion and policy. 1847. 12°. LB.44:
"Wordsworth's Letters on the C^h of Rome."

[————]. Maynooth, the crown, and the country; or,
a protest against the new augmented, permanent ...

endowment of the Maynooth college. Roman Catholic
College of Maynooth. 1845. 8°. [*L*; *NUC*]. LB.
34: "Maynooth Pamphlets [lent between 14 May and
2 December 1845]." See *LY*, 1256, where WW acknow-
ledges receiving these in a letter dated 30 June
1845.

————. Notes at Paris, particularly on the state
and prospects of religion. 1854. 7.75 in. [*CWC*:
MW:Ann]. LB.56: "Notes at Paris--Dr. W."

————. Occasional sermons. Third and fourth series.
1852. 8°. LB.54: "3ᵈ Series Dʳ Wˢ Occˡ Sermons."

[————]. Ode performed in the Senate House, Cambridge,
on the seventh of July MDCCCXXXV at the first Commencement after the installation, and in the pre-
sence, of John Jeffreys, Marquis Camden, K.G.,
Chancellor of the University. Cambridge, 1835.
4°. *SC*.622.

————. On the canon of the Scriptures of the Old and
New Testament, and on the Apocrypha. Eleven discourses ... being the Hulsean lectures for the
year 1847. 1848. 8°. LB.42: "Wordsworth's Canon
of Scripture [lent 11 Sept. 1848]."

————. Sermons on the Irish church. 1852. [*DNB*].
LB.56: "Wordsworths Sermons on the Irish Church."

————. Sermons preached at Harrow School. 1841. 8°.
SC.312.

————. Theophilus Anglicanus; or, instruction for
the young student, concerning the Church and our
own branch of it. 1843. 12°. LB.55: "Theophilus
Ang:"

Wordsworth, Dorothy. A narrative concerning George
and Sarah Green of the parish of Grasmere. [A
manuscript so entitled, edited and published by
Ernest de Selincourt (Oxford, 1936) as *George and
Sarah Green, A Narrative*]. [WL]. LB.11: "Narrative of Greens [lent 11 Aug. 1830]."

Wordsworth, William. See Chaucer, Geoffrey; Hudson, John; Snow, Joseph.

————. Poems. 2 vol. 1807. 12°. *SC*.689: "(*Large-ly annotated, revised, and amended for subsequent editions*)." MC.52: "Wordsworth's Poems 1807: 2 Vols in one:"

————. Poems, by William Wordsworth: including Lyrical ballads, and the miscellaneous pieces of the author. With additional poems, a new preface, and a supplementary essay. 2 vol. 1815. 22.5cm. [OO.SC]. [WL (2 copies): (1) Ann; (2) DWQ]. MC. 52: "Wordsworth's Poems 1815: 2 Vol:" [? MC.52: "Wordsworth's Poems 2nd [? edition; item crossed out]."

————. The poetical works of William Wordsworth. 4 vol. Boston, Cambridge [U.S.A.], 1824. 12°. [L: "*With the Author's Autograph*"]. *SC*.692: "4 vols., 8vo, *Boston*, 1824." LB.27: "American Ed of Wordsworth."

————. The poetical works of William Wordsworth. 5 vol. 1827. 12°. LB.8: "1st & 5th Vols W's poems Decr [1827]."

————. The poetical works of William Wordsworth. Paris, 1828. 8°. [WL (2 copies): (1) Ann; (2) GGW]. *SC*.693: "complete in one Vol., imp. 8vo, *Paris*, 1828." LB.54: "French Ed. of Poems."

————. The poetical works of William Wordsworth. A new edition. 6 vol. 1836-7. 6.75 in. [*CWC*]. *SC*.690: "12 mo ... 1837. Perhaps more than in any other existing data, the growth of the Poet's mind may be perceived in these volumes. They contain a large amount of variorum readings, inspired jottings, and constructive emendations: together with additional short Poems in the Author's pencil autograph. It is most probable these were his pocket companions and *communists* in his later poetical rambles and in his fireside musings."

————. [Another copy of Vol. 5]. *SC*.689: "Poetical Works of William Wordsworth, vol. 5, 1837--*a few pencilled Memoranda inside the cover*."

————. The poetical works of William Wordsworth. 6 vol. 1841. 12°; Vol. 7 added in 1842. LB.37: "3^d, 4th, 5th Aug 3^d [1846] 5 vols Wordsworth Miss F^s [Isabella Fenwick's] Ed 2^d & 6 vol." See *LY*, 1278, 1287, 1289, and 1293; also *CWC*, 119, for a copy of Vol. 7 bearing the inscription: "Wm Wordsworth, Rydal Mount, 6th Decr 1842."

————. The poetical works of William Wordsworth ... A new edition. 6 vol. 1850. 12°. *SC*.694.

————. [Selections]. LB.30: "Burns Hines (Selections &c [)]." [? Select pieces from the poems of William Wordsworth. London: James Burns, [1843]. 16°. See *CWC*, 128]. [? Selections from the poems of William Wordsworth, Esq. chiefly for the use of schools. [Edited by Joseph Hine]. 1831. 12°; a new edition. 1834. 16.5cm.]. [00.SC:Ann].

————. Concerning the relations of Great Britain, Spain, and Portugal, to each other, and to the common enemy, at this crisis, and specially as affected by the Convention of Cintra. 1809. 8°. [WL:Ann]. MC.40: "Wordsworth's Convent: of Cintra: 2 Cop:" MC.62: "Convention of Cintra:"

————. Descriptive sketches. In verse. Taken during a pedestrian tour in the Italian, Grison, Swiss, and Savoyard Alps. 1793. 10.75 in. [*CWC*:Ann:DW]. MC.52: "Wordsworth's Descrip: Sketches:"

————. The excursion, being a portion of The recluse, a poem. 1814. 10.5 in. [*CWC*: "blue-gray boards": Ann]. MC.52: "Wordsworth's Excursion Half B$_n^d$" MC.52: "[Wordsworth's Excursion] Bds:" [? LB.6: "Excursion"].

————. The excursion. 2nd ed. 1820. 8°. [WL:Ann]. [? LB.6: "Excursion"].

————. A guide through the district of the lakes in the north of England, with a description of the scenery, &c. for the use of tourists and residents. Fifth edition, with considerable additions. Kendal, 1835. 8°. *SC*.179.

————. Lyrical ballads. 2n ed. 2 vol. 1800. 8°. [WL:Ann: "2 vols. London, 1798 [*sic*]"]. MC.53: "Wordsworth's Lyr: Ballads 2nd Edit: 2 Vol:"

————. Peter Bell, a tale in verse. 1819. 7 15/16 in. [*CWC*]. MC.52: "Wordsworth's Peter Bell: &c:"

————. The sonnets of William Wordsworth. Collected in one volume, with a few additional ones, now first published. 1838. 6.75 in. [*CWC*]. *SC*.691: "A proportionate share of the preceding remark [i.e. on *SC*.690. The poetical works. 6 vol. 1836-7] applies in this instance also."

————. Thanksgiving ode, January 18, 1816. With other short pieces, chiefly referring to recent public events. 1816. 9 in. [*CWC*]. [WL:Ann]. *SC*.663.

————. The waggoner, a poem. To which are added, Sonnets. 1819. 8.75 in. [*CWC*]. MC.52: "Wordsworth's Waggoner:"

————. The white doe of Rylstone; or the fate of the Nortons. A poem. (The force of prayer; or, the founding of Bolton Priory. A tradition). [In verse]. 1815. 4°. [WL (2 copies):Ann]. MC.52: "Wordsworth's White Doe:"

Worsley, Thomas. The province of the intellect in religion deduced from Our Lord's Sermon on the Mount, and considered with reference to prevalent errors. [With a synoptic table]. 5 pt. 1845-49. 8°. *SC*.314: "5 vols., 8vo ... 1845."

Wortley, Lady Emmeline Charlotte Elizabeth Stuart. The visionary; a fragment, with other poems. 2 pt. 1836-39. 8°. *SC*.588: "1836."

Wotton, Sir Henry. Reliquae Wottonianae; or, a collection of lives, letters, poems; with characters of
sundry personages: and other imcomparable pieces
of language and art. 2nd ed. 1654. 12°. *SC*.180.
MC.60: "Reliquae Wattianae [*sic*]."

Wotton, William. Reflections upon ancient and
modern learning. Second edition, with large additions. With a dissertation upon the epistles of
Phalaris, Themistocles, Socrates, Euripedes ...
and Aesop's fables. By Dr. [Richard] Bentley. 2
pt. 1697. 8°. *SC*.380. MC.81: "Wotton on Learning:"

Wrangham, Francis. See Virgilius Maro, Publius. Bucolics.

[Wren, Matthew]. Considerations on Mr. Harrington's
Commonwealth of Oceana: restrained to the first
part of the Preliminaries. [By Matthew Wren].
1657. 16°. *SC*.36: "(by Sir Christopher [*sic*]
Wren, 12mo, 1627 [*sic*]." MC.33: "On Harrington's
Commonw."

Wright, Edward. Certaine errors in navigation. Detected and corrected by Edw[ard] Wright. With many
additions that were not in the former edition.
3rd ed. 1657. 4°. *SC*.182: "4to, Hog., 1857
[*sic*]."

[? Wright, George Newnham]. Scenes in Ireland. With
historical illustrations, legends, and biographical notices. Embellished with ... engravings.
1834. 12°]. *SC*.181: "Wright, J.N.: Tours in Ireland; Maps and numerous Engravings." [? LB.9:
"Irish Tour"].

Wright, Thomas. See Mapes, Walter.

————. Alliterative poem on the deposition of King
Richard II ... Edited by Thomas Wright. 1838.
8°. *SC*.15.

————. A contemporary narrative of the proceedings against Dame Alice Kyteler, prosecuted for sorcery in 1324, by Richard Ledrede, Bishop of Ossory. Edited by Thomas Wright. 1843. 8°. *SC*.15.

————. The political songs of England, from the reign of John to that of Edward II. Edited and translated by Thomas Wright. 1839. 8°. *SC*.15. LB.41.

————. Three chapters of letters relating to the suppression of monasteries. Edited by Thomas Wright. 1843. 8°. *SC*.15.

Wyatt, Charles Percy. Poems, original and translated. 1837. 8°. *SC*.623.

Wyche, Sir Peter. See Freire de Andrade, Jacinto.

Wycliffe, John. An apology for Lollard doctrines, attributed to Wicliffe. Introduction and notes by James Henthorn Todd. 1842. 8°. *SC*.15.

Xenophon. He Kyrou anabaseos biblia hepta [in Greek]. X. de Cyri expeditione libri septem, a T[homas] Hutchinson. Editio quarta nuper recognita. *Gr. and Lat.* Cantabrigiae, 1785. 8°. [*EU*]. [WL: Ann]. MC.7: "Xenophon: Hutch:"

————. Oratio de Agesilao rege, Hiero sive de regno, Lacedaemoniorum respublica, Atheniensium respublica, Rationes redituum seu de proventibus. Recensuit B[olton] Simpson. [Greek and Latin]. Oxford, 1754. 8°. *SC*.409.

Xiphilinus, Joannes. See Dion Cassius.

Xylandrus, Gulielmus. See Strabo.

Yonge, Walter. Diary of Walter Yonge, Esq. Justice
of the Peace, and M.P. for Honiton, written ...
Edited by George Roberts. 1848. 8°. *SC*.15.

*York, Archbishop of. Sermon. MC.20: "Archb: of
York's Sermon:"

Young, Arthur. [? A six months tour through the North
of England. Containing an account of the present
state of agriculture, manufactures and population,
in several counties of this kingdom. 4 vol. 1770.
8°]--[? Sharp, James. Extracts from Mr. [Arthur]
Young's six months tour through the North of England. 1774. 8°]. MC.72: "Young['s] Northern
Traveller:"

Young, Edward. The works of the author of the Night
thoughts, revised and corrected by himself. 4 vol.
1767. 12°. *SC*.696: "1757, 8vo."

————. The complaint: or, night-thoughts on life,
death, & immortality. 9 pts. in 1 vol. 1743.
26cm. [*DLC*]. [WL:Ann]. MC.47: "Young's Night
thoughts:"

[Young, Samuel]. Vindiciae anti-Baxterianae. [By
Samuel Young]. 1696. 12°. *SC*.189. MC.63: "Vindiciae Anti-Baxterianae:"

Zeune, Johann Carl. See Horatius Flaccus, Quintus.
Opera.

Zwingerus, Jacobus. See Scapula, Joannes.

APPENDIX I:
WORDSWORTH

Books belonging to Wordsworth
in addition to those found in
the Sale Catalogue,
the Manuscript Catalogue,
or the Loan Book

A.   See Arnold, Matthew.

Akenside, Mark.   The poems of Mark Akenside.   [Edited
    by Alexander Dyce].   1835.   8°.   [DD: "Wm Words-
    worth from A. Dyce"].   [HL.MK.243].

Allan, John Harrison.   A pictorial tour in the Medi-
    terranean: including Malta--Dalmatia--Turkey--
    Asia Minor--Grecian Archipelago--Egypt--Nubia--
    Greece--Ionian Islands--Sicily--Italy--and Spain.
    1843.   14.5 in.   [WL:Ann].

Allom, Thomas.   See Rose, Thomas.

Aristotle.   Aristotle's treatise on poetry, translated:
    with notes ... and two dissertations ... by Thomas
    Twining.   The second edition ... by Daniel Twining.
    2 vol.   1812.   8°.   [DD: "William Wordsworth Rydal
    Mount"].

Arnold, Matthew.   The strayed reveler, and other poems,
    by "A."   1849.   8°.   [WR:Ann].

Arnold, Thomas.   Introductory lectures on modern history,
    delivered in Lent term, MDCCCXLII.   With the inaugural
    lecture delivered in December, MDCCCXLI.   Oxford, 1842.
    8°.   [NjP.   From the Collection of Robert H. Taylor].

Atterbury, Francis.   Fourteen sermons preach'd on
    several occasions, together with a large vindica-
    tion of the doctrine contain'd in the sermon
    preach'd at the funeral of Mr Thomas Bennet.
    1708.   7.5 in.   [*CWC*:Ann].

Bacon, Francis.   See Montagu, Basil.   Selections.

————.   [? Essays moral, economical, and political.
    With the life of the author.   1812.   8°].   [*L*].
    Essays.   1813.   [DD: "W.W. to W.W. Jr.   Rydal 6th
    Oct. 1837"].

————. Essays, moral, economical, and political, by
Francis Bacon, Baron of Verulam and Viscount St.
Albans. A new edition, with the Latin quotations
translated. 1819. 8°. [Richard Wordsworth:Ann].

Bailey, Benjamin. The churchman's manual. Calcutta,
1847. [DD: Presentation copy. "Ralnapoona, Cey-
lon Decr 29, 1848"].

Bailey, Nathan. An universal etymological dictionary.
2 vol. 1733. 8°. [WL:Ann].

Barrow, Isaac. See Montagu, Basil. Selections.

Baxter, Richard. The saints' everlasting rest; abridged
by Isaac Crewdson. 5th ed. 1830. 12°. [DD: "W.W.
from the author"].

Beattie, James. The poetical works of James Beattie.
1831. 8°. (Aldine edition of the British Poets.
Vol. 12.) [DD: "Wm Wordsworth from A. Dyce"].

Beckford, William. Italy with sketches of Spain and
Portugal. Paris, 1834. 8°. [DD: "William Wordsworth Rydal Mount"]. [HL.MK.230].

Beckmann, Johann. A concise history of ancient institutions, inventions, and discoveries. 2 vol.
1823. 12°. [DD: "W.W. to W.W. Jr. 7 Apr. 1835"].

Béranger, Pierre Jean de. Chansons. Paris, 1826.
11cm. [NIC:Ann].

Bible. The Holy Byble, conteining the Olde Testament
and the Newe. Authorised and appointed to be read
in churches. 1585. 16 in. [*CWC*:Ann].

————. Bybel--printen, vertoonende de voornaemste
historien en afbeeldtsels der Heylige Schrifture.
Amsterdam, 1659. [WL:Ann].

Bonner, George William. See Kidd, William.

Book of Common Prayer. Oxford, 1823. [DD: "Mary Wordsworth 1828"].

————. 1839. [CSmH.ZZB:Ann].

A British officer of hussars. See Owen, Col. Hugh.

Brown, Thomas, Capt. See White, Gilbert.

Browne, afterwards Hemans, Felicia Dorothea. Poetical
remains of the late Mrs. Hemans. Edinburgh, 1836.
[WL:Ann].

Browne, Sir Thomas. See Montagu, Basil. Selections.

————. Enquiries into vulgar and common errors.
1658. fol. [WR: "which contains a long letter
to Sara Hutchinson, relative principally to many
curious passages in the work, also several MS.
marginal notes and corrections, all in the handwriting of S.T. Coleridge, and autographs of
Charles Lamb and Mary Wordsworth"].

————. Religio medici. Its sequel, Christian morals
... With resemblant passage from Cowper's Task,
and a verbal index. 1844. 8°. [DD: "William
Wordsworth from John Peace April 7, 1844"].

Bruins, Cornelis. Reizen over Moskovie door Persie
en Inde. Amsteldam, 1714. fol. [DD: "W. Wordsworth. This book was given to Reginald Graham
Wordsworth 12th May 1860, having been selected
for him from his Grandfather's Library at Rydal
Mount, previous to the Sale of those Books which
his Father, & Uncle, did not wish to retain. W^m
Wordsworth Esqr & Son of William Wordsworth, P.L.
ob. 23rd April 1850 aet. 80"].

Brydges, Sir Samuel Egerton. Polyanthea. Librorum
vetustiorum, Italicorum, Gallicorum, Hispanicorum,
Anglicanorum, et Latinorum. Parts 1 and 2.
Geneva, 1822. 8°. [WL:Ann].

————. Sonnets and other poems. First published in
  1785. 1789. 8 in. [*CWC*:Ann].

Bunyan, John. The pilgrim's progress. [DD: "W Wordsworth Jn^r from his kind friend C.H. Townsend Jan.
  6th 1821"].

Burns, Robert. Poems of Robert Burns, with his life
  and character. Dundee, 1802. 5.5 in. [*CWC*:Ann].

————. The works of Burns, with his life by Allan
  Cunningham. 6 vol. [really 8 vol]. 8°. [DD:
  "William Wordsworth"]. [*DDSC*.467: "Life and Works
  of Burns, 8 vols., 1834, original cloth"].

Cavendish, Richard. A letter to the Lord Archbishop
  of Canterbury on the actual relations between
  church and state. Suggested by Mr. Baptist Noel's
  essay. 1849. 22cm. [NIC:Ann].

Chaucer, Geoffrey. See Powell, Thomas.

Chiabrera, Gabriello. Delle opere di Gabriello Chiabrera in questa ultima impressione tutte in un
  corpo novellamente unite. Tomo primo ... (Tomo
  quinto). 5 vol. in 2. Venezia, 1782. 15.5cm.
  [*AWC*:Ann].

Clapperton, Hugh. Journal of a second expedition into
  the interior of Africa from the Bite of Benin to
  Soccatoo by the late Commander Clapperton of the
  Royal Navy. To which is added the Journal of
  Richard Lander from Kano to the sea-coast, partly
  by a more eastern route. 1829. 11.25 in. [*CWC*:
  Ann].

A clergyman of the Church of Scotland. See Williamson,
  Dugald Stewart.

Coleridge, Hartley. Biographia borealis. 1833. 8°.
  [WL:Ann].

Coleridge, Henry Nelson. See Coleridge, Samuel Taylor.
     Aids to reflection; Biographia literaria.

Coleridge, Samuel Taylor. See Browne, Sir Thomas;
     Scaliger, Joseph Justus; Seneca, Lucius Annaeus;
     Seneca, Marcus Annaeus.

————. Aids to reflection. Edited by Henry N.
     Coleridge. 2 vol. 1843. 5th ed. 8°. [WL: vol.
     1:Ann].

————. Biographia literaria. 1817. [WL:Ann].

————. Biographia literaria. Second edition, pre-
     pared for publication in part by the late Henry
     Nelson Coleridge, completed by his widow (Sara
     Coleridge). 2 vol. 1847. 8°. [WL:Ann].

————. Poems on various subjects. London, Bristol,
     1796. 8°. [WL:Ann].

Coleridge, Sara. See Coleridge, Samuel Taylor.

Cooke, George Alexander, pub. Cooke's topography of
     Great Britain: or, British traveller's pocket
     directory: being an accurate and comprehensive
     topographical and statistical description of all
     the counties in England, Scotland and Wales.
     Part 17: Containing the 2nd Division of the county
     of Kent. [n.d.] 24°. [*NUC*]. [WL:Ann].

Costa, Paolo. See Dante Alighieri.

Cowper, William. See Browne, Sir Thomas.

Crewdson, Isaac. See Baxter, Richard.

Cunningham, Allan. See Burns, Robert.

Dante Alighieri. La Divina commedia di Dante Ali-
     ghieri con le noti di Paolo Costa. 3 vol. Fir-
     enze, 1835. 16°. [WL:Ann].

De Vere, Sir Aubrey. See Hunt, afterwards De Vere.

The devout communicant, according to the Church of
England; containing the companion for the altar,
and suitable prayers to be used during the cere-
mony. Whitehaven, 1827. 11cm. [RPB.HLKC:Ann].

[Dictionary of mythology. Title-page missing]. [WL:
Ann].

Dobson, Susannah Dawson. See La Curne de Sainte-
Palaye, Jean Baptiste de.

Dockray, Benjamin. Remarks on Catholic emancipation.
[1829]. 22cm. [MA:Ann].

Dunbar, William. The poems of William Dunbar. Now
first collected. With notes, and a memoir of his
life, ed. David Laing. 2 vols. Edinburgh, 1834.
19cm. [Paul F. Betz:Ann].

Dyce, Alexander. See Akenside, Mark; Shakespeare,
William; Skelton, John.

Dyche, Thomas. The youth's guide to the Latin tongue;
or, an explication of Propria quae maribus, quae
genus, and As in praesenti ... By Thomas Dyche ...
The fourth edition. 1766. 16°. [Mark L. Reed:
Ann].

Fairfax, Edward. See Tasso, Torquato.

Falkland, Lord [Cary, Lucius, 2nd Viscount Falkland].
See Teale, William Henry.

Fisher's drawing-room scrap-book, with poetical illustrations by L.E.L. [Letitia Elizabeth Landon].
1833. 4°. [DD: "William Wordsworth Rydal Mount"].
[HL.MK.270].

Frend, William. Patriotism; or the love of our country: an essay, illustrated by examples from ancient and modern history. 1804. 8°. [WL:Ann].

Frome, Samuel Blake. The songs, odes, ballads, duets, and glees, in an opera entitled Sketches from life; or, the wandering bard. 1809. 8.375 in. [*CWC*: Ann].

Fuller, Thomas. See Montagu, Basil. Selections.

Goldsmith, Oliver. The history of Rome. 2 vol. Edinburgh, 1823. [DD: "S. Hutchinson to Wm Wordsworth Jn^r 1824"].

Hall, Joseph. See Holworthy, Samuel; Montagu, Basil. Selections.

Hall, Samuel Carter. The book of British ballads. Edited by S.C. Hall. 1842. fol. [DD: "William Wordsworth from the publisher"].

————. The book of gems. The poets and artists of Great Britain. Edited by S.C. Hall. 3 vol. 1836, 1837,1838. 8°. [DD: "William Wordsworth from the editor"].

Hamilton, Thomas. Men and manners in America. 2nd ed. 2 vol. 1834. 20cm. [*NUC*]. [DD: "Miss Wordsworth with the Author's best acknowledgements"].

Hare, Augustus William. See Hare, Julius Charles.

Hare, Julius Charles. See Niebuhr, Barthold Georg.

[———— and Augustus William Hare]. Guesses at truth. 2nd ed. 2nd series. London, Cambridge, 1848. 6.75 in. [*CWC*:Ann].

Hayes, Samuel, M.R.I.A., of Avondale, Ireland. A practical treatise on planting and the management of
woods and coppices. Dublin, London, 1794. 8°.
[DD: "William Wordsworth"]. [HL.MK.155].

Hazlitt, William. Select poets of Great Britain. To
which are prefixed, critical notices of each author.
1825. 22cm. [NIC:Ann].

Hemans, Felicia Dorothea. See Browne, afterwards
Hemans.

Herbert, George. Poems: with his Country parson. A
new edition to which is prefixed, the life of the
author; from I. Walton. 1809. 12°. [DD: "W.
Wordsworth Junr from his affectionate Mother M.
Wordsworth"].

[Hey, Rebecca]. Recollections of the lakes, and other
poems. 1841. 17cm. [MA:Ann].

[————]. The spirit of the woods illustrated by
coloured engravings. 1837. 8°. [DD: "William
Wordsworth Rydal Mount"]. [HL.MK.149].

Hints towards the formation of character, with reference
chiefly to social duties. By a plain-spoken Englishwoman. 1843. 18.5cm. [Paul F. Betz:Ann].

Hofland, Mrs. The son of a genius; a tale for youth
... a new edition. 1820. 16°. [Mark L. Reed:
Ann].

[Holworthy, Samuel]. Three contemplations of Bishop
[Joseph] Hall, &c. To which is prefixed, an original poem on the crucifixion, by the Editor. 1821.
7 in. [WL:Ann].

Horne, Richard Hengist. [Offprint of "The Prologue"
to the poems of Geoffry Chaucer modernised. 1841.
8°]. [WL:Ann].

Hudson, John, of Kendal, ed. A complete guide to the
lakes, comprising minute directions for the tourist,

with Mr. Wordsworth's description of the scenery
of the country, &c., and four letters on the geology of the Lake district, by the Rev. Professor
Sedgwick. 3rd ed. Edited by the publisher. Kendal, London, 1846. 19cm. [NIC:Ann].

Hunt, afterwards De Vere, Sir Aubrey. Mary Tudor ...
The lamentation of Ireland. 1847. [DD: "Wm Wordsworth Rydal Mount"].

Jonson, Ben. See Sidney, Sir Philip.

Junius, *pseud*. Junius. Stat nominis umbra. A new
edition. Edinburgh, 1807. [WL:Ann].

Keats, John. Endymion. 1818. 8°. [*Book Prices Current, 1908*, Item 4274: "first edition, earliest issue,
with the page of erratum and the 5 line slip of
errata, original boards, uncut (front cover loose),
had the autograph signature of William Wordsworth"].

Kennedy, Rann. A poem on the death of Her Royal Highness the Princess Charlotte of Wales and Saxe
Cobourg. 2nd ed. [n.d.]. 22.5cm. [MA:Ann].

Kidd, William, pub. The picturesque pocket companion
to Margate, Ramsgate, Broadstairs, and the parts
adjacent; illustrated ... by George William Bonner.
1831. 12°. [WL:Ann].

L., L.E. See Landon, afterwards Maclean, Letitia
Elizabeth.

La Curne de Sainte-Palaye, Jean Baptiste de. The literary history of the troubadors, containing their
lives, extracts from their works, and many particulars relative to the customs, morals, and history

of the twelfth and thirteenth centuries. Collected
and abridged from the French of Mr. de Saint[e]-
Palaye by Mrs. [Susannah Dawson] Dobson. 1807.
18cm. [*CWC*:Ann].

Laing, David. See Dunbar, William.

Lander, Richard. See Clapperton, Hugh.

Landon, afterwards Maclean, Letitia Elizabeth. See
Fisher's drawing-room scrap-book.

Landor, Walter Savage. Citation and examination of
William Shakespeare touching deer-stealing. To
which is added A conference of Edmund Spenser with
the Earl of Essex. 1834. 12°. [DD: "William
Wordsworth"]. HL.MK.722: "Exam^n of Shakespere."

————. Gebir, Count Julian, and other poems. 1831.
8°. [WR:Ann].

Latimer, Hugh. See Montagu, Basil. Selections.

A layman. The church establishment considered in its
relation to the state and the community. 1837.
22cm. [MA:Ann].

Lessing, Gotthold Ephraim. Schriften. 7 vol. Berlin,
1827. [DD: "W. Wordsworth Jr. Heidelberg 1830-
31"].

The Lessons of the United Church of England and Ire-
land. 2nd ed. Whitehaven, 1838. [DD: "William
Wordsworth from his affectionate Friend M. Fred
Bentinck"].

Little, Thomas. See Moore, Thomas.

Lofft, Capel. Laura: or an anthology of sonnets (on
the Petrarchan model) and elegaic quatorzains.
5 vol. [in 3]. 1814. 12°. [DD: "To his friend
W. Wordsworth H.C.R. [Henry Crabb Robinson]"].
[HL.MK.138: "3 v"].

The London encyclopaedia, or universal dictionary of
science, art, literature, and practical mechanics.
22 vol. 1829. 8°. [Mrs. Mary Wordsworth Hender-
son (Rydal Mount):Ann].

Macloc, J. New, complete and universal natural history ... With drawings by J. Thompson. 1813. 12°.
[DD: "Wm Wordsworth"].

Mallet, Paul Henri. Northern antiquities. [Translated
by Thomas Percy]. 2 vol. 1770. 8°. [PSC.WWC.
JB:Ann].

Melmoth, William Henry. See Virgilius Maro, Publius.

Milton, John. See Montagu, Basil. Selections.

————. Paradise lost. A poem in ten books. 1669.
4°. [NN.RBD:Ann].

————. [Another copy, with the seventh title-page].
[WR:Ann].

————. [Another copy]. [WL:Ann].

————. Paradise lost. A poem in twelve books. The
author John Milton. The third edition. Revised
and augmented by the same author. 1678. 17cm.
[NN.RBD:Ann].

————. Paradise lost ... correctly printed from the
text of Thomas Newton. 1763. 8°. [WL:Ann].

————. Paradise lost. 9th ed. Edited by Thomas
Newton. 2 vol. 1790. 8°. [DD: "D.W.Q. from
W.W. Rydal Mount Decr 1844"].

————. Paradise regained. 1671. 8°. [WL:Ann].

————. Paradise regained. A new edition. Edited by
Thomas Newton. 2 vol. 1784. [DD: "D.W.Q. from
W.W. Rydal Mount Decr 1844"].

————. Poems. 1645. [WR:Ann].

————. Poems. 1673. [WR:Ann].

————. Poems upon several occasions, English, Italian, and Latin, with translations by John Milton. With notes by Thomas Warton. 2nd ed. 1791. 8°. [Richard Wordsworth:Ann].

Miscellaneous poems and translations. By several hands. 1712. 19cm. [InU.WC:Ann].

Montagu, Basil. Female affection. 1845. 6.25 in. [*CWC*:Ann].

————. Selections from the works of Taylor, Latimer, Hall, Milton, Barrow, South, Browne, Fuller and Bacon. 4th ed. 1834. 18cm. [*NUC*]. [WL:Ann].

————. Thoughts of divines and philosophers. 2 pt. 1832-35. 24°. [WL:Ann].

Montgomery, James. The poetical works of James Montgomery. 3 vol. 1836. 15cm. [WL:Ann].

Montgomery, Robert. Death: with other poems. 1834. [WL:Ann].

[Moore, Thomas]. The poetical works of the late Thomas Little, esq. [*pseud.*]. 12th ed. 1814. 17cm. [NIC:Ann].

Moxon, Edward. Christmas; a poem. 1829. 12°. [DD: "William Wordsworth from the Author December 22 1828 [*sic*]"].

Murray, Thomas Boyles. Golden sayings of the wise king on the conduct of life. With metrical illustrations by the Rev. T.B. Murray ... 2nd ed. 1846. 16cm. [*NUC*]. [DD: "W.W.'S."].

Nelson, Robert. See Teale, William Henry.

Newton, Thomas. See Milton, John. Paradise lost;
    Paradise regained.

The New York review. Vol. 4, no. 7. Jan., 1839. New
    York, London, Paris [1839]. 1 vol. 25cm. [NN.
    BC:Ann].

Nibby, Antonio. Viaggio antiquario ne' contorni di
    Roma. 2 tom. 1819. 8°. [WR:Ann]. [HL.MK.219:
    "Nibby Viaggio 3V [*sic*]"].

Niebuhr, Barthold Georg. Roman history. Translated
    by Julius Hare and Connop Thirlwall. 2 vol. Cam-
    bridge, 1828. 8°. [DD: "William Wordsworth"].
    HL.MK.697: "Niebuhr's Rome 2v."

[Oakeley, Rev. Frederick]. Sertum ecclesiae: the
    church's flowers. 1848. 8°. [*DAP*]. [DD: "Will-
    iam Wordsworth Esqr with respectful compliments
    and thanks"]. [HL.MK.434: "Sertum Ecclesid"].

Ogilby, John. See Virgilius Maro, Publius.

[Owen, Col. Hugh]. The civil war in Portugal, and the
    siege of Oporto. By a British officer of hussars,
    who served in the Portuguese army during the
    Peninsular War. 1836. 8°. [DD: "William Words-
    worth"].

P., X.A. See Peace, John.

[Parker, John Henry]. A glossary of terms used in
    Grecian, Roman, Italian, and Gothic architecture.
    4th ed., enlarged. 3 vol. Oxford, 1845-6. 23cm.
    [*CWC*:Ann].

[————]. [Another copy]. [DD: "To his friend Will-
    iam Wordsworth, H.C. Robinson Rydal Mount 9th Jan:
    1846"].

Parsons, Abraham. Travels in Asia and Africa. 1808.
4°. [Richard Wordsworth: "R. Southey Aug: 31,
1811, Liverpool." "W. Wordsworth/ Belonged to
Rydal Mount Library/ in Ivy Room/ handed down to
M.L. Mair (née Wordsworth) 1882/ White Moss. Rydal Mere." "See pages 204 & 307 for notes [by]
S.T.C. also 14 & 24/. J[ohn] W[ordsworth]"].

[Peace, John]. An apology for cathedral service.
1839. 19.3cm. [Paul F. Betz]. [HL.MK.213: "Apology for Cathedral Service"].

[————]. A descant upon railroads. BY X.A.P. 1842.
7.75 in. [*CWC*:Ann].

[————]. A descant upon weather-wisdom. By __.
1845. 7.875 in. [*CWC*:Ann].

Percy, Thomas. See Mallet, Paul Henri.

Pietas quotidiana; prayers and meditations for every
day in the week; and on various occasions, being
a collection from the most eminent divines. 1825.
16°. [WL:Ann].

Plain-spoken Englishwoman. See Hints.

Powell, Thomas. [Offprints of The nun's priest's
tale (modernised) and certain original poems.
Also a MS. notebook of criticism on these moderni-
sations]. [WL:Ann].

Quillinan, Edward. Woodcuts and verses. Printed at
the private press of Lee Priory, Kent. 1820. 4°.
[DD: "William Wordsworth from Edward Quillinan"].
[HL.MK.256: "Woodcuts & Verses"].

Reed, Henry. See Wordsworth, William. Complete poetical works.

Reynolds, John Hamilton. The Eden of imagination. A poem. 1814. 4°. [WL:Ann].

Richardson, David Lester. Sonnets and other poems. 1825. 8°. [DD: "For William Wordsworth Esqr with the most respectful Compliments of the Author D.L. Richardson"]. [HL.MK.198].

[Robertson, David, pub.]. Songs for the nursery. Glasgow, 1844. 16°. [WL:Ann].

Rogers, Samuel. Human life. A poem. 1820. 12°. [Richard Wordsworth:Ann].

————. [Another copy]. [Paul F. Betz:Ann].

Rose, Thomas. Westmorland, Cumberland, Durham & Northumberland, illustrated from original drawings by Thomas Allom &c, with historical and topographical descriptions, by Thomas Rose. 1832. 19cm. [*NUC*]. [Richard Wordsworth:Ann].

Salis-Seewis, Johann Gaudenz von. Gedichte. Neueste vermehrte Auflage. Zürich, 1823. 12°. [DD: "W. Wordsworth Jr/ gekauft zu L[?] Juni 1830/ gebunden zu Heidelberg/ Mainz 1831"].

Savile, Sir Henry. See Tacitus, Cornelius.

Scaliger, Joseph Justus. Epistola de vetustate et splendore Gentis Scaligerae, et Jul. C. Scaligeri vita. J.C. Scaligeri oratio in luctu filioli Audecti. Item testimonia de gente Scaligera et J.C. Scaligero. Lugduni Batavorum, 1594. 4°. [RPB.HLKC: "autograph of William Wordsworth on title page; initials of Samuel Taylor Coleridge on title page"].

Scaliger, Julius Caesar. See Scaliger, Joseph Justus.

Sedgwick, Adam. See Hudson, John.

Seneca, Annaeus, the Elder. See Seneca, Lucius Annaeus.

Seneca, Lucius Annaeus. L. Annaei Senecae Philosophi,
    et M. Annaei Senecae Rhetoris quae extant opera.
    Raphelengii: ex Officina Plantiniana, 1609. 4.75
    in. [*CWC*: "Blank leaf signed 'W Wordsworth';
    title-page signed 'S.T. Coleridge'"].

Shakespeare, William. The poems of Shakespeare.
    (Memoir of Shakespeare by the Rev. Alexander Dyce.)
    1832. [In the Aldine edition of the British poets.
    58 vol. 1830-53. 8°]. [*L*]. [DD: "Wm Wordsworth
    from A. Dyce"].

Sidney, Sir Philip. Sir Philip Sydney's [*sic*] Defence
    of poetry; and observations on poetry and eloquence
    from the Discoveries of Ben Jonson. [Edited by
    Joseph Warton]. 1787. 8°. [DFo:Ann].

Skelton, John. The poetical works of John Skelton:
    with notes and some account of the author and his
    writings by ... A[lexander] Dyce. 2 vol. 1843.
    8°. [Jonathan Wordsworth:Ann].

South, Robert. See Montagu, Basil. Selections.

Southey, Robert. Chronicle of the Cid; from the Span-
    ish. 1808. 4°. [WL:Ann].

————. Congratulatory odes to His Royal Highness the
    Prince Regent, His Imperial Majesty the Emperor of
    Russia, and His Majesty the King of Prussia. 1814.
    4°. [WL:Ann].

————. Selections from the prose works of Robert
    Southey. 1832. 12°. [WL:Ann].

Spalding, John. The history of the troubles and memo-
    rable transactions in Scotland, from the year 1624

to 1645. 2 vol. Aberdeen, 1792. 19cm. [NN.BC:
Ann].

Spenser, Edmund. A view of the state of Ireland as it
was in the reign of Queen Elizabeth. Written by
way of dialogue between Eudoxus and Ireneus ...
to which is prefix'd the author's Life, and an Index added to the work. Dublin, 1763. 6.5 in.
[*CWC*:Ann].

Stopford, Miss A. St. G. Sad sounds from a broken
harp; or a faint death-cry from Ireland. [Poems].
London, Dublin, 1847. 14cm. [*L*; *DAP*]. [MA:Ann].

Tacitus, Cornelius. The ende of Nero and beginning of
Galba. Fower bookes of the histories of C. Tacitus, etc. [Translated by Sir Henry Savile]. 1612.
fol. [WR:Ann].

[Talfourd, Thomas Noon]. Ion: a tragedy, in five acts
[and in verse]. To which are added a few sonnets.
Second edition. [1835]. 8°. [WL:Ann].

[————]. [Another copy]. [Mark L. Reed:Ann].

————. Vacation rambles and thoughts, etc. 2 vol.
1845. 12°. [WL:Ann].

Tasso, Torquato. La Gerusalemme liberata ... Edizione
quarta. 2 vol. 12°. Parigi, 1783. [*BN*]. [RPB.
HLKC:Ann. Vol. 2 only].

————. Godfrey of Bulloigne, or the recouerie of
Jerusalem. Done into English heroicall verse, by
E[dward] Fairfax. 3rd ed. 1687. 8°. [WR:Ann].

Taylor, Sir Henry. Philip van Artevelde. Part I and
Part II. 1834. 8°. [WL:Ann].

Taylor, Jeremy. See Montagu, Basil. Selections.

Teale, William Henry. Lives of English laymen, Lord
    Falkland, Izaak Walton, Robert Nelson. [Vol. 22
    of The Englishman's Library, 31 vol., 1840–46.
    12°]. [DD: 1842: "Wm Wordsworth from the Author"].

Thirlwall, Connop. See Niebuhr, Barthold Georg.

Thompson, J. See Macloc, J.

Thomson, James. The castle of indolence, an allegori-
    call [*sic*] poem written in imitation of Spenser.
    1747. 9.5 in. [Bound with eight other eighteenth-
    century poems published between 1747 and 1752].
    [*CWC*].

————. The seasons. 4th ed. [Note on flyleaf states:
    "In truth the second edition"]. 1726. 8°. [WL:
    Ann].

————. The seasons. 1730. [Lowndes: two 1730 eds.:
    one 4°, other 8°]. [WL:Ann].

————. The seasons. 1778. 8°. [Lowndes]. [WL:Ann].

Tobin, John. The honey moon: a comedy in five acts.
    1805. 8°. [PSC.WWC.JB:Ann].

Trench, Richard Chenevix. Poems from Eastern sources;
    The steadfast prince; and other poems. 1842. 8°.
    [DD: "William Wordsworth"].

————. Sacred poems for mourners. With an introduc-
    tion by the Rev. R.C. Trench. 1846. 8°. [WL:Ann].

Tupper, Martin Farquhar. Proverbial philosophy; a book
    of thoughts and arguments, originally treated.
    1838. 8°. [WL:Ann].

Twamley, afterwards Meredith, Louisa Anne. The romance
    of nature; or the flower-seasons illustrated ...
    The plates engraved after original drawings from
    nature by the author. 1836. 22cm. [*NUC*]. [DD:
    "William Wordsworth from the Authoress"]. [HL.MK.
    150].

Twining, Daniel. See Aristotle.

Twining, Thomas. See Aristotle.

Virgilius Maro, Publius. The whole genuine works of
    Virgil, the famous Roman poet ... revised, correc-
    ted, and improved by William Henry Melmoth. [NN
    Mor:Ann]. [*L*: "[? 1790] 4°"].

————. The works of Publius Virgilius Maro. Trans-
    lated by John Ogilby. 1650. 8°. [*L*]. [WL: "En-
    closure attached to endpaper, hand of G.G.W.: 'This
    translation of Virgil was found tied up in a bundle
    with the MSS of the translations [of Virgil] of
    W.W.'"].

Voss, Johann Heinrich, the Elder. Luise, ein länd-
    liches gedicht in 3 idyllen. Königsberg, 1823.
    16°. [*ABL*]. [DD: "W. Wordsworth Junr 24 June
    1830"].

Walker, J. and C. Lancashire. Map. 1835. [WL:Ann].

Walker, John. A critical pronouncing dictionary and
    expositor of the English language. A new ed.
    carefully revised and corrected. 1841. 23cm.
    [Bound with the next]. [NN.BC:Ann].

————. A key to the classical pronunciation of Greek,
    Latin, and Scripture proper names. 2nd ed. 1839.
    23cm. [NN.BC:Ann].

Walter, Weever. Letters from the Continent. Edin-
    burgh, London, 1828. 21.5cm. [NN.BC:Ann].

Walton, Izaak. See Herbert, George; Teale, William
    Henry.

Warton, Joseph. See Sidney, Sir Philip.

Warton, Thomas. See Milton, John. Poems upon several occasions.

Watts, Alaric, ed. The literary souvenir; or, cabinet of poetry and romance. 1827. 8°. [WL:Ann].

Watts, Alaric A. Poetical sketches: The profession; The broken heart; etc. with stanzas for music, and other poems. 1824. 16.4cm. [Paul F. Betz: Ann].

Watts, Isaac. Prayers composed for the use and imitation of children. 1759. [WL:Ann].

Wehner, Paul Mathias. Pavli Mathiae VVehneri ... Practicarvm jvris observationvm selectarvm liber singvlaris ... Editio iterata & posthuma, priori longe auctior & correctior. Francofvrti, 1624. 21cm. [CtY.BL:Ann].

Whateley, Richard. See Whately, Thomas.

Whately, Thomas. Remarks on some of the characters of Shakespeare by Thomas Whately ... edited by Richard Whately, D.D. Archbishop of Dublin. 3rd ed. 1839. 8°. [NNMor:Ann].

White, Gilbert. The natural history of Selborne. Edinburgh, 1830. [DD: "W.W. to W.W. Jr. Bath, 20th April 1839"].

————. The natural history of Selborne ... With notes by Captain T. Brown. Edinburgh, 1833. 8°. [DD: "Wm Wordsworth Rydal Mount"].

[Williamson, Dugald Stewart]. Metrical paraphrases of the book of Revelations of Saint John, with a preface and notes by a clergyman of the Church of Scotland. Kirkcudbright, 1838. 23cm. [MA:Ann].

Wordsworth, William. See Hudson, John.

————. The poetical works of William Wordsworth. 4 vol. 1832. 8°. [WL:Ann].

————. The complete poetical works of William Wordsworth: together with a description of the country
of the lakes in the north of England, now first
published with his works ... edited by Henry Reed.
Philadelphia, 1837. 10.125 in. [*CWC*]. [WL:Ann].

————. The poetical works of William Wordsworth.
1845. fol. [Bound by Frederick Westley and given
to WW in 1845]. [WL:Ann]. [WL has four other annotated copies of this edition].

————. [A quarto volume containing An evening walk
(1793), The excursion (1814), and The white doe
(1815), all bound together]. [WL:Ann].

————. A description of the scenery of the lakes in
the north of England. 4th ed. 1823. 8°. [WL:
Ann].

————. Lyrical ballads. 1798. 8°. [WR: "contains
the autograph of Mary Hutchinson, afterwards the
poet's wife"]. [NIC:Ann].

————. Lyrical ballads. 3rd ed. 2 vol. 1802. 8°.
[WR: "with the inscription on the fly-leaf, 'Given
by W.W. to S.H. at Gallow Hill, the Evening before
our Marriage, Oct. 3rd, 1802. M.W.' It also has
the autograph of Sara Hutchinson on both titles"].
[WL:Ann].

ADDENDUM

The Edinburgh Review. October 1815. [WL:Ann]. [PL:
"This is an issue of the *Review* with review of
The White Doe of Rylstone"].

APPENDIX II: COLERIDGE

Books marked in
the Manuscript Catalogue
as belonging to Coleridge

Abulfeda. See Wilken, Friedrich.

Adam, Thomas. Private thoughts on religion and other
    subjects connected with it. 2nd ed. York, 1795.
    12°. [*L*:Ann. *CM*]. MC.28/JC/"2 C [two copies]":
    "Adam's Priv: Thoughts:" MC.108s: "Adams private
    thoughts."

Adamus, Melchior. Vitae Germanorum theologorum, qui
    superiori seculo, ecclesiam Christi voce scriptis-
    que propagarunt et propugnarunt. Haidelbergae,
    1620. 8°. [CF.*CM*]. MC.111s: "Vitae theologorum."

Adelung, Johann Christoph. See Willich, Anthony Flor-
    ian Madinger.

Aesop. Fables of Aesop and other eminent mythologists:
    with morals and reflections. By Sir Roger L'Es-
    trange Kt. The seventh edition corrected. (vol.
    2. Fables and stories moralized. Being a second
    part of the Fables of Aesop, and other eminent
    mythologists ... By Sir Roger L'Estrange, Kt. The
    fourth edition). 2 vol. 1724,30. 8°. [*L*:Ann.
    CN, 3N3487]. MC.81/JC: "L'Estrange's Aesop: 2
    Vol:" MC.109s: "Fables of Aesop--Sir R Lestrange
    2 vols."

African Association, Proceedings of. See WW entry.

Agricola, Rodolphus. Nonnulla opuscula. Antverpiae,
    1511. 4°. MC.9/JC/C: "Rodolphi Agri: op:"

Ahmad, Ardabili. A series of poems, containing the
    plaints, consolations and delights of Achmed Arde-
    beili, a Persian exile. With notes historical and
    explanatory, by Charles Fox. Bristol, 1797. 8°.
    MC.105/[JC]: "Series of Poems--of A. Ardebeili."

Akenside, Mark. The works of Mark Akinside [*sic*] ...
    With his life, a facsimile of his hand-writing,
    and an essay on the first poem, by Mrs. Barbauld.
    2 vol. in 1. New-Brunswick [N.J.], 1808. 12°.
    [*NUC*]. MC.45/Colerigde's [*sic*]: "Works of Aken-
    side."

Alemán, Mateo. The rogue; or, the life of Guzman de
    Alfarache. Translated by ... James Mabbe. 1623.
    fol. [*CN*, 2N2117]. MC.87/JC/H[artley]/C: "Life
    of Guzman de Alfer:"

Alexander, Sir William. See Sidney, Sir Philip.

Alfieri, Vittorio, Count. See Merope.

*Almanac, German. MC.97/X/JC/C: "German Almanack."
    MC.111s: "Ger. Almanack."

*Almanacco-Italiano (1803). MC.102/JC/P ["P" inserted
    above item]: "Almanacco-Italiano (1803)."

Andrewes, Lancelot, Bishop of Winchester. XCVI. ser-
    mons by the Right Honourable and Reverend Father
    in God, Lancelot Andrewes, late lord bishop of
    Winchester. Fifth edition. 1661. fol. [*NUC. CM*:
    Ann]. MC.106/[JC]: "Bp: of Winchester's sermon."
    MC.109s: "Bp Winchesters Sermon."

*Apuleius, Lucius. MC.8/C: "Apulius" [*sic*].

Aquinas, Saint Thomas. See Thomas, Aquinas, Saint.

Ardebeili, Achmed. See Ahmad, Ardabili.

*Aristipp an Lais. [? Müchler, Karl Friedrich. Aris-
    tipp. Berlin, 1781. 15.5cm: "Lais an Aristipp,"
    pp. 79-118]. [InU. *DAL*, I, 104]--[? A compilation
    from Wieland, Christoph Martin. Aristipp und
    einige seiner zeitgenossen (vols. xxxiii-xxxvi of
    his Sämtliche werke, ed. Göschen, Georg Joachim.
    Leipzig, 1800-01)]. [*BN*]. MC.105/[JC]: "Aristipp
    an Lais--Germ[an]."

*Aristoteles. MC.1/JC: "Aristoteles." See *CN*, 3T3276;
    CN, 3N3276; *CN*, 1N and *CN*, 2N *passim*.

*Aristotle. Ethica Nicomachea. See WW entry.

[? Arnauld, Antoine and Pierre Nicole. La logique, ou
    l'art de penser: contenant ... plusieurs observa-

tions nouvelles. Paris, 1662. 12°]. MC.97/C:
"La Logique."

Arouet de Voltaire, François Marie. See Merope.

[————]. La pucelle d'Orléans, poëme divisé en quinze
livres. Par Monsieur de V***. Louvain, 1755. 8°.
MC.100/X/JC/0: "La Pucelle de Voltaire:" MC.111s:
"La Pucelle Voltaire."

Augustine, Saint, Bishop of Hippo. Omnium operum. 10
vol. Parisiis, 1531. fol. MC.28/C: "D: Aurelius
Augustinus 8 vol:" "Mr Irvin[g] [item crossed
out]."

Aurelius Augustinus, Saint, Bishop of Hippo. See
Augustine, Saint, Bishop of Hippo.

*Ausonius, Decimus Magnus. MC.1/C: "Ausonius." See
CN, 3N3276.

Bacon, Francis. The works of Francis Bacon ... To
which is prefixed a life of the author, by Mr.
[David] Mallet. 4 vol. 1740. fol. [*CN*, 1N913].
MC.80/X/JC/H[artley]/C: "Bacon's Works: 4 vol."
MC.113s: "Bacon's Works."

[Baculard d'Arnaud, François Thomas Marie de]. Sidnei
et Silli, ou, la bienfaisance et la reconnaissance.
Histoire anglaise. Suivie d'odes anacréontiques.
Par l'auteur de Fanni. 1766. 12°. MC.96/C:
"Sidnei & Silli:"

Barbauld, Mrs. Anna. See Akenside, Mark.

Barclay, John. Argenis. Amstelodami, 1659. 12°.
[MH:Ann. *CN*, 2N3145]. MC.8/JC/C: "Barclaii Argenis: 2 Cop:"

————. Euphormionis lusinini, sive J. Barclaii partes
quinqz. Oxoniae, 1634. 12°. MC.8/C: "Barclaii
Euphormio:" See *CN*, 3N3276, 3728.

Barclay, Robert. An apology for the true Christian divinity, as the same is held forth and preached by the people, called in scorn Quakers. 1720. 8°. [*CM*]. MC.21/X/JC/C: "Barclay's Apology." MC.110s: "Barclays Apology."

Baron, Robert. Metaphysica generalis. 1657. 12°. MC.33/JC/X/C: "Baronii Metaphys:" MC.114s: "Baronii Metaphy." See *CN*, 1N1126.

Barrow, Isaac. See Euclid.

—————. The works ... Published by ... Dr. [John] Tillotson. 4 vol. 1683-7. fol. [*CM*]. MC.21/C: "Barrow's Works: 2 Vol:" "sent to D[erwent] [item crossed out"]. See *CN*, 1N1655.

Bartholinus, Casparus. Speciminis philosophiae naturalis, disputatio. Hafniae, 1690. 4°. MC.31/JC/ C: "Casp: Bartholinus de Phil:" MC.113s: "Specimen [*sic*] Philosophiae."

[Barzoni, Vittorio]. An accurate account of the fall of the Republic of Venice ... in which the French system of undermining and revolutionizing states is exposed; and the true character of Buonaparté faithfully pourtrayed. Translated from the Italian [of V. Barzoni], by John Hinckley. 1804. 8°. [CaOTV. *CN*, 3N4145]. MC.62/JC/C: "Fall of Repub: of Venice:" MC.112s: "Republic of Venice."

Beaumont, Francis and John Fletcher. Fifty comedies and tragedies. All in one volume. 1679. fol. [Lamb's copy, with notes by STC, is in L; see *CN*, 3N3656. GW: "There is also another edition ... in BM annotated by C."] MC.45/X/JC/C: "Com: & Trag: of Beaumont and Fletcher: Fol." "Hartley took March 4th, 1824." MC.115s: "Beaumont & Flet."

Beddoes, Thomas. See Brown, John.

—————. Observations on the nature of demonstrative evidence; with an explanation of certain difficulties occurring in the elements of geometry: and reflections on language. 1793. 8°. [CaOTV. *CN*, 3N3455]. MC.33/X/JC/C: "Beddoes on demonstrat: Evidence:" MC.110s: "Beddoes on demon: evid."

Bell, Andrew. The Madras School, or elements of tuition. 1808. 8°. MC.82/C: "Bell's Elements of Tuit:" See *CN*, 3N3291.

Bentham, Jeremy. Traités de législation civile et pénale, précédés de principes généraux de législation et d'une vue d'un corps complet de droit: terminés par un essai sur l'influence des temps et des lieux relativement aux lois, publiés en François par [Pierre] É[tienne Louis] Dumont. 3 tom. Paris, 1802. 8°. [*CM*]. MC.98/JC/C: "Traites de Legislation 3 Vol 1st w8 ["1st w8" crossed out]." MC.101/C: "Traites de Legislation: [number of volumes not indicated]." See *CN*, 2N1967.

Bentley, Richard. [? The folly and unreasonableness of atheism ... In eight sermons preached at the lecture founded by the Honourable Robert Boyle. 1693. 8°]. MC.20/C: "Bentley's Sermons:" "sent to Derwent in 1827 [item crossed out]."

Bernard, Sir Thomas. See The reports of the Society for Bettering the Condition ... of the Poor.

Beughem, Cornelius à. Apparatus ad historiam literarium novissimam, variis conspectibus ex[h]ibendus, quorum nunc primus prodit, qui est Bibliographia eruditiorum critico-curiosa. 4 vol. Amstelaedami, 1689-1701. 12°. [*BN*]. MC.12/"3 [? vol.]"/JC/C: "Corn: Abughem [*sic*] Bibliog: 4 Vols:" MC.113s: "Cornetii [*sic*] a Beug Apparatus." [CaOTV. HD: "Bibliographiae eruditiorum critico-curiosae sive Apparatus ad historiam novissimam conspectus secundus. Amstelodami, 1694"].

Biancardi, Sebastiano. Le vite de' rè di Napoli succintamente ... e distese per ordine cronologico. Venezia, 1737. 4°; *and* Continuazione delle vite de' re di Napoli. Venezia, 1739. [CaOTV. HD]. MC.101/JC: "Le Vita [*sic*] de [*sic*] Re di Napoli."

Bible, Dutch. [GW: "*GS* shows a copy (not shown as C's) of 'Nieuwe Testament door H.M. Heeren.' Maastricht. 1691"]. MC.98/X/JC/C: "Dutch Bible:"

*Bible, German. MC.95/X/C: "German Bible." MC.108s: "German Bible." See *CN*, 1T346.

Birch, Thomas. See Milton, John.

Bisse, Thomas. The beauty of holiness in the Common Prayer. 1744. 8°. *SC*.199. MC.22/C: "Beauty of Holin:" "To Derwent [item crossed out]." See WW entry.

Blanc de Lanautte, Alexander Maurice, Count d'Hauterive. State of the French Republic at the end of the year VIII [1800], translated from the French of Citizen Hauterive, chef de relations extérieures, by Lewis Goldsmith. 1801. 8°. [*CN*, 1N933]. MC.63/JC/C: "Goldsmith's French Rep:" MC.110s: "Goldsmith's French Republic."

Blumenbach, Johann Friedrich. Institutiones physio-logicae. Editio nova avctior et emendatior. Got-tingae, 1798. 8°. [*NUC*]. MC.34/JC/C: "Institu: Phisiolog [*sic*]:" See *CN*, 3N3744, 4359.

Boccaccio, Giovanni. Della geneologia [*sic*] de gli dei. Venetia, 1588. 4°. [*CN*, 1N1649; 2N2512, 2737]. MC.95/JC/X/C: "Boccacio [*sic*] Geneal:" MC.114s: "Boccacio [*sic*] Genealogi."

Bochart, Samuel. Geographia sacra, cujus pars prior Phaleg de dispersione gentium et terrarum divi-sione facta in aedificatione turris Babel; pars posterior Chanaan de coloniis et sermone Phoeni-cum agit ... 2 pt. in 3 vol. Frankfurt, 1681. 4°. [*CM*:Ann]. MC.11/X/JC/C: "Bocharti Geogr: Sacr: 3 v." MC.109s: "Geographia Sacra De Bochar-ti."

Böckh, Christian Gottfried. See Bragur.

Boethius, Anicius Manlius Torquatus Severinus. Of the
consolation of philosophy ... Made English and illustrated with notes by the Right Honourable Richard [Graham], Lord Viscount Preston. 1695. 8°.
[*L*. *CM*. *CN*, 3N4050]. MC.27/C: "Consolation of
Philosoph:" MC.105/[JC]: "A.M.S. Boethius--Consol:
of Philosophy." MC.108s: "Consolation of Philosophy."

*Books of music. MC.106/[JC]: "19 Books of Music."

[Bottari, Giovanni Gaetano]. Carmina illustrium poe-
tarum Italorum. [Collected and edited by Giovanni
Gaetano Bottari]. 11 tom. Florentiae, 1719-26.
8°. [LVA.DC:Ann. *CN*, 2N2590]. MC.18/JC/H[artley]/
C: "Carm: Illust: Poet: Ital:" MC.112s: "Carmina
Illus 11 Vols 1st wanting." See *CN*, 3N3305.

Boyer, Abel. The royal dictionary abridg'd. French
and English by Mr. Boyer. [c.1728]. 8°. [CF.
CM]. MC.16/C: "Buoyer's [*sic*] Fren: Dicty Octvo:"

Boyle, Robert. See Bentley, Richard.

Bragur. Ein litterarisches magazin der Deutschen und
Nordischen vorzeit. Herausgegeben von [Christian
Gottfried] Böckh und [Friedrich David] Gräter. 8
Bde. Leipzig, Breslau, 1791-1812. 8°. MC.95/JC/
C: "Bragur:"

Brown, John. The elements of medicine of John Brown,
M.D., translated from the Latin, with comments and
illustrations by the author. A new edition revised and corrected. With a biographical preface
by Thomas Beddoes, M.D. 2 vol. 1795. 8°. [*CM*.
NUC]. MC.36/X/JC/C: "Brown on Medicine: 2nd Vol:"
MC.111s: "Brown on Medicine 2d vol." See *CN*, 1N389.

Brunetti, Cosimo. See Pascal, Blaise.

Buchanan, George. The history of Scotland, written in
Latin by George Buchanan faithful[ly] rendered into
English. 1690. fol. MC.59/JC/C: "Buchanan's
Hist: of Scotl:"

————. Rerum Scoticarum historia. [? Edimburgi, 1582. fol.]. [*NUC*]. MC.114s: "Rerum Scot: Historia." See *CN*, 3N3494.

Bunyan, John. The pilgrim's progress from this world, to that which is to come. 1678. 8°. MC.27/C: "Pilgrims Progress:" "gone to Derwent [item crossed out]."

Burder, George. See Mather, Cotton.

Burn, Richard. See Nicolson, Joseph.

[Burnet, Thomas]. Archaeologiae philosophicae: sive doctrina antiqua de rerum originibus. Libri duo. 1692. fol. [CaOTV.HD. *CN*, 1N1000H]. MC.12/X/ JC: "Archaeologia Philosoph:" MC.109s: "Archaeologia Philosophica."

————. De statu mortuorum et resurgentium liber. Adjecitur appendix de futura Judaeorum restauratione ... Accedunt ... epistolae duae de archaeologiis philosophicis. [Edited by F.W., i.e. Francis Wilkinson]. 1727. 8°. [CaOTV.HD. *L*]. MC.24/JC/ C: "De statu Mortuum [*sic*]." MC.108s: "De Statu Mortuorum."

————. Telluris theoria sacra. Libri duo priores, de diluvio et paradiso (Libri duo) posteriores, de conflagratione mundi, et de futuro rerum statu. 2 vol. 1681-89. 4°. [CaOTV:Ann. *CN*, 1N61, 2N2796]. MC.32/JC/C: "Theoria Sacra." MC.113s: "Theoria Sacra."

Burnett, George. Specimens of English prose writers. 3 vol. 1807. 8°. [*CM*]. MC.79/C: "Burnet's [*sic*] Specim: 3 Vol:"

Burton, Robert. The anatomy of melancholy. Oxford, 1621. 4°. [*CN*, 1N803]. MC.82/JC/C: "Anatomy of Melanch: Qto:" See *CM*.

Butler, Joseph. Fifteen sermons ... preached at the Rolls Chapel. 2 vol. Glasgow, 1769. 8°. [*CM*].

MC.20/C: "Butler's Sermons:" "sent to Derwent 1827 [item crossed out]." See *CN*, 2N3145.

Buxtorfius, Johannes. See WW entry.

[? Cabala: sive scrinia sacra. Mysteries of state and government: in letters of illustrious persons and great agents; the reigns of Henry the Eighth, Queen Elizabeth, K. James, and the late King Charles. 4 vol. in 2. Sulzbaci, 1677-8. 4°.]. [*CM*].--[? Kabbala denudata, seu doctrina Hebraeorum transcendentalis, et metaphysica atque theologica. 4 vol. in 2. Sulzbachi, 1677-8. 4°.]. [*CM*]. MC.62/X/ JC/C: "Cabala:" MC.112s: "Cabala."

Calvin, Jean. See WW entry.

Camilli, Camillo. See Huarte Navarro, Juan de Dios.

[? Canard, Nicolas François. Principes d'economie politique, ouvrage couronné par l'Institut national, dans sa séance du 15 nivôse an IX (5 janvier 1801), et depuis revu, corrigé, et augmenté par l'auteur. Paris, 1801. 8°.]. [*BN*]. MC.95/ JC/C: "Principes d'Economie."

Caramuelius, Aspasius, *pseud.* [Casparus Schottus]. Joco-seriorum naturae et artis, sive magiae naturalis centuriae tres ... Accessit diatribe de prodigiosis crucibus (A[thanasius] Kircheri). [? Amsterdam, 1666]. 4°. [*CM*:Ann]. MC.30/JC/ H[artley]/C: "Joco Seria Nat: et Ar:"

Carew, Richard. See Huarte Navarro, Juan de Dios.

[Carrara, Ubertinus]. Columbus carmen epicum. Romae, 1715. 8°. [CaOTV.HD. *CM*:Ann]. MC.8/X/JC/C: "Columbus: Carm: Ep:" MC.114s: "Columbus: Carmen Epicum."

Casti, Giovanni Battista. Novelle. 3 vol. Parigi, 1804. 8°. MC.95/C: "Nouelle D: Cit[? adino] Casti:"

Catullus, Caius Valerius. Catulli, Tibulli, et Proper-
tii opera ad fidem optimorum librorum recensiti.
Goettingae, 1762. 12°. [*BB*]. MC.2/C: "Catullus:
Gott:" See *CM*.

Caussin, Nicolas. De eloquentia sacra et humana libri
xvi. Lugduni, 1651. 4°. [*CM*:Ann]. MC.14/JC:
"Caussinus de Eloqu:"

Cave, William. Scriptorum ecclesiasticorum historia
literaria, a Christo nato usque ad saeculum XIV
... Editio novissima, ab autore ipsomet ante
obitum recognita et auctior facta. 2 vol. Oxford, 1740, 1743. fol. [*CM*:Ann]. MC.24/C:
"Ecclesiast: Scriptor:" "sent to Derwent [item
crossed out]." MC.58/JC/C: "Historia Ecclesiast
(2 vols Caves)." MC.109s: "Caves Theologia [*sic*]
Literaria." See *CN*, 1N1070, 1071.

Certaine sermons or homilies, appointed to be read in
churches. In the time of the late Queene Elizabeth
of famous memory. And now thought fit to be reprinted by authority from the Kings [Charles I's]
Most Excellent Majesty. 1640. 4°. [NNUT.*McAC*,
V, 545]. MC.20: "Certain sermons [not indicated
as STC's and only item of four bracketed as 'sent
to Derwent 1827' and not crossed out]." See WW
entry and *CM*.

Chamberlayne, William. Pharonnida: a heroick poem.
1659. 8°. MC.50/C: "Pharonniday [*sic*] by Cham:"

Chapman, George. See Homer.

Charles I, King of England. Large declaration concerning the late tumults in Scotland, together
with a particular deduction of the seditious practices of the prime leaders of the Covenanters,
collected out of their owne foule acts and writings, by the King. 1639. fol. [Blackwell Catalogue 527 (1948), Item 99, where it is described
as *"Samuel Taylor Coleridge's copy with his initials on the title-page and with book-plate of*

Derwent Coleridge on *end-paper*"]. MC.59/X/JC/C: "The Kings declaration Late Tumults in Scotland:" MC.115s: "Tumults in Scotland."

Clarendon, First Earl of. See Hyde, Edward.

Clarkson, Thomas. History of the rise, progress and accomplishment of the abolition of the slave trade by the British Parliament. 2 vol. 1808. 8°. [CtY:Ann.*CM*]. MC.106/[JC]: "Clarkson's Slave Trade 5 cop:"

Claudianus, Claudius. Cl. Claudiani quae exstant: ex emendatione Nicolai Heinsy [Nicolaas Heinsius, the Elder]. Amstelodami, 1650. 16°. [TxU. *CM*:Ann. cf. *CN*, 3N3876]. MC.2/H[artley] C[oleridge]/: "Claudiani opera."

Code Napoléon. See Codici Napoleone.

Codici di Napoleone il Grande pel Regno d'Italia. Edizione fiorentina secondo la edizione originale ed ufficiale di Milano. Firenze, 1806. 4°. [*L*:Ann. *CN*, 2N3143]. MC.102/JC/C: "Codici di Napoleone."

[Cölln, Georg Friedrich Wilibald Ferdinand von]. Neue feuerbrände. Herausgegeben von dem verfasser der vertrauten briefe über die innern verhältnisse am Preussischen Hof seit dem tode Friedrichs II ... Ein Journal in zwanglosen heften. Hft. 1-18. Amsterdam & Cölln [Leipzig], 1807, 08. 8°. MC.101/ JC/C: "Reue [*sic*] Feuerbrande:"

Coleridge, John. Miscellaneous dissertations, arising from the xviith and xviiith chapters of the book of Judges. 1768. 8°. MC.26/C: "Coleridge's Dissertat:" "gone to D[erwent] [item crossed out]."

Coleridge, Samuel Taylor. See Schiller, Johann Christoph Friedrich von.

Cooke, Charles. See Shakespeare, William. The poetical works.

Cordero, Graciano. See Pascal, Blaise.

Cove, Morgan. An essay on the revenues of the church
    of England. 1795. 8°. *SC*.207: "8vo, 1797." MC.
    40/JC/C: "Cove on Church Rev:" See *CN*, 1N1048.

Cumberland, Richard. De legibus naturae disquisitio
    philosophica. 1672. fol. [CaOTV.HD. *CM*:Ann].
    MC.31/X/JC/C: "De leg: Naturae:" MC.108s: "Legi-
    bus natura [*sic*]."

D., J. See Duport, James.

Dalyell, Sir John Graham. See Huber, François.

Daniel, Samuel. The Collection of the history of Eng-
    land. By Samuel Daniel. Revised, and by his last
    corrected coppy [*sic*] printed. 1634. fol. [*CM*:
    Ann. *L*]. MC.58/JC/C: "Daniel's Hist: of England:"
    MC.109s: "Daniels Hisꞅy of England."

Dante Alighieri. Opere ... col commento del Pompeo
    Venturi della Compagnia di Gesù. 5 vol. Venice,
    1793. [*NUC*: size of vol. not indicated. *CN*,
    2N3014]. MC.96/X/JC/C: "Dante: Q 3 vols [probably
    "Query 3 Vols"]." MC.111s: "Dante Opere."

Darjes (or Daries), Joachim Georg. Via ad veritatem
    commoda auditoribus methodo demonstrata. Editio
    secunda auctior et emendatior. Jenae, 1764. 8°.
    [CaOTV.HD. *CM*]. MC.33/JC/C: "Via ad Veritat:"

Davy, Sir Humphry. [? Outlines of a course of lectures
    on chemical philosophy. 1804. 8°]--[? A syllabus
    of a course of lectures on chemistry, delivered at
    the Royal Institution of Great Britain. 1802.
    8°]. MC.31/JC/C: "Davy's Lectures:" See *CN*,
    1N1098 and *CM*.

————. Researches, chemical and philosophical, chief-
    ly concerning nitrous oxide, or dephlogisticated

nitrous air, and its respiration. 1800. 8°. MC. 31/X/JC/C: "Davy's Researches:" MC.110s: "Davy's Researches."

Defensio Fidei Catholicae. [? Suarez, Franciscus. Defensio Fidei Catholicae ... adversus Anglicanae sectae errores. Conimbricae, 1613. fol.]--[? Groot, Hugo de. Defensio Fidei Catholicae de satisfactione Christi, adversus Faustum Socinum. With a preface by G.J. Vossius. Salmurii, 1675. 12°]. MC.22/JC/C: "Defen: Fidei Catholic:" MC. 113s: "Defensio ------ [? Christi]."

Demophilus. See Sallust, the Platonist.

Dibdin, Thomas Frognall. See The director.

The director; a weekly literary journal: containing I. Essays, on ... literature, the fine arts. II. Bibliographiana. III. Royal Institution. Analysis of the lectures. IV. British Gallery. Description of the principal pictures. [Edited by T.F. Dibdin]. 2 vol. 1807. 8°. MC.82/X/JC/ H[artley]/C: "Director: 2 v." MC.111s: "The Director 2 vols."

Dobson, William. See Milton, John.

Dodsley, Robert. See Old plays.

[? Du Hamel, Jean Baptiste. Philosophia vetus et nova ad usum scholae accommodata, in Regia Burgundia olim pertractata. Tom. I, qui logicam, moralem, et metaphysicam, complectitur. Tom. II, qui physicam continet. Ed. 4ª. 2 tom. 1685. 12°]. [EU]. MC.31/1 [? vol]/JC/C: "Philosophia Vet: & Nov: 2 Vol:"

Dumont, Pierre Étienne Louis. See Bentham, Jeremy.

Duport, James. Threnothriambos, sive Liber Job Graeco carmine redditus per J.D. [James Duport]. Gr. and Lat. Cantabrigiae, 1653. 8°. MC.6/JC/C: "Threnothriambus [sic]:"

Dupré de Saint-Maur, Nicolas François. See Milton,
John. The state of innocence.

Eckhardus, Primus, Dean of St. Gall. De prima expeditione Attilae, regis Hunnorum, in Gallias, ac de
rebus gestis Waltharii, Aquitanorum principis,
carmen epicum saeculi VI ... [auctore Ekkehardo],
[continuatio carminis epici, auctore F. Molter]
... nunc primum in lucem productum ... a Friderico
Christophoro Jonathan Fischer ... Lipsiae. 1780,
92. 2 pt. in 1 vol. 4°. [*CM*:Ann. *BN*]. MC.9/JC/
C: "De Expeditione Attilae:"

Edwards, Jonathan, the Elder. A careful and strict
enquiry into the modern prevailing notion of that
freedom of will, which is supposed to be essential
to moral agency, virtue and vice, reward and punishment, praise and blame. 5th ed. 1790. 8°. [Ca
OTV.HD. *NUC*]. MC.33/JC/C: "Edwards on the Will:"
MC.111s: "Edwards on the Will."

Ekkehart. See Eckhardus, Primus.

English comedians. Taliclea die grossmüthige. Comoe-
dia [in five acts and in prose]. Theil 2 of schau-
bühne Englischer und Frantzösischer comödianten,
auff welcher werden vorgestellt die schönsten und
neuesten comödien, so vor wenig jahren in Frank-
reich, Teutschland und andern orten ... seynd
agiret ... worden. 3 Thle. Franckfurt, 1670.
8°. MC.99/C: "Taliclea:"

Epicurus. See Gassendi, Pierre.

Erasmus, Desiderius. Adagiorum ... epitome. Editio
novissima; ab infinitis fere mendis, quibus cae-
terae scatebant, repurgata; nonnullisque in locis
adaucta, uti praefatio ad lectorem indicate. Oxford, 1666. 12°. [*CM*:Ann]. MC.9/C: "Erasmi
Adagia:"

————. D. Erasmi Roterdami Apophthegmatum libri octo
cum primis frugiferi, denuo vigilanter ab ipso
recogniti autore, non sine lucro nouae accessionis.
Antverpiae, 1554. 8°. [CaOTV.HD. *BBel*, II, 449].
MC.9/JC/C: "Erasmi Apothegmata [*sic*]." MC.111s:
"Erasmi Apophthegmata."

————. [? Familiarium colloquiorum ... liber. Florentiae, 1531. 8°]--[? D. Erasmi Colloquia; cum
notis tertia parte auctioribus et indice novo, accurante C. Schrevelio. Lugd[uni] Batavorum, 1655.
8°]. [*CM*]. MC.9/C: "Erasmi Colloquia:"

————. Liber utilissimus de conscribendis epistolis,
continens artificium et praecepta in earum compo-
sitione observanda. Editio nova; diligenter ab
erratis expurgatis. Amstelodami, 1670. 12°. [*CM*:
Ann]. MC.9/JC/C: "Erasmus de Epistol:"

Erigena, Johannes Scotus. De divisione naturae libri
quinque. Oxonii, 1681. fol. [*L*:Ann. *CN*, 1N1369.
CM]. MC.30/X/C: "Scotus Erigina [*sic*]:"

Erpenius, Thomas. Rudimenta linguae arabicae. See WW
entry.

Estienne, Charles. Dictionarium historicum, geographi-
cum, poeticum ... gentium, hominum, deorum, gentilium, regionum, locorum ... hac editione auctius
et locupletis redditum. [Geneva], 1603. 4°. MC.
11/C: "Diction: Histor: Geog: Poet:"

Estlin, John Prior. Sermons, designed chiefly as a
preservative from infidelity and religious indif-
ference. Bristol, 1802. 8°. MC.21/C: "Estlin's
Sermons:" "sent to D[erwent]--27 [item crossed
out]."

Euclid. Euclidis elementorum libri xv. Breviter de-
monstrati, opera Is[aac] Barrow. [London], 1659.
8°. [*CM*:Ann]. MC.35/JC/C: "Barrow's Euclid:"
MC.113s: "Euclidis Elementorum."

[? Faber, Basilius (Soranus). Basilii Fabri Sorani
Thesaurus eruditionis scholasticae omnium usui et
disciplinis omnibus accommodatus. 2 vol. Franco-
furti et Lipsiae, 1749. 37.5cm.]. [*NUC*]. MC.13/
X/JC/C: "Thesaurus Erudition Ecclesiast [*sic*]: 2
Vol: Fol:" MC.114s: "Thesaurus 2 Vols fol." See
WW entry.

Fairfax, Edward. See Tasso, Torquato.

Fazello, Tomaso. [? De rebus Siculis decas prima
[- secunda]. 3 vol. Catanae, 1749-53. fol.].
MC.62/C: "Fazellus de Rebus Siculis 4 Vol: 1 wg."

[Feder, Johann Georg Heinrich]. Moralisches vademecum
für soldaten. Göttingen, 1794. [*DAL*, IV, 279].
MC.101/JC: "Moralisches Bade-mecum [*sic*]." See
CM.

Ferrara, Francesco. Storia generale dell' Etna, che
comprende la descrizione di questa montagna: la
storia delle sue eruzioni e dei suoi fenomeni:
la descrizione ragionata dei suoi prodotti e la
conoscenza di tutto ciò, che può servire alla
storia dei volcani. Catania, 1793. 8°. [CaOTV.
HD. *CN*, 2N1888]. MC.102/JC: "Storia Generale Dell'
Etna."

Ficino, Marsiglio. Platonica theologia de imortali-
tate [*sic*] animorum. [Firenze], 1525. 4°. [*L*:
Ann. *IS*, p. 423, n. 100. *CM*]. MC.30/C: "Marsil:
Ficinus:" MC.106/[JC]: "Barsilii [*sic*] Ficini,
Platon: Theologia."

Firmicius Maternus, Julius. See Minucius Felix, Marcus.

Fischer, Friedrich Christoph Jonathan. See Eckhardus,
Primus.

Fletcher, John. See Beaumont, Francis.

Fludd, Robert. Philosophia Moysaica, in qua sapentia
et scientia creationis et creaturarum Sacra vereque

Christiana. Gouda, 1688. fol. [Blackwell Catalogue 527 (1948), Item 158: "Formerly Samuel Taylor Coleridge's copy with his initials in top corner of title-page and on fly-leaf the inscription
'This was among the books of S.T. Coleridge's bequeathed to Derwent Coleridge by Joseph Henry
Green.'" *L: "Goudae*, 1638." *CM*]. MC.35/JC/C:
"Philosophia Moysaica:"

Fontanini, Giusto. See Haym, Niccolò Francesco.

Fox, Charles. See Ahmad, Ardabili.

Fracastorius, Hieronymus. Opera omnia. Venetiis,
   1574. 4°. [*CN*, 3N3737]. MC.30/X/JC/C: "Fran-
   castorii [*sic*] Opera:"

Francesco di Sales, Saint. Il Teotimo o sia il trat-
   tato dell' amor di Dio. 2 vol. Padova, 1790.
   [CaOTV.HD:Ann. *CN*, 3N3560]. MC.99/JC: "Amor de
   [*sic*] Dio: 2 Vol:" MC.112s: "Sales Amor 2 Vols."

Francis (François) of Sales, Saint. See Francesco di
   Sales, Saint.

Fredro, Andrzej Maksymilian. Gestorum populi Poloni,
   sub Henrico Valesio, Polonorum, postea vero Galli-
   ae rege (liber primus). Dantisci, 1652. 4°. MC.
   100/JC/C: "And: Maxim: Fredr: Gesta Pop: Polon:"
   MC.114s: "Fredro Gesta Pollonium [*sic*]."

Frend, William. See WW entry.

*Frider, Peter (Mindanus). MC.32/JC/C: "Mindani Ex-
   perimenta & Medit:" MC.108s: "Experimenta et
   Meditation."

Fromondus, Libertus. Meteorologicum libri sex. Antverpiae, 1627. 4°. MC.105/[JC]: "Libertus Fromondus Meteorolog:"

La galerie de Florence. Florence, 1804. 8°. [CaOTV. HD]. MC.97/JC/C: "La galerie de Florence:"

Galilei, Galileo. Mathematical collections and translations in two tomes. (Englished from the originall Latine and Italian, by T[homas] Salusbury.) 5 tom. 1661-65-62. fol. MC.36/JC/C: "Mathemat: Collections:" See *CN*, 1N937D.

Garzoni, Tommaso. Opere ... cioè il theatro de' varij, & diversi cervelli mondani, la sinagoga de gli ignoranti, & l'hospidale de' pazzi incurabili. Nuovamente in questa nostra impressione con somma diligenza ristampate, & da molti errori espurgate. 3 pt. in 1 vol. Venetia, 1617. 4°. [CaOTV.HD. *CM*:Ann]. MC.95/X/JC/C: "Opere di Tomaso [*sic*] Garzoni:" MC.108s: "Opere Di Tomaso [*sic*] Garzoni."

Gassendi, Pierre. [? Philosophiae Epicuri syntagma, continens canonicam, physicam, et ethicam. 1660. 12°]. [*BN*].--[? Opera omnia. Lugduni, 1658. 6 vol. fol. I-II. Syntagma philosophicum, complectens logicam, physicam et ethicam. III. Philosophia opuscula]. [*BN*]. MC.31/X/JC/C: "In Philosoph: Epicuri:" MC.35/X/JC/C: "Philosophia Epicuri (3rd) [? vol.]." MC.115s: "In Philosophiae Epicuri."

A gentleman, *pseud.* See White, James and Lamb, Charles.

A gentleman of Oxford. See Green, George Smith.

Gilbert, William, of Bristol. The hurricane; a theosophical and western eclogue. To which is subjoined a solitary effusion in a summer's evening. Bristol, 1796. 8°. MC.46/C: "The Hurricane:"

Gilbert, William, M.D. De mundo nostro sublunari philosophia nova. Opus posthumum, ab authoris fratre [also called William Gilbert] collectum pridem et dispositum, nunc ex duobus MSS. codicibus editum [by I[saac] Gruterus]. Amstelodami, 1651. 4°. [CaOTV.HD. *L*]. MC.35/JC/C: "Gilberti Philosophia: Nova."

————. Tractatus, sive physiologia nova de magnete, magneticisque corporibus et magno magnete tellure, sex libris comprehensus. Sedini, 1633. 4°. [*CM*: Ann]. MC.34/JC/C: "Tractatus de Mag: Gilb:"

Glossary, German. See Scherz, Johann Georg.

Göschen, Georg Joachim. See Aristipp an Lais.

Goesius, Wilelmus. Rei agrariae, auctores legesque variae. Amstelredami, 1674. 4°. [CaOTV.HD]. MC.106/[JC]: "Goesii res agraria."

[? Goethe, Johann Wolfgang von. Die leiden des jungen Werters. Leipzig, 1774. 8°]. MC.97/JC: "Leiden."

Goldsmith, Lewis. See Blanc de Lanautte, Alexander Maurice.

Gomez de Quevedo Villegas, Francisco. Obras de Don Francisco de Quevedo Villegas. 2 vol. Brussels, 1660. 4°. [Blackwell Catalogue 513 (1945), Item 808. *CM*:Ann]. MC.98/C: "Quevedo 3 Vol." See *CM* for third volume.

Gottsched, Johann Christoph. Le maître de la langue allemande, ou nouvelle grammaire allemande, mé-thodique et raisonnée, composé sur le modèle des meilleurs auteurs de nos jours, et principalement sur celui de Mr. le Prof. Gottsched. Dixième édi-tion. Strasbourg, 1786. [? 12°]. [CaOTV.HD. *NUC*]. MC.16/JC: "Gottsched Ger: Gram:" MC.108s: "Grammaire Allemande."

Gräter, Friedrich David. See Bragur.

Graham, Richard. See Boethius, Anicius Manlius Tor-quatus Severinus.

Green, George Smith. See Milton, John. The state of innocence.

Green, Robert. [? The principles of natural philoso-phy, in which is shown the insufficiency of the

present systems. Cambridge, 1712. 8°]--[? The
principles of the philosophy of the expansive and
contractive forces, or an inquiry into the principles of the modern philosophy, that is, into the
several chief rational sciences, which are extant.
Cambridge, 1727. fol.]--[? Green, Thomas. An examination of the leading principle of the new system of morals, as that principle is stated and
applied in Mr. Godwin's Enquiry concerning Political Justice, in a letter to a friend. Second
edition ... 1799. 8°. *CM*]. MC.34/JC/C: "Green's
Philosophy:"

Green, Thomas. See Green, Robert.

Groot, Hugo de. See Defensio Fidei Catholicae.

Gruterus, Isaacus. See Gilbert, William.

H., G. See Hakewill, George.

Hakewill, George. An apologie or declaration of the
power and providence of God in the government of
the world. Consisting of an examination and cen-
sure of the common errour touching natures
perpetuall and universal decay. Divided into foure
bookes. 2nd ed. Oxford, 1630. fol. [*CM*]. MC.22/
C: "Hoakwill's [*sic*] Apology" "sent to Derwent
[item crossed out]."

Hall, Joseph. The works of Joseph Hall. 3 vol. 1634.
fol. [*CM*]. MC.106/[JC]: "Hall's Works."

Haller, Albrecht von, Baron. Primae lineae physiolo-
giae in usum praelectionum academicarum auctae.
Gottingae, 1751. 8°. MC.35/JC: "Haller's Phisio-
logy [*sic*]." MC.108s: "Alberti v. Haller Physio-
logiae."

Harrington, James. The common-wealth of Oceana. See
WW entry.

————. The Oceana of James Harrington and his other works; som whereof are now first publish'd from his own manuscripts. The whole collected, methodiz'd, and review'd, with an exact account of his life prefix'd, by J[ohn] Toland. 1700. fol. [*L. CN*, 2N2223]. MC.35/JC/C: "Harrington's Works."

Harris, John. Navigantium atque itinerantium bibliotheca; or, a compleat collection of voyages and travels, consisting of above four hundred of the most authentick writers. 2 vol. 1705. fol. [*CM*]. MC.71/JC: "Harris' Collection of Voy: 2 Vols."

Harrison, Anthony. Poetical recreations. 2 vol. 1806. 8°. MC.46/1/JC: "Harr: Poetical Recr: 2 cop:" [One copy may have been WW's; see WW entry].

Harrison, R. See Seddon, John.

Hartley, David, the Elder. Observations on man, his frame, his duty, and his expectations. (Notes and additions ... by H[ermann Andreas] Pistorius ... translated from the German ... To which is prefixed a sketch of the life and character of Dr Hartley [by the editor, David Hartley, the Younger]). 3 vol. 1791. 8°. [*L*:Ann. *CM*]. [Vol. 3 contains Pistorius' Notes and additions]. MC.31/X/JC/C: "Hartley on Man: 2 Vol:" MC.33/JC/C: "Notes & Add: of Pistorius: 3^d." MC.111s: "Hartley on Man &c."

Hartley, David, the Younger. See Hartley, David, the Elder.

Harvey, Gideon. Sileni Alcibiadis. Ars sanandi, cum expectatione. Opposita arti curandi nuda expectatione: satyra Harveana castigatae ... ed. G[eorg] E[rnst] Stahl. Parisiis, 1730. 8°. [CaOTV.HD. *NUC*. *L*]. MC.36/JC/C: "Ars Sanandi:" MC.111s: "Arts [*sic*] sanandi."

Hauterive, Count d'. See Blanc de Lanautte, Alexander Maurice.

[Haym, Niccolò Francesco]. Notizia de' libri rari nella
lingua Italiana ... anessovi tutto il libro della
Eloquenza Italiana di ... Giusto Fontanini, con il
suo Ragionamento intorno la detta materia. 1726. 8°.
[CaOTV.HD:Ann. *L*]. MC.95/X/JC/C: "Notizia de [*sic*]
libri rari." MC.110s: "Notizia de [*sic*] Libri Rari."

[Hazlitt, William]. An essay on the principles of
human action; being an argument in favour of the
natural disinterestedness of the human mind. To
which are added some remarks on the systems of
[David] Hartley and [Claude Adrien] Helvétius.
1805. 8°. [*CM*]. MC.32/JC/C: "Principles of
Human Action:"

Heinsius, Nicolaas, the Elder. See Claudianus, Claudius.

Herbert, Edward, Baron Herbert of Cherbury. De religione gentilium, errorumque apud eos causis. Amstelaedami, 1663. 4°. MC.26/C: "De Religione
Gentil: Q ?" "sent to D[erwent] [item crossed out]."

Herbert, George. Herbert's remains; or, sundry pieces
of that sweet Singer of the Temple, Mr. G[eorge]
H[erbert] ... now exposed to publick light. 3 pt.
1652. 12°. [NN:Ann. *CM*]. MC.83/X/JC/C: "Herbert's Remains:" MC.112s: "Herbert's Remains."

Hermann, Johann Gottfried Jacob. Godofredi Hermanni
de emendanda ratione Graecae grammaticae pars prima.
Accedunt Herodiani aliorumque libelli nunc primum
editi. Lipsiae, 1801. 8°. [*L*:Ann. *CM*. *CN*,
3N3279]. MC.11/C: "Hermanus de Emenda:"

Herodianus, Aelius. See Hermann, Johann Gottfried
Jacob.

Hesiod. See WW entry.

Heumann, Christoph August. See Melancthon, Philipp.

Heylyn, Peter. The history of the Sabbath. In two
  bookes. 2nd ed. 1636. 4°. [*L*:Ann. *CM*: "8°."
  CN, 1N1000B]. MC.24/JC: "History of the Sabbath."

Hinkley, John. See Barzoni, Vittorio.

Hobbes, Thomas. Examinatio & emendatio mathematicae
  hodiernae. 1660. 8°. [CaOTV. *NUC*. *CN*, 3N3595:
  "4°"]. MC.35/X/JC/C: "Examinatio & Emendatio
  Mathemat:" MC.115s: "Mathematicae Emendatio."

Hogarth, William. See Lichtenberg, Georg Christoph.

Homer. The whole works of Homer; prince of poetts in
  his Iliads, and Odysses. Translated according to
  the Greek, by Geo: Chapman. [1616]. fol. [MoSW:
  Ann. *CM*]. MC.92/JC/C: "Chapman's Homer." See WW
  entries.

————. A translation of the first seven books of the
  Odyssey of Homer. [Tr. Charles Lloyd, the Elder].
  Birmingham, 1810. 12°. [CaOTV:Ann. HD. *CM*: "8°."
  DNB]. MC.91/JC/X/C: "Lloyds Odyssey (7 Bks)." MC.
  111s: "Homer [crossed out] Odyssey Loyd [*sic*]."

Hooker, Richard. The works of Mr. Richard Hooker,
  (that learned and judicious divine) in eight books
  of ecclesiastical polity, compleated out of his
  own manuscrips; never before published. With an
  account of his life and death. 1666. fol. [*CM*.
  NUC]. MC.21/C: "Hooker's Eccles: Polity:" "to
  D[erwent] [item crossed out]." [STC owned the
  1682 ed. (*L*:Ann] of Hooker's *Works*, which included
  Ecclesiastical Polity. See *CN*, 3N3455, 3574].

Hoole, John. See Scott, John.

Howell, James. Epistolae Ho-Elianae ... Familiar letters domestic and forren; divided into six sections:
  partly historicall, politicall, philosophicall,
  upon emergent occasions. The second edition,

enlarged, ... With an addition of a third volume
of new letters. 4 pt. 1650. 8°. [CaOTV.HD.
CM:Ann. *L*]. MC.82/X/JC/C: "Howell's Letters:"
MC.108s: "Epistolae Ho-Elianae Howell."

Huarte Navarro, Juan de Dios. Examen de ingenios.
The examination of mens wits ... Translated out of
the Spanish tongue by M. Camillo Camilli. Englished out of his Italian by R.C. [Richard Carew].
1604. 4°. [*CM*. *L*]. MC.32/JC/C: "Trial of Wits."

Huber, François. New observations on the natural his-
tory of bees ... Translated from the original [by
Sir John Graham Dalyell]. Edinburgh, 1806. 12°.
MC.76/X/JC/C: "Natural History of Bees:" MC.115s:
"Huber on Bees." See *CM*.

Hucks, Joseph. A pedestrian tour through North Wales,
in a series of letters. 1795. 12°. [*CM*]. MC.
70/JC/C: "Hucks' Pedest: Tour:"

Hutton, James. An investigation of the principles of
knowledge and of the progress of reason, from sense
to science and philosophy. 3 vol. Edinburgh, 1794.
4°. [*L*:Ann. *CN*, 1N243]. MC.33/JC/C: "Hutton's
Philosophy: 3 Vol: 1 wanᵍ:"

Hyde, Edward, first Earl of Clarendon. Characters of
eminent men in the reigns of Charles I. and II.
Including the Rebellion. 1793. 8°. [CaOTV.HD].
MC.66/X/JC/C: "Char: of Emin: Men:" MC.112s:
"Characters of Eminent Men."

I., Z. See Jones, Zachary.

Italian grammar. See Lancelot, Claude.

Jackson, Thomas. A treatise of the divine essence and attributes. 2 pt. 1628, 29. 4°. MC.24/JC/C: "Jackson's Treatise on [*sic*] the divine Essence:" See *CN*, 1N1377.

Johannes Scotus Erigena. See Erigena, Johannes Scotus.

Jones, John. A grammar of the Greek tongue, on a new and improved plan. 1805. 8°. [*CM. BB*]. MC.11/X/JC/C: "Jones's Greek Gram:" MC.109s: "Jones' Greek Grammar."

Jones, Sir William. See Manu.

Jones, Zachary. See La Vardin, Jacques de.

Jovius, Paulus. See Sannazaro, Jacopo.

Julianus, Flavius Claudius. Two orations of the Emperor Julian: one to the Sovereign Sun, and the other to the Mother of the Gods; translated from the Greek. With notes and a copious introduction. [by Thomas Taylor]. 1793. 8°. [CaOTV.HD. *L*]. MC.92/X/JC/C: "Orations of Emp: Julian:" MC.112s: "Two Orations Julian."

Junius, *pseud*. The letters of Junius ... Complete in one volume. 1797. 8°. [*L*:Ann. *CM*]. MC.83/JC/H[artley]/C: "Letters of Junius:" MC.114s: "Letters of Junius."

Kant, Immanuel. See Willich, Anthony Florian Madinger.

King, William. An essay on the origin of evil ... translated from the Latin, with ... notes [by E[dmund] Law, Bishop of Carlisle] ... The fifth edition, revised by Edmund [Law], Bishop of Carlisle. 1781. 8°. [CaOTV.HD. *L*]. MC.21/X/JC/C: "King on Evil:"

Kircher, Athanasius. See Caramuelius, Aspasius.

————. Mundus subterraneus, in xii libros digestus, quo divinum subterrestris mundi opificium ... universae denique naturae majestas et divitiae summa rerum varietate exponuntur. 2 tom. (in one). Amstelodami, 1678. fol. [*CM*:Ann]. MC.34/ X/JC/C: "Kircheri Mundus Subt:" MC.113s: "Mundus Subterraneus."

————. Principis Christiani archetypon politicum, sive sapientia regnatrix, quam ... symbolicis obvelatim integumentis ... exponit Athanasius Kircherus. Amstelodami, 1672. 4°. [*BN*]. *SC*.262. MC.34/C: "Christ: Architypon [*sic*]."

————. Prodromus Coptus sive Aegyptiacus. Romae, 1636. 4°. [CaOTV.HD. *L*]. MC.33/JC/C: "Athanasius Kircher Prod:"

[Klopstock, Friedrich Gottlieb]. Der Messias. Ein heldengedicht. Halle, 1749. 8°. MC.96/C: "Messias." See *CM*.

Knight, Richard Payne. An analytical inquiry into the principles of taste. 3rd ed. 1806. 8°. [CSmH: Ann: STC and WW. *CN*, 2N1963; 3N3952]. MC.82/X/ JC/H[artley]/C: "Knight's Prin Taste:" MC.112s: "Knight on Taste."

Krause, Karl Christian. Compendium logices secundum principia S.R.D. Crusii in usum Tironum adornatum. Lipsiae, 1753. 8°. [CaOTV:Ann.HD. *CM*. *ABL*, II, col. 657]. MC.13/JC/C: "Cranse's [*sic*] Logic (compendium logicis)."

Lamb, Charles. See White, James.

Lancaster, Joseph. Improvements in education, as it respects the industrious classes of the community; containing among other important particulars, an account of the institution for the education of one thousand poor children, Borough Road, Southwark,

and of the new system of education on which it is
conducted. Fourth edition, 1806. 8°. [*CM*:Ann].
MC.83/X/JC/C: "Lancaster on Education." MC.113s:
"Lancaster on Education."

Lancelot, Claude, *pseud.* [Le Sieur de Trigny]. A new
method of learning the Italian tongue. Translated
from the French of Messieurs de Port Royal ... by
an Italian master. 1750. 8°. [*BN. CN*, 2N2074].
MC.17/X/JC/C: "Italian Gramm:" MC.115s: "Italian
Grammar."

Latimer, Hugh. Fruitful sermons: preached by the
Right Reverend Father ... Master Hugh Latimer, newly imprinted with others not heretofore set forth
in print, to the edifying of all which will dispose
themselves to the reading of the same. Seene and
allowed according to the order appointed in the
Kings Majesties injunctions. 1635. 4°. [*CM*:Ann.
CN, 2N2438: "folio"]. MC.20/C: "Latimer's Sermons:"
"sent to Derwent in 1827 [item crossed out]."

La Vardin, Jacques de. The historie of George Cas-
triot, surnamed Scanderbeg, King of Albania. Newly
translated into English by Z[achary] I. [for J]
[Jones], gentleman. 1596. fol. MC.62/JC: "History of Scanderb:"

Law, Edmund, Bishop of Carlisle. See King, William.

Lee, Henry. Anti-scepticism: or, notes upon each chapter of Mr. Lock's [*sic*] Essay concerning humane
[*sic*] understanding. 1702. fol. [CaOTV.HD. *CM*:
Ann. *L*]. MC.23/JC/C: "Anti-scepticism:"

Leibnitz, Gottfried Wilhelm von, Baron. Essais de
théodicée sur la bonté de Dieu, la liberté de
l'homme, et l'origine du mal. 2 tomes en 1 vol.
Amsterdam, 1710. 8°. MC.99/X/JC/C: "Essais de
Theodicee:" MC.108s: "Essais de Theodicee." See
CN, 2N1993.

Lesser, Friedrich Christian. Théologie des insectes;
ou, démonstration des perfections de Dieu dans tout

ce qui concerne les insectes. Tr. P[ierre] Lyonnet. 2 tom. A La Haye, 1742. 8°. [CaOTV. *CM*:
Ann. *IS*, p. 429, n. 190]. MC.96/JC/C: "Theologie
des Insectes 2 Vol:"

[? Lessing, Gotthold Ephraim. Fabeln. Drei bücher.
Nebst abhandlungen mit dieser dichtungsart ver-
wandten inhalts. Berlin, 1759. 8°]. MC.99/C:
"Fabeln:"

L'Estrange, Sir Roger. See Aesop.

Lichtenberg, George Christoph. Ausführliche erklärung
der Hogarthischen kupferstiche, mit verkleinerten
aber vollständigen copien derselben von E[rnst
Ludwig] Riepenhausen. 9 Lief [of 12]. Göttingen,
1800-6 [of 1794-1816]. 12°. [*CM*]. MC.97/JC/C:
"Hogarthischen Rupferstiche [*sic*]."

Lloyd, Charles, the Elder. See Homer.

Locke, John. [? An essay concerning humane [*sic*] understanding, in four books. 1690. fol.]--[? A
syllabus of Locke's Essay on the human understanding. 3rd ed. Cambridge, 1802. 8°]. [*CM*:Ann. *L*].
MC.31/X/JC/C: "Locke on understanding:"

————. [? Posthumous works ... viz. I. Of the conduct of the understanding. 1706. 8°]--[? The
works of John Locke ... 7th ed. 4 vol. 1768.
4°]. [*CM*. *L*]. MC.108s: "Conduct of the understanding Locke."

Lucchesi, Jacopo Antonio. See Pulci, Luigi.

[? Luther, Martin. D. Martin Luthers sowohl in
Deutscher als Lateinischer sprache verfertigte
und aus der letztern in die erstere übersetzte
sämtliche schriften. (Mit historischen vorreden
und einleitungen ... herausgegeben von J[ohann]
G[eorg] Walch.) 24 Thle. Halle im Magdeburgis-
chen, 1740-1750. 4°]. MC.101/JC/C: "Lutheri
Samptliche Schrifften [*sic*]: 5 Vol:" See *CN*,
1N385.

Lyonnet, Pierre. See Lesser, Friedrich Christian.

Maffei, Francesco Scipione, Marquis. See Merope.

Maimonides. See Moses, ben Maimon.

[Malebranche, Nicolas]. De la recherche de la verité,
     où l'on traite de la nature de l'esprit de l'homme
     et de l'usage qu'il en doit faire pour éviter l'er-
     reur dans les sciences. Quatrième édition augmen-
     tée. (Défense de l'auteur de la recherche de la
     verité, contre l'accusation de Mons. [Louis] de la
     Ville [*pseud*., Louis Le Valois]). 2 tom. Amster-
     dam, 1688. 12°. [CaOTV.HD. *L*]. MC.97/JC/C: "De
     la Verite: 2 Vol:" See *CN*, 3N3974.

Mallet, David. See Bacon, Francis.

Malthus, Thomas Robert. An essay on the principle of
     population. New edition ... enlarged. 1803. 4°.
     [*L*:Ann. *CM*. *CN*, 1N1832]. MC.34/JC/C: "Malthus on
     Population:"

Mansvelt, Regnerus a. Adversus Anonymum Theologico-
     Politicum [Baruch de Spinoza] liber singularis, in
     quo omnes et singulae Tractatus theologico-politici
     dissertationes examinatur et refellantur, cum prae-
     missa disquisitione de divina per naturam et scrip-
     turam revelatione. Opus posthumum. Amstelaedami,
     1674. 4°. MC.33/JC/C: "Regnerus a Mansuelt [*sic*]:"
     See *CM*.

Mantuanus. See Spagnuoli, Baptista (Mantuanus).

Manu. Institutes of Hindi law; or, the ordinances of
     Menu ... translated from the ... Sanscrit. With
     a preface by Sir William Jones. 1796. 8°. MC.
     38/X/JC/C: "Jones' Hindu Law." MC.112s: "Insti-
     tutes of Hindu Law."

Markham, Gervase. Markham's master-piece: containing
     all knowledge belonging to the smith, farrier, or

horse-leach, touching the curing all diseases in horses. Drawn with great pains and approv'd experience, and the publick practice of the best horse-marshals in Christendom. 1723. 4°. [*CM*:Ann]. MC.36/JC: "Markham's Masterp:"

Mather, Cotton. Essays to do good addressed to all Christians ... a new edition [of the work originally published (in 1710) with the title "Bonifacius ..."], improved, by G[eorge] Burder. 1807. 12°. MC.26/C: "Essays to do good:"

Mela, Pomponius. Pomponii Melae de orbis situ libri III. et Iulii Solini, Polyhistor ... Basle, [1595]. 12°. [KC:Ann. *CM*]. See WW entry.

Melanchthon, Philipp. Loci praecipui theologici. Witebergae, 1577. 8°. [*CM*:Ann. *L*]. MC.24/X/JC/C: "Loci Praecip: Theologici:" MC.111s: "Loci Praecipui."

————. Vita Martini Lutheri, theologi Germaniae principis, breviter exposita ab ipsius collega Philippo Melanchthone. Adjuncta est Petri Mosellano Narratio de disputatione lipsiensi anni 1519. Adjecit praefationem annotationesque subtexuit Christoph Aug[ust] Heumannus D. Gottingae, 1741. 4°. [*BN*]. MC.65/JC/C: "Vita Lutheri &c: Theo: Ger:"

Menu. See Manu.

*Merope. [? Maffei, Francesco Scipione, Marquis. La Merope, tragedia. Terza edizione purgata. Venezia, 1714. 12°]--[? Arouet de Voltaire, François Marie. La Mérope française avec quelques petites pièces de littérature. Paris, 1744. 8°]. [*BN*]. --[? Alfieri, Vittorio, Count. Merope. Tragedia. Venezia, 1798. 8°. (in Il teatro moderno, tom. 24)]. MC.97/JC/C: "Merope."

Milizia, Francesco. De l'art de voir dans les beaux-arts. Traduit de l'Italien de Milizia, suivi des

institutions propres à les faire fleurir en France
et d'un état des objets d'art dont ses musées ont
été enrichis par la guerre de la liberté, par le
G[énér]al [François-René-Jean de] Pommereul. Paris,
an VI [1798]. 8°. [CaOTV.HD. *L*]. MC.102/JC:
"L'Art de voir dans Les beaux-arts." MC.109s: "Le
[*sic*] Art de Voir dans Les Beaux-Arts."

Milton, John. A complete collection of the historical,
political, and miscellaneous works of John Milton:
correctly printed from the original editions. With
an historical and critical account of the life and
writings of the author [by Thomas Birch]; containing
several original papers of his, never before published. In two volumes. 1738. fol. [*CN*, 1N700;
3N3678, 3781]. MC.80/X/JC/C: "Milton's Works 2 V."
MC.109s: "Milton's Prose works 2 vol." See *CM*.

————. Paradise lost. A poem. Written in ten books.
1667. 4°. MC.114s: "Paradise Lost English."

————. Joannis Miltoni Paradisus amissus Latine redditus. Interprete Josepho Trapp. vol. 1 [*containing the first six books*]. 1741. 4°. MC.43/JC:
"Trappe's [*sic*] Milton 1 Vol:" MC.112s: "Trapp's
Milton."

————. Paradisus amissus. Poema Joannis Miltoni
Latine redditum, a Gulielmo Dobson. 2 tom. Oxonii,
1750,53. 4°. MC.43/JC: "Dobson's Milton: 2 Vol:"
MC.112s: "Paradissus [*sic*] Amissus 2 vol."

————. [? The state of innocence and fall of man described in Milton's Paradise lost. Render'd into
prose with ... notes from the French of ... Raymond
[or rather Nicholas François Dupré] de St. Maur.
By a gentleman of Oxford [? George Smith Green].
1745. 8°]. MC.80/X/JC/C: "Prose Parad: Lost:"

Mindanus. See Frider, Peter (Mindanus).

Minsheu, John. Ductor in linguas. The guide into
tongues. Cum illarum harmonia. 1617. fol. [*CM*:
Ann]. MC.11/C: "Ductor in Linguas:"

Minucius Felix, Marcus. Octavius, cum integris omnium
notis ac commentariis, novaque recensione J. Ouze-
lii [Jacobus Oiselius], cujus et accedunt animadversiones. Accedit praeterea liber J[ulii] Firmici
Materni V.C. de errore profanarum religionum.
Lugduni Batavorum, 1652. 4°. [CaOTV.HD. *L. CN*,
1N313]. MC.27/C: "Minucii Felicis Octavius:" "Mr
Irvin[g] [item crossed out]."

Molter, Friedrich Valentin. See Eckhardus, Primus.

Montalte, Louis de, *pseud.* See Pascal, Blaise.

More, Henry. Enchiridion ethicum, praecipua moralis
philosophiae rudimenta complectens. Amstelodami,
1679. 12°. [TxU.Wn. *NUC. CM*]. MC.30/JC/C: "Enchiridion ethicum:" MC.114s: [? "Ethicum"].

[————]. Enchiridion metaphysicum: sive, de rebus
incorporeis succincta & luculenta dissertatio.
1671. 4°. [CaOTV.HD. *L*]. MC.35/JC/C: "Enchiridion Metaph:"

Mosellanus. See Schade, Petrus (Mosellanus).

Moses, ben Maimon. Rabbi Moses Maimonides de jure
pauperis et peregrini apud Judaeos [being cap. II
of Book VII. of the Yadhachazakah]. Latine vertit
et notis illustravit H[umphrey] Prideaux. Oxonii,
1679. 4°. [CaOTV.HD. *L*]. MC.13/JC: "Maimonides
de jur: paup: &c:"

Müchler, Karl Friedrich. See Aristipp an Lais.

Music. See Books of music.

Newcome, William. An historical view of the English
Biblical translations. Dublin, 1792. 8°. MC.24/
C: "Newcome on Bib: Transla:"

Newton, Sir Isaac. See Varenius, Bernardus.

————. Opticks; or, a treatise of the reflexions, re-
fractions, inflexions and colours of light. 3rd
ed., corrected. 1721. 8°. [*CM*:Ann]. MC.35/JC/C:
"Newton's Opticks:"

Nichols, John. See Old plays.

Nicholson (or Nicolson), William, Bishop of Carlisle.
The English historical library; or, a short view
of most of the writers, now extant ... which may
be serviceable to the undertakers of a general history of this kingdom. 3 pt. 1696-99. 8°. MC.58/
C: "Nicholson's Eng: Histor: Libr:" See WW entry.

————. The Scottish historical library: containing a
short view and character of the writers, records,
registers, law-books, &c., which may be serviceable
to the undertakers of a general history of Scotland, down to the union of the two kingdoms, in K.
James the VI. 1702. 8°. [CaOTV.HD. *L*]. MC.58/
X/JC/C: "N's Scot: Histor: Library:" MC.110s:
"Scottish Historical Library."

Nicholson, William. The first principles of chemistry.
1790. 8°. MC.34/JC/C: "Prin: of Chemistry: (Nicholson's):" MC.109s: "Principles of Chemistry."

Nicole, Pierre. See Arnauld, Antoine; Pascal, Blaise.

Nicolson, Joseph and Richard Burn. The history and
antiquities of the counties of Westmorland and
Cumberland. 2 vol. 1777. 4°. [*L*:Ann. *CM*]. MC.
60/X/JC/C: "History of Cumberland and Westmorland
[*sic*]." MC.109s: "History of West & Cumb 2 vol."
See *CN*, 2N2286.

*Num (or Nurn) (or Nova) R--s. [MS. illegible]. MC.
109s.

Nuovo leggendario delle Santissime Vergini. Lucca,
[? 1732]. 16°. MC.95/C: "Nuovo Legendario [*sic*]
D:S: Vergini."

O., W.C. See Oulton, Walley Chamberlain.

Oberlinus, Jérémie Jacques. See Scherz, Johann Georg.

Oiselius, Jacobus. See Minucius Felix, Marcus.

*Old plays. [? [Dodsley, Robert, ed.] A select col-
    lection of old plays. 12 vol. 1744. 8°]. [*CM.
    L*].--[? [Nichols, John, printer, ed.] Six old plays,
    on which Shakespeare founded his Measure for Mea-
    sure. Comedy of Errors. Taming the Shrew. King
    John. K. Henry IV., and K. Henry V. King Lear.
    2 vol. (in one). 1779. 8°]. [*CM. L*]. MC.43/JC:
    "Old Vol: of Plays."

Oulton, Walley Chamberlain. See Shakespeare, William.

*Ovidius Naso, Publius. MC.114s: [? "Letters of Ovid
    &c."]. [MS. unclear].

Paley, William. [? Natural theology; or, evidences of
    the existence and attributes of the Deity collec-
    ted from the appearances of nature. 1802. 8°]--
    [? The principles of moral and political philoso-
    phy. 1785. 4°]. [*NUC*]. MC.32/JC: "Paley's Nat:
    Philoso: [*sic*]." See *CN*, 2N3145.

[Pascal, Blaise]. Les provinciales, ou lettres es-
    crittes par Louis de Montalte [*pseud.*] à un provin-
    cial de ses amis & aux RR. PP. Jésuites, sur la
    morale & la politique de ces Pères; traduites en
    Latin par Guillaume Wendrock [Pierre Nicole] ...
    en espagnol, par le Sr. Gratien Cordero ... et en
    italien, par le Sr. Cosimo Brunetti. Cologne,
    1684. 12°. [CaOTV.HD:Ann. *NUC. CN*, 2N2133].
    MC.99/X/JC/C: "Les Provinciales:" MC.109s: "Les
    Provinciales &c."

Paullini, Christian Franz. Disquisitio curiosa, an
    mors naturalis plerumque sit substantia vermonisa?
    Francofurti et Lipsiae, 1703. 8°. [*CM*:Ann]. MC.
    30/JC/C: "Franc: Paullinus: [*sic*]."

Pausanias. The description of Greece: translated ...
with notes. [by Thomas Taylor]. 3 vol. 1794.
8°. *SC*.147. MC.91/C: "Pausanias' History [*sic*]
of Greece:"

Pedagucci, Pietro Ismaele. See Pulci, Luigi.

Percy, Thomas, ed. Reliques of ancient English poetry:
consisting of old heroic ballads, songs, and other
pieces of our earlier poets ... together with some
few of a later date. 3 vol. 1794. 8°. [*CM*].
MC.48/C: "Percy's Reliques: 3 Vol:" See *CN*, 3N4082.

Petrarca, Francesco. De remediis utriusque fortunae.
[? Strasbourg, 1468]. fol. MC.100/JC: "Petrarca:
de Remediis." MC.114s: "Petrarch's Remedy."

Philippson, Joannes (Sleidanus). De quatuor monarchiis
libri tres. Lugduni Batavorum, 1669. 12°. [*BN*].
MC.9/JC/C: "Sleiden de Monar:" MC.113s: "Jean
Sleidani de Quatuor Monarchiis."

Piccolo, Diego Saverio. Descrizione della peste di
Messina, nel 1743, divisa in principii, avenza-
mente e cessazione. Messina, 1745. fol. [*CM*:
Ann. *BSic*]. MC.96/C: "Descrizione della Pestilen-
za."

Pistorius, Hermann Andreas. See Hartley, David.

*Poems, German. MC.115s: "Dialog [crossed out] Poems
German."

[? Poetae Latini minores ... curavit J.C. Wernsdorfius.
6 tom. Altenburgi et Helmstadii, 1780-99. 8°].
MC.7: "A Pocket vol: of the Minor Latin Poets
given by Anthony Harrison [of Penrith] to S.T.C.
taken by Hartley Coleridge. Jay 2^d, 1829." [In
pencil following: "The autog. [of] the Poet's
daughter"]. [In LB this borrowing is marked:
"1830 March 21 returned"].

Pommereul, Général François-René-Jean de. See Milizia,
Francesco.

Poole, Matthew. Synopsis criticorum aliorumque S.
    Scripturae interpretum. 4 vol. 1669-76. fol.
    MC.22/X/C: "Synopsis Interpret: 4 Vol:" "Gone to
    Mr Irvin[g] [item crossed out]."

Pordage, Samuel. See Willis, Thomas. Two discourses.

Port Royal, Messieurs de. See Lancelot, Claude.

Preston, Viscount. See Graham, Richard.

Price, Richard. [? Sermons on the Christian doctrine,
    as received by the different denominations of Chris-
    tians. To which are added sermons on the security
    and happiness of a virtuous course. 1787. 8°].
    MC.21/C: "Price's Sermons:" "sent to D[erwent]
    [item crossed out]."

Prideaux, Humphrey. See Moses, ben Maimom.

*Primo catalogo. MC.101/JC/C: "Primo Catalogo:"

Proclus, Diadochus. See Sallust, the Platonist.

————. The philosophical and mathematical commentar-
    ies of Proclus ... Translated from the Greek by
    Thomas Taylor. 2 vol. 1792. 4°. [L:Ann. CN,
    1N1728]. MC.34/JC/C: "Comment: of Proclus:"

Prynne, William. A legall vindication of the liberties
    of England against illegall taxes and pretended
    Acts of Parliament lately enforced on the people.
    1649. 4°. MC.38/C: "Vindicat: of Libert:"

Pulci, Luigi. Il Morgante maggiore. [Edited with the
    "argomenti" of Jacopo Antonio Lucchesi and a life
    of the author, by Pietro Ismaele Pedagucci]. 3
    vol. Firenze [or rather Naples], 1732. 4°. [CN,
    3N4389:Ann. L. E]. MC.95/JC/C: "Pulci's Morgante:"

Quevedo, Francisco de. See Gomez de Quevedo Villegas, Francisco.

Rabaut Saint-Étienne, Jean Paul. The history of the Revolution of France translated from the French of M. Rabaut de Saint-Étienne [by James White]. 1792. 8°. [CaOTV.HD. *CN*, 1N177]. MC.63/C: "Hist: of Revol: in France:"

Randolph, Robert. See Randolph, Thomas.

Randolph, Thomas. Poems, with the Muses looking-glasse, Amyntas, Jealous lovers, Aristippus. [Edited by Robert Randolph] ... The fourth edition, inlarged. 5 pt. 1652. 8°. [NN:Ann. *CM. CN*, 3N3828]. MC. 47/X/JC/C: "Randolph's Poems:" MC.113s: "Randolphs Poems."

[? Ranzovius, Henricus, Count. De conservanda vale-tudine liber. Lipsiae, 1576. 8°]. MC.36/JC/C: "De conserv: Valetudine:"

Redi, Francesco. Bacco in Toscana, ditirambo ... con le annotazioni. Firenze, 1685. 4°. MC.101/JC/C: "Bacco in Toscania [*sic*]."

Regnerus a Mansvelt. See Mansvelt, Regnerus a.

Reichard, Heinrich August Ottokar. Guide des voyageurs en Europe. 2 tom. Weimar, 1793. 8°. [CaOTV.HD. *L. CN*, 2N2038]. MC.101/JC/X: "Guide des Voyageurs: 2 Vol:" MC.113s: "Guide to [*sic*] Voyageurs."

The reports of the Society for Bettering the Condition and Increasing the Comforts of the Poor. [Edited by Sir Thomas Bernard]. 5 vol. 1805, 1802, 1805, 1808 [Vols I-II being 1805]. 8°. [CaOTV.HD. GW].

Riepenhausen, Ernst Ludwig. See Lichtenberg, Georg Christoph.

Ritter, Matthias. See Melanchthon, Philipp.

Rossini, Pietro, the Elder. Il Mercurio errante. See WW entry.

*Sagre offerte. MC.98/JC/C: "Sagre Offerte:" MC.113s: "Sagre Offerte."

St. Maur, Raymond de. See Dupré de Saint-Maur, Nicolas François.

Sales, Francis of, Saint. See Francesco di Sales, Saint.

Sallust, the Platonist. Sallust on the gods and the world; and the Pythagoric sentences of Demophilus, translated from the Greek; and five hymns of Proclus, in the original Greek, with a poetical version. To which are added five hymns by the translator [Thomas Taylor]. 1793. 8°. [L:Ann. CM. CN, 3N3902]. MC.92/X/JC/C: "Sallust on the Gods of [sic] the World:" MC.112s: "Sallust on Gods of [sic] the World."

Salusbury, Thomas. See Galilei, Galileo.

Sannazaro, Jacopo. Opera omnia. Accedit vita authoris per Paulum Jovium. Francofurti, 1709. 8°. [CSmH: Ann. CM. BN. CN, 2N2633]. MC.10/JC/C: "Sannazarii Op:"

Sayers, Frank. Disquisitions metaphysical and literary. 2nd ed. 1808. 8°. [CaOTV.HD. CM. L: "Norwich, 1808. 8°"]. MC.32/X/JC/C: "Sayer's [sic] Disquisitions:" MC.111s: "Sayers Disquisitions."

Scaliger, Julius Caesar. Exotericarum exercitationum liber quintus decimus, de subtilitate, a Hieronymum Cardanum. Francofurti, 1612. 4°. [MdBJ:Ann. CM. CN, 1N880, 1125: "Frankfurt, 1607"]. MC.31/C: "Scaliger de Subtilit:" MC.37/JC: "Jul: Caes: Scaliger de subtilitate." See WW entry.

————. Poetices libri septem. [Lyons], 1561. fol.
MC.12/C: "Scaligeri Poet:"

Scapula, Joannes. Lexicon Graecum-Latinum novum. [*CN*,
3N3276: "Lyons, 1663"]. MC.14/H[artley] C[ole-
ridge]: "Scapula:" See WW entry.

Schade, Petrus (Mosellanus). See Melanchthon, Philipp.

Scherz, Johann Georg. J.G. Scherzii glossarium Ger-
manicum medii aevii potissimum dialecti Suevicae.
Edidit ... J[érémie] J[acques] Oberlinus. 2 tom.
Argentorati, 1781-84. fol. [*CM*]. MC.18/JC:
"German Glossary 2 Vol:"

Schiller, Johann Christoph Friedrich von. The Piccolomini; or, the first part of Wallenstein, a drama
in five acts. Translated from the German of Frederick Schiller by S[amuel] T[aylor] Coleridge.
1800. 8°. *Separate title-page*, Part 2: The death
of Wallenstein. A tragedy in five acts. Translated by ... S[amuel] T[aylor] Coleridge. 1800.
8°. [*CWC*]. MC.53: "Coleridge's Wallenstein: 2
Co:" ["2 Co:" crossed out] "1 Copy sent to Derwent
at Mr Hopwoods" "his Fathers desire" [these three
words in pencil; below them, pencilled, with an
arrow pointing to them: "Wordsworth's writing"].

Schottus, Casparus. See Caramuelius, Aspasius.

Schrevelius, Cornelius. See Erasmus, Desiderius.
Familiarium colloquiorum.

Scott, John. Critical essays on some of the poems of
several English poets. With an account of the
life and writings of the author, by Mr. [John]
Hoole. 1785. 8°. [*CM*:Ann]. MC.82/X/JC/C:
"Scot's [*sic*] Crit: Essays:" MC.109s: "Scotts
Critical Essays."

Scott, Sir Walter. Minstrelsy of the Scottish Border.
[*CM*:Ann. ƷW: "2 vol. Kelso, 1802. [*with*] Vol. III.
Edinburgh, 1803." *L*: "8°"]. MC.45/C: "Minstrelsy
of Scot: Border:"

Search, Edward, *pseud*. [Abraham Tucker]. The light
of nature pursued. 7 vol. 1768-78. 8°. [*DNB*:
"'The Light of Nature, Pursued, by Edward Search,'
4 vols., 1768; the remaining three volumes as
'Posthumous Works of Abraham Tucker,' edited by
his daughter [Judith Tucker], appeared in 1778"].
[CaOTV.HD. GW: "The VCL copy can be described as
2 vol [of 3] in 5 pt [of 8], in 5 vol. 1768.
None of the posthumous pts are there"]. MC.32/X/
JC/C: "Light of Nature: 5 Vol:" MC.111s: "Light
of Nature 1st vol."

Seddon, John. Discourses on the person of Christ, on
the Holy Spirit, and on self-deception. [ed. R.
Harrison]. Warrington, 1793. 8°. [CaOTV.HD.
DNB]. MC.28/X/JC/C: "Seddon's Discourses." MC.
110s: "Discourses on P. of Xt." MC.115s: "Seddons
Discourses."

Selchow, Johann Heinrich Christian von. Elementa anti-
quitatum juris Romani publici et privati. Gottingae, 1757. 8°. [*ADB*. *E*. CaOTV.HD]. MC.12/C:
"I:H: Christiani de Selchow Element: Antiq: Juris
Rom:"

————. Elementa juris Germanici privati hodierni, ex
ipsis fontibus deducta. 6th ed. Goettingae, 1779.
8°. [CaOTV.HD. *L*]. MC.34/X/JC/C: "Elementa Juris
German:" MC.110s: "Juris Germ. Elementa."

Selden, John. The historie of tithes. 1618. 4°.
[TxU. *CM*]. MC.25/C: "History of Tithes:"

Seneca, Lucius Annaeus. The tragedies of L[ucius]
Annaeus Seneca, the philosopher; viz. Medea, Phae-
dra and Hippolytus, Troades, or the Royal captives,
and the rape of Helen ... translated into English
verse; with annotations. To which is prefixed the
life and death of Seneca the philosopher; with a
vindication of the said tragedies to him, as their
proper author ... By Sir Edward Sherburne. 1702.
8°. [*CM*:Ann. *DLC*]. MC.92/C: "Seneca's Tragedies:"

Sennertus, Daniel. Opera omnia. [*CM*:*GS*:Ann: "Opera omnia. 4 vol. in two. Lugduni, 1666. fol."]. MC.36/JC/C: "Sennerti Opera: 2 Vol:" See *CN*, 1N1000C.

Shadwell, Thomas. The dramatick works of Thomas Shadwell. 4 vol. 1720. 12°. *SC*.650: "4 vols., 8vo, 1720, *with ... Autog. of the elder Coleridge*." MC. 81/X/JC/H[artley]: "Shadwell's Plays: 4 Vol:"

Shakespeare, William. See Old plays.

————. [? Poems ... With illustrative remarks, original and select. To which is prefixed a sketch of the author's life. [Edited by W.C.O., i.e. Walley Chamberlain Oulton]. 2 vol. 1804. 8°]. MC.43/JC: "Shakespeare's [*sic*] Poems: 2 Vol:"

————. [? Cooke, Charles, publisher. Poetical works ... With the life of the author. 'Cooke's [pocket] edition' of select British poets. 45 vol. [1794-1804. 18°]. [1797]. 12°. [repr. 1800. 12°]. [*SB*, 436. *L*. *CM*]--[? Poems ... [from the text of Geo. Steevens] with a glossary. (Vol. VII of The works of William Shakespeare, containing his plays and poems; to which is added a glossary, 7 vol. 1797, published by G.G. & J. Robinson, roy. 8°]. [*DLC*. *CM*. Lowndes, VIII, 2263. *SB*, 436]. MC.43/X/JC/C: "Shakspeare's [*sic*] Poet: Works:" MC.112s: "Poetical Works of Shakespeare." See *CN*, 2N3145, 3N3289.

Sherburne, Sir Edward. See Seneca, Lucius Annaeus.

Sidney, Sir Philip. The Countess of Pembroke's Arcadia, written by Sir Philip Sidney ... now the sixt time published, with some new additions. Also a supplement of a defect in the 3^d part of this historie, by Sir W[illiam] Alexander. 1627. fol. [*CM*. *BN*]. MC.88/Hartley/C: "Countess of Pembroke's Arcadia:" See WW entry and *CN*, 1N1011.

Simpson, Thomas. A new treatise of fluxions. 1737.
4°. [Blackwell Catalogue 570 (1951), Item 49:
"Samuel Taylor Coleridge's copy with his initials
on the title-page"]. MC.35/JC/C: "Simpson's
Fluxions:"

Sleidanus. See Philippson, Joannes.

Society for ... the Poor. See The reports of ...

Solinus, Caius Iulius. See Mela, Pomponius.

Sotheby, William. Saul; a poem, in two parts. 1807.
4°. [*CM*:Ann]. MC.52/JC/C: "Sotheby's Saul:"

Southey, Robert. Joan of Arc, an epic poem. Bristol,
1796. 4°. [*CN*, 3N4166, 4202]. MC.53/1/JC:
"Southey's Joan of Arc: 2 Cop:"

————. Specimens of the later English poets, with
preliminary notices by Robert Southey. 3 vol.
1807. 8°. *SC*.662. MC.53/JC/H[artley]: "Southey's
Specimens."

*Spagnuoli, Baptista (Mantuanus). MC.8/C: "Baptista
Mantuanus."

Spencer, John. De legibus Hebraeorum ritualibus, et
earum rationibus, libri tres. 2 vol. Cantabrigiae,
1685, 1684. fol. [CF:Ann. *CM*]. MC.27/C: "Spen-
cerus de legibus Hebraeorum: 3 Vol:" "gone to Derwent [item crossed out]."

Stahl, Georg Ernst. See Harvey, Gideon.

*Statius, Publius Papinius. Sylvarum libri quinque.
See WW entry.

Steevens, George. See Shakespeare, William. Poetical
works.

Stonhouse, Sir James. See universal restitution.

Strada, Famianus. Prolusiones academicae orationiae, historicae, poeticae. Oxonii, 1745. 8°. [*CN*, 3N3276]. MC.9/JC/H[artley]/C: "Strada:" MC.114s: "Stradae [*sic*]."

Suarez, Franciscus. See Defensio Fidei Catholicae.

Taliclea. See English comedians.

*Tasso, Torquato. La Gerusalemme liberata. MC.99/C: "Gerusalemme libera [*sic*] 2 Vol:" See WW entry.

————. Godfrey of Bulloigne, or the recoverie of Jerusalem. Done into English heroicall verse ... by E[dward] Fairfax. [? 1600. fol.]. *SC*.417: "Fairfax's Tasso, 1749." MC.48/X/JC/H[artley]/C: "Fairfax' Tasso:" MC.112s: "Fairfixes [*sic*] Tasso." See WW entry.

Taylor, Edward. See entry for WW's copy of Jacob Behmen's (Böhme's) Theosophick philosophy unfolded.

Taylor, Jeremy. Antiquitates Christianae: or, the history of the life and death of ... Jesus. 1675. fol. MC.27/JC/X: "Antiquitates Christ:" "C not marked & omitted to be sent to Highgate."

————. A dissuasive from Popery to the people of Ireland. 3rd ed., revised and corrected by the author. 1664. 8°. MC.22/X/C: "Dissuasive fr: Popery." MC.23/JC: "Taylor on Popery:" MC.112s: "Dissuasive from Popery." See WW entry and *CN*, 2N2209.

————. Ductor dubitantium; or, the rule of conscience in all her generall measures; serving as a great instrument for the determination of cases of conscience. 1696. fol. [*CN*, 1N677]. MC.34/JC/C: "Ductor Dubitant:" MC.115s: "Ductor Dubitant."

————. The rule and exercises of holy living. 1650. 12°. MC.23/H[artley] C[oleridge]: "Taylor's Holy living:" MC.23/X/C: "Taylor's Holy Living." "gone to Keswick ["Southey" in pencil; perhaps Southey's copy] [item crossed out]." MC.26/C: "Taylor's Holy Living: [item crossed out]."

————. Symbolon Ethico-Polemikon [in Greek]: or a collection of polemical and moral discourses. 1657. fol. [Blackwell Catalogue 513 (1945), Item 814 (with STC's initials and Derwent's bookplate). *CM. L*]. MC.23/C: "Taylor's Discourses:" "sent to D [erwent] [item crossed out]." MC.26/C: "Taylor's Discourses: [item crossed out]." See *CN*, 2N2209.

Taylor, Thomas, the Platonist. See Julianus, Flavius Claudius; Pausanias; Proclus, Diadochus; and Sallust, the Platonist.

*Testament, German. MC.97/C: "German Testament:"

Thelwall, John. The natural and constitutional right of Britons to annual parliaments, universal suffrage, and the freedom of popular association: being a vindication of the motives and political conduct of John Thelwall, and of the London Corresponding Society, in general. Intended to have been delivered at the bar of the Old Bailey, in confutation of the late charges of high treason. 1795. 8°. [CaOTV.HD: "[with two other tracts, a poem, and prospectus of a course of two lectures]"]. MC.33/X/JC/C: "Thelwal's [*sic*] Rights [*sic*] of Brit:" MC.110s: "Rights of Britons."

[————]. The peripatetic; or, sketches of the heart, of nature and society; in a series of politico-sentimental journals, in verse and prose, of the eccentric excursions of Sylvanus Theophrastus [John Thelwall]. 3 vol. 1793. 12°. MC.31/X/JC/C: "Peripatetic: 3 Vol: 2 wg: ["2 wg" crossed out]." MC.110s: "Peripatetic 3 Vols."

————. [? Poems on various subjects. In two volumes.
Vol. 1, consisting of tales. 1787. 12°. *No more
published*]--[? Poems written in close retirement
in the Tower and Newgate, under a charge of high
treason. 1795. 4°]--[? Poems chiefly written in
retirement. Hereford, 1801. 8°]--[? 2nd ed.
Hereford, [? 1805]. 8°]. [*L* entry for the last-
named reads: "*A presentation copy from the author
to Mrs. Coleridge*"]. MC.51/JC/C: "Thelwall's
Poems:"

Theophrastus, Sylvanus, *pseud.* See Thelwall, John.

Thomas, Aquinas, Saint. [Opera omnia]. Parisiis,
1660. fol. Vols. 11, 16, 18-20. [CaOTV.HD. *CM*].
MC.27/C: "St. Tho: Aquinas: 5 Vol:" "gone to Derwent [item crossed out]." MC.106/[JC]: "Summa D.
T. Aquinatis."

Thümmig, Ludwig Philipp. Institutiones philosophiae
Wolfianae, in usus academicos adornatae opera L.P.
Thümigii. 2 tom. Francofurti et Lipsiae, 1725,
26. 8°. [CF:Ann. *CM*. *ADB*. *EU*. *CN*, 1N905, 2N2219,
3N3256]. MC.34/X/C: "Wolfe's [*sic*] Institutes:"
MC.35/X/JC: "Wolfe's [*sic*] Institut: 4 Vol:" MC.
114s: "Wolfs Institutes 4 Vols."

Tillotson, John. See Barrow, Isaac.

Timpler, Clemens. Metaphysicae systema methodicum.
Francoforti, 1607. 8°. [*CM*:Ann. *BN*]. MC.32/JC/
C: "Templeri [*sic*] Metaphys:"

Toland, John. See Harrington, James.

Tracts, printed and published by the Unitarian Society
for promoting Christian knowledge and the practice of
virtue. 13 vol. 1791-1802. 12°. MC.25/"2"/JC/C:
"Unitarian Tracts: 6 Vol:" MC.110s: "Unitarian
tracts 4--6."

*Tragoedia per musica. MC.98/C: "Tragoedia per Musica:"

Trapp, Joseph. See Milton, John. Paradisus amissus.

Trigny, Le Sieur de. See Lancelot, Claude, *pseud.*

Trussell, John. A continuation of the Collection of
the history of England. Beginning where Samuel
Daniel esquire ended with the reigne of Edward
the Third: and ending where the honourable Viscount Saint Albans began with the life of Henry
the Seventh. 1641. fol. [*CM. DLC*]. MC.58/JC/C:
"Trusler's [*sic*] Continu: of Daniel's Hist: of
England:" MC.109s: "Trussle's [*sic*] Continuation."

Tucker, Abraham. See Search, Edward, *pseud.*

Tucker, Judith. See Search, Edward, *pseud.*

Unitarian Society. See Tracts.

Universal restitution. [? Universal restitution, a
Scripture doctrine. [by Sir James Stonhouse].
London, Bristol, 1761. 8°]--[? Universal restitution farther defended; being a supplement to the
book intituled Universal restitution a Scripture
doctrine. [by Sir James Stonhouse]. Bristol,
1768. 8°]. MC.26/C: "Universal Restitut:" "gone
to D[erwent] [item crossed out]."

*Unterricht. MC.97/C: "Unterricht."

V***, Monsieur de, *pseud.* See Arouet de Voltaire,
François Marie.

Varenius, Bernardus. Bernhardi Vareni Med. D. Geographia generalis, in qua affectiones generales
telluris explicantur, summa cura quam plurimis in
locis emendata, & XXXIII schematibus novis ...
aucta & illustrata. Ab Isaaco Newton. Cantabrigiae, 1672. 8°. [*CM*:Ann]. MC.106/[JC]: "Bern:
Vareni Geograph:"

Venturi, Pompeo. See Dante Alighieri.

Vida, Marcus Hieronymus. See WW entry.

Vincent, William. The Greek verb analysed. An hypo-
thesis. In which the source and structure of the
Greek language, and of language in general, is
considered. 1795. 8°. [CaOTV.HD:Ann]. MC.13/
JC/C: "Vincent's Greek Verb:"

*Virgilius, Polydorus. MC.9/JC/H[artley]/C: "Polydorus
Virgilius:" MC.108s: "Polidorii Virgilii."

Voltaire. See Arouet de Voltaire, François Marie.

Vossius, Gerardus Joannes. See Defensio Fidei Catholicae.

————. Aristarchus, sive de arte grammatica libri
septem. Editio secunda. 2 tom. Amstelaedami,
1662. 4°. [CM:Ann. BN. EU]. MC.11/JC/C: "Vossii
Aristarchus: de A G--."

————. De vitiis sermonis et glossematis Latino-Bar-
baris, libri quatuor. Amstelodami, 1645. 4°.
MC.11/JC/C: "Vossius de Vitiis Serm:"

————. Elementa rhetorica oratoriis ejusdem parti-
tionibus accommodata; inque usum scholarium Hol-
landiae et West-Frisiae emendatius edita. Amstelodami, 1655. 8°. MC.12/JC/H[artley]: "Vossii Rhetorica:"

————. Gerardi Joannis Vossii. Poeticarum institutionum libri tres. 5 pt. (in one vol.) Amstelodami, 1647. 4°. [LVA.DC:Ann. CM. BN: "3 parties
en 1 vol in-4°"]. MC.14/JC/H[artley]/C: "Vossii
Inst: Poetic:"

Wainhouse, William. Poetical essays. Lat. and Eng.
Bath, 1796. 8°. [CM:Ann]. MC.46/JC/C: "Poetical
Essays: (Wainhouse)."

Walch, Johann Georg. See Luther, Martin.

Walker, John. A dictionary of the English language,
    answering at once the purposes of rhyming, spelling,
    and pronouncing on a plan not hitherto attempted
    ... To which ... is added an index of allowable
    rhymes, with authorities for their usage. 1775.
    8°. [MH:Ann. *CN*, 3N4134]. MC.17/X/JC/C: "Walker's
    Rhim^g [*sic*] Dicty:" MC.109s: "Wather's [*sic*]
    Rhyming Dictionary."

Wendrock, Guillaume, *pseud*. See Nicole, Pierre.

Wernsdorfius, Johann Christian. See Poetae Latini
    minores.

Whiston, William. A new theory of the earth ... where-
    in the creation ... deluge and ... conflagration as
    laid down in the Holy Scriptures are shewn to be
    perfectly agreeable to reason and philosophy. With
    a ... discourse concerning the ... Mosaick history
    of the creation. 1696. 8°. MC.34/JC/C: "Whis-
    ton's Theory:" MC.113s: "Whiston's Theory."

Whitaker, John. Gibbon's History of the decline and
    fall of the Roman Empire, in Vols. IV. V. and VI.,
    quarto, reviewed. 1791. 8°. [CaOTV.HD]. MC.83/
    X/JC/C: "Whitaker's Review of Gibbon's History."
    MC.112s: "Review of Gibbon R Empire."

————. The origin of Arianism disclosed. 1791. 8°.
    [*L*:Ann. *CM*]. MC.33/X/JC/C: "Origin of Arianism:"
    MC.114s: "Origin of Arianism."

White, James. See Rabaut Saint-Étienne, Jean Paul.

[———— and Charles Lamb]. Original letters ... of
    Sir John Falstaff and his friends, now first made
    public by a gentleman, a descendant of Dame Quick-
    ly. 1796. 12°. MC.83/X/JC/C: "Original Letters
    of Sir: J: Falstaff." MC.111s: "Original Let of
    Sir J. Falstaff."

Wieland, Christoph Martin. See Aristipp an Lais.

Wilken, Friedrich. Commentatio ... de Bellorum Crucia-
    torum ex Abulfeda historia. Gottingae, [1798]. 4°.
    MC.12/C: "F: Wilken's Commenta:" [*CM*:Ann]. MC.
    105/[JC]: "Wilken--commentatio de Bell: critt:
    [*sic*]."

[? Wilkins, John. An essay towards a real character,
    and a philosophical language. 2 pt. 1668. fol.].
    MC.13/JC: "Essay on Langu: (Wills's) [*sic*]."

Wilkinson, Francis. See Burnet, Thomas. De statu
    mortuorum.

Willich, Anthony Florian Madinger. Elements of the
    critical philosophy: containing a concise account
    of its origin and tendency; a view of all the works
    published by its founder, I[mmanuel] Kant, and a
    glossary for the explanation of terms and phrases.
    To which are added: Three philological essays,
    chiefly translated from the German of I [for J]
    [ohann] C[hristoph] Adelung. 2 pt. 1798. 8°.
    [*L* lists STC's copy, with MS. notes. GW: "[notes]
    in an unidentified hand." CaOTV.HD: "Author's pre-
    sentation copy to Joseph Cottle"]. MC.33/X/JC/C:
    "Kant's Crit: Philosophy:" MC.110s: "Kant's Criti-
    cal philosophy."

Willis, Thomas. [De anima brutorum]. Two discourses
    concerning the soul of brutes, which is that of
    the vital and sensitive of man ... Englished by
    S[amuel] Pordage. 1683. fol. [*CM*]. See WW
    entry.

————. Pharmaceutice rationalis. [Oxford], 1674.
    4°. MC.36/X/JC/C: "Pharmaceu: Ration:" MC.108s:
    "Pharmaceutice Rationatis [*sic*]."

Winchester, Bishop of. See Andrewes, Lancelot.

Wither, George. Juvenilia; a collection of those
    poemes [*sic*] which were heretofore imprinted and

written by G[eorge] Wither. 1622. 8°. [*CM*]. MC.
49/X/JC/C: "Wither's Poems:" MC.115s: "Withers
Poems."

Wolf, Johann Christoph. Curae philologicae et criticae
in IV S.S. Evangelia et Actus Apostolicos. Editio
secunda. 4 tom. Hamburgi, 1733-32-35. 4°. [MH:
Ann. *CN*, 3N3778, 3793]. MC.14/JC: "Curae Philologicae."

Wolff (or Wolf), Christian, Baron von. See Thümmig,
Ludwig Philipp.

Woodward, John. Naturalis historia telluris. 3 pt.
1714. 8°. MC.32/X/JC/C: "Johan: Woodwardus: Nat:
Hist:"

[Wordsworth, Christopher, Master of Trinity]. Six
letters to Granville Sharp, Esq., respecting his
remarks on the uses of the definitive article, in
the Greek text of the New Testament, 1802. 8°.
[CaOTV.HD:Ann]. MC.13/C: "On Greek Artic:" See
CN, 3N3275.

Wrangham, Francis. Thirteen practical sermons; founded
upon Doddridge's Rise and progress of religion in
the soul. 1800. 8°. [CaOTV.HD:Ann]. MC.21/C:
"Wrangham's Sermons:" "sent to D[erwent] [item
crossed out]."

Young, Thomas. A syllabus of lectures on natural and
experimental philosophy. 4 pt. 1802. 8°. MC.
35/JC/C: "Young's Syllabus of Lect: on Nat: Philosophy:"

Zetznerus, Lazarus. Theatrum chemicum. 3 tom. Ursell,
1602. 8°. [*BB*]. MC.35/JC/C: "Theatrum Chemicum:
3 Vol:"

Zwinger, Theodor, the Elder. Theatrum humanae vitae.
29 vol. in 4. Basileae, 1586-[87]. fol. [MdBJ:
Ann. *CM*. *BB*]. MC.14/JC/C: "Theatrum Hum: Vitae:
4 Vol:"

T